F4

T. S. ELIOT: MAN AND POET

VOLUME ONE

THE MAN AND POET SERIES
General Editor
Carroll F. Terrell

Louis Zukofsky: Man and Poet
Edited by Carroll F. Terrell, 1979

Basil Bunting: Man and Poet
Edited by Carroll F. Terrell, 1980

George Oppen: Man and Poet
Edited by Burton Hatlen, 1981

May Sarton: Woman and Poet
Edited by Constance Hunting, 1982

William Carlos Williams: Man and Poet
Edited by Carroll F. Terrell

Charles Reznikoff: Man and Poet
Edited by Milton Hindus, 1984

H.D.: Woman and Poet
Edited by Michael King

Patrick Kavanagh: Man and Poet
Edited by Peter Kavanagh, 1986

David Jones: Man and Poet
Edited by John Matthias, 1989

Marianne Moore: Woman and Poet
Edited by Patricia C. Willis, 1990

T. S. Eliot: Man and Poet
Edited by Laura Cowan, 1990

In Process

Hugh MacDiarmid: Man and Poet
Edited by Nancy Gish, 1991

Carl Rakosi: Man and Poet
Edited by Michael Heller, 1992

To Terry, Marie,
Betsy, and
Sam

T. S. ELIOT

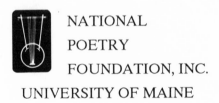

NATIONAL
POETRY
FOUNDATION, INC.
UNIVERSITY OF MAINE

MAN AND POET

VOLUME 1

Edited
with an introduction by
Laura Cowan

Grateful Acknowledgment is made to the following for permission to reprint from previously published materials:

Extracts from uncollected sources reprinted by permission of Mrs. Valerie Eliot and Faber and Faber Ltd. Quotations from the American Editions of *After Strange Gods, Christianity and Culture, The Complete Plays of T. S. Eliot, The Complete Poems and Plays, 1909-1950, Essays on Elizabethan Dramatists, Selected Essays, Selected Prose,* and *The Waste Land Facsimile,* reprinted by permission of Harcourt Brace Jovanovich, Inc. Quotations from *For Lancelot Andrewes, On Poetry and Poets,* and *The Use of Poetry and the Use of Criticism* reprinted by permission of Faber and Faber Ltd. Quotations from *Knowledge and Experience* reprinted by permission of Farrar, Straus and Giroux, Inc. Quotations from *The Sacred Wood* reprinted by permission of Barnes and Noble, Inc.

Extracts from the works of Ezra Pound reprinted by permission of New Directions Publishing Corporation.

Cover illustration: Portrait of T. S. Eliot, pen and ink by Wyndham Lewis. Used courtesy of National Gallery of Victoria, Melbourne.

Published by The National Poetry Foundation
University of Maine, Orono, Maine 04469

Printed by Cushing-Malloy, Inc.
Ann Arbor, Michigan

Library of Congress Number: 88-62932
ISBN: 0-943373-09-3 (cloth)
0-943373-10-7 (paper)

ACKNOWLEDGMENTS

Thanks to the board of the National Poetry Foundation, in particular Burt Hatlen and Connie Hunting, for making this book possible. Walt Litz' and Sam Hynes' help was indispensable during the initial stages of this project. I am also indebted to Pat Burnes, Marilyn Emerick, and Marie Alpert for their encouragement and good will and for providing work-study students as research assistants. I am eternally grateful to the following dedicated assistants: Austin Hummell, Sam Thonet, Laura Lane, Bill Boles, Marcus Librizzi, Bonnie Woellner, Deana McInnis, Kai Shafft, and Sue Nason. Sam Thonet deserves special thanks for compiling the index. Betsy Rose also warrants special recognition for her many hours typesetting and editing. She did her best to lighten my load. Thank you, Carroll Terrell, for your guidance. And thank you, Sylvester Pollet and Marie, for taking care of the final details.

LIST OF ABBREVIATIONS

ASG   *After Strange Gods: A Primer of Modern Heresy*. The Page-Barbour Lectures at the University of Virginia. 1933. New York: Harcourt Brace, 1934.

CC   *Christianity and Culture: The Idea of a Christian Society and Notes Towards the Definition of Culture*. New York: Harcourt Brace, 1960.

Clark   1926 Clark Lectures. *Lectures on the Metaphysical Poetry of the Seventeenth Century, with special reference to Donne, Crashaw and Cowley*. ms. Hayward Bequest, King's College Library, Cambridge University.

CP   *The Complete Plays of T. S. Eliot*. New York: Harcourt Brace, 1967.

CPP   *The Complete Poems and Plays of T. S. Eliot*. New York: Harcourt Brace Jovanovich, 1971.

EAM   *Essays Ancient and Modern*. New York: Harcourt Brace, 1936.

EE   *Essays on Elizabethan Drama*. New York: Harcourt Brace, 1960.

FLA   *For Lancelot Andrewes: Essays on Style and Order*. London: Faber and Faber, 1970.

KE   *Knowledge and Experience in the Philosophy of F. H. Bradley*. New York: Farrar, Straus and Giroux, 1964.

OPP   *On Poetry and Poets*. 1957; rpt. London: Faber and Faber, 1985.

PEY   *Poems Written in Early Youth*. New York: Farrar, Straus and Giroux, 1967.

SE   *Selected Essays*. 1932; rpt. New York: Harcourt Brace, 1978.

SP   *Selected Prose of T. S. Eliot*. Ed. Frank Kermode. New York: Harcourt Brace/Farrar, Straus and Giroux, 1975.

SW   *The Sacred Wood: Essays on Poetry and Criticism*. 1920; rpt. New York: Barnes and Noble, 1960.

TCC   *To Criticize the Critic and Other Writings*. 1965; rpt. New York: Farrar, Straus and Giroux, 1968.

UPUC   *The Use of Poetry and the Use of Criticism: Studies in the Relation of Criticism to Poetry in England*. Charles Eliot Norton Lectures for 1932-33 at Harvard University. 1933; rpt. London: Faber and Faber, 1967.

WLF   *The Waste Land: A Facsimile and Transcript of the Original Drafts Including the Annotations of Ezra Pound*. Edited and with Introduction by Valerie Eliot. New York: Harcourt Brace, 1971.

TABLE OF CONTENTS

"THE THREE VOICES": ELIOT'S INDIVIDUAL WORKS

Early Poetry

The Waste Land

Ash-Wednesday

Four Quartets

Drama

"A DISTINCTIVE ACTIVITY OF THE CIVILIZED MIND": ELIOT'S CRITICISM

LAURA COWAN

*PREFACE**

> We shall not cease from exploration
> And the end of all our exploring
> Will be to arrive where we started
> And know the place for the first time.
>
> *Little Gidding*

The National Poetry Foundation initiated its Man/Woman and Poet Series in 1978 in order to bring attention to neglected twentieth century writers. *Louis Zukofsky: Man and Poet* (1979) was its first collection and subsequent volumes have followed almost annually. The series met with such success that it seemed misguided to exclude more well-known writers. When the Foundation began plans for five centennial conferences to celebrate the births of leading modernists, it seemed only logical to issue commemorative volumes in conjunction with these conferences.

T. S. Eliot: Man and Poet is the eleventh book in the Man/Woman and Poet Series and the fourth commemorative centennial work. Its tone is--appropriately--celebratory. More than one hundred years after his birth (and twenty-five years after his death), Thomas Stearns Eliot remains arguably the leading English or American poet of the twentieth century and the author of undeniably its most influential poem. His poetry and criticism were so rapidly and completely enshrined that they--and the New Critical principles of interpretation that they engendered--dominated both poetry and its analysis until well into the 1970s. The echoes of his influence still resound.

This volume emerges at a crucial time in Eliot scholarship. The publication of *The Waste Land* facsimile in 1971 exploded many preconceptions about Eliot's work and the subsequent publication of his letters (Volume One was published last year [1989]) promises to further disturb accepted truths about him.

---

*Other collections in the Man/Woman and Poet Series have ended with an annotated bibliography. The magnitude of the Eliot bibliography (1977-1986) prohibits our including it here. It will be published as Volume 2 of *T. S. Eliot: Man and Poet* (edited by Sebastian Knowles and Scott A. Leonard).

Eliot scholarship has also ironically benefited in many ways from the challenges to New Criticism by structuralist, psychoanalytic, Marxist, deconstructionist, and other post-structuralist theories. In addition to giving us new ways to read his works, these approaches' gradual abrogation of New Criticism's reign allows us to discern Eliot's decisive role in its formation and also to disentangle Eliot's poetry and criticism from the complicated critical apparatus that both supported and fettered our understanding of him. We are discovering that the doctrines he inspired were not always his own. Valuable insights have also resulted from defenses against Eliot's vigorous, contemporary detractors.

The infinite variety of the twenty-two essays in this collection testifies to the wealth of contemporary criticism and also to the still rich potential of Eliot's work. The articles, which cover his poetry, plays, and criticism, range widely in both subject and method. Their techniques include Edward Lobb's contextualist examination of tropes in Eliot's early poetry, Shyamal Bagchee's linguistic analysis of several modifiers which recur throughout Eliot's oeuvre, James Miller's psychological and biographical interpretation of *Four Quartets*, Joseph Bentley's and Jewel Spears Brooker's examination of the manuscript of *The Waste Land* and its revisions, and Richard Shusterman's philosophical comparison of Eliot's cultural criticism to the writing of Marxist theorist, Theodor Adorno. It is a tribute to Eliot that one of the most celebratory essays in the volume is Russell Murphy's personal reminiscence--which itself defies Eliot's long-revered principle of impersonality.

The essays' topics also often question traditional wisdom about Eliot or his works. J. P. Riquelme, James Longenbach, and Sanford Schwartz all treat the contested ground of Eliot's relationship to the Romantic poets and their tradition. In its examination of Eliot's interest in the supernatural and its account of the "uncanny" effect of much of his verse, Longenbach's essay also subtly revises the view of Eliot as an exclusively rational poet who early separated from his contemporary Symbolist tradition. Riquelme also highlights the uncanny.

Several essays revise our notions of Eliot by directly confronting Eliot's current assailants. Ronald Bush challenges both Eliot's New Critical defenders and his Marxist critics by associating him with an American, Emersonian tradition. Through an analysis of Eliot's post-World War II essays, Jeffrey Perl defends him against those who condemn him as politically reactionary and anti-Semitic and who reify his views according

to his early essays. Richard Shusterman refutes these same
naysayers by proving that Eliot's actual arguments against the
dominant bourgeois liberal ideology of his time can be
appropriated by today's radical cultural critique.

Other works contribute to our understanding of Eliot
by treating neglected subjects. Cleo Kearns, for example, examines *Four Quartets* in light of his much maligned, but little
examined, Christian beliefs. Sanford Schwartz, Jewel Spears
Brooker, and James Longenbach all examine the relationship
between Eliot's poetry and the theories in his dissertation, which
has only recently been recognized as important to his works.
Mohammad Shaheen and Joan Fillmore Hooker's analyses of
Eliot in French and Arabic prove the extent and substance of his
influence. Harvey Gross' discussion of the affinities between
Four Quartets and Thomas Mann's *Doctor Faustus* enlarges our
understanding of modernism and the historical forces shaping
literature during World War II.

Many essays bring new perspectives on traditional
subjects. This is true of David Moody's, Hugh Kenner's, and J.
P. Riquelme's treatment of Eliot's formal innovations and his
use of allusions, topics which were the most prominent in early
reactions to his verse. Louis Martz gives us an entirely new
reading of *Ash-Wednesday* by placing it in a tradition of love
poetry commencing with Calvacanti, Dante, and Petrarch
instead of the Christian tradition in which it is usually studied.
Barbara Everett turns away from more usual philosophical or
theological readings of *East Coker* and examines the curious status of the poem's place-name title. W. B. Worthen and Richard
Badenhausen both contribute to the scholarship on Eliot's
drama. Worthen analyzes the function of the text in the *mise-en-
scène* and the roles that actor, character, and spectator play in
Murder in the Cathedral. Badenhausen concentrates particularly
on the Chorus' relationship to its audience and studies Eliot's
transition from poet to dramatist.

It is part of the revaluative nature of this collection
that its essays do not categorize easily. They are divided,
nonetheless, into separate sections, in order to help the reader.
(However, the index probably offers greater assistance.) The
form is circular. It begins with "A Shape and A Significance," a
general section most of whose essays treat Eliot's career as a
whole, or at least many of its different phases. The authors in
the next section, "The Whole of Literature: A Simultaneous
Existence," examine Eliot's works in respect to foreign works or
authors. Discussions which focus on particular works make up

"The Three Voices." The collection's emphasis on *Four Quartets* and Eliot's theoretical works (and in particular, his dissertation) reflects the current status of Eliot scholarship--where these two once slighted areas have gained prominence. The essays in the final section, "A Distinctive Activity of the Critical Mind," con- centrate mostly on his theoretical writings, which are inherently more general. In our end is our beginning.

"A SHAPE AND A SIGNIFICANCE": ELIOT'S WORKS IN GENERAL

A. D. MOODY

ELIOT'S FORMAL INVENTION*

"The water whirls up the bright pale sand in the spring's mouth."
That line from Pound's canto 4 might be a way of imaging his
idea that emotion is the source of form (15). In a later canto he
wrote:

> This liquid is certainly a
>   property of the mind
> nec accidens est   but an element
>   in the mind's make-up
> est agens and functions   dust to a fountain pan otherwise
>   Hast 'ou seen the rose in the steel dust
>   (or swansdown ever?)
> so light is the urging, so ordered the dark petals of iron   (74/449)

This is to conceive of form and order not as an end-product, but
as an energy; to think not of the empty shell, but of the living
forces that shaped it. "Every force evolves a form," as Guy Dav-
enport has remarked.

     In Eliot's poetry it is certainly the force of emotion
that evolves the form. I take that to be self-evident. But if
demonstration were called for, one might start with "Preludes,"
and observe a simple and powerful emotion shaping a heap of
sordid images into a coherent world, and evolving a poetic form
which is the specific form of the soul constituted of those
images. The form is what brings everything in a poem together,
so that we can see it as a whole and find that we understand it.

     To apprehend the inner, shaping form of a poem, or
of a play or novel, is one of the major pleasures of reading,
indeed the ultimate satisfaction. Yet we as readers and critics of
Eliot perhaps take it too much for granted. To attend directly to
it for once may be an appropriate thing to do in this centennial
year, since to investigate the form of his poetry, its changing and
evolving form, is to concern ourselves with both the substance

---

*This paper was a keynote lecture at the National Poetry Foundation's T. S. Eliot Centennial Confer-
ence, August 18-20, 1988, Orono, Maine. Copyright © 1990 by A. D. Moody.

and the essence of his achievement, and to recognise what is of lasting value in the inheritance he has left us.

The emphasis in my title is upon Eliot's invention of form. I might as well have said his innovation of form. To invent can mean to discover, or to rediscover, something latent or lost. It would not mean, when we are talking of Eliot, to make up forms no-one had ever thought of, though the form of his *Four Quartets* may be an invention in that sense. His inventiveness was mainly a matter of reworking existing poetic forms, and discovering new possibilities in them. Existing forms and influences were his primary resource--and not at all a source of anxiety. Prufrock, the character, is made deeply anxious by the social forms that would make him a mere creature of circumstance. But Eliot, in dramatizing Prufrock's predicament, draws upon a range of literary forms with genuine freedom and inventiveness.

"The Love Song of J. Alfred Prufrock" is the proper place for this inquiry to begin, because it exhibits the form of Eliot's early poetry at its most developed. But before going into it in detail it may be helpful if I give some bearings, to indicate where I am heading. I see Eliot's formal development as a continuous progress through the whole of his career as a poet, from 1909 to 1942. Within it three main phases or stages can be made out. The first begins with his discovery of Laforgue in 1908 or 1909, and continues into the ur-*Waste Land*, that is, the poem as drafted in 1921. This is the phase of *dramatic* lyricism. The second begins with his finding a new style and form as he completed *The Waste Land* at the end of 1921 or in early 1922, and it includes his "dream poetry" of the 1920s, *The Hollow Men, Ash-Wednesday* and "Marina." This is the phase of *pure* lyricism. In retrospect it can be seen to have been a transitional style and form; but Eliot himself thought for a time that with "Marina" he had reached the end of his development as a poet, and turned towards writing for the theater. But then, somehow, out of *Murder in the Cathedral* came *Burnt Norton*, and thence his third and most important phase, that of his *Four Quartets*. This is the phase of *metaphysical* lyricism, in which thought has taken over from the dramatic.

The relation of the last phase to the first can be gauged by comparing some remarks made in 1917, the year in which the Prufrock volume was published, with remarks made in the 40s, after *Four Quartets*. Writing in 1917 about the relation of vers libres to traditional meters, Eliot said: "[T]he most interesting verse which has yet been written in our language has been done ... by taking a very simple form, like the iambic pentameter, and constantly withdrawing from it" (TCC 185). "Prufrock" would be an example of that. But in 1947, in his British Academy lecture on Milton, there is a different emphasis: "In studying *Paradise Lost* we come to perceive that the verse is continuously animated by the departure from, and return to, the regular measure" (OPP 183). That return has the effect of making the regular measure the norm. And there are indeed many passages in *Four Quartets* which are regulated by blank verse or by some other set form. Eliot also had something to say about "intricate formal patterns" in the 1917 essay (TCC 189). Their decay, he thought, had gone too far, along with the decay of the Mind of Europe, for a modern poet to be able to do much with them. But in 1942, in *The Music of Poetry*, he blandly said: "It is sometimes assumed that modern poetry has done away with forms" such as the sonnet, the formal ode, the sestina. "I have seen signs of a return to them," he went on, saying nothing of his own return to them in the *Four Quartets*, "and indeed, I believe that the tendency to return to set and even elaborate patterns is permanent" (OPP 30). Had the Mind of Europe been so much restored in just twenty-five years? In 1917 he had thought that

> only in a closely knit and homogeneous society, where many men are at work on the same problems, such a society as those which produced the Greek chorus, the Elizabethan lyric, and the Troubadour canzone, will the development of such forms ever be carried to perfection. (TCC 189)

Eliot did not imagine, I am sure, that he was living in such a society in 1940-42, the years of his wartime quartets, each of which has a section in some set form. The change had taken place in his own mind. He could by then conceive of a Christian society, a communion of saints, closely knit and homogeneous, and at work on the same problems. So a baroque lyric after St. John of the Cross and Crashaw, a sestina after Arnaut Daniel, and terza rima after Dante, had become forms which could be returned to and further developed. He had gone far from "The Love Song of J. Alfred Prufrock."

The form of "Prufrock" is the product of two opposed tendencies. There is the tendency to disintegrate regular forms, both in the line and in the strophe; and there is the tendency to fall back into the iambic pentameter and a set pattern of rhyme. Prufrock begins his monologue with a paragraph that might be said to depart in every possible direction from the iambic pentameter, only to arrive at the closures of his rhymes--

> Oh, do not ask, "What is it?"
> Let us go and make our visit.

And again:

> In the room the women come and go
> Talking of Michelangelo.

Those couplets have the iambic pulse, but they are not full pen-
tameters. The only wholly regular pair of iambic pentameters--
but they don't rhyme--are these:

> I should have been a pair of ragged claws
> Scuttling across the floors of silent seas.

But this is the moment of escape, if only into fantasy, and it is
odd that the escape should be *into* a regular measure. Through
the previous seventy lines Prufrock has maintained a consistent
irregularity, changing form from line to line and stanza to
stanza, as if to avoid being formulated and pinned down. Yet in
those two lines he virtually formulates himself.

   Along with the evasion of the iambic pentameter and
the retreat into it, there is a drifting into regular strophic forms
despite a deft irregularity in the handling of them. There are the
three stanzas beginning with some variation upon "I have known
them all already, known them all," and ending with a variation
upon "So how should I presume?" (CPP 5). Each of these stanzas has a different number of lines and a different rhyme
scheme. Then there are the two longer, more developed stro-
phes, beginning upon "And would it have been worth it, after
all," and ending with "That is not what I meant, at all" (CPP 6).
Here again, the second strophe nervously won't settle into the
same pattern as the first; and the rhymes, at once irregular and
predictable, further disturb any sense of reassuring order.

   Until the final section, beginning at "No! I am not
Prince Hamlet," the writing is consistently restless, disturbed,
unsettled. Apart from the one moment--"I should have been a
pair of ragged claws"--the poem can't or won't rest in the iambic
pentameter. And while it seems to be moving into set strophic
forms, it can't or won't settle in them. The form of the poem is
then this unresolved conflict, between a feeling for some definite
form, and a drawing back from any that begins to materialise.
That conflict is the very life of Prufrock and of the poem, being
the occasion of his wit and the cause of his inventiveness. His
decadence, or disintegration, is dynamic.

   In the final section of the poem, however, the form
no longer holds. The tension of conflicting impulses is relaxed,

and there is, not a resolution, but a separating out and a breaking down. First there is the pastiche of dramatic blank verse, the Prince Hamlet strut, which sends itself up in its rhymes. Then there are the very different closing rhymes, in which self-mockery gives way to self-pity:

> I grow old . . . I grow old . . .
> I shall wear the bottoms of my trousers rolled.
> . . . .
> We have lingered in the chambers of the sea
> By sea-girls wreathed with seaweed red and brown
> Till human voices wake us and we drown.

In this final part of the poem, what was before a genuinely dramatic lyricism, has separated out into self-mocking dramatic posturing, and self-consoling lyricism. The real drama in which Prufrock lived and suffered so inventively is dissipated in the mere posturing, and he ends in a lyric mode which is thoroughly conventional. Yet again, and terminally, he has escaped or lapsed into a fixed formula and a set form.

That separating out of the dramatic and lyric elements--surely an ironic completion of the form in "Prufrock"--is, rather surprisingly, the basis of the form of *The Waste Land*. The form of parts 1-3, at least, is that of fragments of dramatic writing cohering, if at all, around centers of lyric feeling. The dramatic writing, mostly pastiche, is doing the dead in different voices, and exhibiting, in used up literary forms, the deathliness of what passes for living. The absence of originality and inventiveness in these passages makes their point. The lyric writing, on the other hand, does have originality, and becomes progressively more vital and innovative, to the point of being the dominant element in part 5. Instead of ending up, as Prufrock does, in one of Romanticism's clichés, *The Waste Land* finds a way out of its dead ends through a development of the lyric mode. When we consider the poem in its entirety, from the early drafts through to the published state, we find a progression from lifeless pastiche and imitation of past literary forms towards what Eliot rightly called his new form and style. And it is this progression, from the dramatic monologue to a purely lyric voice, and to a new form of the lyric, which constitutes the form of *The Waste Land*.

The narrative of a doomed fishing voyage out of Gloucester was justly damned by Pound for its dead regular iambic pentameter. He also struck out the inferior couplets, (after Rochester rather than Pope), doing Fresca at her toilet; and he salvaged, by skillful surgery, the passage which Eliot had written in strict quatrains after Dryden and Gray, giving Tiresias' observation of the typist and clerk. Among the drafts there were also an Exequy, an Elegy, a Dirge, and various songs, extending the series of waxworks. Those lifeless imitations disappeared, yet there remains a good deal of pastiche in the final version. Marie, Madame Sosostris, the prophet in the desert and the Dantescan vision of the Unreal City, are as much pastiche as "The Chair she sat in" (CPP 39) and the Pub monologue, or "By the waters of Leman I sat down and wept" (CPP 42). The difference between these passages of pastiche and those which were cut out of the poem is partly in their greater intensity and concentration of effect. But it is even more that they are not mere imitations. The typist and clerk episode--in its more concentrated form, with everything that was only filling out the quatrains removed--creates its own world, and instead of being an inferior form of verse presents an inferior form of life.

A striking aspect of the personages of the poem, as Eliot called them, is that, while they are dramatic voices, they are not involved in any significant action. They are the isolated fragments of a static predicament, and the more they speak the more they say the same thing. The significant action of the poem, and its effective development, is carried on in the lyric parts, the centers of feeling; beginning with " 'You gave me hyacinths first a year ago' . . . I knew nothing, / Looking into the heart of light, the silence" (CPP 38). The ambiguities of that knowing nothing are resolved in "A Game of Chess":

"What is that noise now? What is that wind doing?"
                    Nothing again nothing.

                                                    "Do
"You know nothing? Do you see nothing? Do you remember
"Nothing?"

    I remember
Those are pearls that were his eyes.
"Are you alive, or not? Is there nothing in your head?" (CPP 40-1)

The Thames-daughters' song takes up the theme with apparent finality:

"On Margate Sands.
I can connect
Nothing with nothing.
The broken fingernails of dirty hands.
My people humble people who expect
Nothing."   (CPP 46)

Then, in "What the Thunder Said," the negative becomes specific, and is developed into an expression of positive desire. First there is the insistent "Here is no water but only rock / Rock and no water . . . rock without water" (CPP 47). Out of that develops what Eliot called "the water-dripping song" (after the song of the hermit-thrush):

> If there were water
> And no rock
> If there were rock
> And also water
> And water
> A spring
> A pool among the rock
> If there were the sound of water only
> Not the cicada
> And dry grass singing
> But sound of water over a rock
> Where the hermit-thrush sings in the pine trees
> Drip drop drip drop drop drop drop
> But there is no water   (CPP 47-48)

When *The Waste Land* was published Eliot said that so far as he was concerned it was a thing of the past, and that he was feeling towards a new form and style. But in fact his new form and style was already achieved in the "water-dripping song," which he had been working towards through the sequence of lyrics on the theme of "nothing." Taken together, they bear out Pound's axiom that emotion originates form. Their form, as it happens, follows another of Pound's axioms: that the effective presentation of an intellectual and emotional complex requires a strict economy of words; and, as to rhythm, "compose in the sequence of the musical phrase" ("A Retrospect" 95). Robert Creeley summed it up as "Form is an extension of content." In the "bad nerves" section of "A Game of Chess," there is a sense of quatrains disintegrating under the strain of neurosis. In contrast, the Thames-daughters' short, broken phrases assume a formal shape, composing a sketchy sonnet after the fashion of those in the *Vita Nuova*. In the "water-dripping song" there is no extrinsic shape at all, but simply a succession of phrases imaging an emotional sequence, and with the music arising naturally from the pulses of feeling.

Eliot once used the term "dream songs" for this kind of writing--Berryman, I assume, borrowed it from Eliot, and made it his own. It is an apt term for songs arising in that dreamlike state when ordinary reality dims, and in its place we see what we feel, or see the world as we inwardly feel it. "Dream

songs" are phantasmagoric, that is, visionary projections of what
is intensely desired or intensely suffered, as the "water-dripping
song" projects both an oppressive aridity and the water that is
no water. Later, the Unreal City is transmogrified into "falling
towers," as a "city over the mountains / Cracks and reforms and
bursts in the violet air" (CPP 48). It was actually to some sections of *The Hollow Men* that Eliot applied the term "dream
songs," but with "On Margate Sands" and much of "What the
Thunder Said" we are already in the realm of that later
sequence, and of *Ash-Wednesday*. The alien world of the dramatic voices has either been transcended, or transformed into
nightmare (as in "A women drew her long black hair out tight"),
or else it is viewed with the philosophic or moralising detachment of the responses to the thunder.

What was new in Eliot's poetry after *The Waste Land*
was the virtual exclusion of the realm of common reality and
drama. Instead, the inner feelings were freed from its oppres-
sions, as in "Marina":

> Those who sit in the style of contentment, meaning
> Death
> Those who suffer the ecstasy of the animals, meaning
> Death
>
> Are become unsubstantial, reduced by a wind,
> A breath of pine, and the woodsong fog
> By this grace dissolved in place. . . . (CPP 72)

"Marina" reformulates the ordinary world so as to give a shape
and form to desire, and it would appear to place us in a realm of
pure lyricism. Yet that striking assertion of a meaning, "meaning
/ Death," points up what most distinguishes *The Hollow Men*
and *Ash-Wednesday* from *The Waste Land*. In this phase of
Eliot's poetry, feeling is not in fact all, for the feelings are being
interpreted and ordered by the understanding. The images are
not only charged with feeling, but even more with meaning, as in
The Hollow Men: "There, the eyes are / Sunlight on a broken
column," or--

> Let me also wear
> Such deliberate disguises
> Rat's coat, crowskin, crossed staves
> In a field. . . . (CPP 57)

In later sections the meaning is spelt out, though in an abrupt
and abbreviated manner, by allusions to Dante, a citation of the
Lord's Prayer, and some philosophical assertions:

Between the potency
And the existence
Between the essence
And the descent
Falls the Shadow

For Thine is the Kingdom. . . . (CPP 59)

Throughout *Ash-Wednesday* it is the same. We find intense feelings not so much seeking their form as seeking their meaning. The Garden, which might have been the Hyacinth Garden, becomes the desert; but instead of the hermit-thrush singing, we are told that the desert "Is now the garden / Where all loves end." Then the meaning is further developed in the variation, "the Garden / Where all loves end" (CPP 62).

Eliot had become convinced that emotion was not enough, and that the sensibility was not, by itself, a source of form and order. Rather, it needed to be saved from itself by being ordered according to an intellectual understanding. Eliot's disapproval of D. H. Lawrence was based on his judgment that Lawrence lacked understanding of what came to him from below consciousness. Certainly that was where a writer had to start, with "the deeper, unnamed feelings which form the substratum of our being" (UPUC 149); but then the poet's business was to shape the feelings into a significant pattern. For Eliot, of course, the pattern followed the Christian interpretation of experience, as in Dante and the Desert Fathers. This profoundly altered the nature of his lyric writing, and in a problematic way. What happens to the lyric when its form, instead of arising from the shaping emotion, is given also by a quite distinct intellectual process? We naturally suspect that the intellect will interfere with the emotion and that the form will be forced. But in *Ash-Wednesday* I detect no disparity between the feeling and the form. Certainly it is a willed form, but then longing and willing are what the poem is all about. "Our peace in His will" is just the order the feelings have been seeking (CPP 67). There is nothing wrong with the form then.

The problem is rather that there is something lacking, that the form is imperfect. The intellectual element, which does play an important part in the poem, is not fully realised. We are not given the intellectual process by which the feelings are brought to that Dantescan order. We are given the answer, as it were, but not shown how it is reached. If emotion is not enough, but needs to be supplemented by the intellect, then pure lyricism cannot be enough either. The intellect must find its own voice and be seen to play its part within the poem. But the pecu-

liar quality of *Ash-Wednesday* and of the Ariel poems is that they
are metaphysical poetry written in a lyric mode. That is a
notable achievement, and yet the metaphysics requires more
than the lyric mode.

The metaphysics required the form of *Burnt Norton*
and the three later quartets. That seems obvious now; but I
think it was not at all obvious to Eliot when he moved on from
"Marina" to "Coriolan" and *The Rock* and *Murder in the Cathedral*. The line of development he was following there was into
dramatic writing, doing voices again. It was only in the course of
writing for the theater that Eliot discovered a form for his metaphysical poetry. He himself said that *Burnt Norton* began with
some passages that would not work in the stage-production of
Murder in the Cathedral; but the connection goes further and
deeper. In the choruses for *The Rock* he had experimented with
a great range of styles, lyric, dramatic, didactic, philosophical,
devotional; but it was in the nature of that work that the choruses did not form a unified whole. In *Murder in the Cathedral* a
similar range of styles is deployed in a more structured form,
which roughly adumbrates that of *Burnt Norton*. The Chorus
speaks for the sensibility which feels sensitively what is happening but does not understand it. The Priests give a more intelligent account of affairs. But Thomas goes beyond them in
declaring a metaphysical understanding of the pattern in his
existence. There are other styles in the play, particularly those of
the Tempters and of the Knights in their self-justification to the
audience. But the one that matters most in the end is the transformation of the Chorus into a communion of believers affirming the pattern which Thomas has revealed in their experience.
These several distinct styles and voices are the basis of Eliot's
quartet form. The voice of the sensitive sensibility; the voice of
the analytic intelligence; the voice of metaphysical understanding; and the visionary voice, seeing and accepting what has been
understood--these are the four instruments which make up his
quartet.

Burnt Norton begins philosophically: "Time present
and time past . . . What might have been and what has been /
Point to one end, which is always present" (CPP 117). These
abstractions modulate into a daydream mingling memory and
imagination, experience and mystery: "the roses / Had the look
of flowers that are looked at," and "the leaves were full of children, / Hidden excitedly, containing laughter" (CPP 118). When
this first movement closes with a repeat of the philosophical
statement, led into by "human kind / Cannot bear very much

reality," I am reminded of the structure of parts 1 and 2 of *The Waste Land*: a center of intense experience is surrounded by, and as it were challenged by, other and alien voices. But in *Burnt Norton* what questions the imagination and its visionary moment is more than disillusionment (the cloud passing). It is that generalising and summing up of human experience in universal propositions. That is the dominant mode, the leading instrument, in *Burnt Norton*. But then the philosophical mode develops beyond mere abstract propositions. In the third movement, the thinking, instead of being opposed to memory and imagination, is applied to their realm of experience:

> Here is a place of disaffection
> Time before and time after
> In a dim light: neither daylight
> Investing form with lucid stillness
> Turning shadow into transient beauty
> With slow rotation suggesting permanence
> Nor darkness to purify the soul

Instead this observer discovers only

> Men and bits of paper, whirled by the cold wind
> That blows before and after time
> . . . .
> Eructation of unhealthy souls
> Into the faded air, the torpid
> Driven on the wind that sweeps the gloomy hills of London. . . .
> (CPP 120)

This is the seeing, as in a vision, what the philosophy had asserted about "the enchainment of past and future" (CPP 119). Then in the fourth and fifth movements there is the effort to see with the aid of imagination what it means to be "At the still point of the turning world" (CPP 121). This is led up to by a memory taken over into thought, with the effect of making the intelligence momentarily lyrical:

> After the kingfisher's wing
> Has answered light to light, and is silent, the light is still
> At the still point of the turning world.

In such a passage all the instruments of the quartet are playing in unison.

That order of composition is reached by a progressive development of the dominant philosophical mode. First it declares propositions or basic principles. Then experience, "the moment in the rose-garden," is meditated upon in the light of those ideas. And the meditation leads to an altered perception of experience, a different way of seeing the world, one in which memory and imagination have been informed and transformed by the philosophical process. Thus, instead of regretting what the black cloud carries away, the poem ends

> Sudden in a shaft of sunlight
> Even while the dust moves
> There rises the hidden laughter
> Of children in the foliage
> Quick now, here, now, always--
> Ridiculous the waste sad time
> Stretching before and after.   (CPP 122)

There the voice of experience, which includes memory and imagination, is brought into harmony with the voices of analytical and metaphysical thought, and is no longer being questioned by them, or having its motifs taken over and transformed. It is still the voice of desire, but now it sees the world in their way. That is what Eliot's quartet form is for: to bring his experience of life into harmony with his understanding of it, to restore "the experience / In a different form" (CPP 133).

   Burnt Norton appeared as the concluding poem in *Collected Poems 1909-1935*, and it was the culmination, and the completion, of twenty-five years' work. No one could have expected "Prufrock" and *The Waste Land* to lead to this; and yet the progression can be seen, with hindsight, to have been natural and inevitable, with each stage preparing and requiring the next. The Thames-daughters' song and the water-dripping song led on to *The Hollow Men* and *Ash-Wednesday* and "Marina." Then the new role given to meaning in those dream songs led on to the fully realised metaphysical poetry of *Burnt Norton*. At each new stage, moreover, there is a resuming of what had gone before. *The Waste Land* achieved a new form on the basis of the separation of the dramatic and lyric elements at the end of "Prufrock." *The Hollow Men* is a virtual resumé, in the new form and style of dream song, of *The Waste Land*. The garden of *Burnt Norton* picks up not only the garden imagery of *Ash-Wednesday*, but also resumes, in its moment of illumination and deception, *The Waste Land*'s Hyacinth Garden and water-dripping song. It is as if *Burnt Norton* were starting again from those states of heightened sensibility and going on to treat them in the new metaphysical manner. The result is not a departure from lyricism, but a reaching through thought for a new kind of lyricism. Not the lyricism of the dream state, in which subconscious feelings take shape in image and rhythm; but the lyricism of thought itself, when it is a reshaping of experience into a vision, as in "Time and the bell have buried the day" (CPP 121), and "Sudden in a shaft of sunlight / Even while the dust moves" (CPP 122).

It might appear that in *Burnt Norton* the form owes more to the philosopher in Eliot than to emotion. But what moved his mind in its thinking if not his emotional sources? The shaping intelligence is moved by a profound need to explicate experience, and actually to see it as having a meaning and a pattern. The need arises in the sensibility, not in the intellect; and the function of the thinking in the poem is to think out the sensibility and to resolve it into the order which it seeks but could not attain on its own. The sense that life cannot satisfy his desires is not a product of argument, but is rather what is argued out in such a way as to erect it into a principle to live by. One could say that the form of *Burnt Norton*, and the basis of *Four Quartets*, is the ultimate form attained by Eliot's mind; but it might be more exact to say that it is the form in which his sensibility most fully articulated itself.

Looked at either way, it is a form that only Eliot could have invented, because you would have had to be Eliot, and to have worked through the stages of his development, to arrive at that specific and unparalleled form. Other poets, Eliot's contemporaries, developed other forms, and their forms, Pound's and Williams' especially, have proved serviceable for younger poets in a way that Eliot's has not. It would be too simple to conclude that Pound and Williams opened up new possibilities for poetry, while Eliot rather ended a tradition. To have extended the possibilities of verse as Eliot did, and to have invented a wholly new form, is not to be the end of anything. And still I find it hard to imagine poets now taking up Eliot's quartet form as Olson and Duncan and Ginsberg carried on from *The Cantos* and from *Paterson*.

Of course he himself further developed his quartet form in the three wartime quartets. He did not simply repeat the form of *Burnt Norton*. *East Coker* and *The Dry Salvages* depart from that first quartet in a number of ways. There is a greater diversity of style, going with the wider range of material and the enlarged sense of history; and there are variations in the form, the most significant of which bind the two quartets together into a single work, a continuous progression from "In my beginning is my end" through to "The life of significant soil." *Little Gidding* not only continues the sequence, but resumes the other three in such a way as to compose the four quartets into a whole.

When we see them in that way, then we can see *Four Quartets* as not only completing, but as making a whole of Eliot's poetic *oeuvre*. We can find a shape and form in his poetry taken all together, as in an ideal "Collected Poems 1909-1942," and this form corresponds to his quartet form. First there is the extraordinarily sensitive sensibility, dramatising its feelings in phantasmagorical, and lyrical, visions and revisions. Second, there is the effort to order the sensibility intellectually, in order both to confirm its findings from experience, and to direct it towards a realm beyond experience. Thirdly, there is the attainment in a poetic form of an intellectual vision of experience, a vision which would carry the feelings with the mind into a realm beyond sense. Eliot's power of formal invention was such that he created, not just a series of poems each having its own specific form, but his own poetic macrocosm.

WORKS CITED

Pound, Ezra. *The Cantos of Ezra Pound*. New York: New Directions, 1970.
_____ . *Pavannes and Divisions*. New York: Alfred A. Knopf, 1918.

RONALD BUSH

"TURNED TOWARD CREATION":
*T. S. ELIOT, 1988**

Begin with Paris in November 1922 and with the American poet
John Peale Bishop. Bishop, five years out of Princeton and travelling on an extended honeymoon, has paid a visit to Ezra Pound
in Montparnasse. Previously, his good friend, Edmund (Bunny)
Wilson, editor at *Vanity Fair* and *The New Republic*, had raved to
him about a forthcoming masterpiece by T. S. Eliot. Proofs of
The Waste Land were made available to Wilson by the New
York journal, the *Dial*, which was to bring the poem out in
November and wanted to follow up with an essay in December,
trumpeting its praise. We shall have occasion to glance at Wilson's essay in a moment. Wilson's first response, though, was as
interesting. On September 5th, supplied with notes he had not
yet had time to read, he had written to Bishop that "the poem,
as it appears to me from two or three cursory readings, is nothing more or less than a most distressingly moving account of
Eliot's own agonized state of mind during the years which preceded his nervous breakdown. Never have the sufferings of the
sensitive man in the modern city chained to some work he hates
and crucified on the vulgarity of his surroundings been so vividly
set forth. It is certainly a cry *de profundis* if ever there was one--
almost the cry of a man on the verge of insanity" (Letters 94).
      Bishop, primed by this letter, read the now published
Waste Land with enthusiasm and contrived after visiting Eliot's
friend Pound to invite him to dinner. The dinner was a success,
and sometime before November 29, he wrote: "Dear Bunny." "I
wished many times that you might have been here to see the
great 'Amurcan' poet work out. There was a lot of his past that
came out after he had begun to get into his cups which was fairly
soon, as well as a few points about 'Tears' Eliot (as some Paris
wit has recently christened him)" (qtd. in Spindler 80). Con-

---
*This essay was originally given as a paper at the National Poetry Foundation's T. S. Eliot Centennial
Conference, August 18-20, 1988, Orono, Maine.

cerning Eliot, Bishop in fact had a good deal to say. For example:

> Eliot is tubercular and disposed toward epilepsy. On one occasion
> he decided to kill himself in Pound's house but funked at the final
> moment. The psychological hour in *Lustra* [Pound's 1916 collec-
> tion of poems] gives E.P.'s reaction to T.S.E.'s wedding which was
> substituted on the spur of the moment for a tea engagement at
> Pound's. It seems that Thomas and Vivienne arrived in the hall-
> way and then turned back, went to the registrar's and were wed, to
> everybody's subsequent pain and misery. She . . . is an invalid. . . .
> \ Eliot's version of her is contained in [the lines beginning] 'The
> Chair she sat in like a burnished throne.' . . . [The pub scene, on
> the other hand,] reflects the atmosphere immediately outside their
> first flat in London. Eliot, it seems, is hopelessly caught in his own
> prudent temperament. . . . Mr. Eugenides actually turned up at
> Lloyds with his pocket full of currants and asked Eliot to spend a
> weekend with him for no nice reasons. His place in the poem is, I
> believe, as a projection of Eliot, however. That is, all the men are
> in some way deprived of their life-giving, generative forces.

Needless to say, all of this made an impact on Bishop's reading
of *The Waste Land*, so much so that he told Wilson to
"disregard" his recent inquiries. "I think," he wrote,

> I have cleared up the meaning of the poem as far as it is possible.
> . . . It's my present opinion that the poem is not so logically con-
> structed as I had at first supposed and that it is a mistake to seek
> for more than . . . personal emotion in a number of passages. The
> Nightingale passage is, I believe, important: Eliot being Tereus
> and Mrs. E., Philomela. That is to say, that through unbalanced
> passion, everybody is in a hell of a fix; Tereus being changed into a
> hoopoe [i.e., a hawk] and T. S. E. a bank clerk. Thomas' sexual
> troubles are undoubtedly extreme. (qtd. in Spindler 81-82)

Bishop's letter, which as far as I know has never been
cited, will have to be accounted for. But I leave that accounting,
as well as the task of sorting out the truth of what Pound told
Bishop, for another place. What concerns me here are the
dynamics of transmission beginning with this moment very close
on the composition of *The Waste Land* and opening out into its
first public reception. For we know that Wilson answered
Bishop's letter immediately, and that his response, written a little short of three months after he advised Bishop that *The Waste
Land* was "nothing more or less than a most distressingly moving account of Eliot's own agonized state of mind," was to leave
a large mark (*Letters* 98). Between September and November,
Wilson studied Eliot's notes, supplied to him with the Liveright
proofs but unavailable to Bishop, who read the poem in the

October *Criterion* or the November *Dial*, both without notes.
And on the heels of his study Wilson changed his tune. Writing
on November 29, 1922, he was as ever patronizing to Bishop,
who, older than Wilson, had passed through Princeton a year
behind him. He began the letter expressing interest in Pound's
"gossip," but assuring his friend that, as he would discover if he
read Wilson's "long thing" in the *Dial*, he had "the wrong dope
about the nightingale." The bird, he assured Bishop, was the
reflection of the " 'sylvan scene' in *Paradise Lost*," just as
Tereus, the barbarous king, was "not Eliot, but the things which
are crucifying Eliot," which Bishop would realize once he read
Titus Andronicus, act IV, scene i (*Letters* 99). And while he was
at it Bishop would have to refresh his memory of *The Spanish
Tragedy, Anthony and Cleopatra, The Golden Bough*, etc.

The rest, as the saying goes, is history. And as we are
in the process of discovering, history tends to ride on ideological
rails. Wilson's essay, which appeared in the December 1922
Dial, contained an extremely sensitive assessment of the personal and cultural resonances of *The Waste Land*, but it was
dominated by an urge to explain to the public at large, as Wilson
had already explained to Bishop, the significance of Eliot's
"complicated correspondences" and "recondite references and
quotations" ("Poetry of Drouth" 616). Wilson's patronizing,
moreover, though an expression of his personality and of his editorial persona, was also part of his institutional charge. As was
pointed out many years ago, the editors of the *Dial*, Scofield
Thayer and J. S. Watson, Jr., had in 1922 both awarded Eliot a
large prize and commissioned Wilson's essay to advance the
magazine's mission. They bought the *Dial* to make the American
spirit "count in the great world of art and affairs" (see Wasserstrom 86 and Sieburth).[1] And, co-opted into this project, *The
Waste Land* in Wilson's description came to signify something
different from what Eliot later called--not without guile--"the
relief of a personal and wholly insignificant grouse against
life . . . a piece of rhythmical grumbling" (WLF 1). Whatever the
disjunctions of its formal and thematic cross purposes, in Wilson's account it was made to announce the achievement of
American mastery, and therefore of classical standards of mastery and high seriousness in general.

Nor did the appropriation stop there. One of the
many themes Wilson attributed to the poem came to serve the
interests of many who followed him. In "our whole world of

---

1. Sieburth, though, seems reluctant to point out how the *Dial*'s appropriation of Eliot runs against
much in the poet's grain.

strained nerves and shattered institutions," he speculated, *The Waste Land*'s symbolic landscape of "spiritual drouth" was especially telling ("Poetry of Drouth" 616). "The reflections which reach us from the past," he added, "cannot illumine such a dingy scene."

Wilson's keynote here is "Our ... shattered institutions," our contemporary crisis of tradition and belief. And his characterization came to resonate with the changing emphases of Eliot's own concerns. To rehearse an old story: although in 1920 Eliot was quite willing to concede that poetry deals with "philosophical ideas, not as matter for argument, but as matter for inspection," by 1929 he had withdrawn his concession (SW 162). In his essay on Dante of that year he insisted that in some sense we must assume that the poet "means what he says" and that "one probably has more pleasure in the poetry when one shares the beliefs of the poet" (SE 230-31). And by then he had already indicated (in a preface added to the 1928 reprinting of *The Sacred Wood*) that his own interests had evolved. He was now less interested, he said, in poetry considered by itself than in "the relation of poetry to the spiritual and social life of its time and other times" (SW viii). Which is to say that he then considered it his task to ponder the relation of poetry to a particular order of belief--an order of belief that (to quote the same preface) elevated the poetry of Dante over that of Shakespeare because "it seems to me to illustrate a saner attitude towards the mystery of life" (SW x).

But if by the early thirties Eliot himself was ready to re-envision his earlier work along the lines Wilson had laid down, his disciples were even more so. Eliot, at least, had his moments of candor. When his friend Paul Elmer More, for example, suggested in an essay of 1932 that there was a cleavage between Eliot "the lyric prophet of chaos" and Eliot the critical exponent of classicism, he was taken aback (27). In public, with much qualification, he implied that the contradiction was only apparent (see ASG 30-31). But in private, in an unpublished letter dated 26 October 1932 and now at Princeton University Library, he was more forthcoming. There, he simply wrote that More had raised a problem to which he could not find an answer, and that the contradiction would only be resolved when no one was interested any longer in his prose or his verse.

F. O. Matthiessen, however, had none of Eliot's qualms. In the first prominent full-length study of Eliot, published in 1935, Matthiessen found himself "unable to understand" More's naiveté and patiently explained that Eliot's classicism "steadily illuminates the aims of his verse" and that both were rooted in the themes of religious belief (98-99). Then two years later Cleanth Brooks, an admirer of Matthiessen's, published one of the landmark essays by which New Criticism domesticated modernism. Despite the force of its corrosive ironies, Brooks explained, *The Waste Land* was in fact a calculated unity. Its "theme" was "the rehabilitation of a system of beliefs" which had been reduced to clichés, and its method of indirection, though lamentably "violent and radical," was necessary if the poet were to bring Christian truth back to life (171). Thus was the shape and ideological import of *The Waste Land* fixed for a generation. What Edmund Wilson, albeit tentatively and against his own initial instincts, had been impelled by the politics of his sponsor to begin, the New Critics consolidated into dogma. And as *The Waste Land* became part of the academic curriculum the testimony of Wilson's friend Bishop was forgotten.

2

It is one cause for optimism in this centennial year of Eliot's birth that at last the New Critical appropriation of *The Waste Land* has lost its grip on literary history, and that energies in the poem that were obvious to its first readers are once more being acknowledged. During the last ten years a number of careful and thoughtful studies have examined Eliot's early poetics and discovered not conformity with his later political and philosophical positions, but philosophical, formal and psychological disjunctions of considerable force. In 1984, for instance, Michael Levenson's *A Genealogy of Modernism* examined the developing premises of Eliot, Ford, Conrad, Hulme and Pound and concluded that they had changed radically over the course of modernism's first decade. The writings of these figures, according to Levenson, built on themselves in "conflicting and sometimes contradictory" ways, and these contradictions rather than any ideological uniformity conditioned their creative work (192). The case of *The Waste Land* was particularly interesting. It was, Levenson says, an attempt to restore the equilibrium of religious authority conditioned by a form derived from the philosophical pluralism of Eliot's doctoral dissertation. Wittingly or not, Eliot guaranteed that any unity achieved by his poem would be "provisional." And thus inexorably "the principle of order in *The Waste Land* depends on . . . an ever-increasing series of points of

view, which struggle towards an emergent unity and then continue to struggle past that unity" (193).

There is also the resurgence of biographical and psychological interpretation, which started with the publication of
The Waste Land drafts, and which lately has grown more subtle
and better informed. Although this kind of criticism obviously
eschews the broad theoretical and cultural questions raised by
Eliot's poem and its reception, it does serve also to limit certain
kinds of excesses. Once we have recognized the divided impulses
driving Eliot's composition, for example, and the fact that the
"different voices" of his working title ("He do the police in different voices") had strong unconscious sources, it becomes more
difficult to credit an account like Brooks', which gives us a poem
sprung full-bodied from its author's conscious mastery. The New
Critical line, we remember, was anticipated and pilloried by
Eliot's close friend Conrad Aiken, who in a *New Republic* review
that appeared four months after *The Waste Land* was published
took pains to insist that "the poem is not, in any formal sense,
coherent," that it is anything but "a perfect piece of construction" (194-95). In Aiken's words, Eliot's "powerful, melancholy
tone-poem" succeeds "by virtue of its ambiguities, not of its
explanation" (98). And one would hope that as letters like John
Peale Bishop's continue to appear, it will become easier for us to
remember Aiken's admonishment and harder to accept any new
totalitarian account.

I say one would hope, however, with some melancholy. For it is already becoming apparent that a new set of
shibboleths have come into play that reinforces the New Critic's
Eliot, this time not to praise the poet but to bury him. Simplify-
ing, we may identify the source of these pressures with a certain
strain of post-structuralist theory, which has come to ascribe to
postmodernism more and more of the oppositional values that
were once seen as the essence of modernism, and consequently
has depicted the modernists themselves as homogeneous and
reactionary. This kind of thing gets tricky with Joyce, Woolf, and
even Pound, of course, and these three are intermittently designated postmodernists *avant la lettre*. But Eliot is a sitting duck
because he himself prepared the ground in the latter phase of
his career. Thus we find Fredric Jameson in his book *Fables of
Aggression: Wyndham Lewis, the Modernist as Fascist,* blithely
identifying Eliot's "aesthetic and political neoclassism" with
Lewis' celebration of Hitler and cautioning us that our admiration of the modernists indicates we live in a time "when new and

as yet undeveloped forms of protofascism are in the making around us" (116, 23).

The chief exponent of this new school (and perhaps the chief obstruction to acknowledging modernism's contingent and contradictory history) is probably Terry Eagleton. Eagleton, in his 1976 *Criticism and Ideology*, shaped the Marxist commonplaces of today when he argued that *The Waste Land*, though it mimes the experience of cultural disintegration, in fact silently alludes by its "totalising mythological forms" to a "transcendence of such collapse" (150). By means of its "elaborate display of esoteric allusion" and its "closed, coherent, authoritative discourse," the poem, Eagleton asserted, produces "an ideology of cultural knowledge" consonant with the "authoritarian cultural ideology" espoused by Eliot's prose (151).

Eagleton's position, it seems to me, is simply Brooks' stood on its head. No less than Matthiessen or Brooks, Eagleton derides the idea of what Paul More called a "Cleft Eliot." For Eagleton, too, Eliot and modernism are in practice and theory monolithic; only he would argue that they are also malign. This in the face of the stark ideological contradictions that pervade the production and reception of modernist writing beginning with the case of that arch-modernist Nietzsche, whose example since 1900 has underwritten thinkers as diverse as Derrida and Mussolini.

Yet in the late 1980s, Eagleton's terms seem pervasive. Consider the case of Richard Poirier, who once celebrated the subtlety of modernist writing, but who in *The Renewal of Literature* apes Eagleton and characterizes especially Eliot's modernism as a "snob's game" (98). The modernists, Poirier now claims, having inculcated in us a respect for 'difficulty-as-a-virtue,' conned us into swallowing on updated terms the old elitist notion that literature is "a privileged and exclusive form of discourse" and cuts us off from the springs of our imaginative power as readers (99). Poirier's argument is particularly ironic because it relies on the sponsorship of Ralph Waldo Emerson and the American tradition, from which Eliot is pointedly excluded. And yet it is this last pinch of extremity that may provide us leverage to use Poirier against himself and suggest a way of approaching Eliot that will resist the reductive force of his most recent metamorphosis.

I observed above that although Edmund Wilson attributed to *The Waste Land* the theme of failed belief, there were other strains in his 1922 *Dial* review. A second, less remarked, was an identification of Eliot's "constricted emotional experience." And when, nearly ten years later, Wilson set about revising his essay for inclusion in *Axel's Castle*, the latter theme seemed to him weighty enough to begin his discussion. For in the meanwhile, Wilson had concluded that not only was Eliot a major representative of modern tendencies in literature, he was also first and foremost "characteristically American . . . . a typical product of our New England civilisation" (87). "One of the principle subjects of Eliot's poetry," Wilson noted, "is really that regret at situations unexplored, that dark rankling of passions inhibited, which has figured so conspicuously in the work of American writers of New England and New York from Hawthorne to Edith Wharton." "In this respect," Wilson continued, Eliot "has much in common with Henry James. Mr. Prufrock and the poet of the 'Portrait of a Lady,' with their helpless consciousness of having dared too little, correspond exactly to the middle-aged heroes of 'The Ambassadors' and 'The Beast in the Jungle,' realising sadly too late in life that they have been living too cautiously and too poorly."

Wilson's remarks quite rightly have become a cornerstone of Eliot criticism. But a phrase I have omitted has not, and I suspect its provocation might serve the present moment well. One of the characteristics by which Eliot most clearly disclosed his New England heritage, Wilson suggested, involved a "combination of practical prudence with moral idealism." It is the latter I would stress now. Eliot's idealistic striving, as I have argued elsewhere, colored everything he did and wrote (see Bush, "Emerson" and "Hawthorne"). Not only did it form the self-conscious subject of most of his poetry (in the form of a drama in which men live in an idealistic dreamworld only to awaken to their own betrayal of real lovers), but it motivated his philosophy and his poetics as well, launching his resistance to Emersonian excess from a platform of intellectual absoluteness and aloofness no less quintessentially American than Emerson's own. No matter how hard the later Eliot tried to accept received dogma and received ritual, his striving betrayed an Emersonian quest to renew and purify the spirit. It was the negative side of this quest that his sister Ada recognized when she confided in Eliot's friend Frank Morley shortly after her brother's conversion. "She was both interested and concerned about Tom's 'Way of contemplation,'" Morley recounts, which she imagined "might divorce him from 'human' relationships and drive him into a shadow-world of 'dramatism,' into increasing tendencies of outward 'acting' and inward 'mysticism'" (110).

But Eliot's Emersonianism had positive qualities as well--the very qualities that Poirier endorses in his new book but which, taking Eliot's preaching for practice, refuses to credit in Eliot's creative work. I am thinking now of the impulse toward imaginative renewal which gives Poirier his title and which most of us took for granted in modernism until it became fashionable to think otherwise. If Eliot's poetry returns us to the work of his great predecessors, it also, as Wilson concluded in 1922, lends "to the work of his great predecessors a new music and a new meaning" ("Poetry of Drouth" 616). And if his most famous essay calls on us to write and read with a feeling for "the whole of literature of Europe from Homer" onward, it adds that this knowledge must exist as a "simultaneous order" which is "modified by the introduction of the new (the really new) work of art"--modified, that is, by the "great labour" by which we remake the tradition for ourselves (SW 49-50).

W. H. Auden wrote in the introduction to *The Faber Book of Modern American Verse* that no true European could have written these phrases. And if "Tradition and the Individual Talent" alone weren't enough to make us nod agreement, Eliot articulates the same Emersonian yearning to make it new even more clearly in a little known lecture he gave to the Arts League of London at about the same time. This lecture, which Eliot called "Modern Tendencies in Poetry" when he published it in an obscure Indian journal, was meant, he said, to complement "Tradition and the Individual Talent."[2] As in its more familiar counterpart, in it he employs the metaphor of poet as catalyst. But in it--far more than in the reprinted piece--he takes pains to explain what it means to have a perception of the pastness of the past and of its presence. Responding to the objection that poetry is less future-looking than science because "while past work in science appears of value only because of its being the basis of present conclusions and future discoveries, past poetry retains a permanent value equal and alongside of contemporary and future work," Eliot replies,

> The life of our 'heritage' of literature is dependent upon the con-
> tinuance of literature. If you imagine yourself suddenly deprived of
> your personal present, of all possibility of action, reduced in con-
> sciousness to the memories of everything up to the present, these
> memories, this existence which would be merely the totality of
> memories, would be meaningless and flat, even if it *could* continue

---

2. The essay was published in *Shama'a* (India). As Donald Gallup notes in his *T. S. Eliot: A Bibliogra- phy* (206), a five-line excerpt was "printed under the heading 'T. S. Eliot in Poetry' in the *Bulletin of the Arts League of Service* ... with a note that the lecture 'will form the theme of an essay on Poetry ["Tradition and the Individual Talent"] which will be published shortly by "The Egoist." ' "

to exist. If suddenly all power of producing more poetry were
withdrawn from the race, if we knew that for poetry we should
have to turn always to what already existed, I think that past
poetry would become meaningless. For the capacity of appreciating poetry is inseparable from the power of producing it, it is poets
themselves who can best appreciate poetry. Life is always turned
toward creation; the present only, keeps the past alive. (12; qtd. in
Longenbach 209)

"Life is always turned toward creation." The phrase
is one Emerson would be proud of. And the statements that precede it inescapably recall, if one is in an Emersonian mood, lines
from "The Divinity School Address" and "Self-Reliance":

[truth] is an intuition. It cannot be received at second hand. Truly
speaking, it is not instruction, but provocation, that I can receive
from another soul. What he announces, I must find true in me, or
reject; and on his word, or as his second, be he who he may, I can
accept nothing. . . . Let this faith depart, and the very words it
spake and the very things it made become false and hurtful. Then
falls the church, the state, art, letters, life. . . .

. . . [I]mitation is suicide. . . . though the wide universe is full of
good, no kernel of nourishing corn can come to [a man] but
through his toil bestowed on that plot of ground which is given to
him to till. (Emerson 104, 147-48)

Still, I don't want to press the point too far. Even in
the essays Eliot wrote before *The Waste Land*, the passage I
have isolated represents one mood among many, and is usually
counterpointed both by a sense, not un-Emersonian, that the
truth we create has been created in other forms before, and by a
definitely un-Emersonian suspicion of the creative imagination.
Yet even when Eliot was most resistant, the mood recurred,
remaining part of his fundamental stance as late as *Four Quartets*:

And so each venture
Is a new beginning, a raid on the inarticulate
With shabby equipment always deteriorating. . . . (CPP 128)

It therefore seems at present far more salutary to
risk overemphasizing this mood and to represent Eliot as an
American, a maker, a "toiler" who fashioned a tradition with
"great labour" and knew that the next man would have to repeat
the labour for himself, than to continue revering the stolid master of the Anglophile New Critics, whose achievement was to
wrench literature back from the barbarians and revitalize the
great tradition. Doing so we keep the internal contradictions of
man and poet in focus and make it harder to fall prey to the

reductions of either right or left. And more importantly we keep in view the real power *The Waste Land* shares with *Ulysses, The Cantos, Women in Love, To the Lighthouse,* and the Yeats of *The Tower.* For that power derives not just from the renewed authority these works aspire to, but from their simultaneous awareness that such authority can never achieve permanent or legitimate embodiment. And if it is true that this precarious tension could disintegrate into something politically unpleasant, it is also true that without it the works I have named would lose much of their energy, an energy that with few exceptions has not been surpassed. In the words of a recent study of modernism by Alan Wilde, it is necessary to "assert, in response to those who see the shape of modernist literature as organic, its failure to fuse its contradictory elements" (37). What moves us in this literature, Wilde says, is the spectacle of "desire straining against the constraining form it has itself devised as the only possible response to its own impossible hope for fulfillment." And if anything, this spectacle is more impressive in the age of postmodernism. In the supermarket of postmodernist tolerance, whose characteristic gesture is a "willingness to live with uncertainty, to tolerate, and in some cases, to welcome a world seen as random and multiple," the moral idealism that Edmund Wilson recognized in *The Waste Land* continues to have its attractions (43).[3]

WORKS CITED

Aiken, Conrad. "An Anatomy of Melancholy." *New Republic* 7 Feb. 1923. Rpt. in *The Waste Land: A Casebook.* Ed. C. B. Cox and Arnold Hinchliffe. London: Macmillan, 1969. 93-99.
Brooks, Cleanth. "The Waste Land: An Analysis." *Southern Review* 3.1 (Summer 1937): 106-136. Rpt. in *Modern Poetry and the Tradition.* Cleanth Brooks. Oxford: Oxford UP, 1965. 136-72.
Bush, Ronald. "Nathaniel Hawthorne and T. S. Eliot's American Connection." *Southern Review* 21.4 (October 1985): 924-33.
_____. "T. S. Eliot: Singing the Emerson Blues." *Emerson: Prospect and Retrospect.* Ed. Joel Porte. Cambridge: Harvard UP, 1982. 179-97.
Eagleton, Terry. "Capitalism, Modernism and Postmodernism." *Against the Grain: Essays 1975-1985.* London: Verso, 1986. 131-47.
_____. *Criticism and Ideology.* 1976. London: Verso, 1985.
Emerson, Ralph Waldo. *Selections from Ralph Waldo Emerson.* Ed. Steven E. Whicher. Boston: Houghton Mifflin, 1957.

3. About the relative value of modernist and postmodernist art, even Terry Eagleton has had second thoughts. See his 1985 essay, "Capitalism, Modernism and Postmodernism," in which he grudgingly acknowledges the impressiveness of modernism's "struggle for meaning" in the light of the postmodern artwork's disturbingly casual acceptance of its own commodity status (1986: 140, 143).

Gallup, Donald. *T. S. Eliot: A Biography*. New York: Harcourt, Brace and World, 1970.

Jameson, Fredric. *Fables of Aggression: Wyndham Lewis, the Modernist as Fascist*. Berkeley: U of California P, 1979.

Levenson, Michael. *A Genealogy of Modernism: A Study of English Literary Doctrine 1908-1922*. Cambridge: Cambridge UP, 1984.

Longenbach, James. *Modernist Poetics of History: Pound, Eliot, and the Sense of the Past*. Princeton: Princeton UP, 1987.

Matthiessen, F. O. *The Achievement of T. S. Eliot: An Essay on the Nature of Poetry*. 1935. New York: Oxford UP, 1972.

More, Paul Elmer. "The Cleft Eliot." *The Saturday Review of Literature* 12 Nov. 1932. Rpt. in *T. S. Eliot: A Selected Critique*. Ed. Leonard Unger. New York: Rinehart, 1948. 24-29.

Morley, Frank. "A Few Recollections of Eliot." *T. S. Eliot: The Man and His Work*. Ed. Allen Tate. New York: Delta, 1966.

Poirier, Richard. *The Renewal of Literature: Emersonian Reflections*. New York: Random House, 1987.

Sieburth, Richard. "Pound's *Dial* Letters: Between Modernism and the Avant-garde." *American Poetry* Winter 1989: 3-10.

Spindler, Elizabeth Carroll. *John Peale Bishop: A Biography*. Morgantown: West Virginia U Library P, 1980.

Wasserstrom, William. "T. S. Eliot and The Dial." *Sewanee Review* Winter 1962: 81-92.

Wilde, Alan. *Horizons of Assent: Modernism, Postmodernism, and the Ironic Imagination*. Baltimore: Johns Hopkins UP, 1981.

Wilson, Edmund. *Axel's Castle: A Study in the Imaginative Literature of 1870-1930*. 1931. London: Collins, 1967.

_____. *Letters on Literature and Politics*. New York: Farrar, Straus and Giroux, 1977.

_____. "The Poetry of Drouth." *Dial* 73.6 (Dec. 1922): 611-16.

JAMES LONGENBACH

*UNCANNY ELIOT**

Considering that in less than six years he would publish one of the great poems of the twentieth century, it seems peculiar that in his Ph.D. dissertation, *Knowledge and Experience in the Philosophy of F. H. Bradley* (1916), Eliot quotes only one line of poetry. The line is not taken from Dante or Shakespeare, not even from Tourneur or Tennyson. In his chapter "On the Distinction of 'Real' and 'Ideal' " Eliot quotes the opening line from the twenty-sixth of Elizabeth Barrett Browning's *Sonnets From the Portugese*: "I lived with visions for my company." Actually, Eliot misquotes the poem, citing the opening line as "I lived with shadows for my company" (KE 55). As he did so often, Eliot was quoting from a poem committed to memory; like Dante's meeting with the spirit of Arnaut Daniel in the twenty-sixth canto of the *Purgatorio* or Tennyson's search for the ghost of Hallam in the seventh lyric of *In Memoriam*, Barrett Browning's sonnet was one of Eliot's sacred texts.

Throughout his entire life Eliot was fascinated by visionary experiences. He lived with shadows for his company, ransacked literature for spectral manifestations, and incorporated these ghostly presences into his own poetry. In one of his first publications, an essay titled "Gentlemen and Seamen" (1909), he described Salem as a town "populous with ghosts" (115-16); in "To Walter de la Mare" (1948), one of the last poems he wrote, he invoked that violet hour when "two worlds meet" and "when the lawn / Is pressed by unseen feet, and ghosts return" (106-07). In less guarded moments Eliot even admitted that he himself sometimes experienced an uncanny "sense of dispossession," and there is evidence to suggest that like Pound and Yeats he participated in spiritualist experiments.[1] Yet Eliot was always careful to distinguish his interest in

---

*This essay is a longer version of a paper given at the National Poetry Foundation's T. S. Eliot Centennial Conference, August 18-20, 1988, Orono, Maine.
1. Eliot wrote about his "sense of dispossession" to William Force Stead on 9 August 1930; the letter is quoted in Ronald Schuchard 1046. Schuchard's essay treats the moral and explicitly horrific aspects of

the chimera of the mind from debased forms of spiritualism; in
The Waste Land he juxtaposed the truly horrifying apparition of
Stetson with the comical Madame Sosostris, and in *Four Quartets* he ridiculed tarot cards and palm readings as "features of
the press." at the same time that he insisted that "what the dead
had no speech for, when living, / They can tell you, being dead"
(CPP 136, 139).

Eliot's interest in collecting, explaining, and representing ghostly experience led him to develop a casual taxonomy
for what Freud has taught us to call the "uncanny." Not only did
he depict such phenomena in his poetry and plays, but in his
philosophical writings he explored an epistemology that could
account for the experience of hallucination. Both these
achievements involved a special sensitivity to the doubleness of
texts and experiences which in the dull rounds of everyday life
appear comfortably univocal. As Freud suggests in his essay on
"The 'Uncanny,' " it is a repetition, a return of the repressed,
that creates an uncanny feeling. "Nothing is more dramatic than
a ghost," Eliot once said (SE 39), and although his work is pop-
ulated with specters, its more potent uncanny power emanates
from the doubleness that arises from Eliot's manipulation of
repetition, disjunction, and allusion. Over the course of his
career--from Harvard philosopher to the poet of *The Waste
Land* to the sage of *Four Quartets*--Eliot employed these devices
for different effects, but his fascination with doubleness produced a body of work that vibrates at the very edge of controlled
nightmare.

During the academic year 1913-1914 Eliot was
enrolled in Josiah Royce's graduate seminar in the Comparative
Study of Various Types of Scientific Method. On February 24th,
1914, he told his classmates in a report on "Description and
Explanation" that in no theory of knowledge is illusion ever
ultimately explained. An illusion, he went on, is real from the
point of view of the visionary, but non-existent from any other
point of view; in passing from the realm of illusion to reality, the
illusion disappears, and yet it continues to exist as what Eliot
calls an "unreal object"--its status is double, both real and
unreal. No existing theory of knowledge could account for these

---

Eliot's interest in uncanny experience. In his *T. S. Eliot: A Life*, Peter Ackroyd claims that Eliot
"attended seances which had been organized by Lady Rothermere, at which P. D. Ouspensky, the
'mystic' presided" (113).

"unreal objects" because to do so would necessitate the maintenance of two points of view at the same time.[2]

Eliot did not elaborate on this point, but his emphasis on the double perspective required to understand illusion remained a constant refrain in his philosophical prose. On May 5th, 1914 he presented an essay titled "Classification of Types of Objects--A Priori or Empirical?" and there he said that hallucinations should be defined as objects perceived simultaneously from two points of view. In his dissertation he named such objects "half-objects": "i.e., we intend something which from our point of view is wholly inexistent. In order to acknowledge the existence of hallucinations we have partially to concede their truth" (KE 115). As Sanford Schwartz has pointed out, the "half-object arises from the conflict between two points of view: the external or objective point of view, through which the psychologist observes the external behavior of another, and the internal or subjective point of view, through which he identifies with the other as a subject like himself" (185-86). In order to investigate a patient's hallucination, the psychologist must perceive it from both his own point of view (from which it does not exist) and the point of view of the patient (from which it undeniably does). The half-object floats inside this double perspective: "they do not belong to any point of view," says Eliot, "but depend for their existence upon our apprehending two points of view at once, and pursuing neither" (KE 159-60).

Freud's essay on "The 'Uncanny' " (1919) helps to clarify this point. Examining a novella by E. T. A. Hoffman, Freud concludes that an "uncanny" (*unheimlich*) feeling arises in literature or in life because of the sense of doubleness created by repetition: "it is only this factor of involuntary repetition which surrounds what would otherwise be innocent enough with an uncanny atmosphere, and forces upon us the idea of something fateful and inescapable when otherwise we should have spoken only of 'chance.' " The inescapable urge to repeat something arouses an uncanny feeling because it recalls "the sense of helplessness experienced in some dream-states" (17:237).[3] The repetition creates a doubleness that is the uncanny, and it is for

2. The manuscript of Eliot's "Description and Explanation" is part of the Hayward Bequest of T. S. Eliot material in the King's College Library, Cambridge University. For an account of Eliot's participation in Royce's seminar, see Harry Todd Costello.
3. See also Otto Rank, *The Double*, which is one of Freud's texts in "The 'Uncanny.' " Rank points out that the double originated in the idea of the soul, an assurance against death, but as the soul was depicted iconographically as the double of the body, it was quickly transformed into a harbinger of death. In addition to Freud and Rank see the introduction to John T. Irwin's *Doubling and Incest/Repetition and Revenge: A Speculative Reading of Faulkner*, which provides a genealogy of the double in American literature (Poe, Twain, James, Faulkner, Jeffers) into which Eliot's work may be comfortably situated.

this reason that a glimpse of identically dressed twins or a moment of déjà vu makes us uneasy; as Eliot suggests, we are forced to perceive the world from two points of view at once, and the two perspectives overlap. The spiritual apparition of a dead person--or even the idea of a living person's soul--creates an uncanny feeling because it emphasizes doubleness: faced with the ghostly double we realize we are not univocal and self-moti-vated--other hidden forces deep within us are miming our thoughts and living out a second life that we are not equipped to understand. In *Beyond the Pleasure Principle* (drafted at the same time as the essay on the uncanny) Freud pointed out that the compulsion to repeat was sometimes strong enough to override what he had previously thought of as the indomitable pleasure principle; our uncontrollable urges to repeat, to double, show "an instinctual character and, when they act in opposition to the pleasure principle, give the appearance of some 'daemonic' force at work" (18:35).[4]

Like many Victorian philosophers and scientists, Freud was a member of the Society for Psychical Research; he sought plausible explanations for experiences that positivistic science had previously relegated to an intolerable world of fantasy. Sanford Schwartz rightly points out that Eliot's theory of the half-object is an "expression of Eliot's enduring interest in the process of social integration," but it is also an expression of Eliot's interest in psychic phenomena; like Freud he wanted to find a way to treat the ancient belief in the power of ghosts seriously (184).[5] He knew that it was in attempts to account for illu-

---

4. Freud was not the only theoretician of the workings of repetition; the most commonly invoked essay is Kierkegaard's *Repetition* (1843). While very little study of repetition in poetry has been undertaken, the last decade has produced important studies of repetition in narrative fiction: see especially Peter Brooks, *Reading for the Plot: Design and Intention in Narrative* and J. Hillis Miller, *Fiction and Repetition: Seven English Novels*.

Although I have avoided Tzvetan Todorov's vocabulary since his taxonomy of the "fantastic" in literature is too rigid to accommodate the particular qualities of Eliot's poetry, I should mention his work in order to avoid any confusion between his use of the word "uncanny" and mine. For Todorov, a "fantastic" moment occurs in literature when a character or the reader is faced with an inexplicable experience and cannot decide if it is manifested by super-natural or material causes: "The fantastic lasts as long as this uncertainty lasts; once the reader opts for one solution or the other, he is in the realm of the uncanny or the marvelous" (*The Poetics of Prose* 179). In Todorov's terminology, the "marvelous" is a fantastic experience ultimately explained by supernatural causes, while the "uncanny" is such an experience explained by exclusively material causes. My use of the word "uncanny" is close to what Todorov means by the "fantastic": that doubleness, the inability to decide between the mate-rial and the supernatural, is the quality that both Freud and Eliot describe. Todorov's argument with Freud's description of the "uncanny" is based on a strategic misreading of Freud as a doctrinaire materialist; I would argue that what Todorov calls the "fantastic" is precisely what Freud means by the "uncanny" and that Todorov is mistaken when he states that "psychoanalysis has replaced (and thereby has made useless) the literature of the fantastic" (*The Fantastic: A Structural Approach to a Literary Genre* 160). Freud's less rigid category of the "uncanny" contains the possibility of Todorov's three categories (fantastic, marvelous, uncanny), and Todorov has reduced the territory occupied by Freud's "uncanny" in order to clear space for his own hierarchy of categories.

5. For an account of the organization of the Society for Psychical Research (1882) and the rise of the scientific study of spiritual phenomena in the late nineteenth century see Samuel Hynes, *The Edwardian Turn of Mind* 132-47.

sion that existing theories of knowledge broke down, and his dissertation was the product of an effort to forge an epistemology that could account for the peculiar doubleness of an apparition: the fact that apparitions both do and do not exist forces the epistemologist to concede that there are "degrees of reality" in experience.

Just as Freud is careful to point out that even the most everyday experiences can appear uncanny, however, Eliot maintains that "degrees of reality" are present in all our perceptions. While ghosts and apparitions are useful for explaining the theory of the "half-object," that same doubleness is apparent in even the most mundane of our experiences; a ghost literalizes doubleness and consequently signifies the power of the uncanny. "The *I* who saw the ghost," Eliot writes in his dissertation, "is not the *I* who had the attack of indigestion" (KE 121). Here Eliot stresses that the doubled point of view required to explain an illusion is not simply the contradiction of the deluded patient and the undeluded doctor; that same doubleness exists within the individual who sees the ghost because after the illusion passes he then approaches it from a new point of view. In more candid moments Eliot admits that this internalized doubleness provokes a sense of disappointment as the vision fades and the visionary himself must approach it as a half-object. That is his point when he quotes from Barrett Browning's sonnet (referring to her only as "the poet"):

> When the poet says
>
> *I lived with shadows for my company*
>
> she is announcing at once the defect and the superiority of the world she lived in. The defect, in that it was vaguer, less of an idea, than the world of others; the superiority, in that the shadows pointed toward a reality, which, if it had been realized, would have been in some respects, [a] higher type of reality than the ordinary world--compared to which the ordinary world would be less real. . . . (KE 55-56)

Eliot was even more interested than Barrett Browning in remaining in the company of shadows; he disregards the sestet of her sonnet in which the beloved comes to replace the fading visions and "put man's best dreams to shame." The undercurrent of Eliot's rational explanations of hallucinations is that he considered visionary experience to be the ultimate task of the poet. And as a poet he cultivated these experiences in order to reach, like his version of Barrett Browning, a "higher type of reality than the ordinary world."

          Several passages in *The Waste Land*, each with roots
in Eliot's prose writings, show how his theory of hallucination
became manifest in the portrayals of ghostly experience in his
poetry. Eliot began a 1913 essay on "Degrees of Reality" with a
discussion of hallucination that was later recast in his dissertation: "The child 'thinks it sees' a bear. The meaning of this
phrase is by no means self-evident, for we have, I believe, no criterion for saying that the child does or does not see a bear. . . . It
is therefore not altogether true or altogether false to say that the
child sees a bear" (KE 115-16). The hallucination is not an
"error," says Eliot, because from the point of view of the child
"the hallucination has a greater degree of substantiality than an
error" (KE 117). In both his 1913 essay and his dissertation
Eliot then refers his readers to Pierre Janet's studies of hysterics
in *The Major Symptoms of Hysteria* (1907), in which hallucinations are repeatedly said to have "the sensation of touch and
weight" (KE 115). Eliot's point is that these specters are "real"
in their own sense because they are experienced: all significant
truths are private truths, he concludes in "Degrees of Reality";
as soon as they become public they cease to be truths (15).[6]
          In the long narrative passage that originally preceded
the "Death by Water" lyric in the drafts for *The Waste Land*,
Eliot returned to his discussion of spectral bears. Echoing Tennyson's "Ulysses" and Poe's *Narrative of Arthur Gordon Pym of
Nantucket*, this passage tells the story of a sea voyage off the
coast of Cape Cod which becomes a voyage into a different
degree of reality. The narrative begins quite naturalistically but
ends in an hallucination of bears which is as "real" as the snap-
ping canvas and the smell of oil:

> Something which we knew must be a dawn--
> A different darkness, flowed above the clouds,
> And dead ahead we saw, where sky and sea should meet,
> A line, a white line, a long white line,
> A wall, a barrier, towards which we drove.
> My God man theres bears on it.
> Not a chance. (WLF 67-69)

As the ship sails into this vision the narrative abruptly ends, and
the sailor is transformed into Phlebas the Phoenician. After
Pound persuaded Eliot to cut the narrative, only the sudden
moment of metamorphosis remained; but in its original form
"Death by Water" was designed to show the mechanism of hallucination as Eliot described it in his prose--not reality giving

---

6. In 1934 Eliot implied that he had heard Pierre Janet (who along with Charcot was important for
Freud's early work in hysteria) lecture at the Sorbonne in 1910 ("A Commentary" 452).

way to some intangible dream, but one "degree" of reality shifting into another. Like Eliot's theory of the half-object, the narrative implies a doubleness, two realities, two modes of perception existing at once. It is this very doubleness, as Freud suggests, that gives the passage its uncanny power; had it drifted off into an unnatural diffuseness, the narrative would not seem so threatening.

          This cancelled passage is particularly useful for revealing Eliot's manipulation of illusion in *The Waste Land*, but the mechanism is equally as visible in lines which remain in the published version of the poem. These lines from "What the Thunder Said" cross the story of Christ and the apostles on the road to Emmaus from Luke 24:15 ("And it came to pass that, while they communed together and reasoned, Jesus himself drew near, and went with them. But their eyes were holden that they should not know him") with Ernest Shackleton's account of his final Antarctic expedition ("during that long and racking march of thirty-six hours over the unnamed mountains and glaciers of South Georgia it seemed to me often that we were four, not three. I said nothing to my companions on the point, but afterwards Worsley said to me, 'Boss, I had a curious feeling on the march that there was another person with us.' Crean confessed to the same idea" [211]):

> Who is the third who walks always beside you?
> When I count, there are only you and I together
> But when I look ahead up the white road
> There is always another one walking beside you
> Gliding wrapt in a brown mantle, hooded
> I do not know whether a man or a woman
> --But who is that on the other side of you? (CPP 48)

In these lines the doubleness of the illusion is particularly emphasized; it is not an alien creature but an additional human figure, a twin, both male and female, walking beside the speaker's companion. Eliot cited Luke and Shackleton in his notes to *The Waste Land* but the passage was more likely inspired by a passage in Gibbon which Eliot invoked in a 1919 review of Yeats' essays. Eliot was dissatisfied with Yeats' brand of ghosts because they were too dreamy; they lacked the real power to terrorize because they did not linger at the cusp of everyday reality. To support this point Eliot invokes a fifth-century heretical sect which Gibbon "names the *fantastic*": "This party of philosophers held that the visible Jesus, who grew to manhood and mixed with mankind, was a phantasm; at a certain moment the son of God assumed by the banks of Jordon full-

grown the similitude of humanity. He was not really incarnate,
but divinely deceived the world" ("Foreign Mind" 552-53). The
same ambiguity--flesh and spirit, companion and specter, reality
and dream--is what makes our experience of *The Waste Land* so
especially uneasy. If we could point to any of the nightmarish
episodes in the poem and say that they were clearly "unreal"
phenomena, the poem would not retain its uncanny power.

Throughout *The Waste Land* the actual geography of
London is crossed with the mythic landscape of the "Unreal
City" to create just this effect; the apparition of the ghostly Stetson is startling because he appears in what begins as an utterly
naturalistic (and geographically accurate) description of the
crowd flowing over London Bridge and down King William
Street to St. Mary Woolnoth. The same is true of the sudden
apparition of spiritual splendour in Christopher Wren's church
of Magnus Martyr. In a 1921 "London Letter" to the New York
Dial Eliot lamented the proposed demolition of this and other
Wren churches, revealing that his depiction of Magnus Martyr
in *The Waste Land* was firmly rooted in his own quotidian experience: "the loss of these towers, to meet the eye down a grimy
lane, and of these empty naves, to receive the solitary visitor at
noon from the dust and tumult of Lombard Street, will be
irreparable and unforgotten" (691).[7] When Eliot recast this
experience in *The Waste Land* it became explicitly spiritual,
marked by a tension between naturalistic description and the
gradual diffusion into another reality (first hinted at by the allusion to Baudelaire's "Les Sept vieillards": "Fourmillante Cité,
cité pleine de rêves, / Où le spectre en plein jour raccroche le
passant!"):

> O City city, I can sometimes hear
> Beside a public bar in Lower Thames Street,
> The pleasant whining of a mandoline
> And a clatter and a chatter from within
> Where fishmen lounge at noon: where the walls
> Of Magnus Martyr hold
> Inexplicable splendour of Ionian white and gold. (CPP 45)

Like the narrative deleted from "Death by Water" this passage
offers (in the highly compressed form Pound would allow) the
almost imperceptible translation from one degree of reality to
another. The passage is remarkable in *The Waste Land* because

7. In this account of the Wren churches Eliot directs his readers to same pamphlet he cites in the note
to line 264 of *The Waste Land* ("Proposed Demolition of Nineteen City Churches") and quotes
Ugolino's line from canto 33 of the *Inferno* ("*quand'io sentii chiavar l'uscio di sotto*" [and below I heard
them nailing up the door]), which appears in his note to line 412 of *The Waste Land* (*Dial* 70 [June
1921]: 691).

it is one of the few that rises to the plane of spiritual redemption rather than descending to the plane of what Eliot called "seldom explored extremities of torture" ("Beyle and Balzac" 392). As he wrote of Barrett Browning in his dissertation, these lines realize "a higher type of reality than the ordinary world," but do so in the naturalistic terms of that ordinary world.

Eliot praised Dostoevsky because the "point of departure" for his hallucinatory scenes is always "a human brain in a human environment"; there is no unreal "aura" imposed on the scene ("Beyle and Balzac" 392). Eliot followed the same practice in *The Waste Land,* and Freud likewise concluded in his essay on "The 'Uncanny' " that an uncanny experience retains its unsettling effect "not only in experience but in fiction as well, so long as the setting is one of material reality; but where it is given an arbitrary and artificial setting in fiction, it is apt to lose that character" (17:251). Freud relies on a remarkable etymology borrowed from Schelling to support his observations: the German word *heimlich* refers not only to something "belonging to the house" but to something "hidden and dangerous," and consequently, in Freud's words, "*heimlich* is a word the meaning of which develops in the direction of ambivalence, until it finally coincides with its opposite, *unheimlich*" (17: 225). In either a ghost story or in experienced reality, Freud then explains, the "uncanny is in reality nothing new or alien, but something which is familiar and old-established in the mind and which has become alienated from it only through the process of repression" (17:241). A vision of a ghost disturbs us because it is the return of something we know all too well; it reminds us of our uncontrollable urge to repeat what we have worked hard to repress. As Eliot explains in his 1919 essay's reference to Dostoevsky, the ghostly *appears* fantastic because "most people are too unconscious of their own suffering to suffer much" ("Beyle and Balzac" 392).

Dostoevsky was one author who taught Eliot this lesson, but the Tennyson Eliot read as a child offered him his earliest model for a poetry that transforms common experience into otherworldly experience without imposing an egregiously fantastic aura. *Idylls of the King* was the last long poem by a major English poet that Eliot had to face when he wrote *The Waste Land,* and when he was casting around for ways to unify his collection of fragments, it was natural that he chose the same motif Tennyson used in his long poem: the quest for the Holy Grail. In depicting that quest Tennyson was always careful to present even the most fantastically mythic experience in explicably naturalistic terms. Occasionally the effect of this effort is comical; when in Arthur's hall "the sweet Grail / Glided and past, and close upon it peal'd / A sharp quick thunder," Tennyson's notes inform us that "it might have been a meteor"; in the same way, "thunderless lightnings striking under sea" are glossed as "communication by submarine cable, telegraph," and these lines, which Merlin speaks when the youth Gareth asks him to tell "the truth" about the apparently magical city of Camelot, are glossed with the phrase "refraction by mirage":

> Son, I have seen the good ship sail
> Keel upward, and mast downward, in the heavens,
> And solid turrets topsy-turvy in air:
> And here is truth. (224, 353, 301, 371, 311, 43)

Tennyson wrote his poem in an age that demanded scientific explanations for inexplicable phenomena, and Freud, nurtured in the same age, provided better explanations than the laureate. But following Tennyson, Eliot was also a poet simultaneously visionary and skeptical; he glossed the apparition of the ghostly crowd flowing over London Bridge with the phrase "[a] phenomenon which I have often noticed" (CPP 51). And when he wrote his version of the grail quest he was careful to keep his expressions of the *unheimlich* close to home.

That doubleness, the ghostly landscape coterminus with the natural, permeates all of *The Waste Land*; the poem throbs, as Tiresias is described, "between two lives" (CPP 43). As a whole *The Waste Land* is more calculatedly terrifying than the poems of *Prufrock and Other Observations* or *Poems 1920* because only in the longer poem did Eliot consistently reveal his sensitivity to the natural otherness of even the most daily of experiences; in *The Waste Land* he is willing (as he describes Tiresias in the drafts) to "trace the cryptogram that may be curled" within the ordinary city of London (WLF 43). In "Prufrock" and "Portrait of a Lady," in contrast, the very problem he depicts is his speakers' unwillingness to unearth the "buried life" (CPP 9) that lurks within the taking of a toast and tea, the horror of facing the doubleness of all experience. In an early unpublished poem called "Mandarins" Eliot portrays several figures of Boston society and remarks that their lives are calm because they are unaware of the life that goes on in different planes; they do not see their shadows, their doubles, on the screen. In a wonderful passage that he deleted from the published version of "Prufrock" Eliot shows his timid protagonist making that fateful step. After staying up all night Prufrock looks out into the street and sees a man sitting on the curb. But

Prufrock immediately perceives the man as his own double, an embodiment of his madness, and as the man begins to sing, Prufrock's carefully constructed world begins to fall apart. In the published version of the poem that world remains intact because Prufrock does not face the possibility of his dual existence. While he addresses that other self in the opening line ("Let us go then, you and I,") he expends all his energy keeping that threatening double suppressed.

The doubleness of the ghostly experiences Eliot presents in his poetry is one source of its uncanny power, but even *The Waste Land*, his most ghostly poem, is not overpopulated with specters. The poem's unrelenting dis-ease comes from another kind of uncanny doubleness, one linked to Eliot's theory of hallucination and yet more subtle. Freud points out, as I have said, that not only a supernatural event evokes an uncanny feeling; "the frightening element can be shown to be something repressed which *recurs*" (17:241). This involuntary repetition produces an unsettling effect because it suggests some hidden order that controls us, some mysterious logic that we cannot comprehend; we like to think that lightning never strikes twice, but when it does we tend to think that something more than chance is at work. In his 1934 essay on Marston, Eliot outlined a strikingly similar conception of uncanny doubling:

> It is possible that what distinguishes poetic drama from prosaic drama is a kind of doubleness in the action, as if it took place on two planes at once. In this it is different from allegory, in which the abstraction is something conceived, not something differently felt, and from symbolism (as in the plays of Maeterlinck) in which the tangible world is deliberately diminished--both symbolism and allegory being operations of the conscious planning mind. In poetic drama a certain apparent irrelevance may be the symptom of this doubleness; or the drama has an under-pattern, less manifest than the theatrical one. We sometimes feel, in following the words and behaviour of some of the characters of Dostoevsky, that they are living at once on the plane that we know and on some other plane of reality from which we are shut out: their behaviour does not seem crazy, but rather in conformity with the laws of some world that we cannot perceive. (EE 173)[8]

The application of this kind of doubleness of logic or action is immediately apparent in Eliot's own plays. *The Family Reunion* (1939), the most uncanny of his finished plays, is replete with passages in which a character suddenly steps outside the action

---

8. See Ronald Bush's discussion of this essay in *T. S. Eliot: A Study in Character and Style* 94, 169-73. Eliot began to develop this theory of dramatic doubleness long before he wrote this essay. See "The Noh and the Image," "Beyle and Balzac," and "Wanley and Chapman."

of the play and begins to speak as if from a different script. The
effect is initially irritating (even comical), as if the character had
suddenly forgotten his role, but it soon becomes clear, as Eliot
suggests of Marston, that a hidden logic is at work, doubling the
visible action on the stage. This doubling gives that sense of an
otherworldly presence controlling the action. For instance, just a
few moments into *The Family Reunion*, when the characters are
engaged in an inane discussion of the implications of Harry's
return to Wishwood, Agatha suddenly erupts in a sequence of
unrelated lines that do not make her seem crazy, but rather possessed by a second reality with its own peculiar logic:

> Thus with most careful devotion
> Thus with precise attention
> To detail, interfering preparation
> Of that which is already prepared
> Men tighten the knot of confusion
> Into perfect misunderstanding; . . . (CPP 230)

It is passages such as these--not the apparitions of the ghostly
Eumenides (which Eliot himself recognized as an embarrassment on the stage)--that give the play its uneasy spirituality.[9]
Harry is a haunted man, but it is not the apparition of ghosts
that convince us of his nightmare; rather it is his and Agatha's
ability to act in two planes of dramatic reality at once.

Eliot did not sketch out this theory of dramatic doubleness until after *The Waste Land* was completed, but several of
his early essays adumbrate it, and his early poetry is permeated
by just this kind of doubleness. In the unpublished Clark Lectures of 1926 (*Lectures on the Metaphysical Poetry of the Seventeenth Century, with special reference to Donne, Crashaw and
Cowley*) Eliot examines its workings in Chapman's verse, but as
an aside reveals a more crucial inspiration for his own poetry;
this same doubleness, he explains, may be felt in Browning's
"Childe Roland to the Dark Tower Came" and in a certain line
of Nerval's: "Crains, dans le mur aveugle, un regard qui t'épie!"
In *The Symbolist Movement in Literature*--the book that introduced Eliot to Laforgue in 1908--Arthur Symons quotes this
same line and comments that it reveals Nerval's readiness "to
believe in the mystery behind the world" (11). Symons pointed
out this doubleness, this sense of two worlds, in Nerval's poetry,
and from the beginning of his career Eliot set out to incorporate
it into his own. The first verse paragraph of "The Fire Sermon"

9. See Eliot's discussion of the difficulty of staging the ghostly Eumenides effectively in "Poetry and
Drama" (OPP 90).

in *The Waste Land* ends with a line from Verlaine ("Et O ces voix d'enfants, chantant dans la coupole!"):

> White bodies naked on the low damp ground
> And bones cast in a little low dry garret,
> Rattled by the rat's foot only, year to year.
> But at my back from time to time I hear
> The sound of horns and motors, which shall bring
> Sweeney to Mrs. Porter in the spring.
> O the moon shone bright on Mrs. Porter
> And on her daughter
> They wash their feet in soda water
> *Et O ces voix d'enfants, chantant dans la coupole!* (CPP 43)

The unrelenting spookiness created by these lines is the product of their radical disjunction--the same kind of disjunction between the normal speech of *The Family Reunion* and Agatha's incantatory effusion. The disjunction creates that uncanny sense of doubleness, and the reader cannot read the text as a univocal expression. In *The Waste Land* so many different voices are present, so many different modes of discourse or planes of logic collide, that the sense of otherworldly presence is constant. The opening verse paragraph of "The Fire Sermon" is consequently one of the most uncanny parts of the poem even though it contains no ghostly apparitions. The passage begins with naturalistic description, but that logic is immediately disrupted by the presence of "nymphs" on the riverbank. The landscape suddenly becomes urban, strewn with bottles, sandwich papers, cigarettes, and the juxtaposition with the lovely refrain from Spenser's "Prothalamion" ("Sweet Thames, run softly, till I end my song" [CPP 42]), so unsuited to that landscape, does not seem merely ironic; like Agatha's speech it makes us wonder if there is some other presence in this desiccated landscape, a power in the verse to perceive it, that we cannot fathom. The subsequent quotation from Marvell (which is itself disrupted by a second voice which gives us "The rattle of the bones, and chuckle spread from ear to ear" [CPP 43] instead of the expected "Time's winged chariot hurrying near") and the reference to the myth of the Fisher King build the sense of a bizarre "under-pattern" in the verse to an almost unbearable pitch. As Eliot suggests in his essay on Marston the lines do not seem merely irrational; they are all the more frightening for appearing part of a hidden logic that we do not understand. By the second reference to Marvell (beginning with the lines quoted above) the disjunctions have run rampant, and we are swept from the rat's foot to motor cars to Mrs. Porter and finally to the utterly inexplicable epiphany of Ver-

laine's children chanting in the dome. The dramatic doubleness
that Eliot presents simply in *The Family Reunion* is here
expanded to a bewildering array of voices, each asserting the
presence of its own plane of reality. We have reached, as
Symons said of Nerval, "the mystery behind the world."

Of course we have intuited the second logic working
in these lines (though knowledge of it does little to reduce the
lines' uncanny power, especially if read aloud); Eliot's manipulation of the grail myth at least partially unites these disjunctive
voices, and once we know that the line from Verlaine's sonnet
describes Parsifal's arrival at the grail castle, the logic is clearer.
Yet the quest's point of destination still seems an utterly otherworldly place. Like Browning's quester in "Childe Roland to the
Dark Tower Came," the quester in *The Waste Land* begins
somewhere recognizably close to home and ends in a place that
is utterly different and yet not too far away. Part of the
strangeness of both Browning's and Eliot's poems is due to their
macabre imagery; but as Eliot recognized in the Clark Lectures
the peculiar power of "Childe Roland to the Dark Tower Came"
is not due to the references to water rats and babies' shrieks but
to the fact that Browning's quester is repeating a journey that
many other questers have taken before him. The sense of doubleness, of ghostly precursors, is overwhelming; the quester fears
that he will set his "foot upon some dead man's cheek" as he
walks, and when he finally reaches the round squat tower, the
lost souls of his predecessors stand about him and create a
paradoxically "living" frame for the quester's own death:

> There they stood, ranged along the hill-sides, met
>   To view the last of me, a living frame
>   For one more picture! in a sheet of flame
> I saw them and I knew them all. And yet
> Dauntless the slug-horn to my lips I set,
>   And blew *'Childe Roland to the Dark Tower came.'* (1:592)

The final line adds another uncanny doubleness to the poem
because it repeats a line from Edgar's mad song in *King Lear*
(3.4.171-73). The quotation emphasizes the sense that this quest
has been undertaken before, but now the feeling of doubled
experience is complicated by a doubling from another literary
text: we are torn between reading the quest as the rendering of
experience and the echo of an anterior text. This kind of doubleness is obviously rampant in *The Waste Land*; the scene in a
London pub which ends "A Game of Chess" is wonderfully
realistic in its depiction of East End accents and sensibility, but
when the dialogue slips into Ophelia's mad song ("Good night,

ladies, good night" [CPP 42]) the text is suddenly doubled, and
we are inextricably poised between the poem as a rendering of
modern life and the poem as a web of echoes from previous
renderings.

The doubleness of Browning's poem is of a slightly
different nature than Eliot's; in *The Waste Land* the doubleness
is more particularly dramatic, and in addition to multiple images
of the dead and multiple echoes of the past, there are multiple
voices. Other passages in Eliot's early poetry show this dramatic
doubleness more simply. When the voice of "Prufrock" suddenly
stops its gentle whining to intone "In the room the women come
and go / Talking of Michelangelo" (CPP 4), or when the tired
voice of "Gerontion" startles us with

> In depraved May, dogwood and chestnut, flowering judas.
> To be eaten, to be divided, to be drunk
> Among whispers; (CPP 21-22),

we once again have that sense of some other logic besides that
of the character's personality controlling the direction of the
lines; the effect is as if we had seen a ghost, a double from
another world, and we must begin to read the poem's doubled
narrative. This *dramatic* function of disjunction is what gives
Eliot's poetry the haunted quality that other masters of juxtaposition do not attain. In Eliot there is always the shock produced
by shifting from one mode of logic or discourse to another; in
Pound's work the so-called ideogrammatic method is pedagogical rather than dramatic, and if the shock comes at all it is not
emotional but intellectual, a momentary puzzling over what *Sor-
dello* could possibly have to do with So-chu churning in the sea.

In contrast to Pound's juxtapositions of textual fragments, the final lines of *The Waste Land* will produce an
uncanny feeling every time they are read aloud because even if
we know what the collection of disjunctive phrases means, their
very sound so challenges our conventional conception of coherence that we immediately feel the presence of an unseen master
speaking in a common language we do not understand. The juxtaposition of foreign tongues alienates us from the poem but at
the same time draws us in with the uncanny feeling that something other than nonsense is being transmitted from beneath the
veil. The line Eliot borrows from Baudelaire ("You! hypocrite
lecteur!--mon semblable,--mon frère!" [CPP 39]) is frightening
enough when it occurs in the *Fleurs du Mal*; but placed at the
end of "The Burial of the Dead" the line adds the ultimate
touch of horror to an increasingly horrific passage simply by lit-

eralizing the shift from the City of London to the Unreal City in a shift into a different language. And when we know what the line means it becomes all the more frightening because it confirms what we have suspected all along: that this poem really is a mirror, our brother, our image, the irrepressible return of all our darkest longings.

Some of this same kind of dramatic doubleness is apparent in Eliot's later poetry, but it is of a different order. No poem he wrote after *The Waste Land* is so radically disjunctive and no poem is quite so hair-raising. The doublings in *Four Quartets* are more controlled, and the second world we sense is clearly a Christian heaven. *Sweeney Agonistes*, itself written on the cusp between the Eliot of *The Waste Land* and the Eliot of *Ash-Wednesday*, shows how its author redirected his interest in expression of the uncanny. The two fragments of the play operate in just the way Eliot suggests that Marston's plays operate: while Dusty and Doris, Klipstein and Krumpacker each speak a ridiculously simple (and consequently earth-bound) language, Sweeney interjects a new mode of speech into the play, and that mysterious speech gives us the sense of some power beyond the dramatic action:

> I knew a man once did a girl in
> Any man might do a girl in
> Any man has to, needs to, wants to
> Once in a lifetime, do a girl in.
> Well he kept her there in a bath
> With a gallon of lysol in a bath. (CPP 83)

After these unprecedented lines all Swarts can say is "[t]hese fellows always get pinched in the end," and while he and the other characters bring Sweeney's statement down to their level of journalistic intrigue, we are left with the feeling that Sweeney was talking about something far more mysterious than a common murder. Sweeney's incantatory ravings finally become so overpowering that the other characters join his plane of reality and together they intone the nightmare patter-song with which the second fragment ends:

> You've had a cream of a nightmare dream and you've got the
>   hoo-ha's coming to you.
> Hoo hoo hoo
> You dreamt you waked up at seven o'clock and it's foggy and it's
>   damp and it's dawn and it's dark
> And you wait for a knock and the turning of a lock for you know
>   the hangman's waiting for you.
> And perhaps you're alive

And perhaps you're dead
Hoo ha ha
Hoo ha ha
Hoo
Hoo
Hoo
KNOCK KNOCK KNOCK
KNOCK KNOCK KNOCK
KNOCK
KNOCK
KNOCK (CPP 84-85)

At this point the effect on the reader is more inexplicable than the effect of Sweeney's ravings on the other characters: we are victims of a conspiracy, each character having jumped to the degree of reality he showed no evidence of comprehending--now only we are left below. An unpublished scenario for what would have been the completed version of *Sweeney Agonistes* provides some of the answers we crave. Eliot specified elsewhere that there must be eighteen knocks at the end of the patter-song--a doubling of the eighteen chimes of the Angelus, announcing the annunciation. Just that knowledge helps us to divine the alien logic of the play. Eliot's scenario tells us that when the knocks at the door to the flat are answered, there stands Pereira (the landlord), who wants to evict Dusty and Doris from the flat. Sweeney invokes the Rent and Mortgage Interest Restriction Act of 1923 to show that Pereira cannot do so, and then reveals himself as the "Superior Landlord." After Pereira leaves the characters in the flat continue to wait for Mrs. Porter, who when she finally arrives does not knock but announces her presence by singing a bawdy ballad in the street. After she enters she and Sweeney begin to have an argument. Although they are clearly antipathetic to each other, says Eliot, they are nevertheless drawn together because each is the only person on the other's plane of vitality. But as their debate continues, Sweeney speaks less and less, drinks more and more, and finally pulls something out of his pocket (presumably a knife). He lets out a dull roar as Dusty and Doris shriek hysterically and Mrs. Porter collapses on the floor. She is carried out of the room, presumably dead, and Sweeney continues drinking, the only character who is quite unperturbed by the event.

Here is the mysterious "doing in" of a girl for which we were prepared; yet Sweeney's behavior remains inexplicable. Dusty and Doris scramble to hide the body as yet another knocking is heard at the door, but Sweeney remains calm, as if he somehow knows that panic is unnecessary. After the women get rid of a tenant who had come to complain of the noise, we hear Mrs. Porter's voice singing the bawdy ballad in the next room. As Eliot describes the play's final tableau, we witness the "resurrection" of Mrs. Porter, who returns to the stage as vital and lively as ever. The other characters are stunned by this event--except for Sweeney and Mrs. Porter herself, who act as if they knew everything in advance and are merely accepting the roles given to them by fate. As the curtain falls in Eliot's scenario, all the characters form a procession, raise their wine glasses, and sing.[10]

Throughout the play, two dramatic actions were to have transpired at once. One is the murder mystery and slapstick comedy of Dusty and Doris, and the other is a story of Christian redemption that only Sweeney and Mrs. Porter understand. Eliot epitomized this doubleness when he placed two contrasting epigraphs on the published fragments of the play, one from the *Choephoroi* ("ORESTES: You don't see them, you don't--but *I* see them: they are hunting me down, I must move on") and the other from *St. John of the Cross* ("Hence the soul cannot be possessed of the divine union, until it has divested itself of the love of created beings" [CPP 74]). In *Sweeney Agonistes* Eliot took the dramatic doubleness he exploited in *The Waste Land* (with the number of doublings reduced for easier comprehension on the stage) and, while retaining some of the nightmarish quality of that second world, transformed the nightmare into an explicitly redemptive spiritual reality. The doubleness of the drama is now the Christian doubling of the city of God and the city of man. In Eliot's later plays, especially *The Family Reunion* and *The Cocktail Party*, this Christian doubling becomes so schematic that it is difficult not to chafe at Eliot's insistence that only some people (Harry and Agatha in *The Family Reunion*, Henry and Celia in *The Cocktail Party*) are predestined to feel the pressure of that second world; the rest of us are left down below with Dusty and Doris.[11]

---

10. Eliot's scenario for the completed version of the Sweeney play (which would have been titled *The Superior Landlord*) is part of the Hayward Bequest, King's College Library, Cambridge University. His remark about the eighteen knocks at the end of the published fragments occurs in a letter to Hallie Flanagan, 18 March 1933; see Hallie Flanagan, *Dynamo*, 82-84. In a close examination of the manuscript of Eliot's scenario, Michael Sidnell has concluded that it was composed in 1934 when Eliot was considering the completion of the published Sweeney fragments. See *Dances of Death: The Group Theatre of London in the Thirties* 263-65).

11. In *The Use of Poetry and the Use of Criticism* (1933) Eliot explained how *Sweeney Agonistes* was designed to reinforce distinctions between social classes: "There was to be an understanding between the protagonist and a small number of the audience, while the rest of the audience would share the responses of the other characters in the play" (UPUC 153). Eliot's distinct hierarchy of characters in his later plays appears all the more insidious when we realize that they match the class distinctions he outlines in *The Idea of a Christian Society* (1939): distinct from the Christian Community (the "great mass" of humanity) is the Community of Christians, composed of the more spiritually and intellectually developed members of both the clergy and laity.

When Eliot became committed not only to the Anglican church but to the idea of explicitly Christian poetry, all his ghosts became holy. Yet *Four Quartets* retain some of the uncanny power that his later plays sacrifice to pedagogical clarity. The ghostly presences in the opening movement of *Burnt Norton* are nearly as affecting as any of those in the early poetry:

> Shall we follow?
> Quick, said the bird, find them, find them,
> Round the corner. Through the first gate,
> Into our first world, shall we follow
> The deception of the thrush? Into our first world.
> There they were, dignified, invisible.
> Moving without pressure, over the dead leaves. . . . (CPP 117-18)

This movement away from the world of abstract philosophizing into "our first world" where the unspecified "they" appear is only momentary; it passes as quickly as it comes, and the rest of the quartets are there to explain these moments and console us when they do not come. In these lines we suspect that the first world (which makes our world of everyday life the second world) is an explicitly Christian reality, but Eliot complicates this doubling with another form of textual doubling. In the beginning of *Burnt Norton* the uncanny effect is not made by disjunction but by repetitions. While we follow the "[o]ther echoes" that "inhabit the garden" Eliot also tells us that his "words echo / Thus, in your mind" (CPP 117). The incessant repetitions of the opening lines, focusing on the word "present," create a wash of unspecified meaning so that each word has its own ghost or double; the word "present" is made to mean both the opposite of past and the opposite of absence, and it refuses to settle comfortably into either meaning. This kind of doubling becomes more and more complicated as the quartets progress, each poem doubling itself and each poem doubling the one before it by following the same structural and thematic pattern.[12]

Eliot remained just as fascinated by ghosts and hallucinations when he wrote *Four Quartets* as when he studied epistemology at Harvard. The ghosts of *Burnt Norton* ("they") recall the spirits of children who gather around the barren old women in Kipling's story "They." In 1941 Eliot told John Hayward that the story had lodged in his memory "for 30 years." And along with the story Eliot remembered some lines from Elizabeth Bar-

---

12. My brief examination of the linguistic doubleness of *Four Quartets* only touches on an important problem that others have examined in greater detail. For a subtle and specific analysis of the problem see Bush 193-98; for a more generally theoretical (and slightly exaggerated) account see William V. Spanos.

rett Browning which Kipling quoted in "They": "the quotation form E. B. Browning," he told Hayward, "has always stuck in my head" (qtd. in Gardner 29).[13] The opening movement of *Burnt Norton* echoes *Alice in Wonderland* and Eliot's own *Murder in the Cathedral* and "New Hampshire," but it also owes something to the one poet he invoked in his dissertation twenty years before *Burnt Norton* was published. The speaker of Barrett Browning's "The Lost Bower" explains how as a child she found a secret garden in the woods, and there she heard "a sound, a sense of music which was rather felt than heard,"

> Heart and head beat through the quiet
> Full and heavily, though slower:
> In the song, I think, and by it,
> Mystic Presences of power
> Had up-snatched me to the Timeless, then returned me to the Hour.
> (152-53)

The rest of the poem details the speaker's life-long attempt to recapture that lost moment of dispossession, and as Helen Gardner has suggested, the poem presents the underlying themes of *Burnt Norton* in miniature.

In his prose writings Eliot drew attention to the work of Elizabethan dramatists and Harvard philosophers as the impetus for his own interest in the doubleness of uncanny experience; but it was in the poets of the nineteenth century he read in his early youth--Barrett Browning, Browning, Nerval, and Tennyson--who first excited his desire to plumb the depths of the other world. Eliot followed his Romantic and Victorian precursors in being a poet both visionary and skeptical. On the one hand he maintained a healthy post-Enlightenment distrust of the supernatural; but on the other hand, he wanted to preserve the inspired poet's right to plumb the depths of foreign worlds that lurk deep within or far beyond the minds of human beings. Wallace Stevens epitomized this typically Romantic and post-Romantic tension when he wrote in "Effects of Analogy" that while the purpose of poetry may be to rationalize mysticism, the poet's "ambition is to press away from mysticism toward that ultimate good sense which we term civilization" (116). Before Stevens, Arnold named the Romantic poet's dilemma even more severely in "Stanzas from the Grande Chartreuse": while Arnold confesses that "rigorous teachers seized my youth, / And purged its faith, and trimmed its fire," he longs to transcend such good sense and join the "last of the people who believe," the few

---

13. Gardner discusses Barrett Browning's "The Lost Bower" on 39-41.

strange men who managed to escape the Enlightenment's chas-
tening lesson (304). Arnold could not linger in the high, secluded
world of the Grande Chartreuse, and neither could Eliot. The
author of *The Waste Land*, we have seen, found his netherworld
not on mountaintops but in the streets of London. That descent
was not a rejection of the Romantic sublime but a literalization
of the doubleness present in virtually every post-Enlightenment
poet's spiritual yearnings. Coleridge remembered in the
Biographia Literaria that when he and Wordsworth began the
Lyrical Ballads they conceived of a series of poems "composed
of two sorts" (2:6). Coleridge devoted his energies to "persons
and characters supernatural" and yet "real" in the sense that
"they have been to every human being who, from whatever
source of delusion, has at any time believed himself under
supernatural agency." While Coleridge emphasized the reality of
the unreal, Wordsworth did the opposite; he was "to give the
charm of novelty to things of every day, and to excite a feeling
analogous to the supernatural" (2:7).

   While Eliot felt this doubleness in the work of
authors as disparate as Dostoevsky and Chapman, his awareness
of the uncanny effects of nineteenth-century poetry highlights an
important feature of Romanticism and reminds us of Eliot's
place in that tradition. At the same time, it is important to see
that Eliot's interest in the uncanny was not exclusively literary.
Freud emphasized that in "an arbitrary or unrealistic setting"
the uncanny loses its power "not only in fiction but in experience
as well" (17:242). In addition to the nineteenth-century poets he
loved, Eliot found the inspiration for his own manipulation of
the uncanny in his own experience--in the life of a bank clerk in
the City of London who walked down Lombard Street to St.
Magnus Martyr, in the life of a middle-aged man of letters who
looked back on his spent youth and felt the ghosts of what might
have been gather about him. As both theorist and poet Eliot
spent his life trying to explain the peculiar power of illusion, and
to treat such a topic in exclusively literary terms is to contain it,
to reduce its implications within a world that the literary critic
has the vocabulary to control. Freud himself tells us that "all
supposedly educated people have ceased to believe officially that
the dead can become visible as spirits, and have made such
appearances dependent on improbable and remote conditions;
their emotional attitude towards their dead, moreover, once a
highly ambiguous and ambivalent one, has been toned down in
the higher strata of the mind into an unambiguous feeling of
piety" (17:242-43). Here Freud steps to the very edge of his own

reality, vacillating between a desire to explain the real power of the uncanny and the need to explain it away. Perhaps that is the doubleness in which readers of poetry are always caught. Eliot played the role of the sober critic very well, but if he had not felt the pull of *The Waste Land*'s other world himself, his poetry would not continue to entrance, and we, *hypocrite lecteurs*, would not hear our voices, alternately angry and consoled, returning to us from somewhere deep within the page.

WORKS CITED

Ackroyd, Peter. *T. S. Eliot: A Life*. New York: Simon and Schuster, 1984.

Arnold, Matthew. *The Poems of Matthew Arnold*. Ed. Kenneth Allott. 2nd ed. London: Longmans, 1979.

Brooks, Peter. *Reading for the Plot: Design and Intention in Narrative*. New York: Knopf, 1984.

Browning, Elizabeth Barrett. *The Complete Poetical Works*. Boston: Houghton Mifflin, 1900.

Browning, Robert. *Robert Browning: The Poems*. Ed. John Pettigrew. New Haven: Yale UP, 1981. 2 vols.

Bush, Ronald. *T. S. Eliot: A Study in Character and Style*. New York: Oxford UP, 1984.

Coleridge, S. T. *Biographia Literaria*. Ed. James Engell and W. Jackson Bate. Princeton: Princeton UP, 1983. 2 vols.

Costello, Harry T. *Josiah Royce's Seminar, 1913-1914: As Recorded in the Notebooks of Harry T. Costello*. Ed. Grover Smith. New Brunswick: Rutgers UP, 1963.

Eliot, T. S. "Beyle and Balzac." *Athenaeum* 4648 (30 May 1919): 392-93.

_____."Classification of Types of Objects--A Priori or Empirical?" ms. Hayward Bequest, King's College Library, Cambridge University.

_____. "A Commentary." *Criterion* 13 (April 1934): 451-54.

_____. "Degrees of Reality." ms. Hayward Bequest, King's College Library, Cambridge University.

_____. "Description and Explanation." ms. Hayward Bequest, King's College Library, Cambridge University.

_____. "A Foreign Mind." *Athenaeum* 4653 (4 July 1919): 552-53.

_____. "Gentlemen and Seamen." *Harvard Advocate* 87 (25 May 1909): 115-16.

_____. "London Letter." *Dial* 70 (June 1921): 686-91.

_____. "The Love Song of J. Alfred Prufrock." ms. Eliot's Poetry Notebook. Berg Collection, New York Public Library.

_____. "Mandarins." ms. Eliot's Poetry Notebook. Berg Collection, New York Public Library.

_____. "The Noh and the Image." *Egoist* 4 (Aug. 1917): 102-103.

_____. *The Superior Landlord*. ms. Hayward Bequest, King's College Library, Cambridge University.

_____. "To Walter de la Mare." *A Tribute to Walter de la Mare*. Ed. T. S. Eliot. London: Faber and Faber, 1948. 106-7.

_____. "Wanley and Chapman." *Times Literary Supplement* 1250 (31 Dec. 1925): 907.

Flanagan, Hallie. *Dynamo*. New York: Duell, Sloan and Pearce, 1943.

Freud, Sigmund. *The Standard Edition of the Complete Psychological Works*. Ed. James Strachey. London: Hogarth Press and the Institute of Psycho-Analysis, 1981. 23 vols.

Gardner, Helen. *The Composition of* Four Quartets. London: Faber and Faber, 1978.

Hynes, Samuel. *The Edwardian Turn of Mind*. Princeton: Princeton UP, 1968.

Irwin, John T. *Doubling and Incest/Repetition and Revenge: A Speculative Reading of Faulkner*. Baltimore: Johns Hopkins UP, 1975.

Kierkegaard, Soren. *Repetition*. Trans. and Ed. Howard V. and Edna H. Hong. Princeton: Princeton UP, 1981.

Miller, J. Hillis. *Fiction and Repetition: Seven English Novels*. Cambridge: Harvard UP, 1982.

Rank, Otto. *The Double*. Trans. and Ed. Harry Tucker. Chapel Hill: U of North Carolina P, 1971.

Schuchard, Ronald. "Eliot and the Horrific Moment." *Southern Review* 21 (1985): 1045-56.

Schwartz, Sanford. *The Matrix of Modernism: Pound, Eliot, and Early Twentieth-Century Thought*. Princeton: Princeton UP, 1985.

Shackleton, Ernest. *South: The Story of Shackleton's Last Expedition 1914-1917*. London: Heinemann, 1919.

Sidnell, Michael. *Dances of Death: The Group Theatre of London in the Thirties*. London: Faber and Faber, 1984.

Spanos, William V. "Hermeneutics and Memory: Destroying T. S. Eliot's *Four Quartets*." *Genre* 11 (1978): 523-73.

Stevens, Wallace. *The Necessary Angel*. New York: Vintage, 1951.

Symons, Arthur. *The Symbolist Movement in Literature*. Ed. Richard Ellmann. New York: Dutton, 1958.

Tennyson, Alfred, Lord. *Idylls of the King*. Ed. J. M. Gray. New Haven: Yale UP, 1983.

Todorov, Tzvetan. *The Fantastic: A Structural Approach to a Literary Genre*. Trans. Richard Howard. Ithaca: Cornell UP, 1975.

_____. *The Poetics of Prose*. Trans. Richard Howard. Ithaca: Cornell UP, 1977.

*The heavens have been shut
up in wait*

ELIOT AND THE VOICES OF HISTORY*

Eliot preferred to be anonymous; it's said that on being recognized on a London bus he'd crisply get off at the next stop. One time, though, it was a cab-driver who recognized him, and he chose not to make a scene. The dialogue, by his account, went as follows:

> "You're T. S. Eliot, aren't you?"
> "Ah."
> "Just last week, do you know who was sitting where you're sitting now? Bertrand Russell!"
> "Ah."
> "So I said, 'Well, Lord Russell, what's it all about?' And do you know, he couldn't tell me!"

That was too good not to be recounted again and again; Eliot's widow says it was one of his favorite stories. For its theme is how self-assumed Omniscience got confronted by a man with a simple wish for one clarifying sentence ... which Omniscience was powerless to formulate. It's like having the Voice from the Burning Bush struck dumb.

Had Russell possessed the wit he might have responded in the Voice of the Eliotic Thunder: DA *Datta Dayadhvam Damyata*, which is more or less What It's All About, and would be especially persuasive from the back of a cab (CPP 49). Perhaps he did think of it but feared being asked to translate, which would have consumed an evening while the meter ran. (I mean the meter of the taxi.) Eliot's impish mind would not have missed the analogy between the taxi-driver and the Quester of *The Waste Land*, who in Jessie Weston's rescension of the myth finds relics in a ruined chapel and wants to know what they are: whereupon the heavens open and rain falls. The heavens have been shut up in wait for someone--anyone--with merely the desire to know.

---

*This essay was originally given as a paper at the National Poetry Foundation's T. S. Eliot Centennial Conference, August 18-20, 1988, Orono, Maine.

It had been part of Eliot's implication, perhaps, that by 1921 England no longer contained that desire. For its literati read the *Times Literary Supplement* and could not be stumped. If you wrote, "Those are pearls that were his eyes," they murmured smartly, "*Tempest!*" If you wrote, "The Army of unalterable law," they responded, "Meredith: 'Lucifer in Starlight' "; then they hissed "plagiarist!" (Yes, that did get said, when Eliot built Meredith's line into a minor poem, "Cousin Nancy.") And if you put *The Waste Land* before them they knew on what prior wealth this "poem" was drawing, and could be relied on to find its "parodies" "cheap," its "imitations" "inferior." (F. L. Lucas, the bookman's bookman, said so, in '22. And Jack Squire, a bookman who stood for Traditional Values, added that a grunt would have served about as well. [118]).

And if you'd asked, "What's it all about?" meaning not *The Waste Land* but our circumambient "it," they'd have invoked Rural Certainties, Traditional Values, even Iambic Pentameter. (Bertrand Russell, to his credit, hadn't resorted to that.)

But such "cultivation" reduces Literature, our communal memory, to the status of Trivial Pursuit. It's noteworthy how it's now the theme of a relentless weekly contest in the *TLS*, where people who can Spot the Author gain Book Coupons. But the Thunder's words to the Quester would earn no coupons. Far from filling a quizmaster's "Aha!" slots, they ravel down from prehistory through history to our present consciousness, and never are they neat, no, simply omnipresent. Their syllables come literally from prehistory and are all but impenetrable.

Eliot had drawn on the great discovery we identify now with Sir William Jones, a man Dr. Johnson had known. It was not true, thought Sir William Jones, that etymologies lie inert in a tidy field, Greek deriving from Hebrew, Latin from Greek, English from all of the above. No, what we now call the Indo-European tongues descend from a lost speech to which our best clue is the Sanskrit of India. In 1882, the year James Joyce was born, Walter Skeat, one pioneer in the tradition of Jones, published the final volume of his *Etymological Dictionary*, with a list of 461 Aryan (Sanskrit) roots. Skeat's book was just a short generation old when Eliot, a graduate student, undertook Sanskrit at Harvard, knowing that beyond Sanskrit stretched the unknowable, "that vanished mind of which our mind is a continuation." By another decade he was making his Thunder speak Sanskrit.

So the DA root is from prehistory, and utters the bestowing impulse. Then one compound, *Datta* says "Give," and other words specify what is to be given: *Dayadhvam*, "Give Sympathy," *Damyata*, "Give Guidance." In a world now infinitely more bureaucratized, English has borrowed "data" from dead Latin to signify items given, just scraps like the fact that Shakespeare wrote *The Tempest*. We consign them to a computer program we call a Data Base Manager, and perish amid their proliferation.

And that's not all; we can further persuade ourselves that *Dayadhvam* and *Damyata* command an encompassing force that leaves "Give Sympathy" and "Give Guidance" sounding pendantic. That may well be an illusion derived from our ignorance of Sanskrit; Eliot once alluded to the pleasure he took, in his student days, from repeating to himself passages of Dante he did not yet know how to construe or translate. Still, those English phrases are but ways to analyze, and they use unproducible abstractions, "sympathy," "guidance," such glibness as Bertrand Russell under pressure from the taxicab driver had failed to conjure up. Nor are the "Sympathize" and "Control" of Eliot's own note much better: words, words, words. What *The Waste Land* strives to isolate is the starkly inarticulable: what can't be explained if you don't know it already: so to speak, F. H. Bradley's Immediate Experience, no longer Immediate once we try to think "about" it.

For such is the way our deepest certainties are, according to Eliot, who by Jeffrey Perl's showing was in a strict sense a Radical Skeptic. For Knowing, the opposite of Skepticism, is the art of isolating what is knowable. Your Practical Cat you can perhaps make shift to isolate (though does anyone *know* a cat?). But try to isolate some object of profounder knowledge, and lo, it disappears. That hints at flower-child, countercultural lore, an unsettling thought if your degree is from the old Harvard.

(It follows, by the way, that Eliot's verse can't be explained; the best the explainer can offer is such hinting as may help reposition a reader's mind. It's odd indeed that Eliot of all poets became the New Criticism's patron saint; less odd, then, that John Crowe Ransom didn't greatly care for his work, or that Yvor Winters liked it very much less.)

So Eliot talks of a poet's usable knowledge being in his bones; "the historical sense compels a man to write not merely with his own generation in his bones, but with a feeling that the whole of the literature of Europe from Homer and within it the whole of the literature of his own country has a simultaneous existence and composes a simultaneous order" (SE 4). Having something "in your bones" and having a complex "feeling," those appear to be synonymous; two pages later Eliot is distinguishing it (or them) from "erudition," which he also calls "pedantry" (SE 6). Another time he said, "At the moment one writes, one is what one is, and the damage of a lifetime, and of having been born into an unsettled society, cannot be repaired at the moment of composition." No use, at that moment, resolving to be "classical"; no use signing up for an extension course.

So we've a moral obligation not to be ignorant, but what we've learned in partially freeing ourselves from ignorance we cannot really say. Pound, with his gift for being less mysterious, once said that real knowledge begins when one has "forgotten which book." Repeatedly, in "Tradition and the Individual Talent," Eliot brushes aside "Blue-book" knowledge: the kind that helps you on examinations, and later with those *TLS* competitions. Not that he'd have willingly been without such knowledge, else he'd not have been able to write the Notes to *The Waste Land*, those few enigmatic pages which, as he once remarked, were to achieve "greater popularity than the poem itself." But the knowledge that had fed the poem itself was of a different, unformulable order.

Some of the notes do offer Blue-book facts, as when they tell us in what older book this or that detail of *The Waste Land* may also be found. As information goes, that is information, or perhaps data-base management. But the connection of "The Chair she sat in, like a burnished throne" with *Antony and Cleopatra*, II, ii, 190, is a perfectly pointless tit-bit to offer any reader who doesn't already know it (CPP 39). Such notes tell us what we don't need if we know it already but can't use if we don't, and insofar as the notes are part of the poem their poetic force lies in their enactment of futility. Everyone who has tried to "teach" *The Waste Land* knows that.

And if it seems elementary, it's to Eliot's credit that he has made it seem so. That issue at least he forced into a corner, that sharp distinction between what you have in your bones (having perhaps even "forgotten which book") and what you're just now snacking up, or just now regurgitating ("Ah, yes, *Antony and Cleopatra*; Enobarbus' speech."). He had come to England from what he once called "a large flat country which nobody wants to visit;" in that, he said, America resembled Turgenev's Russia. Eliot coined the phrase apropos of Henry James; we

may remember how when James in 1904 revisited the flat land
of his birth, he rode the ferry to New Jersey and watched shore
houses

> waiting, a little bewilderingly, for their justification, waiting for the
> next clause in the sequence, waiting in short for life, for time, for
> interest, for character, for identity itself to come to them, quite as
> large spread tables or superfluous shops might wait for guests and
> customers. . . . (8)

--waiting, in short, to be haunted by the voices of history.

But that phrase has a romantic ring, not an Eliotic.
Henry James can talk as though all that America has lacked is
time. For buildings and furniture to marinate in time is what
makes them of interest, and here time has been in insufficient
supply. Moreover, Americans--especially New Yorkers--tend to
pull down an edifice well before time has begun to soak into its
pores. James does seem susceptible to the romance of old
houses that have stayed in place for centuries. It's an endearing
susceptibility. By now, were he alive, he might judge the time
just ripening for a coy sidle toward the Flatiron Building.

Eliot, though: when he writes of "old stones that
cannot be deciphered" one detects little romance (CPP 128).
The journey to a sacred place leads "behind the pig-sty to the
dull façade / And the tombstone" (CPP 139). If history, as he
says, may be freedom, it may also be servitude, unless we realize
the truth that

> We cannot revive old factions
> We cannot restore old policies
> Or follow an antique drum. (CPP 143)

That's pretty plain speaking, in an idiom close to that of a *Times*
leader. Though when Eliot's verse speaks plainly there are generally reservations close to the surface. Plain speech is apt to be
a practical compromise. And his way of speaking profoundly, on
one occasion, was to quote the Thunder which can barely be
understood. "Intolerable," indeed, was the "wrestle / With
words and meanings," its issue, at best, ways of putting it, "not
very satisfactory" (CPP 125).

A genre to which he was drawn in the 1930s was that
defined by Thomas Gray, the genre of the "Elegy in a Country
Churchyard." Fully nine Eliot poems take their titles from a
place, and voice meditations which the place helps to compose;
they are the five short "Landscapes" and the four ambitious
"Quartets." One thing curious about all nine poems is the
absence of other people, other voices. The virtual Babel of *The*

Waste Land has been superseded by circumambient silence in which the poet hears only his own low voice; and when, exceptionally, *Little Gidding* does assign a long speaking part to another voice, it is the voice of an ambiguously identified ghost.

Of the "Landscapes," three are American--"New Hampshire," "Virginia," "Cape Ann"--and two from Great Britain--"Usk" and "Rannoch, by Glencoe." "Virginia" moves like an incantation:

> Red river, red river,
> Slow flow heat is silence
> No will is still as a river
> Still. Will heat move
> Only through the mocking-bird
> Heard once? Still hills
> Wait. Gates wait. Purple trees,
> White trees, wait, wait,
> Delay, decay. Living, living,
> Never moving. Ever moving
> Iron thoughts came with me
> And go with me:
> Red river, river, river. (CPP 94)

It's notable how this small poem closes in on itself; of its fifty-eight words fully eight occur twice, two thrice, one ("wait") four times, one ("river") six times. It hears its own words, and it hears a mocking bird, once; all else simply waits. Apart from "me" and "iron thoughts," which I brought here and will take away again, the only hint of human presence is the one word, "gates." We might expect an American poet to hear, in the Virginia of Washington and Jefferson, quickening voices out of American history: the more striking, then, is this sheer depopulated silence, amid which the colors of the flag can be barely collected from a red river, white and purple trees. It was in Virginia, in 1933, that Eliot spoke to a lecture audience of Landscape: "a passive creature," he said, which "lends itself to an author's mood." That was also where he called the American Civil War "a disaster from which the country has never recovered, and perhaps never will." He remarked, too, on human over-readiness to assume that ill effects are obliterated by time. Virginia, the poem hopes we'll remember, was not only the forging place of the Union but the heart of the Secession. They cancelled: hence a vacancy of "wait, wait / Delay, decay."

Then in "Rannoch by Glencoe," a place he visited shortly after returning from Virginia, Eliot found what Elisabeth Schneider finely calls "the dark side of unity of culture, the moment of time none can redeem, a Waste Land contracted into the single scene of a present indelibly but invisibly marked by the past" (163). Rannoch was the site of the massacre that terminated Jacobite hopes; that foreclosed, so to speak, the English Civil War:

> Here the crow starves, here the patient stag
> Breeds for the rifle. Between the soft moor
> And the soft sky, scarcely room
> To leap or soar. Substance crumbles, in the thin air
> Moon cold or moon hot. The road winds in
> Listlessness of ancient war
> Languor of broken steel,
> Clamour of confused wrong, apt
> In silence. Memory is strong
> Beyond the bone. Pride snapped,
> Shadow of pride is long, in the long pass
> No concurrence of bone. (CPP 94-95)

Stags breed but to be shot; the very scavengers starve. Truly, "[i]f all time is eternally present / All time is unredeemable" (CPP 117), and history is the nightmare Stephen Dedalus called it, a nightmare from which we can foresee no awakening.

The broken steel, the clamour of confused wrong, are constituents of knowledge we must bring to Glencoe; a visitor deprived of that knowledge would see only the soft moor, the soft sky. (It can be tenuous knowledge, by the way; the *Encyclopedia Britannica*'s entry on Glencoe gives the location of the district and its dimensions and reports a monument to a Gaelic schoolteacher, but omits all mention of the only compelling reason to go there.)

The *Quartets*, of course, bear the names of places, moreover, places we are unlikely to have heard of save as students of T. S. Eliot. In that, they resemble the Churchyard at Stoke Poges, where Gray chose to locate meditations Westminster Abbey couldn't have prompted. Burnt Norton: a manor in the Cotswolds, at one time "burnt"; unlike Rannoch or Canterbury or Saint Paul's, it has escaped being claimed by "history," which is not to say that it doesn't possess a history. Not only have I never visited it, I have known only two people who had, of whom one was Eliot himself. He was there in 1934 and found empty gardens, an alley bordered by trees, a drained lily-pool. He saw, the poem tells us, the pool mysteriously filled "with water out of sunlight" (CPP 118). "Then a cloud passed, and the pool was empty": nothing as dramatic as thunder giving tongue, just a trick of the light, but it seemed to take away hidden presences. One theme of the poem is the presence of those presences--

escaped being claimed by history

> dignified, invisible,
> Moving without pressure, over the dead leaves,
> In the autumn heat, through the vibrant air, . . .

Meanwhile the very roses "[h]ad the look of flowers that are looked at," a tricky line that can collapse into tautology, since if flowers have a "look" they are being "looked at," but a line that somehow conveys the possibility of other lookers-on than ourselves. The unknown dead? Partly. Partly too, denizens of "what might have been," in the infinity of worlds we never entered, through that door "we did not open," because we elected to open whatever door led us to our Now. One door Eliot had opened was the one that led to residence in England. So among the "dignified, invisible" presences will have been an Eliot who might have stayed in America, might even have joined the faculty at Harvard. He'd have sparred with that phantom in 1932, when he gave the Norton Lecture at Harvard and even stayed in Eliot House. That American visit did unleash much poetry. He published *Burnt Norton* in 1935.

For Eliot, Burnt Norton was a chance encounter. East Coker, though, was part of his personal history: the place from which his American ancestor departed for America, leaving behind the stay-at-home Eliots to whom Sir Thomas Elyot belonged, whose "Boke Named the Governour" the poem quotes. (That Boke, as Eliot would not have failed to notice, got reprinted in Everyman's Library, a series to which he himself had gained admission not as his time's most influential poet but as introducer of the *Pensées* of Pascal.) And the Dry Salvages-- *Les Trois Sauvages* "off the N.E. Coast of Cape Ann, Massachusetts"--(here Eliot did for once supply a note) sport a "beacon" (as he specifies) by which he'd sailed in his youth, long ago when

> The boat responded
> Gaily, to the hand expert with sail and oar. . . . (CPP 49)

Last, Little Gidding, back in England, is a place of pilgrimage for British and Anglican Eliot; also a place where Charles I sought refuge amid the wreckage of his fortunes. Though it comes closest of the four to involvement in formal History, it's by no means a tourist trap, with obvious associations such as Eliot wanted above all to avoid.

So, as he'd done in "Virginia" and "Rannoch," he can import his own associations, for delicate entangling with an obduracy of place. By contrast, Henry James, yearning for those Jersey houses to offer a producible past, can seem not just romantic but nearly blatant. Yet Eliot, being aware of being James' countryman, conjured in his fourth quartet that most Jamesian of apparitions, a ghost. Of Jamesian ghosts, the most famous is perhaps one that Eliot alludes to in *The Family Reunion*, the specter that haunts the Jolly Corner back in New York, to personify the crippled thing New York has come to, the impaired being New York would have made of the protagonist had he stayed there. Its impairment is theatrical: missing fingers, a covered face. Having spelled this out, we recognize that in *Burnt Norton* we've already encountered a theme from "The Jolly Corner": the footfalls of "What might have been," echoing through passages, towards doors. And as long ago as the "Gerontion" of 1919 Eliot had likened history to a Jamesian haunted house, with

> many cunning passages, contrived corridors
> And issues, [where it] deceives with whispering ambitions,
>   Guides us by vanities. (CPP 22)

So now, after the "American" quartet--the one that wrestles with Mark Twain on his own ground, the shores of the great River--it is time for Eliot in England, fire-watching in an "English" war he'd not have known had he stayed in Harvard, to encounter, after deaths by air, earth, water and fire, the ghost his longest poem has been aching to produce: the "other" voice for so long so conspicuously silent. It has, as in "The Jolly Corner," a down-turned face, and proves to be "some dead master,"

> Whom I had known, forgotten, half recalled
> Both one and many; in the brown baked features
> The eyes of a familiar compound ghost
> Both intimate and unidentifiable. (CPP 140)

Horace Gregory once told me something Eliot had confided to him, that the "dead master" was principally Yeats, another ghost-specialist who had "left his body on a distant shore" (the French Riviera) early in 1939. But--Eliot had added to Gregory --it was "also myself":

> So I assumed a double part, and cried:
> And heard another's voice cry: 'What! are *you* here?'
> Although we were not. I was still the same,
> Knowing myself, yet being someone other--
> And he a face still forming. (CPP 141)

Another ghost in this compound is the ghost of Dante, whose speciality was confronting the dead, and whose measure haunts a passage which, as we know by Eliot's own word, embodies a prosodist's contradiction in terms, unrhymed

of unprofitable encounters

terza rima: phantom rhymes, in short. Like Hamlet's father, the ghost has come from a place of fire, and the fire-bombing of the place he's come to makes the two worlds, he remarks, "much like each other." And he goes on to paraphrase the most general lesson of human experience, of history: the gifts life reserves for the old age of whoever lives to grow old.

> First, the cold friction of expiring sense
> Without enchantment, offering no promise
> But bitter tastelessness of shadow fruit
> As body and soul begin to fall asunder. (CPP 142)

That harks back to Tantalus, to the grapes Apelles painted, and to Tennyson's Percivale, questing for the Grail, who drank from a clear brook and ate goodly apples, whereupon "all these things at once / Fell into dust": a detail Eliot had recalled in *Ash Wednesday*, where his protagonist

> cannot drink
> There, where trees flower, and springs flow, for there is
> nothing again. (CPP 60)

So we've known already hints of these disappointments, but in old age we may expect to know them continually. And the ghost presses on:

> Second, the conscious impotence of rage
> At human folly, and the laceration
> Of laughter at what ceases to amuse. (CPP 142)

--where "laceration" remembers the epitaph Swift wrote for himself.

> And last, the rending pain of re-enactment
> Of all that you have done, and been; the shame
> Of motives late revealed, and the awareness
> Of things ill done and done to others' harm,
> Which once you took for exercise of virtue.
> Then fools' approval stings, and honour stains.
> From wrong to wrong the exasperated spirit
> Proceeds, unless restored by that refining fire
> Where you must move in measure like a dancer.

That remembers Dante, and the Yeats of the play Eliot so admired, *Purgatory*, and the far younger Yeats whose vision of the afterworld was an eternity of being "busied by a dance." It all remembers fairy tales too, where injunctions and admonitions come in threes.

Once again it is James whose vision seems trivial by comparison: merely a complaint that its post-Civil-War obsession with bankable gold has kept his native land from cultural maturity. James, who Eliot greatly admired, had brought from the large flat country a subtlety, an authority, against which Eliot habitually measured his own. "Ghost psychology of New England old maid," Wyndham Lewis once wrote of James, and there's justice in that, as there is in Lewis' companion phrase: "Stately maze of imperturbable analogies." And here we're up against James' great limitation, that in his subtle explorations of the social and the psychological he had, it seems, save as a nasty smell, no intimation of the spiritual.

"History" Eliot's ghost subsumes into human experience: nothing specifically Greek nor English nor American: no Spenglerian Rise and Fall but a destiny we all share. The man who was born a century ago in St. Louis was at various times many things--schoolmaster, banker, publisher, essayist, editor, London Clubman, vicarious archdeacon--and might have been many more--I've suggested Harvard Professor. Easily, he might have been locked into a ready fate: the American Unitarian, primly broadminded. He evaded that; evaded, too, dogmatic adhesions; developed a mind like the one he ascribes to James, "so fine no idea could violate it" ("In Memory of Henry James" 856-57). An "Idea" was what the cabby had hoped for from Bertrand Russell, that incarnate belfry aswarm with symbolic logic and dry slogans. What Eliot gave the cabby was his proximity; what the cabby gave Eliot resembles what the ghost in *Little Gidding* gave him: on a street in London, inexhaustible testimony.

WORKS CITED

Perl, Jeffrey M. *Skepticism and Modern Enmity: Before and After Eliot.* Baltimore: Johns Hopkins UP, 1989.

Schneider, Elisabeth W. *T. S. Eliot: The Pattern in the Carpet.* Berkeley: U of California P, 1975.

Wilson, Edmund, ed. *The Shock of Recognition.* New York: Farrar, Straus, Cudahy, 1943.

RUSSELL ELLIOTT MURPHY

ELIOT'S GRANDCHILDREN:
THE POET OF THE WASTE LAND AND
THE GENERATION OF THE SIXTIES*

In *The Ethics of Reading*, J. Hillis Miller writes that literature must itself be regarded as a cause, or it will succumb to being increasingly regarded as nothing more than a series of socio-political effects. Surely, we who devote our lives to literature enough to have made it our field of study must agree that the choices we make professionally and personally, privately and publicly, are themselves largely an effect of the cause that literature is. We know, in other words, that literature has had the effect it produced in producing us because it is intended as a means of shaping experience and altering viewpoints and values --know this because our lives bear testimony to that fact. And so it stands to reason that we should honor those who use those means well, as we are now here doing honor to the poet T. S. Eliot.

But it is not enough for us merely to say as much unless we wish to find ourselves in jeopardy of convincing the convinced, whereas our task is to inculcate the word within the world. We can no longer simply assert the ethical and communal value of literature and of literary studies as if that is the given, a universally accepted commonplace. Rather whether or not literature, in and of itself, serves any overriding cultural value is now the very point in question, as Miller's work and our own occasional lemming-like anxieties as a profession attest. So, I reiterate, we cannot simply assert as much any longer, or even argue it in highly technical terms that duly impress our fellow professionals but leave the common reader with feelings of either confusion or anxiety, confirming his doubts about his own abilities to comprehend serious literature in an intelligent way. No, it is more important--perhaps *most* important--for us to demonstrate

---

*Presented Friday, August 19, 1988, at Session Seven of the National Poetry Foundation's T. S. Eliot Centennial Conference, Orono, Maine.

the value of literature in real terms by drawing upon the best source, our own lived experience of it. Our lived experience of literary works as authentic shaping forces in our lives.

Perhaps the current theoretical bias in mainstream literary studies will ultimately serve its purpose by encouraging the rest of us to begin demonstrating the practical value of a literary experience by relating our own experiences to and for the benefit of the interested reader. Were such an undertaking ever to be widely accepted as something more than a left-handed approach to matters literary, we might see literature again assume a place of more than just passing leisure-time prominence in the general community, for literature would have as its spokesmen the very products of its effectiveness speaking in real terms about those very effects.

Until that moment comes, however, we must content ourselves with opportunities such as this one. I can speak in those real terms because Eliot's poetry did indeed have a profound effect on me during a particularly trying period both for myself and for my generation, the 1960s, as that recent decade transpired here in America. It was a trying period for me personally simply because, born in 1944, I came of age during it. I do not feel that I need to explain to anyone how it was a trying period for my generation and for my nation.

If it is presumptuous to speak for a generation, which is what I am apparently about to do, then I nevertheless have for my precedent none other than T. S. Eliot. The only difference, though a major one, is that Eliot very quickly disclaimed that role as forming any part of his intentions and as quickly eschewed even the role of Lost Leader which then equally rapidly fell to him.

The claims I make to being a spokesman for my generation are modest nevertheless, for I willingly admit that mine is a personal view, a practice not as common today as it used to be (in the sixties, for example) and therefore one open to neither confirmation nor refutation by others. So I hope to put the poet of *The Waste Land*--and other poetry--in perspective not in terms of how he affected my generation, but in terms of how he affected me during that awful decade we call the sixties. That I also happen to be of that generation born in the 1940s and just coming of age as John F. Kennedy was entering the White House gives me that peculiar slant, the *à la mode*. There are, furthermore, affinities between the so-called generation of the sixties and Eliot's generation, which coming into its own during the teens and for which the twenties were a combination coming-out, mourning party, was provided therefore with a similarly exciting and unstable contemporary world ill-suited to concrete values and focused human endeavor; but those affinities are, to my mind, rather obvious ones, after all. In both periods, the old order was changing, or already had, yielding way to the new with something less than grace, nor very much of hope.

But perhaps as much can be said of any two generations. The outstanding difference, of course, is that my generation had Eliot's *The Waste Land* to turn to for our metaphorical reference points, while Eliot's apparently had nothing and no one, only the detritus of a botched culture.

I know that that view of the worldview *The Waste Land* expresses is no longer fashionable, but I also know that it was Eliot's generation's view of his great poem, and that it certainly was mine, for it had become, during my formative years, something of the nature of a popular-culture commonplace, as familiar a catch phrase as the Lost Generation, which we wrongly attributed to Hemingway. Even we schoolboys and schoolgirls, we schoolpersons, knew the story some great poet named Eliot told. Culturally, he said, we had become a wasteland. We did not know exactly what that meant, but it did not sound particularly attractive or hospitable; in fact, it sounded so unattractive and so inhospitable that when Eisenhower's FCC chairman Newton Minnow called television a vast wasteland, we all knew exactly what he meant.

We were just children then, but how wonderful that a government official would make a literary allusion to illustrate how vacuous television, that nemesis of reading and intelligence, was. How strange, too, that everyone recognized it as such. (What a marvellous comment on the impact Eliot's poem had had on his society.) As a working class kid growing up in East Providence, Rhode Island, and attending public schools there, I knew enough about *The Waste Land* only to know that a man named T. S. Eliot had written it, that he also had written lines prophesying that our world would end--shortly, it seemed, to us nuclear age children--not with a big bang but a whimper, and that, like Picasso's strange-faced women, he typified all that was new and rare about our modern world's uniquely distorted vision of things, a vision which our history seemed somehow to be justifying with its violence and war, hatred and coldness.

It was not quite the 60s yet, and all was not lost, after all. There was still Milton Berle and Lucy and Jackie Gleason's *The Honeymooners*, but there, like the cadaverous incarnation of a lost gentility, from time to time we'd see in the pages of *Time* or hear about on the news or in school T. S. Eliot, his limpid smile speaking reams about the sorry state of the world and about the emptiness of our lives just beneath the surface of the news and popular entertainment. With the sort of pride in our technology that not even Sputnik could shake, only challenge, we knew that we were moving faster, flying higher, communicating better and more quickly than any other epoch in human history; but poets like Eliot pointed to the dark side of our common reality. He seemed to know that all that progress and self-congratulatory promotion was nothing compared to the emptiness we felt when the lights were turned off.

It wasn't until much later that I would learn the meaning of that smile of his. First there was a decade to traverse. It was, as many of you must remember, a time when events caught up so much with the mythic that there was no longer any time but the present, no longer any news but the news. Kennedy was in the White House. There was the Bay of Pigs, but there was also the successful naval blockade of Soviet missile shipments to Cuba. There was the Berlin Wall, but there were Kennedy's rousing words to West Berliners. There was the growing threat of nuclear war, but there was also the Nuclear Non-Proliferation Treaty. There was Selma, but there were sit-ins. Even the spirit of modernism with its dilemmas and its uncertainties and its ironies seemed caught up in and overcome by a wave of new enthusiasms without any use for subtle expressions of the anxieties of the past. Eliot was not forgotten, but the contemporary world was too alive for his vision of a dead land to appeal to the young as a suitable image. When we wanted to imagine that we were feeling creatures, there was Bob Dylan; Eliot spoke of another era, our grandfathers', who had given up all hope. Our fathers had won the war against fascism, and we knew that we would inherit the stars.

So when I first actually encountered Eliot's poetry in a sophomore literature class at the University of Massachusetts, I remember being impressed by what was obviously an incredible work of literature, for like any student I identified greatness with difficulty; but Eliot did not speak to me and my sense of social reality as well as, say, Pete Seeger or Joan Baez did. The poem was "The Love Song of J. Alfred Prufrock." I don't think I understood it or that it was even taught particularly well. I thought it was an awfully sad poem about very bored, confused people, told by a man who somehow wanted to feel something again but knew, or had convinced himself, he could not any longer. Otherwise, that sort of literature simply did not connect with the lives of young people for whom the major questions were whether or not the Soviets were going to bury us, or we them.

And then suddenly even that didn't matter anymore. Kennedy was dead, there was rioting in our major cities, more and more horror stories were coming out of Southeast Asia. In the jungles, things are getting bad. We're going to have to do something. We're going to have to get involved. We do, more and more. There is Student Power; there is Black Power; there is Flower Power. There are drugs and reports of bad trips become as common as the trench confessions of Pound's and Eliot's day. There are the Beatles and the Rolling Stones, Janis Joplin, Jimi Hendrix, Eugene McCarthy. Someone shoots Martin Luther King, Jr. Soon another Kennedy is dead, and the police riot at that summer's Democratic National Convention in Chicago. In Miami, the Republicans have already nominated Richard Nixon. And somewhere in the midst of all that, T. S. Eliot passed quietly away.

We spent the last few minutes of a class in modern poetry discussing *The Waste Land*, I recall, and that was it. Any questions? There were none. Who would dare? By then the poem was the Stalin of graduate studies, so formidably entrenched in the canon, what was there left to say, let alone ask? As a descriptive work, it had become a literary artifact; certainly it no longer provided a fictive paradigm for the state of the contemporary world or our view of modern history. In fact, it was not too difficult to find oneself longing for those simpler days of yesteryear when everything was chaotic in a manageable kind of way; and I can recall a teaching assistant meeting at which someone quoted Erich Segal saying that Bob Dylan had inherited Eliot's mantle. And Eliot did seem--*all* the moderns did seem, if I may say so--dated. I had already seen D. W. Griffith's *Intolerance*, and had studied it and Sergei Eisenstein enough to know that, beyond its considerable literary value, *The Waste Land* had become something of a commonplace model for the structural ideals of modernism, its use of fragment and juxtaposition, counterpoint and irony rather old hat by now, although we respected Eliot for having done it first. What the poetry said of the past and *its* present we hardly cared to know anymore, having come at last, as a culture, to admit that we admired the classics only because they were dead things by dead people.

In late 1969, I was looking around for a suitable graduate course for the coming Spring 1970 semester, over and

above the ones one had to take. A young professor who had
already published a well-received book on Gerard Manley Hopkins, Paul Mariani, was offering a seminar in Christocentricity in
four modern poets--Hopkins, Hart Crane, Robert Lowell, and
Eliot. Good lapsed Catholic that I was, I signed up. We had just
finished studying the *Four Quartets* when, in early May, Kent
State occurred.

I cannot describe the horror that filled us all when
we heard that young American soldiers had shot and killed four
young American students protesting the war. Those of you who
were on a college campus must remember those days as vividly
as I, for it seemed as if some great internal cataclysm was about
to come to a head, and that history would sweep us and our
enemies up into one vast and impersonal storm until blood
washed this land clean of thought and cause.

> We cannot revive old factions
> We cannot restore old policies
> . . . .
> These men, and those who oppose them
> And those whom they opposed
> Accept the constitution of silence
> And are folded in a single party. (CPP 143)

Classes were cancelled, campuses across this country
closed down, and students and faculty milled around before
spray-painted libraries wondering what was going to happen
next. At a nighttime rally on the Amherst common, a speaker
announced that there was rioting in downtown Madison, that
students had stolen a plane and bombed a nearby Army base.
My heart feared for the fate of my nation and the future of my
children.

> Who then devised the torment? Love.
> Love is the unfamiliar Name
> Behind the hands that wove
> The intolerable shirt of flame
> Which human power cannot remove. (CPP 144)

I cannot say that I will ever forget those days, but I
can say that Eliot's words in *Little Gidding* that history is here
and is now and is redeemed by the intersection of the timeless
with time and through the will of a God who does not recognize
our banners or sympathize with our causes, and yet whose hand,
with Love, weaves the broadcloth as well as the shirt of fire--

> With the drawing of this Love and the voice of this Calling

--that those words of Eliot and other words like them sustained me by convincing me that it indeed is so (CPP 145).

I cannot say how they convinced me. I can only say that they convinced me. Let us say now that perhaps that confirmation of belief is one of the causes that literature engenders. That in its convictions, or lack of same, and in our reading or misreading of them, literature expresses ourselves, and we each hear our convictions expressed. That then the effect on me is mine to keep or lose or miss or share.

Or let us say instead that that is what Eliot's own convictions did for at least this one of his spiritual grandsons; we say the same thing. For I would be troubled to hear anyone try to prove to me that that lesson, or should we call it consolation, which I obtained from T. S. Eliot is not the effect of conviction expressed in non-dogmatic ways--and that, to me, is literature. That, to me, is art.

And so I came to understand, too, that Eliot's smile, coming as it did in pictures taken years after his penning of *The Waste Land*, was not the limpid smile of the cynic hardly bothering to sneer at a race too stupid to recognize the source of its doom, but the blissful smile of the benevolent sage who has realized the source of our salvation.

SHYAMAL BAGCHEE

ELIOT'S "ONLY" (AND "ALL")

> this wobbliness of words is not
> something to be deplored.
>
> --T. S. Eliot

Eliot wrote in *Ash-Wednesday* 3, "but speak the word only," and indeed he did speak the word "only" on a remarkable number of occasions (CPP 63). And in "The Love Song of J. Alfred Prufrock," the protagonist claims, "I have known them all already, known them all:--" (CPP 5). Without disputing the extent of Prufrock's knowledge, I wish to point out merely that we, the readers of Eliot's poetry, may not yet know fully well all the "all"s and "only"s the poet used in his writings. In this essay I wish to examine briefly Eliot's use of these two modifiers in his poems. The primary object of attention will be the restrictive word "only," and for contrast we will also observe his use of "all."

If we go back to the line from *Ash-Wednesday* 3, quoted above, we will note that it contains not only one pun--on the word "word," as has been pointed out by Elisabeth Schneider (120)--but two puns: on the word "word" as well as on the word "only." I deliberately overlook, in this particular case, the further ambiguity one may detect in the two possible syntactical senses of the line: "speak only the word," and "speak the word only." After all, Eliot is here quoting from Matthew and has not himself invented the syntax. In any case, the word "only" is not rare in Eliot's poetry and one can find quite a number of instances where the poet speaks this word. It seems to me clear that, *pace* "Lines for Cuscuscaraway and Mirza Murad Ali Beg," Eliot's words were *not* "Restricted to What Precisely / And If and Perhaps and But" (CPP 93).

"Only"--the second word in Eliot's notorious "Notes on *The Waste Land*"--is a curiously prominent, although not a dominating, feature of his diction. For example, the word occurs as many as thirty-eight times in *Four Quartets* where its possible

or near cognates, like "mere," "merely," and "barely," are also
to be found. I am not suggesting that all of Eliot's "only"s are
equally significant for the meaning of his poems. Similarly, not
all the "all"s are of particular importance. But there are
instances, and there are quite a few of these, where especially
the location of the modifiers creates complexities for the reader,
and these can be resolved only by paying close attention to the
poet's positioning of the particular modifier in the text.

E. M. Forster once complained (and I am not about
to quote *his* famous "only") that Eliot's poems are "not epi-
curean" (89), that there is a pronounced element of "inhos-
pitality" in Eliot's writing (95). And among the various traps that
one encounters in the poems is the modifier "only" that *usually*
clarifies meaning by restricting reference. Normally this is what
"only" does; but frequently in Eliot's poems the word does not
appear to be doing so. More often than not the obscurity or
ambiguity is caused by Eliot's peculiar placement of the modifier
both within the verse structure and the syntax. For example, a
considerable number of "only"s in Eliot's works are to be found
at the end of a line of verse while it appears to modify nothing in
that particular line but attaches curiously to the sense of the
next.

Consider these two instances from "The Hollow
Men," the only times the word appears in that poem:

> Those who have crossed
> With direct eyes, to death's other Kingdom
> Remember us--if at all--not as lost
> Violent souls, but only
> As the hollow men
> The stuffed men. (CPP 56)

And much later, in reference to the "[m]ultifoliate rose," the
poet writes: "The hope *only* / Of empty men" (CPP 58; italics
added). In each case the word is to be found at the end of a line
of verse to the meaning of which it either does not attach ("not
as lost / Violent souls, but *only*," the modified particular follows
in the next line) or attaches oddly creating syntactical ambiguity.
"The hope only / Of empty men"--does that mean "The only
hope of empty men" or what it in effect says: that *only empty
men* have such hopes? In the latter case the hoped for multifoli-
ate rose takes on dark colorations, since the hope now is nearer
to delusion, empty dream, even vanity. Forster's comment on
this prevalence of the ambiguous element in Eliot's poetry is, "if
he sees a reader floundering he might amuse himself by setting
an additional trap. And I am afraid there is a little truth in this"

(13). Forster's view is shared by many readers of Eliot. But there are also readers who, like Nicholas Urfe in John Fowles' *The Magus*, dislike uncomplex poetry. At the moment I do not want to take a side in this dispute because it seems to me that as far as some of Eliot's "only"s are concerned there is quite another matter to consider.

In spite of the obscurities and difficulties caused by the syntactical and verse locations of the modifier, it is reasonable to assume that Eliot's primary purpose in using "only" was a justifiable one: that is, to clarify or modify or restrict reference. The excessive use of this particular modifier in Eliot's later poetry is, I think, related to the impulse toward perspicuity or lucidity that was a part of high modernist poetics. In Eliot's case the tendency may have also been an inherited cultural trait -- something derived remotely and in a mutated form perhaps from the Puritan background that was his and against which he systematically struggled.

So, while the relatively colorless word "only" might not be part of "the generic Eliotan" diction, to use Hugh Kenner's helpful phrase, to an extent the motive behind its frequent use is generically modernist. While "only" gives us much less of the flavor of Eliot's more typical poetic language than, say, "defunctive," "piaculative," "anfractuous" or "sempiternal" (even if we are to leave out "polyphiloprogenitive"), it gives us a clue to a hidden aspect of Eliotan poetics: the valorization of precision and clarity. Nevertheless, as his poetry also makes clear, this impulse toward lucidity gets imbricated in other, differently orientated impulses. In other words, what the modifier "only" can clarify, and occasionally does clarify in context, becomes undercut by other literary projects and convictions which, too, Eliot held or sought to generate. For example, there was the method of indirection inherent in the *Symboliste* tradition with which Eliot's poetry often aligned itself. Also, Eliot was convinced that the poetry of our times needed to be obscure. This is apparent in, say, his 1921 essay "The Metaphysical Poets" where he writes:

> Our civilization comprehends great variety and complexity, and this variety and complexity, playing upon a refined sensibility, *must* produce various and complex results. The poet *must* become more and more comprehensive, more allusive, more indirect, in order to force, to dislocate if necessary, language into his meaning.[1] (SE 289; italics added)

---

1. Paradoxically, a poet may succeed in dislocating language simply by trying too hard to be exact and precise, as Eliot occasionally does by using "only" excessively. In his quirky but brilliant study, *The*

Of course, we get to the very nub of a major problem of poetics here and it will be wise not to seek to answer glibly, one way or the other, the question whether or not a poet is entitled to have *his* meaning at the cost of distorting language that is essentially not his personal property. And, also, it is not as if Eliot himself has not struggled with this issue in his criticism. At the moment it should suffice to note that the urge toward clarity and precision that is manifest in Eliot's use of "only" is frequently contradicted by the odd and indirect syntax in which he places the word, perhaps impelled by his other conviction that the modern poet "must" be truthful through indirection.

In "The Hollow Men," nevertheless, the syntax can be unravelled and "only" can be seen as serving a useful function in determining the poem's meaning. For example, the overwhelming gloom that many readers find in Eliot's pre-conversion poetry--and which, for some, is gloomiest in this poem--is lifted somewhat when one observes carefully the function of "only" in the first instance of its use. The poem particularizes its utterance by limiting the consciousness to the hollow men, the stuffed men. No matter how many hollow men there might be in the world, they are not all of humanity, at least the poet does not *say* so. Even the hollow men seem to know that there are at least two other categories of human beings: "Those who have crossed / With direct eyes" and those who are "lost / Violent souls" (CPP 56). No matter how "lost" they might be, or have been, the Dantesque violent souls are neither hollow nor stuffed. And since the poem gives us three *extremes* (those with "violent souls," those with "direct eyes," and those with empty insides stuffed with straw) and because the speaking voice is particularized to be identified with only the hollow men, there can be little textual reason to read unredeemed universal gloom into the poem. And in this task of differentiation the word "only" adds precision and clarity.

The objectification and identification of the speakers "only / As the hollow men / The stuffed men," make it possible for us to see the poem, at least at one level, as Eliot's attempt to "do" another "voice." Even if the world is declared to end with a whimper, the clear particularity of the voice that makes the simpering prophecy places useful restrictions in the reader's path and limits the possibilities of careless misreading. It is in charac-

---

Tell-Tale Article: A Critical Approach to Modern Poetry, George R. Hamilton pointed out that Eliot's desire to achieve clarity of emphasis and effect led him to use the definite article in an abnormally high proportion--a full 10% of his vocabulary. On the other hand, far more lucid writers, like Addison and Pope, have required a much smaller number of "the"s in their writing--about 5.6% according to Hamilton. So much for Eliot's classicism!

ter for the hollow men to be borrowing their philosophy from a jingle (and for Eliot to be borrowing from Kipling's "Danny Deever"). So, the poem does not declare, as a fact, that the world is to end with a whimper (or with a bang for that matter)-- rather, to use Foucault's word, it locates the "énonciation" superbly and accurately. That this should be the case is not surprising because, as some readers have noticed, "The Hollow Men" contains a very large number of precise and specific references: *"We"* are the hollow men; it is *"our"* voice that you hear; the rats are *"in our dry* cellar"; *"there"* are the eyes; *"[t]his"* is the dead land; the eyes are *not "here"*; *"we"* are gathered on *"this* beach" (CPP 56, 58).

    Eliot did not come to recognize the possibilities of the modifier "only" early or easily. In fact, the opposite modifier, "all," with its vast comprehensive reference, is far more commonly found in the early works than one finds the restrictive and spare "only." The word "only" is all but absent in *Poems Written in Early Youth,* occurring in an undistinguished fashion among phrases that, for example, speak ungrammatically about one century being "more great" than another. Eliot's 1917 volume of poems, containing "The Love Song of J. Alfred Prufrock," uses the word "only" four times, two of these rather casually in the relatively slight pieces "Cousin Nancy" and "Hysteria." "Prufrock" does not use "only" even once and this, I think, is remarkable. The indecisive, hesitating protagonist cannot perhaps be expected to reach, in his utterances, towards the precision of "only." Rather, the diffused effect of the vaguely comprehensive modifier "all" is more congenial to his vocabulary. He uses the latter word twelve times, at places attributing it to the voice of the feared woman, a voice that Prufrock himself creates--at least as long as we grant that the entire poem exists primarily in his own head.

    It seems curious that reported speeches by the peremptory woman and prophetic Lazarus, and the vocabulary of the vacillating Prufrock should all contain the word "all." Since the impressions of character intended to be produced by the three figures are presumably quite distinct, Eliot's use of "all" may at first appear indiscriminate. Nevertheless, a little thought will show the flexibility of meaning and suggestion inherent in this modifier. And because of its semantic tractability "all" contrasts the typical pointedness of "only."

    William Empson's brief look at "all," in what he labels "a brief interlude" in *The Structure of Complex Words,* is instructive. "All" is really not a complex word and Empson devotes to it fewer than four full pages in his 450 page study. The word's different uses can be described only in a "vague and distant way," he says (102). Although there is "no variety of Senses in the word, which in itself is merely a logical connective," Empson points out also that its relatively loose connotative potential permits it to be used variously to suggest a wide range of emotional contexts: "Combativeness (claiming all, arguing all else away, etc.) pride (ruling all, disdaining all, etc.) love (offering all, disvaluing all but ...) and self-sacrifice (standing as representative of all, giving up all for them)."

In "Prufrock" it is difficult to be certain that Eliot was fully aware of this word's serviceability. Nor can we be sure that Eliot was merely being imprecise or was confused about fine dramatic distinctions that his monologue could or ought to have made by a better management of diction. Compare, for example, the situational adequacy of "all" in Robert Browning's "My Last Duchess": "Sir, 'twas all one! ... / ... / ...--all and each / Would draw from her alike the approving speech," and "This grew; I gave commands; / Then all smiles stopped together" (252). Note particularly the speaker's *consciousness* of both the diffused nature of all--indicating his disapproval of his wife's lack of discrimination--and the finality of his exact but understated command that leads him to juxtapose tellingly the words "all" and "together" in the last line quoted above. By stopping "all" her smiles the Duke brings "together" or aggregates in one ruthless act of arrogation all the shapeless and directionless (as it appears to him) fluidity of her gracious nature.

As the poem stands, "all" functions reasonably well in "Prufrock." When Prufrock claims that he has "known them all already, known them all," he appears to express several kinds of attitudes at once. The repeated use of "all," couched in the repeated phrase "known them all," provides the speaker with a bit of much needed self-assurance, the repetition consolidating by insistent assertion a sense of control over the otherwise overwhelming and threatening world around him. For, even if no one else is there to hear these words as they are spoken, the speaker himself hears them and in so *hearing* perhaps finds in them the reassurance he desperately needs. On the other hand, who can be entirely sure that Prufrock really does *not* know what he claims to know? After all, hypersensitivity about other people's opinion or a lack of social aplomb does not constitute irrefutable evidence of intellectual feebleness. On the other hand, again, what is it exactly that Prufrock knows? The plural "them" (like the vaguely comprehensive "all") is imprecise in its reference: does it stand for the various points in "time" mentioned in lines immediately preceding and succeeding this speech fragment--"in a minute there is time," "a minute will reverse," "the evenings, mornings, afternoons" (CPP 5)? Certainly, "them" must refer also to the "voices" that are "dying with a dying fall" and others that refuse to be silenced: "They will say . . . They will say" (CPP 4).

Lazarus, coming back from the dead, can be more certain of his knowledge and, therefore, can indeed be in a position to tell us "all." (Compare with the line in *The Waste Land*, "I Tiresias have foresuffered all," one of only four uses of "all" in that poem [CPP 44]). Yet he does not tell us anything; Prufrock's projection of the prophet, actually his rehearsing of the lines of the prophet he conjures up as an image of his alter ego,[2] simply crumbles and fades away in the presence of the pooh-poohing woman whose use of the word "all" is, significantly, in the negative: "That is not what I meant at all. / That is not it, at all" (CPP 6). The repetition of the negative phrase here undermines the diffuseness of "all" and seems to give it an absolute validity and a rigidity of denotation that it otherwise lacks: in other words the peremptory (and perhaps unsubtle) woman empties out the various and varied semantic content of the word "all"--until it means nothing at all, and she is entirely firm in her nay saying.

So, in "Prufrock" the word "all" functions to highlight both the indecisiveness, the hesitations and veerings of the protagonist, as well as the firm assurance of those who know (the prophet) and those who claim to know (the woman). "All" has, of course, always been a privileged word in the vocabulary of proud characters who are often too impatient to make fine distinctions. Consider, for example, Shakespeare's Coriolanus: "All the swords / In Italy, and her confederate arms, / Could not have made this peace" (1434; V.iii. 207-209) or "Cut me to pieces, Volsces, men and lads, / Stain all your edges on me" (1436; V.vi. 110-111). No wonder, in Eliot's *Coriolan*, too, we hear: "Cry what shall I cry? / All flesh is grass" ("Difficulties of a Statesman," CPP 87). We might conclude, then, that when we read, for example, Eliot's phrase, "Where all love ends" (*Ash-Wednesday* 2) we should ponder the possibilities of meaning inherent not only in "love" and "end," but also in the modifier "all" (CPP 62).

---

2. On Prufrock's "rehearsing" of the Lazarus "speech" see my essay, " 'Prufrock': An Absurdist View of the Poem" (432-33).

But an account of the probable adequacy of "all" does not quite explain the absence of "only" in "Prufrock." Just consider the possibilities, the potential, of the unutilized "only" in this poem. What about "[D]o not ask, 'What is it?' / Let us [only] go and make our visit" (CPP 3)? One imagines the syllabic disbalance of the lines would have added an element of healthy modernist discordance. But what we have in the poem is peculiarly suitable for sketching in the persona's identity--the first line lengthened by a soulful "Oh," creating a near couplet that is appropriately enervated and jingly. Again, why not "I am [only] an attendant lord"? After all, the speaker, however abject, appears here finally to have arrived at some pointed form of self-knowledge. But Eliot disregards the possibility, gives his speaker merely the awkwardly truncated phrase "Am an attendant lord," and proceeds remorselessly to make a helpless Prufrock dilate meticulously and obtusely upon his dejected state. Similarly, would not the effect of an earlier line in the poem be improved if it was made to read: "In [only] a minute there is time" (CPP 5)? Once again, we cannot say with any certitude that Eliot's avoidance of "only" in this early poem was part of an elaborate rhetorical strategy (to mock the protagonist) rather than the evidence of a lingering diffuse style. Perhaps the truth is simply that while he may have "modernized" himself all on his own, Eliot had not yet encountered Pound's more exact editorial scissors. There is, then, some mystery surrounding this absent "only," and one might justifiably say, "So intimate, this ['only'], that I think [its] soul / Should be resurrected *only* among friends / Some two or three" (CPP 8; italics added). That, incidentally, is the first occurrence of the word in *Collected Poems*. We really do not know why Eliot did not write: "I should have been [only] a pair of ragged claws" (CPP 5).

We can be a bit more certain when Eliot actually chose to use the word. As I have remarked already, the frequency of the use of *only* increased as Eliot matured as a poet. In *The Waste Land* he used *only* fourteen times--as opposed to just four uses of *all*, one of these occurring in the ordinary phrase "all right" (CPP 42, l. 161), printed erroneously as "alright" in two of the earliest editions of the poem (the manuscript had "allright" as one word [WLF 18]). I am, of course, not considering here the three instances of "already" and "always" also to be found in the poem (CPP 42, l. 160; 48, ll. 360 and 363).

It is interesting to note that all the "only"s in the finished poem have been retained from the earliest versions of the respective sections. This shows, seemingly, a certain self-confidence in Eliot's handling of this limiting and well-focused modifier. But the self-confidence is not necessarily justified in every instance because while, say, the simple line of colloquial speech, "And her only thirty-one" (CPP 42), creates no problem of interpretation, the precise meaning of some of the "only"'s--especially in "What the Thunder Said" (ten uses)--is far from clear, in spite of the frequent repetition of the highly particularizing word. For example, what is described as "only rock" turns out to be a landscape complete with a winding road, mudcracked houses and, of course, mountains (CPP 47, l. 331). In terms of the quality of feeling evoked by this waterless scenery, the passage is entirely appropriate to the sense of the poem; but it is evident that "only" attaches here logically to the water that is absent, rather than to the rock which co-exists with other objects the poet describes--and that the image value of these other objects is important to the poem. Clearly, Eliot felt the need to supplement "Here is no water but *only rock*" with a more accurate "If there were *only water* amongst the rock" seven lines later (CPP 47). Similarly, in the next stanza Eliot tells us first that what the scene needs is "the sound of *water only*," but soon afterwards admits that his water-music needs *both* the "sound of water over a rock" and the song of the "hermit-thrush . . . in the pine trees" (CPP 48).

    Nevertheless, I do not wish to argue that logical consistency is always essential to a poem--even though "only" is primarily important as a precise logical sign. No doubt, the very element of improbability with which a "city over the mountains" springs up in a landscape described initially as "endless plains . . . / Ringed by the *flat horizon only*" is vital to the phantasmagoric and nightmarish feelings intended to be conveyed by these lines of *The Waste Land* (CPP 48, ll. 368-69). Here a prominently misapplied "only" enhances the mystery as well as the requisite indeterminacy of the passage. Elsewhere, however, "only" functions well to *eliminate* mystification--as in the Perilous Chapel section. Playing fast and loose at once, Eliot first exploits the mythical possibilities of the chapel by talking about "reminiscent bells," the upside-down bats, the women with long black hair, and so on (CPP 48). But having established the possibility of these romance reverberations, having put together the "ingredients of a witches' broth," the poet tells us, in the following stanza, that the "empty chapel [is] only the wind's home," notwithstanding the "faint moonlight" and "tumbled graves" (CPP 49). The desiccation of the landscape--both internal and external--is absolute, rendering fallow not only metaphysics but also superstition, evacuating both the gods and the ghosts. "Dry bones," therefore, "can harm no one" (CPP 49). But that is small consolation, for the black clouds gather only over *distant* mountains. If we now go back to part 1, the invitation to the "shadow" under the "red rock" ("Only / There is shadow under this red rock, / [Come in under the shadow of this red rock"]), we will hardly find it satisfying any more (CPP 38). What we need is water, only water; neither the "shadow" nor the "black clouds" will suffice.

Out of the five or so "only"s which failed to make it into the final version of *The Waste Land*, only one could have contributed, albeit in a minor way, to the poem's total meaning. This "only" is to be found in the following two lines Eliot placed between the discarded long section about a sailing accident with which the "Death by Water" section began and its last brief Phlebas section which survived:

> And if *Another* knows, I know I know not,
> Who only know that there is no more noise now. (WLF 61)

Interestingly, Pound, who cancelled out all the preceding eighty lines of the section, seems to have wanted these two retained as the opening lines of the short fourth section of *The Waste Land*. The decision to leave out this "only" was apparently the poet's who thought the lines to be either "too tum-pum" (And / An, I know / I know not, knows / know / know / know / no, etcetera) or their reinforcement of the idea of silence after drowning gratuitous. Here, then, is an example of Eliot's judicious editing-out of "only."

Remarkably, also, the use of the all-embracing "all" became sharper and more sharply focused as time passed. For example, *Four Quartets* presents quite a high incidence at twenty-nine (29) uses, but this is not as high as "only" (used in thirty-eight [38] places) and occurs in a dramatically reduced proportion when compared with the increase in the frequency of "only." But now the application of "all" is by and large restricted responsibly to occasions where "all" is essential to sense, as in "All shall be well and / All manner of things shall be well" (*Little Gidding*)--the repetition emphasizing the high necessity of the inclusiveness of reference (CPP 142-143). On the other hand, the phrasal use of "all" as in the ordinary expression "at all"--so insistently present in "Prufrock"--nearly disappears in the *Quartets*. By contrast, a great number of "all"s cluster around a shared sense of movement, desertion, locomotion or deracination, indicating an association of the word, in the poet's imaginative vocabulary, with the turning world: "And destitution of all property" (*Burnt Norton* [CPP 120]); "The houses are all gone under the sea" (*East Coker* [CPP 126]); "They all go into the dark" (*East Coker* [CPP 126]); "Pray for all those who are in ships" (*The Dry Salvages* [CPP 135]); and "the end of all our exploring" (*Little Gidding* [CPP 145]). To these we might add two further instances from *East Coker*: "the bold imposing façades are all being rolled away" and "the faith and the love and the hope are all in the waiting" (CPP 126, 127).

"Only," normally restrictive in its reference, does not need to be limited--or be given a specialized sense--like the word "all." And as I have already observed, "only" bounces back to full form in the *Quartets*: "Only through time time is conquered" (*Burnt Norton* [CPP 120]); "Words move, music moves / Only in time" (*Burnt Norton* [CPP 121]); "The wisdom only the knowledge of dead secrets" (*East Coker* [CPP 125]); "Our only health is the disease" (*East Coker* [CPP 127]); "The dripping blood our only drink, / The bloody flesh our only food" (*East Coker* [CPP 128]); "These are only hints and guesses, / Hints followed by guesses" (*The Dry Salvages* [CPP 136]); "Where action were otherwise movement / Of that which is only moved / And has in it no source of movement" (*The Dry Salvages* [CPP 136]); "only a shell, a husk of meaning / From which the purpose breaks only when it is fulfilled / If at all" (*Little Gidding* [CPP 139]) and "The only hope, or else despair / Lies in the choice of pyre or pyre--" (*Little Gidding* [CPP 144]).

There are many instances of rich, complex and even worrisome uses of "only" in *Four Quartets*. What about "that which is only living / Can only die" (*Burnt Norton* [CPP 121])? At first one might regard this as yet another example of perverted syntax in Eliot. But these lines are different from, say, the lines in *The Waste Land*: "Only / There is shadow under this red rock" (probably meaning that the shadow here can be found only under this red rock). For *Burnt Norton* asks us to contemplate the various modes of living that may or may not be life, and the various modes of dying that may or may not be death. One can, presumably, do more than "only" live, in which case one will not have to "only" die. There is a range of meaning--all of life and all of death--from which Eliot makes his deliberate, strict, limited choice of reference. The topic has been of a lifelong interest to the poet; compare, for example, the lines in *The Waste Land* where the topic is adumbrated, but without using "only": "He who was living is now dead / We who are living are now dying" (CPP 47, ll. 328-29). Clearly, Eliot's tone and import here are quite different from those in, say, Eugene O'Neill's straightforward socialist poem, "Fratricide" (1914), where we find the lines: "Who pays the price that some must pay? / ... / The poor who only live to die" (44).

Only rarely do "all" and "only" occur together in an Eliot passage. When they do, as in the following lines of *East Coker* 2, it is reasonable to assume that the poet is conscious of the juxtapositioning and its semantic and structural potential:

> For the pattern is new in every moment
> And every moment is a new and shocking
> Valuation of *all* we have been. We are *only* undeceived
> Of that which, deceiving, could no longer harm.
> In the middle, not *only* in the middle of the way
> But *all* the way, in a dark wood, in a bramble. . . .
>   (CPP 125; italics added)

"Pattern," indeed, is the key here, and it is renewed every moment in this reflexive piece of verse. Once we notice the shifts that are patterned, our "valuation" of the poet's craft is drastically ("shocking") affected. In line 3 of the quotation we find both "all" and "only"; the pattern is varied in lines 5 and 6 where words occur in two separate lines and in a reversed order --first "only" and then "all." But where the words occur together in the *same line of verse* (line 3), they really belong to two *different sentences*, the line containing the end fragment on one sentence and the beginning of the next. The different poetic uses to which verse lines and sentences can be put was not unknown to Eliot. He had written, as early as 1917 for example,

> How can the grammatical exercise of scansion make a line ...
> more intelligible? Only by isolating elements which occur in other
> lines, and the sole purpose of doing this is the production of simi-
> lar effect elsewhere. But repetition of effect is a question of pat-
> tern. ("Reflections on Vers Libre," SP 33)

For Eliot poetry was always a matter of "pattern." And pattern might be detected even in "irregularity" as Eliot maintained when he distinguished usefully between "the irregularity of carelessness" and "the irregularity of deliberation" (SP 34). What is evident in the section of *East Coker* under review is precisely this "irregularity of deliberation." So, while "all" and "only" belong to a single verse line but two different sentences in line 3, in lines 5 and 6 they belong to the same sentence but to two different lines of verse. The meaning, too, modulates correspondingly. In the first instance "every [new] moment"--precise, particular, isolated--paradoxically evaluates the entire, continuous span of life: "all we have been." In the second example the reference to only the middle of the way is withdrawn, revised and expanded to include "all the way." Here, then, the controlled drama of "only" and "all" and the patterned production of verse signify the processes of transmutation of thought into poetry. We might say of Eliot's best poetry what he said of Shakespeare and Dante: that like them he "offer[s] poetry in detail as well as in design" (SE 148).

But not all poetry makes its point in obscurely patterned ways that require the skill and maturity of sensitive but strenuous readers. The effect of the *absent* "only" in the last, self-sufficient line of *Ash-Wednesday* is quite clear even on first reading: "And let my cry come unto Thee" (CPP 67). Only the "cry," the word, the voice, is capable of making the passage. After all, this is the "Only the hardly, barely prayable / Prayer" mentioned in *The Dry Salvages* (CPP 132). Similarly, the cryptic formula of *Burnt Norton* ("that which is only living / Can only die") is much more simply and effectively conveyed in *Little Gidding* (CPP 144): "We only live, only suspire." The first and the last *Quartets* link up of course, but they show also a gradual relaxing of semantic tension. Perhaps this progress is related to the difference in tone between the distant, fastidious voice in *Burnt Norton* that refers to those who "only" live as mere objects--"that which," not even a humanizing "who"--and the generous, culpable "we" in the section on "Love" at the end of *Little Gidding*. To know, Eliot now realizes, is to look for.

"Every great writer contributes something to the meaning of the key words which he uses, those which are characteristic of his personal style," Eliot maintained (TCC 74). As Eliot's use of "only" and "all" demonstrates, sometimes these key words are quite ordinary words indeed.

WORKS CITED

Bagchee, Shyamal. " 'Prufrock': An Absurdist View of the Poem." *English Studies in Canada* 6 (1980): 430-443.

Browning, Robert. *Browning's Complete Poetical Works*. Ed. Horace E. Scudder. Boston: Houghton, 1895.

Empson, William. *The Structure of Complex Words*. Ann Arbor: U of Michigan P, 1967.

Forster, E. M. *Abinger Harvest*. New York: Harcourt, Brace, 1936: 89-96. Excerpted in *T. S. Eliot: A Selected Critique*. Ed. Leonard Unger. New York: Russell & Russell, 1966.

Hamilton, George. *The Tell-Tale Article: A Critical Approach to Modern Poetry*.
    New York: Oxford UP, 1950.
O'Neill, Eugene. *Poems 1912-1944*. Ed. Donald Gallup. New Haven: Yale UP,
    1979. New Haven: Ticknor & Fields, 1980.
Schneider, Elisabeth W. *T. S. Eliot: The Pattern in the Carpet*. Berkeley: U of
    California P, 1975.
Shakespeare, William. *The Riverside Shakespeare*. Ed. G. Blakemore Evans.
    Boston: Houghton, 1974.

"THE WHOLE OF LITERATURE: A SIMULTANEOUS
EXISTENCE": ELIOT AND FOREIGN WORKS

HARVEY GROSS

COMPOUND GHOST, TRIPLE DEVIL, TERMINAL BOOKS

1

On the twenty-first of June, 1943, Thomas Mann wrote to his dear friend and favorite correspondent, Agnes Meyer:[1]

> Then today . . . came your gift of a book, these Beethoven Quar-
> tets, in which I have read deeply and wished to understand. You
> could have thought of nothing better to make me happy. Whether
> I am linguistically equal to these poems and whether I can get
> hold of all their implications is another question. But I have your
> elevating judgment and thus know that conquest will reward every
> exertion. (Strange, that in one of the pieces [*Burnt Norton*, 1. 74]
> Eliot uses the German word '*Erhebung*': as if one could best grasp
> the expression of this idea with the German word.)
>
> By the way, I know him as an essayist. An article of his, on
> Henry James, if I am not mistaken, had made a great impression
> on me, and it also seems these poems have a strong intellectual or
> better: spiritual impact. I have long believed that poetry and the
> higher kind of prose will always come closer and merge with each
> other.
>
> I am feeling strangely out of sorts by the slow progress with
> the preparatory starts of my new 'novel.' I have actually begun to
> write, because it was no longer bearable *not* to write; and I find
> out that I was perfectly ready for it and feel myself in a state of
> steady, quiet excitement. The title reads:

Doctor Faust

The strange life of Adrian Leverkühn

told by a friend

> This evil story, permeated with the German Middle Ages, moves
> through the medium of a thoroughly rational, humanistically
> inclined reporter, and thereby gains a leavening of cheerfulness
> which it needs--and which I need. The writer (he writes now, 1943,

---

1. Agnes E. Meyer (1887-1970) and Thomas Mann exchanged more than three hundred letters. Before her death she presented Mann's letters to the library of Yale University; they constitute an autobiography of Mann's years in exile, and reveal a remarkable degree of intimacy and personal candor. This and all subsequent translations, unless specifically noted, are my own.

in Germany) is one of the Nazis' pensioned off high school teachers and is called Serenus Zeitblom, Ph.D. In this style nearly all
names are significant. Now imagine the rest!

Your Thomas Mann (323-24)

"These Beethoven-Quartets" were, of course, T. S.
Eliot's *Four Quartets*. They had been published by Harcourt,
Brace only a few weeks previously, on May 11, 1943, and the
copy Agnes Meyer sent was hot off the press.[2] That Mann recognized the presence of Beethoven in *Four Quartets* may have
been the intuitive response of a writer whose own work was
informed by music both as a principle of structure and as a
major metaphor. However, in all probability, Mann read the
review of the *Quartets* that had appeared in *Time* on June 7,
1943. The anonymous reviewer noted the Beethoven-Eliot connections: "Readers familiar with the great 'last quartets' of
Beethoven will suspect that Eliot derived from them his title,
much of his form, elements of his tone and content" (96).

We cannot be sure how much and exactly what Mann
derived from his reading of *Four Quartets*. He admits his linguistic limitations; more important, he felt inadequate to respond to
their "implications" (in his German, *Beziehungen*): their vast
network of reference, allusion, denotation, and verbal resonances. This inadequacy was not simply a matter of language but
of differences in culture. In a subsequent letter, written to Bruno
Walter, Mann observes, "But Joyce, for example, to whom I feel,
in a certain way, quite close, is to the sensibility nurtured in the
classic-romantic-realistic tradition just as much an affront as
Schoenberg and his followers. Incidentally, I also cannot read
Joyce, because to do so one must be born into English culture"
(416).

Mrs. Meyer's gift of the *Quartets* arrived one month
after Mann began writing *Doctor Faustus*. Mann tells us, in *The
Story of a Novel*, that "On May 23, 1943, a Sunday morning . . .
also the date on which I had my narrator, Serenus Zeitblom, set
to work, I began writing *Doctor Faustus*" (30). In his letter to
Mrs. Meyer, Mann shifts from his discussion of Eliot to anxious
talk about his own overwhelming preoccupation with the opening sections of *Doctor Faustus*. My juxtaposition of *Faustus* with
the *Quartets* will suggest, I hope, not so much questions of putative 'influences,' but rather questions of more demonstrable and
significant critical interest.

---

2. Mrs. Meyer, herself a Harcourt Brace author, may have sent Mann an advance copy. See Gallup for
the curious history of the publication of the *Quartets*.

heuristic shock

My cryptic title, "Compound Ghost, Triple Devil," may serve to indicate something of the substance and range of these questions. The "Compound Ghost" appears in section 2 of Eliot's *Little Gidding*, the last of the *Quartets*; the "Triple Devil" manifests himself in chapter 25 of *Doctor Faustus*. These are the two texts of our concern, and I believe that to confront them with each other generates a heuristic shock: to recognize their similarity of subject and background and to view one through the grid of the other initiates a journey of discovery. As an historical datum it is intriguing and provocative that Mann was aware of the *Four Quartets*; however, this datum is only of limited usefulness. Our journey of discovery must begin with the establishment of the immediate historical background, continue with the recognition of what I have already called "similarity of concern," and conclude with some theoretical consideration of *Four Quartets* and *Doctor Faustus* as 'terminal' works in the canon of literary Modernism.

Our first identifiable connection is that *Little Gidding* and *Doctor Faustus* were written against the background of World War II. Mann worked on *Doctor Faustus* from May 1943 to January 1947. The narrative compounds two movements of historical time, the past life of the German modernist composer, Adrian Leverkühn, and the present time of its telling, the catastrophic final years of the Third Reich. The intersection of past and present is also a certain concern of *Four Quartets*: *Little Gidding*, the concluding poem of the sequence, was written in a time dense with the terrible events of the War. For Eliot the great fire bombings of London--which he witnessed as an air raid warden--were apocalyptic moments in the larger pattern of the past and present which makes up history: "History is now and England" (CPP 145). And the bombings provided *Little Gidding* with its dominant symbol of fire and its related religious iconography.

Our second connection, a "similarity of concern," is the crucial role music plays in both works. For Mann and Eliot music was a complex seminal metaphor, a principle of structure, and at times (to use a phrase of Susanne Langer) even approached the status of "a real semantic." Following Symbolist tradition Eliot believed that poetry could "communicate before it was understood," and that the substance of this communication was analogous, perhaps even equivalent, to musical experience. The music in Eliot's poetry inheres in the operations of the auditory imagination; in the arrangements of syntax, prosody, and patterns of imagery. These are, of course, various

religious iconography

aspects of technique; however, it is significant that when Eliot was trying to explain what he was up to in *his* later work, he mentions Beethoven: "To get *beyond poetry*, as Beethoven, in his later works, strove to get *beyond* music" (qtd. in Matthiessen 90). And it is worth noting that a critic as logically rigorous as F. R. Leavis, in his analysis of *Four Quartets*, remarks: "The musical analogy made explicit in the title, *Four Quartets*, has a marked felicity, and prompts the commentator on the co-present four to reflections that yield him light for an intelligent reading" (158). Music, Leavis argues, gathers to itself the form and power of a quiddity; if we propose to interpret the *Quartets* "we have to ask: 'What end--"in my beginning is my end"--is the intrinsic principle of life that determines *the thisness of this music*'" (my italics 159).

"This thisness of this music" might also stand as motto for Mann's *Doctor Faustus*. I need hardly stress or elaborate the fact of its total involvement with music; it is impossible to recall any literary work in which music functions so variously and at so many levels of meaning and structure. Its hero is the distinguished modernist composer--in Mann's pointedly archaic German, *Tonsetzer*--Adrian Leverkühn. The "politically suspect" art of music is deeply implicated in the tragedy of Nazi Germany, and we are reminded of Settembrini's severe platonic pronouncement on the art that rejects the word and courts the irrational and the demonic. In placing the equivocal nature of music at the ideological center of *Doctor Faustus*, Mann follows Nietzsche in recognizing the danger that music posed to the German soul. Germans, Nietzsche believed, were constantly menaced by *Abstraktion* and *Innerlichkeit*, and the related temptations of beer, metaphysics, and music. The German, Nietzsche quipped, "thinks that the Lord God Himself sings songs" (Götzen-Dämmerung 33).

Our third connection that links *Doctor Faustus* and *Four Quartets* is that they are examples of what Erich Kahler called "terminal books" (20). Central to the terminal work--and here I elaborate on Kahler's notion--is its self-conscious preoccupation with problems of style and technique. Kahler notes, "The traditional art forms have grown problematic through external, social and cultural revolution, as well as through internal evolution, evolution of technique; art has become its own subject matter" (21). In the career of the artist, the terminal work usually marks an extreme stylistic breakthrough beyond which neither the artist nor his epigones can go without aesthetic disaster.

In the larger career of nineteenth and twentieth-century Modernism, *Four Quartets* and *Doctor Faustus* mark a concluding phase of Modernism itself. The dispute over when Modernism began and ended has not yet been settled, but certainly these late masterpieces can be read as a valediction to that epoch which began with Baudelaire, Wagner, and Nietzsche. Indeed, Eliot and Mann make this emphatic: Mann bases his biography of Adrian on biographical details taken directly from Nietzsche's life; Eliot's *Quartets*, in their substance and structure, acknowledge "the thought and theory" of symbolism and its program that all art approach the condition of music. These works are gestures of farewell to the Modernist epoch; they also represent, on the parts of Mann and Eliot, final examples of major work. After the *Quartets* Eliot turned to writing for the stage and published only a few minor lyric poems. *Doctor Faustus* was Mann's last novel in the 'epic' mode of the Joseph books and *The Magic Mountain*. In the concluding eight years of his incredibly productive life, Mann wrote ironic fables like *The Holy Sinner* and partially completed the unfinished comic novel from his youth, *Felix Krull*.

2

We have discussed the major extrinsic features that connect *Four Quartets* and *Doctor Faustus*. When we turn to examine the two texts and their demonic protagonists, we discover that they share intrinsic features of genre and thematic concern. The appearance of the "familiar compound ghost" to the poet in *Little Gidding*, and the manifestation of the devil, who comes to Adrian Leverkühn in three questionable shapes, derive from celebrated literary originals (CPP 140). Eliot's text from *Little Gidding* is modelled on canto 15 of the *Inferno* where Dante encounters his former teacher, Brunetto Latini. Adrian's dialogue with the devil is strongly reminiscent of Ivan Karamazov's hallucinated conversation with the devil who emerges as "a gentleman parasite" from his brain fever. Ivan recognizes him as an *alter ego*--more exactly an *alterum id*--and understands the devil as the spokesman for his instincts, his baser self. He tells his apparitition, "You're me with a different face; you keep telling me what I think and are unable to tell me anything new" (767). In language uncannily similar, Adrian complains to *his* devilish visitor, "Ihr sagt lauter Dinge, die in mir sind und aus mir kommen, aber nicht aus Euch" ["You say nothing but the things which are in me and come out of me, but not out of you."] (300).

Adrian's infernal visitor and Eliot's compound ghost say "nothing but the things" that their interlocutors consciously know or have troubled them at some deeper stratum of awareness. Hell is no longer the traditional realm below ground, the literal commonwealth of the damned; conversations with demons and devils take the form of the self's encounter with itself. For Eliot and Mann and the modern literary imagination, hell is internalized, a condition of the self in division and torment. Goethe's Faust laments, *"Zwei Seelen wohnen, ach, in meiner Brust / Die eine will sich von der andern trennen* ... ["Two souls, alas, dwell in my breast / Each seeks to separate from the other"]. But the ghost who confronts Eliot and the devil who appears to Adrian contain more than two souls struggling with each other. Eliot's ghost, as I mention below, is "a congeries of spirits ... a collection of disembodied souls ... " (Olney 303). Adrian's protean visitor is also a collection of various selves, not only from Adrian's fictive past, but from the past of his creator, Thomas Mann. Despite the devil's animadversions on psychology ("Psychologie--daß Gott erbarm, hältst du's noch mit der? Das ist ja schlechtes, bürgerliches neunzehntes Jarhhundert!" ["Psychology--God pity us, do you still hold with it? That is indeed bad bourgeois nineteenth century!"]), both Mann and Eliot subscribe, with certain important reservations, to the modern psychologized view that sees hell as emblematic of the distress of the divided consciousness (332).

We turn to Eliot's text, lines 78-149 from *Little Gidding* which describe the speaker's encounter with the "familiar compound ghost" (CPP 140-42). The passage begins "[i]n the uncertain hour before the morning" and ends when "day was breaking" and the ghost departs "with a kind of valediction ... on the blowing of a horn."

These lines, in the intricacy of their orchestration and the close logic of their narrative movement, form the longest sustained section of the *Quartets*. Eliot remarked that they were the most difficult to compose and cost him the most in technical effort (see Gardner 171-96). The price was well worth paying; the passage is arguably the high point of Eliot's craftsmanship and can be favorably compared to any passage of similar length by the other masters of English blank verse--Shakespeare, Milton, or Wallace Stevens.

Eliot fits the strong and weak syllables of English blank verse into the stanzaic container of Dante's *terza rima*.

Instead of rhyme Eliot alternates masculine and feminine endings, creating the interlocking effects of *terza rima*:

> In the uncertain hour before the morn*ing*
>   Near the ending of interminable *night*
>   At the recurrent end of the unend*ing*. . . . (CPP 140)

Eliot also follows Dante's *endecasillabo* except in those lines when he uses, without variation, lines of regular unrhymed iambic pentameter. We hear the steady blank verse pulse in lines of carefully measured expository emphasis and word order:

> So I find words I never thought to speak. . . .
>
> Let me disclose the gifts reserved for age. . . . (CPP 141)

We also hear the blank verse music in lines where Eliot intends a deliberate mimetic effect: thus the poet and his "familiar compound ghost" move together in this heavily stressed line:

> We trod the pavement in a dead patrol. . . .

Enclosing the rhythms of *terza rima* and the blank verse pulse are the larger shaping and controlling rhythms of Eliot's distinctive syntax. The passage opens with a series of delaying prepositional phrases that blocks off grammatical closure until the appearance of the *I* in the ninth line. Each of the delaying phrases offers suggestions of time and place, and there gradually builds up a powerful sense of early morning urban desolation. The time is after one of the night air raids on London.

> After the dark dove with the flickering tongue
>   Had passed below the horizon of his homing. . . . (CPP 140)

The dark dove with its "flickering tongue" remembers that superb fighter aircraft the Spitfire and the decisive role it played in The Battle of Britain. The dove with "[f]lame of incandescent terror" also figures in the iconography of Christian salvation and damnation. It is the leading symbol for Incarnation, the presence of God in history; it descends as the Holy Spirit in pentecostal fire, and it speaks in tongues to all the nations. Penetecostal fire may be infernal or purgatorial; we must choose the latter to avoid the former:

> The only hope, or else despair
>   Lies in the choice of pyre or pyre--
>   To be redeemed from fire by fire. (CPP 144)

The self must make the descent into hell before being "restored by that refining fire;" the episode is modeled, as we note previously, on Dante's meeting with his teacher Brunetto Latini in canto 15 of the *Inferno*. Eliot's poetic self encounters

> the sudden look of some dead master
> Whom I had known, forgotten, half recalled
>   Both one and many; in the brown baked features
>   The eyes of a familiar compound ghost
> Both intimate and unidentifiable. (CPP 140)

The identity of this "familiar compound ghost" has generated considerable critical speculation: who among Eliot's dead masters might he have been? Mallarmé, certainly ("To purify the dialect of the tribe"), perhaps Irving Babbitt; perhaps Yeats or Joyce (CPP 141).[3] But obviously a compound ghost cannot, by definition, be a single figure; it seems to me that James Olney is exactly right when he says:

> But might one not also, and perhaps more fruitfully, consider [the compound ghost] to be past Eliots; for is that not what a compound ghost would be--a congeries of spirits standing for our heritage and our ancestral significant moments; a collection of disembodied souls representing our personal, professional, national, human past and informing our individual present? (303)

Succeeding lines confirm this interpretation when Eliot's poetic self "assumed a double part, and cried / And heard another's voice cry: 'What are *you* here?' / Although we were not" (CPP 141). Eliot is himself the compound ghost and the elements in the compounding originate in his own biography, in his "thought and theory," and in the poet's eschatological yearnings--when "the exasperated spirit" must move like a dancer in the refining fires of purgatory (CPP 142). Most important is what the ghost has to say about "thought and theory." Eliot preached all his life about what he practiced, and although in later years he made ironically deprecating assessments of his critical writings, he never gave up the profession of criticism. The critical questions broached in *Four Quartets* center on language and "the intolerable wrestle / With words and meanings" (CPP 125). How can a poet in a time when language itself seems to have undergone "a process of deformation and decay" fashion for himself a verbal style that does not seem stale and exhausted? (Heidegger 11). Eliot's ghost identifies the renovation of language as the compelling historical task of his career as poet and critic:

---

3. See *Le Tombeau d'Edgar Poe*: *"Donner un sens plus pur aux mots de la tribu. . . ."*

> Since our concern was speech, and speech impelled us
>   To purify the dialect of the tribe
>   And urge the mind to aftersight and foresight. . . . (CPP 141)

The poetic idiom of the later nineteenth century, with its stale diction and metronomic rhythms out of touch with the "real language of men," could not serve the experience and the inspiration of a poet starting out in that first energetic moment of Modernism, the crucial decade 1910-1920.[4] Like Wordsworth, Eliot repudiated the poetic practice of his literary fathers: "For last year's words belong to last year's language" (CPP 141). "Modernizing himself"--as Ezra Pound put it--Eliot grew aware that certain problems of diction and prosody led to a technical impasse; that, in effect, immanent processes of the historical movement itself had led to an exhaustion of previous subjects and compositional procedures (Pound 40). Thus Eliot sought, through renovation of poetry's basic material, language itself, a breakthrough to a new style. Our following example, the opening lines of "Gerontion," shows how Eliot deconstructed accentual-syllabic meter and built a prosody that gives the illusion we are hearing the rhythms of colloquial speech:

> Here I am, an old man in a dry month,
> Being read to by a boy, waiting for rain.
> I was neither at the hot gates
> Nor fought in the warm rain
> Nor knee deep in the salt marsh, heaving a cutlass,
> Bitten by flies, fought. (CPP 21)

the illusion of colloquial speech

I mentioned "the illusion of colloquial speech" because the achievement of this verse, its syntactical directness and rhythmic compression, is the product of a simplicity reached through great and conscious artifice (see Gross 182-84). It is not a question of whether the verse is 'free' or metered; the *terza rima* of our passage from *Little Gidding*, with its sustained iambic pulse, also creates an intense and immediate presence: the poet's voice with all its characteristic inflections of tone. It is this presence, sounding through the figure of the old man in "Gerontion," through the myriad characters that inhabit *The Waste Land*, and through our "familiar [and] intimate" compound ghost that validates, at least for this reader, the undeniable authenticity of Eliot's craft and vision.

The ghost shifts the talk from theory of language and as Eliot speaking to Eliot, offers to "disclose the gifts reserved

---

4. It is in this same decade that Schoenberg published his first atonal compositions (*Three Piano Pieces*, opus 11), and Kandinsky painted the first purely non-representational paintings.

for age" (CPP 141). If we had any previous doubts about the identity of the ghost, that he is, as James Olney suggests, "past Eliots," they are dispelled here. We remember it was Eliot's persistent conceit to speak through figures considerably older than his own biographical age. The balding, sexually unconfident Prufrock, the blind and impotent Gerontion, the epicene Tiresias (in *The Waste Land*) who functions as the withered conscience of a ruined culture, the "agèd eagle" of *Ash-Wednesday* (CPP 60): are these not prototypes of Nietzsche's epigones or late-comers, men born with gray hairs who "behave as practical pessimists, as men guided by a sense of imminent catastrophe [and who] . . . feel and live an *ironical* existence" (Schlechta 152).

The Eliot of *Little Gidding* was only fifty-four, but already feels as frighteningly imminent the decay of his senses:

> the cold friction of expiring sense
> Without enchantment, offering no promise
> But bitter tastelessness of shadow fruit
> As body and soul begin to fall asunder. (CPP 141-42)

Two oxymorons ("cold friction . . . bitter tastlessness") make vivid the encroaching loss of sexual desire, a loss already figured in similar tropes in the earlier (1920) "Gerontion":

> I have lost my sight, smell, hearing, taste and touch:
> How should I use them for your closer contact?
> These with a thousand small deliberations
> Protract the profit of their chilled delirium,
> Excite the membrane when the sense has cooled. . . . (CPP 23)

In these lines the poet speaks through Gerontion, "a deliberate disguise"; the baroque rhetoric of the lines, derived from the Jacobean dramatists, serves to distance or alienate the poet's authentic self from his speaking mask.

But the compound ghost of *Little Gidding* speaks without the heavy mediations of rhetorical disguise and textual allusion; he directly tells how creative power and desire both depend on the full response of the senses. Eliot's other selves theorized about the "objective correlative," or maintained they could find "no substitute for sense." Like Keats, Eliot was a great poet because his language succeeded in communicating through image and rhythm the immediacy of 'felt experience.' This is particularly striking in those passages where Eliot is dealing with certain root experiences, the approach to the substance of mystic vision, sudden moments of expanded consciousness "[in] which everything in the world appears unified in the light of one fundamental experience" (see Sullivan 154):

He reads us as a writers do

> For most of us, there is only the unattended
> Moment, the moment in and out of time,
> The distraction fit, lost in a shaft of sunlight,
> The wild thyme unseen, or the winter lightning
> Or the waterfall, or music heard so deeply
> That it is not heard at all, but you are the music
> While the music lasts. . . . (CPP 136)

The epiphanic moments reveal themselves through what the eye sees, the nose smells ("the wild thyme *unseen*"), and what the ear, through the transforming power of the "auditory imagination," holds in memory.

Before the ghost fades "on the blowing of the horn," he enumerates the other recognitions that will darken the poet's later years: frustration, regret, and shame over failures in his moral life (CPP 142). It is these enumerations and the anguish of their psychological probings that intensify the autobiographical lineaments of our compound ghost. Certain exegetes have detected in these lines,

> the shame
> Of motives late revealed, and awareness
> Of things ill done and done to others' harm
> Which once you took for exercise of virtue . . . .

Eliot's declaration of remorse for his reactionary--some have said proto-fascistic--politics, and for the bigotry displayed in such texts as *After Strange Gods*. However, I would hesitate to see in these lines such specific intentions; Eliot reads us a generalized litany of atonement for such sins as we all have been guilty of.

In the penultimate tercet the ghost offers the poet the redemptive hope of purgatory:

> From wrong to wrong the exasperated spirit
> Proceeds, unless restored by that refining fire
> Where you must move in measure, like a dancer. . . .

The sub-text here is canto 26 of the *Purgatorio* where the troubadour poet Arnaut Daniel addresses Dante in his native Provençal.[5] He asks that Dante remember his punishment, then disappears into the fire that refines the souls of the lustful. *Poi s'ascose nel foco che li affina* ["Then he hid himself in the fire which refines them"] (342). The final line which the ghost speaks offers an exquisite example of the mimetic rhythm:

> Where you must move in measure, like a dancer. . . .

---

5. Obviously a favorite text of Eliot: he cites it in *The Waste Land* (l. 428); and a phrase from it, *Ara Vos Prec*, provided the title for the 1920 collection of his poems.

Subtle tensions between quantity and accent--some unstressed syllables are long and some stressed syllables are short--animate the line with the movement of what it evokes: the dance itself.

3

it is fascinating and instructive to observe the autobiographical hide-and-seek that Thomas Mann is so fond of playing in the unreliable border-region between the empirical and imaginative truth.

Erich Heller

In 1953, two years before Mann's death, a young Munich painter Fabius von Gugel visited Thomas and Katia Mann. He came to show them a portfolio of his work, a set of fantastic illustrations for Grimm's fairy tales. Mann was deeply affected by the illustrations, and he told von Gugel (here I translate from the account given in Peter de Mendelssohn's massive biography, *Der Zauberer*),

that the drawings strongly reminded him of one of his own experiences, of a vision that he had had as a young man. A vision? asked the painter. Indeed a vision. Gugel was positive that Thomas Mann used this word with emphasis, and not hallucination, dream, fantasy, imagination, or something similar, but emphatically: vision. It had been in his early years, when with his brother he had been spending the summer weeks in Palestrina. There in the stone hallway [of their pension], in the heat of the afternoon, he had suddenly caught sight of a stranger sitting on the black sofa whom he knew had been none other than the Devil. (292-93)

Mann was remembering an experience that he had had fifty-six years before, and that had been filtered through the traumatic process--a four-year period of strain and personal agony--that was the writing of *Doctor Faustus* itself. Mann and his brother Heinrich had indeed spent the summers of 1895 and 1897 in the Italian town of Palestrina; in his letters Mann described the atmosphere of the town as uncomfortable, even a bit sinister. It was a place where a sudden vision of evil, of the demonic might manifest itself.

We doubtless have questions about the precise nature of the 'reality' of the episode. Mann would have been quite capable of putting the young painter on; too many of Mann's critics tend to forget that he was also a great comic writer, a modern master of irony and parody. Such critics as

Georg Lukács, who for ulterior political motives wished to claim Mann for nineteenth century, or even 'socialist' realism, never recognized what Mann himself acknowledged: his affinities, particularly on the level of style, with such avant-garde writers as Joyce.[6] At its most typical the style they shared is learned, allusive, and ironic; in the words of Harry Levin, "an act of evocation, peculiarly saturated with reminiscences." (qtd. in *The Story of a Novel* 91).

The devil who appears to Adrian Leverkühn is "saturated with reminiscences," autobiographical as well as literary. Mann conflates the substance of his alleged 'vision' with two elements of obvious literary ancestry: the previously mentioned episode from *The Brothers Karamazov* and the account of Faust's meeting and pact with the devil taken from its legendary source, the *Urfaustbuch* of 1587. In the fictional time scheme of the book, it is the year 1911 (a year important for Modernism), and Adrian was living with his friend Schildknapp in the spook-haunted town of Palestrina. The devil has come on his traditional mission: to seek Adrian's confirmation of the Faustian bargain and explain to him its terms and consequences. Like Eliot's ghost Mann's devil is a composite figure, but in the larger space of the novel, Mann presents his devil as three distinct personalities. During the long and passionate course of their dialogue, Adrian watches the devil become, in turn, a pimp, a musical theorist, and a theologian.

In their first confrontation the devil has the appearance of a street tough who wears a sports cap over one ear and whose trousers are indecently tight. Later in the chapter we learn he had been *"Esmeralda's Freund und Zuhalt"*--Esmeralda's friend and pimp (311). In a previous metamorphosis, that of a guide and porter, he had steered Adrian to the Leipzig brothel where Adrian meets the prostitute who was later to infect him with syphilis. Appropriately, the devil-as-pimp delivers a lecture on the clinical features of a neuro-syphilis and how, as the disease progresses, Adrian's creative powers will expand. Sounding a familiar Nietzschean note--the Nietzsche of the half-mad *Ecce Homo*--the devil, in a corrupt apostrophe, extols the three-way relationship between art, disease, and criminality:

> Do you believe in anything that possesses *ingenium* that does not partake of hell? *Non datur*. The artist is the brother of the criminal and the madman. Do you think that any fully living work ever came into being without its maker having learned to understand

---

6. Nor did Lukács ever recognize himself as the model for Naphta in *The Magic Mountain*: he could never admit that Communism and Fascism were the two faces of the same totalitarian coin.

the nature of the criminal and the madman? What's morbid and
what's healthy? Without the morbid life in all its living days would
not become manifest . . . . (315)

Even as the devil raves, his features change and
soften: he is now "one of the intelligentsia who writes on art, on
music, for the popular newspapers; a theoretician and critic who
himself composes, insofar as thinking allows him to" (317). The
theoretical wisdom the devil expounds is largely that of Theodor
Adorno, who was Mann's neighbor in Los Angeles during the
writing of *Doctor Faustus* and who served as Mann's adviser on
musical matters. Mann incorporated several sections of
Adorno's then unpublished *The Philosophy of Modern Music*
directly into the text of *Doctor Faustus*; and the difficult problems of style and technique which the devil and Adrian rehearse
are presented as Adorno formulated them and often in
Adorno's own words.[7]

The devil offers an analysis of the stylistic dilemma
in music based on what he calls "the technical niveau." Modern
composers no longer possess the spectrum of tonal arrangements which was available to composers of the romantic and
classic periods. Certain combinations, like the chord of the
diminished seventh, have gone stale. "Every composer of the
better sort carries within himself a canon of the forbidden, the
self-forbidding, which by degrees includes all the possibilities of
tonality, therefore all traditional music" (319). This exhaustion
of technical means cannot be attributed to changes in culture
and society, but has been determined by the history of music
itself. The devil argues that music follows neither the laws of
nature nor of psychology; it develops in accordance with immanent historical process--a process which "no one reverses."

Consequently, the very idea of a self-sufficient musical work is no longer tenable; those traditional genres, sonata
and symphony, which depended on tonality and "its once bind-
ingly valid conventions" could no longer sustain themselves.
Late nineteenth-century composers like Brahms approached the
problem of style through conscious archaism--as in the baroque
passacaglia which concludes his Fourth Symphony. Or a composer like Mahler constructed, one might say 'deconstructed,'
his symphonies with a vast network of quotations and allusions.
Such practices, Charles Rosen observes "acknowledge the existence of a previous classical style, an aspiration to recreate it,
and an affirmation that such a recreation is no longer possible.

---

7. Therefore in the discussion which follows for "devil" read "Adorno."

on naive or independent terms. The control of style is now not merely willed but self-conscious" (27-28).

The devil allows that Adrian through the "self-conscious control of style" might function as a composer despite the alleged exhaustion of all technical means and strategies. Such functioning would be in the nature of a holding operation: Adrian would write compositions that were "the solving of technical puzzles. Art becomes critique. That is something quite honorable, who denies it?" (319-20) Or Adrian, at his own suggestion, might "recognize freedom above and beyond all critique. He could heighten the play by playing with forms out of which . . . life has disappeared." And the devil sneers that such free play would be parody which "might be fun, if it were not so melancholy in its aristocratic nihilism" (322).

Art beomes critique and parody. The dialectical twist of Modernism is that art becomes the critique of itself: we have had in the twentieth century music about music, poetry about poetry, and during the last two decades, *ad nauseam*, criticism about criticism. Doubtless the devil is pleased that "die Situation ist zu kritisch, als daß die Kritiklosigkeit ihr gewachsen wäre!" [The situation is too critical to be dealt with without critique!] (320). In the novel, Adrian with the devil's help, "breaks through" the technical impasse of the outworn tonal system with his 'invention' of the twelve-tone method of composition. But it remains a fascinating, still open question whether the new styles and syntaxes which emerged in that first richly creative moment of Modernism enabled the artist to transcend critique and parody. From the devil's point of view, Eliot's *The Waste Land* and Joyce's *Ulysses* are parody-anthologies of western literature -- from Homer on down. Mann's own *The Magic Mountain* 'takes off' the traditional German *Bildungsroman*; and Schoenberg's *Pierrot Lunaire* is, in a distorted and morbid way, an example of the romantic song cycle.

In his third avatar the devil takes on the features of Eberhard Schlepfuss, the demonic theologian whose teachings had intrigued Adrian and Zeitblom when they were students at Halle. (Eliot's ghost can foresee for the poet the refining fire of purgatory, and the cycle of *Four Quartets* ends on a quiet note of redemption,

When the tongues of flame are infolded
Into the crowned knot of fire
And the fire and the rose are one. [CPP 145])

For Adrian the matter of damnation and salvation is complex, ambiguous, the subject of the severest scrutiny. It is in this discussion with Schlepfuss that Mann releases the awesome power of the original Faust myth and the enormity of the pact with the devil, the nature of hell, and the unbearable punishments of the damned. The question Adrian puts to Schlepfuss is the one *Doctor Faustus*, in the *Urfaustbuch* of 1587, puts to his familiar:

> Doctor Faustus dreamed that he had seene a part of hell: but in what manner it was, or in what place he knew not: whereupon he was greatly troubled in minde, and called unto him Mephostophiles his spirit, saying to him, my Mephostophiles, I pray thee resolve me in this doubt: what is hell, what substance is it of, in what place stands it, and when was it made. . . .

Adrian gets no direct answer from Schlepfuss. Despite the theologian's rhetorical fireworks about the realm of the damned, he admits that the nature of hell can be described only in feints of language: "Mit symbolis, mein Guter, muß man sich durchaus begnügen, wenn man von der Höllen spricht, denn dort hört alles auf,--nicht nur das anzeigende Wort, sondern überhaupt alles,--dies ist sogar das hauptsächliche Charakteristikum. . . . [One must be absolutely content with symbolism, my good fellow, when one speaks of hell; for there everything stops--not only the word that describes, but absolutely everything: this is indeed its chief characteristic. . . .] (326).

Schlepfuss disappears and the pimp returns to bring the palaver to its conclusion. Our twentieth-century Faust need not repair to a crossroad in the woods where he must draw magic circles and invoke cabbalistic symbols to raise the devil. The pact in blood is, so to speak, signed when Adrian takes up with the devil's creature, Esmeralda; and he receives from her "die Illumination, das Aphrodisiacum des Hirns . . ." (331) which is the pathological stimulant to his creative powers. Like the original Faustus Adrian will become a great "nigromancer," but the magic he will make will be in the manipulation of notes, the weaving of motifs, the intricate use of the twelve-tone technique. Finally, as in the original Faustian bargain, Adrian is to be denied all the warmth and consolation of human love. Adrian objects: "Wie? Das ist neu. Was will die Klausel sagen?" And the devil replies, "Uns bist du, feine, erschaffene Creatur, versprochen und verlobt. Du darfst nicht lieben" ["How so? That is new. What does the clause say?" And the devil replies, "You are ours, my fine creature, promised and betrothed. You may not love."] (331).

At this point Adrian faints in an agony of disgust and the glacial cold spewn by the devil-as-pimp. When he recovers he hears the reassuring voice of his friend Schildknapp. It is he who sits in the corner of the sofa and not the Triple Devil who has just held him in an "unexpected but long expected discourse."

4

Without seriously mis-reading our texts--though some of our subtler theorists insist that all reading *is* mis-reading--we see that *Little Gidding* and *Doctor Faustus* display salient features of "terminal books." They are late works in the careers of their creators; Eliot's *Little Gidding* is his last major work of lyric poetry. *Doctor Faustus* is written in blood, in the anguish of exile and the shame of what the scum of the earth did to Mann's Fatherland. But beyond all innovations of technique and intricacies of musical form, these terminal works are religious in the deepest and most profound sense. They conclude in prayers: Eliot finds reconciliation and hope of redemption:

> When the tongues of flame are infolded
> Into the crowned knot of fire
> And the fire and the rose are one. (CPP 145)

Mann's prayer is for mercy: mercy that must go beyond hope and despair, "a miracle beyond the power of belief."

WORKS CITED

"At the Still Point." *Time* 7 June 1943: 96.

De Mendelssohn, Peter. *Der Zauberer*. Frankfurt am Main: S. Fischer Verlag, 1975.

Dostoevski, Feodor. *The Brothers Karamazov*. Trans. Andrew H. MacAndrew. New York: Bantam, 1981.

Gardner, Helen. *The Composition of Four Quartets*. London: Faber, 1978.

Gross, Harvey. *Sound and Form in Modern Poetry*. Ann Arbor: U of Michigan P, 1964.

Heidegger, Martin. *An Introduction to Metaphysics*. Trans. Ralph Mannheim. New York: Anchor Books, 1961.

The Historie of the damnable life, and deserved death of Doctor John Faustus. Trans. William Rose. Ed. William Karl Pfeiler. Indiana: U of Notre Dame P, 1963.

Kahler, Erich. *The Orbit of Thomas Mann*. Princeton: Princeton UP, 1969.

Leavis, F. R. *The Living Principle*. New York: Oxford UP, 1975.

Mann, Thomas. *Briefe aus den Jahren, 1937-1947*. Ed. Erika Mann. Frankfurt am Main: S. Fischer Verlag, 1963.

_____. *Gesammelte Werke*. VI. Frankfurt am Main: S. Fischer Verlag, 1980.

_____. *The Story of a Novel*. Trans. Richard and Clara Winston. New York: Knopf, 1961.

Matthiessen, F. O. *The Achievement of T. S. Eliot*. Boston: Houghton Mifflin, 1935.

Nietzsche, Friedrich. *Götzen-Dämmerung: Sprüche und Pfeile*.

_____. "Vom Nutzen und Nachteil der Historie für das Leben." *Friedrich Nietzsche: Werke in Zwei Bänden*. Ed. Karl Schlechta. München: Carl Hanser Verlag, 1967.

Olney, James. *Metaphors of Self*. Princeton: Princeton UP, 1972.

Rosen, Charles. "Influence: Plagiarism and Inspiration." *On Criticizing Music*. Ed. Kingsley Price. Baltimore: Johns Hopkins UP, 1981.

Sullivan, J. W. N. *Beethoven: His Spiritual Development*. New York: Knopf, 1927.

Urfaustbuch, The Historie of the damnable life, and deserved death of Doctor Iohn Faustus . . . translated into English by P. F., Gent., London, 1592.

JOAN FILLMORE HOOKER

VISIONS AND REVISIONS:
"GERONTION" IN FRENCH*

> Dans une traduction on peut étudier
> l'itinéraire parcouru de chose à dire à chose
> dite, au lieu que dans une oeuvre person-
> nelle le donné de l'inspiration et l'expression
> finale sont confondus pour le lecteur. D'où
> les lumières exceptionnelles que jette sur
> l'esthétique, la technique, etc. d'un écrivain
> son oeuvre de traducteur.
> --Pierre Leyris, "Quelques mots sur la
> traduction littéraire" (122 n.)

When I read that Pierre Leyris' French translation of Gerard
Manley Hopkins' "Pied Beauty" was "an impossibility if ever
there was" and saw it for myself in George Steiner's *After Babel*
(412-13), I was astonished.

> Glory be to God for dappled things--
> For skies of couple-colour as a brinded cow;

had become

> Gloire à Dieu pour les choses bariolées,
> Pour les cieux de tons jumelés comme les vaches tavelées;

and

> With swift, slow; sweet, sour; adazzle, dim;
> He fathers-forth whose beauty is past change:
> Praise him.

had become

> De lent-rapide, d'ombreux-clair, de doux-amer,
> Tout jaillit de Celui dont la beauté ne change:
> Louange au Père!

---

*This essay is a longer version of a paper given at the National Poetry Foundation's T. S. Eliot Cen-
tennial Conference, August 18-20, 1988, Orono, Maine.

Agreeing with Steiner that "Translation of this distinction does not only penetrate the barrier between languages. It seems to break through the barriers of uncertainty which marks any complex speech-act" (413), I had to find out whom else Leyris had translated, as well as to see other Leyris translations of Hopkins' poems.

In addition to an entire book devoted to translations of Hopkins' prose and poetry and to translations of the works of myriad other British and American writers, dating back to and including Shakespeare, this prolific translator's *oeuvre* includes several books of translations of T. S. Eliot's poems, generally revised for successive printings or editions. Thus, not only had Leyris immersed himself in the entire non-dramatic poetic canon, but he had had the advantage of personal discussions with Eliot, by letter and *viva voce*, and with Eliot's close friend John Hayward. The latter, in cooperation with Eliot and acting as his surrogate, provided additional notes for the French translation of *The Waste Land*; and, again in consultation with the poet, he also provided notes for Leyris' translation of *Four Quartets*.

The collaboraton among the three men resulted in French translations that provide illuminating readings of Eliot's poems. Both Englishmen knew French well. In fact, Eliot wrote some of his earlier poems in Paris while deeply immersed in the language; and his poetry was avowedly informed by the language and imagery of such French Symbolist poets as Jules Laforgue. The poet was thus in a position to respond authoritatively to Leyris' translations of his poems.

Although Leyris eventually became the official French translator of T. S. Eliot's poems, twenty-four other translators provide a variety of readings of the English poems, a variety that is further enriched by the fact that the official translator is an inveterate tinkerer. Between periodical and book publication, between printings and editions of books, Leyris would characteristically fine-tune his French versions of Eliot's poems.

Until the summer of 1987, I thought that Donald Gallup's exhaustive bibliography had led me to copies of every version of every known French translation of the poems. But when a colleague gave me a copy of Pierre Leyris' 1947 volume of T. S. Eliot's poems in French translation, I discovered with great surprise and keen interest that it differed significantly from my own copy of what was ostensibly the same *Poèmes 1910-1930*. Miniscule differences in publication data did not reveal the fact that, between the two printings, Leyris had often considerably revised his translations. Thus there had been no way, either for Eliot's bibliographer or for anyone else, to become aware of this additional printing. Lacking distinguishing publication data, I will identify the particular text referred to by designating my new copy, acquired in Santa Cruz, as SC *Poèmes* and the earlier acquired copy, obtained in New York, as NY *Poèmes*.

The Santa Cruz discovery provides us with a fourth Leyris version of "Gerontion," in addition to the three previously known. There exist also Jean Wahl's translations of two excerpts of the poem that appeared in the periodical *Fontaine* in 1943. These five versions provide an opportunity for readers to compare two translators' versions of the same lines, as well as to become aware of progressively more felicitous translations, revealing a window looking intimately into the kindred processes of creation and translation. The analysis involved also enables us to see what sort of light a translation may cast on an original poem. Translation and translation analysis force readers to linger over words, to examine contexts, to sense nuances, to see both *how* a translation is made and *what* it is as a translation. We shall return to Jean Wahl's and Pierre Leyris' translations of "Gerontion"; but first I would like to set forth my rationale for ordering his translations as I do by looking at his renderings of the final lines of Eliot's "Preludes."

Those final lines of Leyris' translations of "Preludes" lay down some of the theoretical groundwork of this sort of translation study: we see the various versions against the translator's "intention," that is, against the English original; and we see the tip of the iceberg of the creative process in the strange sorts of lapses, or blind spots, where some sort of interference from the unconscious or preconscious may affect a poet's or a translator's choices.

Below are Eliot's final lines, followed by Leyris' consecutive French versions of them, with italics indicating successive variations:

> Wipe your hand across your mouth, and laugh;
> The worlds revolve like ancient women
> Gathering fuel in vacant lots. (CPP 13)

> Essuyez votre main à vos lèvres; riez.
> Les mots tournent en rond ainsi que des vieillardes
> Qui glanent des débris sur un lotissement. (SC *Poèmes* [1947] 43)

Essuyez votre main à vos lèvres; riez.
Les mots *tournoient tels* des vieillardes
Glanant du bois aux terrains vagues.
               ("Trois Poèmes de T. S. Eliot" [1946] 174)

Essuyez votre main à vos lèvres; riez.
Les mots *tournent en rond pareils à* des vieillardes
Qui glaneraient du bois aux terrains vagues. (NY *Poèmes* [1947] 43)

Essuyez votre main à vos lèvres; riez.
Les mots tournent en rond pareils à des vieillardes
Glanant du bois *dans quelque* terrain vague. (*Poésie* [1969] 25)

That the last-discovered version, in SC *Poèmes*, is the most radically different of the four and the least felicitous suggests that it is also the earliest version. One can therefore conclude that variant printings of lines in other poems that Pierre Leyris translated reflect the same sequence of revision--even though the second version above was printed earlier than the first.

    While he was working on the translations to be included in *Poèmes*, during what must have been an extended period preceding their 1947 publication, Leyris had an opportunity to provide translations of three Eliot poems for *Fontaine*, in 1946. Looking at the translation for *Poèmes* [1947] that must already have been in the printer's hands, he recognized that "lotissement" was wrong for "vacant lots"; it means, in fact, a lottery, a portioning out by drawing lots. Somehow the slip did not get corrected for the first printing of *Poèmes* [1947]; nor did the translator notice his "mots" slip for "worlds." In fact, the facing English text in *Fontaine* omits the *l*, reading "The *words* revolve. . . ." Probably, having read *worlds* as *words*, the translator submitted the English text in that form. When, however, there was to be a second printing, Leyris had an opportunity to refine those lines and make many other changes throughout the entire text of the book. Thus, "lotissement" became "terrains vagues," an accurate rendering of Eliot's "vacant lots."

    What seems to confirm this ordering is that the galley that Leyris submitted to his publisher for his expanded and revised volume, *Poésie* [1969], with his typed and inked revisions and his instructions to the printer, is made up of pages taken from the same text as NY *Poèmes*; he would scarcely have taken as the basis for the new edition earlier versions of translations that he had revised and refined. In a 1987 letter the translator expressed his mystification about his "mots" / "mondes" slip:

Je ne sais pas comment cette bévue est venue. Est-ce un lapsus de
ma part lors d'une des innombrables "fair copies" établies avant

l'impression? Est-ce une faute d'impression que je n'ai vue sur
épreuves?

In the same letter he attributes to the passage of time his forgetting the order in which he wrote and revised his translations.

With the order of the versions established, we can
now turn to T. S. Eliot's "Gerontion" as translated by Pierre
Leyris and, in two excerpts, by Jean Wahl. Wahl's excerpts
appeared in the journal *Fontaine* in 1943, while Leyris' versions
appeared in *Poésie 47*,[2] in SC and NY *Poèmes 1910-1930*, also in
1947, and in *Poésie* in 1969. Thus, as with "Preludes," we again
have four versions by Leyris. And for the same reasons that I
saw the translations of "Preludes" for SC *Poèmes* as predating
the periodical version, I see SC *Poèmes* as containing the earliest
Leyris translation of "Gerontion."

As an Eliot poem with strong echoes of the language
of Jacobean drama, "Gerontion" poses interesting problems for
the translator. These problems--both more difficult and more
complicated--are very different from those one faces in the
Laforguean "Prufrock," for example, where the French idiom,
strong in Eliot at the time of composition, informed the very
phrasing of his lines. With "Gerontion," the chief problem is
how to transform that Jacobean sound into a French one while
retaining the character of the original.

The syntax and vocabulary imposed by its Jacobean
language suggest not only the age of the speaker through their
often formal, despairing, and weary tone, but an earlier era as
well. Such locutions as "In the juvescence of the year / Came
Christ the tiger" exemplify the point (ll. 19-20, CPP 21). First of
all, "juvescence" is apparently a coinage: the *OED Supplement*,
volume 4, gives its first known use as in this very line in *Ara Vos
Prec*, the Eliot collection in which "Gerontion" first appeared in
1920. Its meaning, however, is recognizable; but the form's
strangeness to eye and ear gives it an archaic air that Eliot
apparently wanted. Secondly, the syntactic order is not that of
everyday speech. One would more naturally put the subject first
and write, "Christ the tiger came in the juvescence of the year."
This reordering of Eliot's sentence into "normal" syntax points
up the elevated decorum that characterizes Gerontion's inner
speech.

In translating these words, Leyris meets the challenge that the poem's decorum poses by using "jouvence." The
word in French, while not a coinage, is rare, used only to refer to

---

2. Leyris' *Poesie 47* version of "Gerontion" is reproduced in full in my *T. S. Eliot's Poems in French Translation* 223-24.

the fountain of youth, "la fontaine de jouvence." Thus, the translation of the word has a strangeness for French ears also when used in connection with a time of year. To further formalize his language, the translator shifts tenses to the historical past: "Dans la jouvence de l'an / *Vint* Christ le tigre" (*Poésie* [1969] 37). Such a tense would never occur in conversation; it is a written tense. Eliot, with Leyris following him, uses language and form and syntax to enhance the effect of dislocation in time that the whole poem conveys.

One wonders why Eliot, who so valued casting poetry in spoken language, in "the dialect of the tribe," would turn to this kind of vocabulary and syntax in this particular poem (CPP 141). The answer can only be that the distancing effect of such language and syntax seemed to him to enhance the effect of unhappy isolation, weariness, and despair that the poem as a whole suggests. It is noteworthy that the passion in the poem is all in the past tense; and that, although he apostrophizes "Christ the Tiger," Gerontion has essentially no one to address but himself. In the course of the poem he evolves from being "an old man in a dry month" (l. 1, CPP 21) into "an old man, / A dull head among windy spaces" (ll. 15-16), into "An old man in a draughty house" (l. 32, CPP 22), into "an old man driven by the Trades / To a sleepy corner" (ll. 73-74, CPP 23), and finally into the depersonalized "Tenants of the house, / Thoughts of a dry brain in a dry season" (ll. 75-76). Gerontion is thus atomized, just like De Bailhache, Fresca, and Mrs. Cammel in the preceding stanza, who are "whirled / Beyond the shuddering Bear / In fractured atoms" (ll. 68-70). Even the personal pronoun has disappeared and, in the final sentence--significantly, itself a fragment--the verb as well: "Tenants of the house, / Thoughts of a dry brain in a dry season."

Eliot's lines convey, in a tone of weary defeat, an unheroic picture of an old man in decayed surroundings. Taking his translation of these lines through several versions, Pierre Leyris gradually refined his language. Setting forth the original lines, followed by Leyris' in the chronological order I have proposed, the following presents a sequence of thematic variations and the variant translations of each (I have italicized the translator's revisions throughout):

Here I am, an old man in a dry month, (CPP 21)

Me voici là, vieil homme que je suis, par un mois sec (SC *Poèmes*)

Me voici, *vieillard dans* un mois de sécheresse, (*Poésie 47*)

> Me voici, vieillard, dans un mois *de sécheresse*, (NY *Poèmes*)

> Me voici, *un* vieillard dans un mois de sécheresse, (*Poésie* [1969])

The first revision contains the most changes. "Me voici là" perhaps lacks the starkness that their context lends to the English words "Here I am." Leyris dropped the "là" for good. "Par un mois sec" he also permently jettisoned; the four monosyllables go too quickly for the mood that gets established right away in the English. "Here I am" comes across as spondaic: "Here I am" followed by "an old man in a dry month." "An old man" is literal and stark. "Que je suis," with its suggestion of light dismissal, simply does not work in the same way; it is too close to a lightly bantering or self-ironic tone. But Eliot is leading us into something a good deal darker. Leyris' revisions therefore bring him closer to that affect of the original. His solution is ingenious. "Me voici," which he retains throughout, means exactly "Here I am"; but he elongates the rhythm of the words that follow so that his first printed revision lends those first two words a gradual darkening. "I" now has "vieillard" in apposition. Removing the word "homme" tends to depersonalize or unsex the speaker; the rhythm is not affected by the change from "vieil homme" to "vieillard." This change would seem to provide an instance of a translator's achieving an effect in a target language that has eluded the writer of the original poem.

     While "par" or "dans un mois sec" translates Eliot's "in a dry month" more literally than "dans un mois de sécheresse," "in a month of dryness" adds emphasis and avoids the clipped speed of the literal French. Diphthongs in English extend the length of time it takes to utter words; "dry" is quite simply said more slowly than "sec," while "sécheresse" is spoken more slowly than "dry." The added comma in NY *Poèmes* further retards the rhythm; but finally, in *Poésie*, Leyris adds "un" to "vieillard," perhaps to retard the line further and to compensate for removing the comma, so that the appostion to the "Me" in "Me voici" is not "vieillard," but the entire balance of the line: "vieillard dans un mois de sécheresse."

     The lines that conclude the first stanza continue this theme:

> I am an old man, / A dull head among windy spaces.
> (ll. 15-16, CPP 21)

> Que suis-je qu'un vieillard / Un cerveau vide parmi les espaces
> venteux. (SC *Poèmes*)

Me voici donc, vieillard / *Tête* vide parmi les espaces venteux.
(*Poésie* 47)

Me voici donc, vieillard / Tête vide parmi les espaces venteux.
(NY *Poèmes*)

Vieil homme que je suis, / Tête vide parmi les espaces venteux.
(*Poésie* [1969])

The translator has restored the "Vieil homme que je suis" in his final version that he jettisoned in his first revision of the stanza's first line. The intervening lines, however, have plunged the speaker more deeply into a realization of his state. Here, to preserve psychological equilibrium--or to try to regain it perhaps--the self-ironic and self-deprecating words create aesthetic distance; and the two utterances of the dominating theme frame the first stanza and prepare for the turn in the movement that follows, a turn in which the speaker reaches towards affirmation, albeit unsuccessfully: "Signs are taken for wonders. 'We would see a sign' " (l. 17, CPP 21).

A look at these changes provides a sharper vision of the original; we are reading a critical and interpretative rendering of "Gerontion" in the form of a translation that attempts to come as close as possible to replicating it *in poetic form*.

The next reprise of the thematic vein that reverberates throughout the poem comes at the end of the third stanza, with its allusion to the Eucharist:

An old man in a draughty house
Under a windy knob. (ll. 32-33, CPP 23)

Rien qu'un vieillard en ce logis à courants d'air
Sous une butte venteuse. (SC *Poèmes*)

Vieillard en ce logis *battu de* courants d'air
Sous un *morne* venteux. (*Poésie* 47)

Vieillard en ce logis battu de courants d'air
Sous un morne venteux. (NY *Poèmes*)

Vieillard en ce logis battu de courants d'air
Sous *cette butte* venteuse. (*Poésie* [1969])

These lines again reflect the translator's tinkering habit, although the changes are indeed minor. The final version's increased specificity, "cette" rather than "une butte" or "un morne," reflects the general principle of translation that one way of compensating for unavoidable loss of specificity in translation is to increase specificity elsewhere. The change from "butte" to "morne" and back to "butte" shows Leyris hesitating as he seeks to translate English "knob," which refers usually to an isolated hill: "A prominent isolated or rounded mound or hill; a knoll; a hill in general; esp. in U.S." (*OED*). Because "knob" is more American than British, Leyris' switch from "butte" to "morne" may well have been dictated by a desire to find a less common word than "butte"; "morne" is used in French colonies, according to Littré's dictionary, especially the West Indies. But this specificity and exoticness went perhaps too far. Back he went to the more general word for an isolated hill, finally lending specificity with "cette."

Finally, there is Eliot's last depiction of defeated old age and aridity and Leyris' successive versions:

> An old man driven by the Trades
> To a sleepy corner.
>
> 　　　　　　Tenants of the house,
> Thoughts of a dry brain in a dry season. (ll. 73-76, CPP 23)

> Un vieillard balayé par les vents alizés
> Dans son recoin d'oubli.
>
> 　　　　　　Habitants du logis
> Pensers d'un cerveau sec en temps de sécheresse.
> 　　　　　　(SC *Poèmes*; *Poésie 47*; NY *Poèmes*)

> *Et* un vieillard *chassé* par les vents alizés
> Dans un coin *somnolent.*
>
> 　　　　　　Habitants du logis,
> *Pensées* d'un cerveau sec en temps de sécheresse. (*Poésie* [1969])

While the changes in Leyris' 1969 book are minor, they are important refinements. "Oubli" ("forgetting") skews Eliot's suggestion. Gerontion is talking neither about forgetting nor about being forgotten; he is talking about a dulling and losing of consciousness, echoing the loss he has earlier complained of--the loss of faculties, "sight, smell, hearing, taste and touch"--that would occur in sleep or death. "Somnolent" is more apt than "d'oubli"; it translates "sleepy" exactly.

"Thoughts" is a more general word than "penser" is when the latter is a noun; "penser" is used poetically or to suggest the manner or faculty of thinking. "Pensées" better suggests the kind of dreamy and despairing and intense emotional states of mind that the speaker's thoughts generate and that in turn generate more intensely realized emotional states.

Thus these successive versions of Pierre Leyris'
"Gerontion" bring him ever closer to the tone, texture, and resonance, as well as meaning, of Eliot's English original. Comparing these selected and parallel lines shows something of the
translator's own creative process; it can also bring readers closer
to Eliot's English, through its focus on individual words, their
contexts, and the sounds and rhythms that carry them.

Besides comparing successive versions of a single
translator's work, one can compare translations by more than
one translator. In the instance of "Gerontion," we have the two
excerpts by Jean Wahl (166-67) mentioned earlier. Wahl translated the first seven lines in his first exerpt, which appears
below, following Eliot's English and followed by Leyris' translation in its 1969 version:

TSE: Here I am, an old man in a dry month,
JW: Me voici, vieil homme dans un mois de sécheresse,
PL: Me voici, un vieillard dans un mois de sécheresse,

Being read to by a boy, waiting for rain.
Ecoutant l'enfant qui lui fait la lecture, attendant la pluie.
Ecoutant le garçon me lire, attendant la pluie.

I was neither at the hot gates
Je n'étais pas aux portes brûlantes
Je n'étais pas au brûlant défilé

Nor fought in the warm rain
Je n'ai pas combattu dans la pluie chaude
Je n'ai pas combattu dans la pluie chaude

Nor knee deep in the salt marsh, heaving a cutlass,
Ni le genou enfoncé dans le marais salé, levant un coutelas,
Ni, embourbé dans la saline jusqu'au genou,

Bitten by flies, fought.
Mordu par les mouches, combattu.
Levant un glaive, mordu par les mouches, combattu.

My house is a decayed house,
Ma maison est une maison délabrée.
Ma maison est une maison délabrée;
                        (ll. 1-7, CPP 21; *Fontaine*; *Poésie* [1969])

One can read each writer's entire versions, as well as the first
and subsequent lines in trios and see subtle differences in significant areas: rhythm, language, and tone. Comparing transla-

tions of poems with each other and with an original, we see the importance of musical qualities to the success of a translation.

In the lines quoted above, for example, Eliot's first sentence establishes the passivity that characterizes Gerontion. The first verb is the verb *to be*: "Here I *am*." Next follow two participial phrases: "*Being* read to *by* a boy, *waiting* for rain." The passive character of the sentence receives the reinforcement the passive construction gives it. Moreover the sentence describes passive activities: listening and waiting.

The translators' versions differ chiefly in their translations of the participial constructions. Wahl's version retranslates as, "Listening to the boy who reads to him," while Leyris' retranslates as, "Listening to the boy read to me." Retranslation often points up differences in tone that might otherwise go unnoticed. The greater formality of the more "written" language in Wahl's version diminishes the sense of inner speech that Eliot's lines suggest. Leyris, on the other hand, with the colloquial suggestion of "Ecoutant le garçon me lire," not only retains that suggestion, but further, his words' laconic quality establishes in the second line of his translation the tone of weariness and despair and the movement toward stasis and ultimate disintegration that characterize the poem.

The contrast between the "*dry* month" and (absent) "*rain*" prepares for the series of negatives that follows, the heroic activities that Gerontion has *not* engaged in, all emphasized by the periodic structure: "I was neither . . . / Nor fought . . . / Nor . . . / . . . , fought." Both translators preserve the negatively climactic structure, ending their second sentences with "combattu"; but Leyris better preserves the anticlimactic effect the language has by translating in more heroic terms what the speaker has not done. When Wahl translates "hot gates" with words that we can read as "hot doors" as readily as "hot gates," the force of Eliot's allusion to Thermopylae may be lost. While Leyris loses the specific allusion, "brûlant défilé" preserves the notion of heroic action by introducing an allusion to a convention of epic poetry, heroic action in a "brûlant defilé," a "burning (mountain) pass"; his meaning is not literally Eliot's, but poetically it is *juste*.

The same is true of the last two lines. Wahl is more literal, his lines retranslating as "Nor the knee sunk deep in the salt marsh, raising a cutlass / Bitten by flies, fought." Leyris' lines retranslate as, "Nor, bogged down" (with a further suggestion in "embourbé" of being in a sticky situation) "in the salt marsh up to the knee, / Raising a blade, bitten by flies, fought."

French "glaive" is a literary and poetic term for English *glaive* or *sword*. Leyris' less-than-literal rendering intensifies the contrast Eliot's English sets up between the unheroic present and the heroic past that Gerontion--negatively, in terms of his own experience--presents. Again, because of translation's inevitable loss in intensity, compensating intensification provides a corrective balance. So much for language and tone.

But syntax, too, comes into play in the translator's struggle for equivalence. Wahl's Gerontion has only his knee (not) sunk in the salt marsh. Leyris' antiheroic persona imagines himself as a whole (not) sunk up to the knee in that marsh; his rendering creates a more global effect than does Wahl's. The syntactic compression of "embourbé dans la saline jusqu'au genou" matches the intensifying compression of "knee deep in the salt marsh." Syntactically and rhythmically it is closer to Eliot's words than Wahl's "le genou enfoncé dans le marais salé," where, for example, "salt marsh" receives four syllables in Wahl's version, compared with trisyllabic "saline" in Leyris' version. After looking closely at these distinctions between the two translators' versions of these lines and after rereading their translations in conjunction with the original, we can see that much more than lexical accuracy is involved in competent poetic translation; also involved is *poetic* equivalence, which necessarily engages the translator in considerations of nuance, rhythm, and tone.

The second excerpt of "Gerontion" that Jean Wahl translated is the Jacobean passage with its anaphoric series of *think*'s. In it Gerontion moves away from his effort to denigrate the perversion of the sacred and begins to attempt to justify his own miserable plight, summed up in the poem's first stanza. He does this sort of rationalizing by generalizing and globalizing his situation, blaming circumstances for his own personal failure to achieve significance or transcendence. He begins with a question:

TSE: After such knowledge, what forgiveness? Think now
    History has many cunning passages, contrived corridors
    And issues, deceives with whispering ambitions,
    Guides us by vanities. . . . (ll. 34-37, CPP 22)

JW: Après une telle connaissance, quelle rémission?
    Pensez maintenant comme l'histoire a des passages astucieux,
    Des corridors agencés ainsi que des sorties,
    Nous trompe avec des ambitions murmurantes,
    Nous guide par des vanités.

PL: Après un tel savoir, quel pardon? Dis-toi bien
        Que l'Histoire a maints passages subtils, maints corridors
        Et issues dérobées, qu'elle nous égare
        D'ambitions chuchotantes, nous leurre de vanités; . . .

By the end of the stanza, finding no forgiveness, Gerontion is shaken by tears born of wrath.

Leyris' translation of the lines following Gerontion's question seems a good deal more faithful to Eliot's text, both in content and tone, than does Wahl's version. Wahl's "Pensez maintenant" literally means "Think at this moment," while Leyris' "Dis-toi *bien*" preserves Eliot's sense of "Think well," or "Think indeed": *now* has an emphatic, not temporal, function in the line. Literal translation has skewed the semantic, contextual function of Eliot's poetic language. Leyris' use of personal pronouns further demonstrates the fact that the art of translation also involves an act of interpretation that can affect readers' interpretations as well. Where Eliot's English must conflate second-person pronouns with *you*, French enables Leyris to use both the singular *toi* and plural or formal *vous*. Wahl, on the other hand, uses *vous* for all the stanza's second-person pronouns. Leyris thereby more clearly distinguishes different referents for his pronouns than Eliot can and than Wahl does. "Dis-toi" suggests that the speaker addresses "Christ the tiger," *tu* being the intimate pronoun for addressing God.

Eliot's "History" is naturally capitalized, coming as it does at the beginning of a line; but what for Eliot may have been an accident of poetic form only, Leyris makes into a virtue of his art as translator. His version--and he capitalizes "Histoire" in three of his four renderings of these lines--makes more emphatic Eliot's personifying of "history" by making it a proper name. The device also fits in with the conventions of an earlier writing style, which a good translator should emulate or for which he should find some equivalent diction in the target language. Wahl's version dilutes Eliot's words. Both Wahl's "astucieux" and Leyris' "subtils" translate Eliot's "cunning," although the shorter word is more aurally apt; but Wahl's "Pensez comme l'histoire a des passages austucieux" retranslates more weakly than the original: "Think now" (at this time) "how history has cunning passages." Leyris' line retranslates more closely and more forcibly: "Dis-toi bien / Que l'Histoire a maints passages subtils" becomes "Tell yourself indeed" (realize and remember well) / "That History has many subtle passages, many corridors." Wahl drops "many," perhaps because he has chosen multisyllabic "astucieux" for "cunning." But by choosing "subtils" for "cunning," Leyris keeps the equivalent syllabic count and his "maints" for "many" preserves a strong echo of the English word. Moreover, "astucieux" is more cerebral than "subtils," which, like "cunning," refers to the material as well as to the mental.

Thus Leyris better preserves the extended pun involved in these lines, where "passages" suggests texts, as well as physical routes that lead from one place to another. One can profitably read these lines with triple vision, seeing both the course of history in all its confusion, the personified History that is a tempting and voluptuous woman, and even the sort of building that might be a setting for a Jacobean revenge tragedy. Leyris' choices of "subtils" and "issues dérobées" permit his readers to perceive the same effects in the French. "Issues" in French means both "exits" and "conclusions" or "outcomes," while Wahl's "sorties" is limited to "exits." "Dérobées" is again a word with a double sense, referring both to disrobing and to concealment or theft. Wahl's "agencés" means simply "arranged." Both the strength and resonance of the English are diminished in Wahl's translation and retained in Leyris'.

Leyris goes on to replicate the elevated style that is in the cadences of the English poem:

> Think now
> She gives when our attention is distracted
> And what she gives, gives with such supple confusions
> That the giving famishes the craving. (ll. 37-40)

> oui, dis-toi bien
> Qu'elle donne lorsque notre attention se trouve distraite
> Et ce qu'elle donne, le donne en confusions si souples
> Que le don affame l'affamé. . . .

The rhythms of the two passages follow the same pattern of emphasis and contain similar sounds where Leyris uses loan words or cognates, as in "attention" / "attention"; "distracted" / "distraite"; "confusions" / "confusions"; "supple" / souples"; "famishes" / "affamé." Syllabic counts are also close, like the word-stress, where the emphasis seems to fall in the same way: "And what she gives, gives." / "Et ce qu'elle donne, le donne." Wahl's version is musically quite different:

> Pensez maintenant qu'elle donne quand notre attention est distraite
> Et ce qu'elle donne c'est avec si souple confusion
> Que le don affame l'affamé. . . .

Although Wahl retains here the aural felicity in the cognates, the intensifying urgency of Leyris' quick monosyllables, "Oui, dis-toi bien," is slowed by Wahl's elongated and not quite apt "Pensez maintenant." "Se trouve distraite" in Leyris' version suggests the very confusion that Eliot's words suggest: our attention *finds itself* distracted. "Se trouve" translates as "is," as does "est"; but Wahl's wording loses that growing sense of urgency in these lines as they build climactically. Wahl's first line above seems much too long; and why does he eschew the opportunity to repeat "give," unlike Eliot and Leyris? He thereby loses an occasion for the poetic replication that is prevalent throughout the English stanza. That Wahl makes "confusions" singular introduces the possibility of French readers' understanding it to mean "with embarrassment," one of the meanings of the French word in singular form.

   The poem's next sentence illustrates some subtle effects of diction. Eliot's

> Gives too late
> What's not believed in, or if still believed,
> In memory only, reconsidered passion. . . . (ll. 40-42)

becomes, for Wahl and Leyris respectively,

> Donne trop tard
> Ce qu'on ne croit pas, ou si on le croit,
> C'est en mémoire seulement, en passion re-méditée. . . .

and

> Qu'elle donne trop tard
> Ce à quoi vous ne croyez point, ou si vous y croyez encore
> Ce n'est qu'en souvenir, en passion ruminée. . . .

While Wahl's is rather more literal, it is too literal. Leyris adds "Qu'elle" ("That she") at the beginning. The effect is of a mind thinking, in an idiomatic French way; the effect of Wahl's is somewhat alien to the French language. In English we do omit subjects of verbs; the French rarely do. Again, "Ce qu'on ne croit pas," while a literal translation, is weaker in French because open to a weaker interpretation than "What's not believed in," which Leyris makes unmistakable with "Ce à quoi vous ne croyez point": "That in which you don't believe at all." Wahl's line could be read as meaning "That which one doesn't think to be so." Eliot's sense of not believing *in* is weakened. Again, intensifying and specifying compensate for the inevitable weakening of language when translated.

    In this passage Leyris shifts his pronoun from *nous*
to *vous*, while Eliot has written in passive constructions
(uncharacteristic of French) that suppress the pronoun. The
translator's choice is perhaps debatable; for me, however, the
choice achieves in French what Eliot's passive constructions
accomplish in English. As Gerontion contemplates the implications of what he is saying, he withdraws, using syntax--passive
constructions--to gain psychic distance. Leyris, having moved
from *toi*, presumably used to address "Christ the tiger," to *nous*
--Eliot's "us"--then moves to *vous*, keeping the idiom characteristically French while at the same time achieving that same
distance that Eliot manages in English with the passive. Again,
the translator strives for compensatory equivalence. *Vous*
generalizes the experience described. Then, in the second half of
the line, Leyris has the emphatic "ou si vous y croyez encore,"
retranslating as "or if you still believe *in it*," while Wahl's half
line retranslates, "or if one believes *it*," a much less emphatic
locution. Wahl concludes Eliot's sentence with, "C'est en
mémoire seulement, en passion re-méditée," while Leyris ends
with, "Ce n'est qu'en souvenir, en passion ruminée." "Re-
méditée," a more cerebral word than Leyris' "ruminée," is more
literally exact. But Leyris' word is again an intensifier to compensate for general loss in force; moreover, it puts the activity of
reconsideration into the viscera, where context would have it
belong. Wahl's choice of "mémoire" is more aurally apt than
Leyris' "souvenir" for "memory." One can only guess that he felt
it to have richer resonances. And it is inhibiting to be too critical
when Leyris has written in his "avant-propos" to *Poèmes*,

> Si le fruit de ce travail d'écoute est d'un bonheur inégal, c'est
> d'un égal malheur qu'il eût été sans l'exquise bienveillance de Mr.
> Eliot. Qu'eussions-nous fait, privé de ces entretiens de Londres
> qui nous ont éclairé tant de registres cachés, épargné tant de
> pièges? (16)

Eliot's next sentence,

> Gives too soon
> Into weak hands, what's thought can be dispensed with
> Til the refusal propagates a fear. . . . (ll. 42-44)

is again more literal in Wahl's hands:

> Donne trop tôt
> En des mains faibles ce dont pense-t-on on peut se passer
> Jusqu'à ce que le refus engendre multiple peur.

Not only is "ce dont pense-t-on on peut" an awkward tongue-stopper, but "multiple peur," while intensifying Eliot's word with the added adjective, also diminishes its force, with its added length. Leyris' line ends with "frayeur," a stronger word than "peur," one that connotes *dread*:

> Qu'elle donne trop tôt
> A des mains sans vigueur, ce dont on pense
> Pouvoir se dispenser, mais l'heure vient
> Où le refus engendre la frayeur. . . .

The latter version has more grace and economy with its tighter construction, and the expression "sans vigueur" for "weak" acts as an intensifier by negatively suggesting the absence of strength, thus creating an effective contrast.

The stanza concludes with four short sentences:

> Think
> Neither fear nor courage saves us. Unnatural vices
> Are fathered by our heroism. Virtues
> Are forced upon us by our impudent crimes.
> These tears are shaken from the wrath-bearing tree. (ll. 44-48)

The effect is cumulative: imperative "Think" is followed by three sentences with quick subject-verb beginnings that build incrementally to culminate in Gerontion's tears. Wahl's and Leyris' lines follow:

> JW: Pensez que ni la crainte ni le courage ne nous sauve.

> PL: Dis-toi
>   Que frayeur ni courage ne sauraient nous sauver.
>   Des vices monstrueux naissent de notre héroïsme.

> JW: Des vertus nous sont imposées par des crimes sans pudeur.

> PL: Nos crimes sans pudeur nous imposent des vertus.

> JW: Ces larmes naissent des secousses de l'arbre aux colères.

> PL: Ces larmes, c'est l'arbre de colère qui les déverse.

As the stanza moves towards its conclusion, Gerontion increasingly experiences a personal and general sense of anomie. Wahl again follows the text rather literally, retaining Eliot's passive constructions that go against the grain of the French language. Leyris, in contrast, does not hesitate to switch to active constructions. But to achieve a French equivalent of the elevated diction of the English words, he omits articles before "frayeur" and "courage," a device that occurs in French in proverbial expressions, when one wants one's language to have an effect analogous to the proverbial, when words are placed in antithetical pairs to lend vivacity to one's language, or when a general conception is involved (Grevisse 270, 272). Leyris thus here lifts his diction to an elevated level, at the same time that he preserves, through syntax, an impression of a human sensibility experiencing the kind of disintegration that the speaker feels to be occurring.

The improvisational effect is one that Leyris achieves, for example, by beginning his last line as Eliot does, with "These tears" ("Ces larmes"). But while Eliot goes on with the passive structure mentioned earlier, "These tears *are shaken* from the wrath-bearing tree," Leyris brilliantly uses the active, suggesting both the way French works and the way a French person uttering such a sentence in a moment of intense feeling would utter it, spontaneously and colloquially: "Ces larmes, c'est l'arbre de colère qui les déverse" ("These tears, it's the tree of wrath that pours them"). While Wahl's "secousse" perfectly translates English "shake," a retranslation of his line shows that it is weaker than the English; it occurs in a string of prepositional phrases that his opting for the passive imposes: "These tears *are born of* the shakings *of* the tree *of* angers." The retranslation is unfair to the French, considering that English has no ear for the active form of "to be born" in this context, as French has, with "naître." But "Ces larmes naissent des secousses de l'arbre aux colères" still does not redeem it, when compared with Leyris' version. The latter ends, for example, with "déverse"; when tears are shaken from a tree, one imagines them falling in drops, while when they are dumped in volume, literally *poured*, "déverser" is the French verb. Yet again, Leyris opts to intensify his translation, effectively ending the stanza with that overwhelming word.

Finally, that Wahl omitted the second of these four lines may not be the result of carelessness; it is entirely possible that the parallelism among those last sentences caused the printer to omit it inadvertantly. My interest is in the overall fidelity of a translation, and in this instance, as in most, Leyris seems to me to achieve a closer approximation of the rhythms and affects of Eliot's original.

Wahl's excerpt leaves off at this point, while Leyris' translation continues into its fifth stanza. Gerontion continues to address "Christ the tiger," who "springs in the new year":

> Us he devours. Think at last
> We have not reached conclusion, when I
> Stiffen in a rented house. Think at last
> I have not made this show purposelessly
> And it is not by any concitation
> Of the backward devils.
> I would meet you upon this honestly. (ll. 49-55, CPP 22)

The speaker moves from the generalized and emotional observations of the preceding stanza to contemplation again of his own specific situation, continuing, however, to use the elevated language and anaphoric "think" twice more as the poem modulates into his reflections about what he has lost: his passion and his five senses. The turn in this stanza is from a plea that this "show" of thought and feeling has not been made "purposelessly," to what seems--in the light of the atomizing concluding stanzas--to be, in this stanza's final line, a purely rhetorical question from one who has lost these things: "How should I use them for your closer contact?" The diction likewise "winds down," from the inversion of "Us he devours" and the obsolete "concitation" ("stirring up" or "rousing," according to the *OED*) / "Of the backward devils," to the simplicity of the stanza's stark and mostly monosyllabic last lines:

> I have lost my sight, smell, hearing, taste and touch:
> How should I use them for your closer contact? (ll. 60-61, CPP 23)

Pierre Leyris' translation participates in the same modulation, from the inversion of "Bondit le tigre au nouvel an" to the simplicity of

> Vu, ouïe, goût, odorat, toucher, j'ai tout perdu:
> Comment en userai-je pour mieux t'approcher?

The final two stanzas of "Gerontion" modulate from a summary statement to a question--whether the spider and weevil will call off their usual activities, impliedly because Gerontion has been aroused by reflective passion, including thoughts about his own death--to the resolving lines in which we see through Gerontion's eyes the atomizing of the world, his world, his self:

> Gull against the wind, in the windy straits
> Of Belle Isle, or running on the Horn.
> White feathers in the snow, the Gulf claims,
> And an old man driven by the Trades
> To a sleepy corner.
>
> Tenants of the house,
> Thoughts of a dry brain in a dry season. (ll. 70-76)

In Leyris' first version in SC *Poèmes*, he wrote,

> Mouette contre le vent
> Dans les goulets venteux de Belle-Isle ou courant
> Droit sur le Horn, duvet blanc dans la neige,
> Le Gulf réclame, et c'est
> Un vieillard balayé par les vents alizés
> Dans son recoin d'oubli.
>
> Habitants du logis
> Pensers d'un cerveau sec en temps de sécheresse.

The next three versions closely resemble each other, most changes occurring in the second, a few minor adjustments in the third, and a few significant revisions in the fourth. For the first time, in the fourth, he, like Eliot, includes the above passage with the lines that precede it, rather than creating a separate stanza at that point. Most significantly, he removes a verb where Eliot has one, creating a participial form. Thus the translation intensifies the deverbalization that accompanies the depersonalization that we have noted. The revisions are italicized in the following quotation from *Poésie*:

> Mouette contre le vent
> Dans le venteux *détroit du Labrador,* ou *dérivant*
> *Par le travers* du Horn, *plumes* blanches dans la neige,
> Le Gulf *exigeant sa rançon,*
> *Et* un vieillard *chassé* par les vents alizés
> Dans *un coin somnolent.*
>
> Habitants du logis,
> Pens*ées* d'un cerveau sec en temps de sécheresse.

Where Eliot has "the Gulf reclaims" in the first quoted sentence, Leyris first translates literally "Le Gulf réclame," followed by "et c'est," which creates an additional verb. Finally, however, he suppresses "et c'est" and transforms "réclame" into participial "exigeant." "Et c'est" had disappeared from his other two revisions as well; but finally, for *Poésie* in 1969, he went beyond Eliot's degree of deverbalization to reinforce the effect in French of the poet's lines.

In this final movement toward stasis, in which mankind, generalized in "De Bailhache, Fresca, Mrs. Cammel," the world, of which the gull, the wind, Belle Isle, and the Horn are emblematic, and finally Gerontion himself--all are conflated in "Tenants of the house," which are just those "Thoughts of a dry brain in a dry season."

"The itinerary covered from thing to say to thing said," to translate from this essay's epigraph by Pierre Leyris, has taken us through as many as four versions of certain lines of T. S. Eliot's poems, as well as through comparisons of two translators' versions of the same lines. Looking at the translations as translations, I have seen Leyris' as both consistently superior to those of Jean Wahl and progressively more poetic and faithful as he refined them over the years. That he was deeply immersed in Eliot's poetry, that he worked on his translations with the close collaboration of the poet and of John Hayward, that he has been a prolific professional translator for many years--all these factors, in addition to his own gifts, contribute to the remarkable success of his translations.

Looking at them as we have here, however, also casts light on the English poems we have touched on or examined in depth. Analyzing translations can modify our own readings of originals, because, to evaluate the translations, we must evaluate comparatively the sound, nuance, context, meaning, and syntax involved in the poems in both languages. Such study brings readers closer to the poet's own conception, his expression of it, and the aesthetic working of his poetic form. And while the translator cannot create a *perfect* translation, being unable to write the original work over again in exactly the same verbal form, he may at times approximate an original with great exactitude, and at others even add poetic value to it. Translation analysis enables us to participate in and observe the kindred processes of creation, translation, reading, and criticism.

In his translations Pierre Leyris has created what are distinguished French poems in their own right. They also do honor to the poetic art of T. S. Eliot.

APPENDIX

Gerontion

Me voici, vieil homme dans un mois de sécheresse,
Ecoutant l'enfant qui lui fait la lecture, attendant la pluie.
Je n'étais pas aux portes brûlantes
Je n'ai pas combattu dans la pluie chaude
Ni le genou enfoncé dans le marais salé, levant un coutelas,
Mordu par les mouches, combattu.
Ma maison est une maison délabrée.

* * *

Après une telle connaissance, quelle rémission?
Pensez maintenant comme l'histoire a des passages astucieux,
Des corridors agencés ainsi que des sorties,
Nous trompe avec des ambitions murmurantes,
Nous guide par des vanités.
Pensez maintenant qu'elle donne quand notre attention est distraite
Et ce qu'elle donne c'est avec si souple confusion
Que le don affame l'affamé. Donne trop tard
Ce qu'on ne croit pas, ou si on le croit,
C'est en mémoire seulement, en passion re-méditée. Donne trop tôt
En des mains faibles ce dont pense-t-on on peut se passer
Jusqu'à ce que le refus engendre multiple peur.
Pensez que ni la crainte ni le courage ne nous sauve.
Des vertus nous sont imposées par des crimes sans pudeur.
Ces larmes naissent des secousses de l'arbre aux colères.

Translated by Jean Wahl, 1943

Gerontion

> *Tu n'es ni jeune ni vieux, c'est*
>
> *comme si*
>
> *Tu sommeillais après le déjeuner*
> *Rêvant de ces deux âges*
> --Shakespeare, *Mesure pour Mesure*

Me voici, un vieillard dans un mois de sécheresse,
Ecoutant ce garçon me lire, attendant la pluie.
Je n'étais pas au brûlant défilé
Je n'ai pas combattu dans la pluie chaude
Ni, embourbé dans la saline jusqu'au genou,
Levant un glaive, mordu par les mouches, combattu.
Ma maison est une maison délabrée;
Dans l'encoignure de la fenêtre est accroupi
Le Juif, son possesseur, qui fut mis bas

Dans quelque estaminet d'Anvers, empustulé
A Bruxelles, rapiécé et dépiauté à Londres.
Le bouc grinche la nuit dans le pré d'au-dessus:
Rocailles, lichen, chiendent, ferraille et fientes.
La femme vaque à la cuisine, fait le thé,
Eternue à la fraîche, tisonne le feu qui crache.
                              Vieil homme que je suis,
Tête vide parmi les espaces venteux.

Les signes sont tenus pour des prodiges. "Un signe,
Nous voulons voir un signe!"
La Parole dans la parole, incapable de dire une parole,
Emmaillottée d'obscur. Dans la jouvence de l'an
Vint Christ le tigre.

Au lascif mois de mai, cournouilles, châtaignes, faînes de Judée
A manger, boire et partager
En chuchotant; par Monsieur Silvero
Aux mains flatteuses, qui à Limoges
Marcha toute la nuit dans la chambre à côté;
Par Hakagawa, saluant parmi les Titiens;
Par Madame de Tornquist qui, dans la chambre obscure
Remuait les bougies; par Fraülein von Kulp
Qui, la main sur la porte, se retourna. De vaines navettes
Tissent le vent. Je n'ai pas de fantômes,
Vieillard en ce logis battu de courants d'air
Sous cette butte venteuse.

Après un tel savoir, quel pardon? Dis-toi bien
Que l'Histoire a maints passages subtils, maints corridors
Et issues dérobées, qu'elle nous égare
D'ambitions chuchotantes, nous leurre de vanités; oui, dis-toi bien
Qu'elle donne lorsque notre attention se trouve distraite
Et ce qu'elle donne, le donne en confusions si souples
Que le don affame l'affamé. Qu'elle donne trop tard
Ce à quoi vous ne croyez point, ou si vous y croyez encore
Ce n'est qu'en souvenir, en passion ruminée. Qu'elle donne trop tôt
A des mains sans vigueur, ce dont on pense
Pouvoir se dispenser, mais l'heure vient
Où le refus engendre la frayeur. Dis-toi
Que frayeur ni courage ne sauraient nous sauver.
Des vices monstrueux naissent de notre héroïsme.
Nos crimes sans pudeur nous imposent des vertus.
Ces larmes, c'est l'arbre de colère qui les déverse.

Bondit le tigre au nouvel an. Et nous dévore. Dis-toi enfin
Que ce n'est pas pour nous la conclusion, du fait
Que mon corps se raidit dans un logis à bail. Dis-toi enfin
Que ceci n'est pas un éclat que je ferais hors de propos
Ni à l'instigation de démons rétrogrades.

Moi qui fus proche de ton coeur, j'en fus chassé,
Perdant la beauté dans l'effroi, l'effroi dans l'inquisition vaine.
J'ai perdu ma passion: pourquoi devrais-je la garder
Quand ce qui est gardé forcément s'adultère?
Vue, ouïe, goût, odorat, toucher, j'ai tout perdu:
Comment en userais-je pour mieux t'approcher?

Ces considerations et mille autres pareilles
Prolongent l'agrément de leur délire glacé,
Excitent la musqueuse, le sens ayant froidi,
De leurs sauces poivrées, multiplient les aspects
Dans une exubérance de miroirs. L'araignée,
Que fera-t-elle? Suspendra-t-elle son ouvrage?
Le charançon surseoira-t-il?
Fresca, Madame Cammel, De Bailhache, emportés
Par delà le circuit de l'Ourse grelottante
En poussière d'atomes. Mouette contre le vent
Dans le venteux détroit du Labrador, ou dérivant
Par le travers du Horn, plumes blanches dans la neige,
Le Gulf exigeant sa rançon,
Et un vieillard chassé par les vents alizés
Dans un coin somnolent.

                              Habitants du logis,
Pensées d'un cerveau sec en temps de sécheresse.

                                    Translated by Pierre Leyris, 1969

WORKS CITED

Eliot, T. S. "Charybde et Scylla: lourdeur et frivolité." Conférence du 25 mars 1952. *Annales du Centre Universitaire Méditerranéan* [Nice] 5 (1951-52): 71-82.

_____. *Four Quartets*. New York: Harcourt, 1943.

Gallup, Donald. *T. S. Eliot: A Bibliography*. London: Faber, 1969.

Germain, André, trans. "Preludes." By T. S. Eliot. *Ecrits Nouveaux* [Paris] 9 (1922): 32-33.

Grevisse, Maurice. *Le Bon Usage: Grammaire française avec des remarques sur la langue française d'aujourd'hui*. Gembloux [Belgium]: Duculot, 1961.

Hooker, Joan Fillmore. *T. S. Eliot's Poems in French Translation: Pierre Leyris and Others*. *Studies in Modern Literature* 26. Ann Arbor: UMI Research Press, 1983.

Leyris, Pierre, trans. "Gerontion." By T. S. Eliot. *Poésie 47* [Paris] 8.38 (1947): 2-7.

_____. Letter to author. 26 Oct. 1987.

_____. Letter to T. S. Eliot. 25 Mar. [no year]. Hayward Bequest, King's College Library, Cambridge University.

_____. Letters to John Hayward. 5 and 26 Feb., 9 Mar., 16 May [1946], [late 1949/early 1950], [Apr. 1950?]. Hayward Bequest and Papers, King's College Library, Cambridge University.

_____. Personal interviews. 8 and 12 Nov. 1980.

_____, trans. *Poèmes accompagnés de proses et dessins*. By Gerard Manley Hopkins. 1957. Paris: Seuil, 1980.

_____, trans. [NY] *Poèmes 1910-1930*. By T. S. Eliot. Collection poétique bilingue. Paris: Seuil, 1947.

_____, trans. [SC] *Poèmes 1910-1930*. By T. S. Eliot. Collection poétique bilingue. Paris: Seuil, 1947.

_____, Galley proofs for *Poésie*. Annotated and pasted up revision of translations in [NY] *Poèmes 1910-1930*, sent by translator to author, 6 Dec. 1980.

_____, trans. *Poésie: Premiers poèmes, La Terre vaine, Les Hommes creux, Mercredi des cendres, Poèmes d'Ariel, Quatre quatuors*. By T. S. Eliot. 1969. Paris: Seuil, 1976.

_____, trans. "Preludes." By T. S. Eliot. "Trois Poèmes de T. S. Eliot." *Fontaine: revue mensuelle de la poésie et des lettres françaises* [Paris] 48-48 (1946): 171-74.

_____. "Quelques mots sur la traduction littéraire considérée tantôt comme une fin en soi, tantôt comme un instrument pédagogique." *Babel: International Journal of Translation* 8 (1962): 121-22.

Littré, Paul-Emile. *Dictionnaire de la langue française*. 4 vols. Monte-Carlo: Cap, 1969.

Steiner, George. *After Babel: Aspects of Language and Translation*. New York: Oxford UP, 1976.

Wahl, Jean, trans. "Gerontion." By T. S. Eliot. (Two excerpts.) *Fontaine: revue mensuelle de la poésie et des lettres françaises* [Paris] 27-28 (1943): 166-67.

MOHAMMAD SHAHEEN

ELIOT IN MODERN ARABIC POETRY

No other foreign poet has achieved as much popularity as T. S. Eliot has done in modern Arabic poetry. While Ezra Pound, for example, is a name which merely rings a bell in Arabic, Eliot is comparatively a common name--at least, to the educated Arab reader. This popularity has inspired investigation. In a recent survey "Eliot in Modern Arabic Literature," Mahir Fareed begins his account by remarking "For one reason or another, our men of letters have been fascinated by reiterating the name of Eliot on various occasions, but to the extent of becoming tedious enough to make people grumble" (173). Fareed quotes Louis Awad as saying that we still talk about Eliot as if English poetry stopped with him (173). He further quotes a well-known poet, M. I. Abi-Sinnah's remark that deep concern with Eliot in the last few years has been at the expense of the rich modern tradition of poetry all over the world (173). Also Fareed points to the misunderstandings spotted by Ali Shalash concerning the exaggerated popularity of Eliot in Arabic which seems to make the Arab reader believe that there is no other great modern poet besides Eliot (173).

However, before we discuss the rationale behind this popularity and assess the impact of Eliot on Arabic poetry, a reference to Eliot's introduction into Arabic may be helpful: An early study of Eliot in Arabic by Louis Awad forms a part of a book entitled *Modern English Literature* published in Cairo in 1950. In his study, Awad views Eliot as the greatest English poet. It is surprising that twelve years later, Awad expresses his dissatisfaction with Eliot's popularity (as we see above). Perhaps Awad did not anticipate that Eliot would be a dominant figure in the Arab literary scene. Also Awad wrote a poem (presumably when he was a student in England during World War II) in which the impact of Eliot is obvious. The poem entitled "Love in Saint Lazar" uses explicit references to "Prufrock" and other Eliot poetry, and it was designed to be a contribution to modern Arabic poetry written in the vein of free verse.

About six years later (1956) Rashad Rushdi pub-
lished his book *Studies in English Poetry* in which important allusions to Eliot are made. In 1961 Rushdi wrote an article on the
"objective correlative" in Eliot; and a few years later he wrote
another article on the same subject but with Eliot's reference to
Shakespeare as a demonstration. The result was that Rushdi
made Eliot appear to the Arab reader as the critic of the objective correlative.

The first major account of *The Waste Land* in Arabic
was by Nabila Ibrahim in which she makes Eliot the poet of the
greatest poem in English literature. Despite its factual mistakes
this account remains a pioneering effort which was followed by a
long series of studies and analyses of the poem. Nabila Ibrahim
wrote another article "The Woman Image in Modern Western
Literature" in which she makes a resumé of *The Cocktail Party*.
Another valuable account is by Mustafa Badawi; his book *Studies in Poetry and Theatre* devotes a whole chapter to Eliot, the
poet. Badawi quotes and translates relevant passages from
Eliot's poetry.

Studies, analyses, commentaries and various writings
and translations continued to appear on Eliot in Arabic in the
sixties through the seventies. Interestingly enough, Eliot has
been particularly promoted by *Aswat*, published in London in
the early sixties. However, all important literary journals in Arabic considered it important to promote the poet's popularity in
the Arab world. Also many dissertations have been written on
Eliot. In his survey mentioned above Mahir Fareed records that
at least twenty M.A. and Ph.D. theses on Eliot have been completed in various Arab universities, and obviously more must
have been written since the survey was made in 1981.

*   *   *

What is the rationale behind all this popularity? I believe there
are different factors which contributed to this matter. One may
be described as historical. Arabs suffered from Western imperialism, particularly French and British, and only after World War
II did those Arab countries under imperialism gain their inde-
pendence. In the fifties memories of the past were still fresh and
they became more so when Britain invaded Egypt in 1956.
Algiers was still fighting French imperialism. All these circumstances generated a hostile attitude towards the West. It is not
surprising then to find Eliot's condemnation of Western civiliza-

tion in *The Waste Land* so attractive to the Arab world. Arab poets and readers as well celebrated Eliot as the authorial voice which could penetrate into the heart of Western darkness, and articulate the decay of its civilization.

In a sense Eliot filled in a gap for the Arab reader which may be identified with the gap that Eliot filled in the West after World War I. Many Arab writers were under the impression that Eliot wrote *The Waste Land* sometime in the forties or fifties.

Another reason behind his popularity lies in the way Eliot's poetry--and particularly *The Waste Land*--seems to yield suggestive images and motifs. Arab poets, for example, found in the dead city of *The Waste Land* a compelling poetic picture: their poetry too is full of motifs which present the city as a hostile force. In general terms, Arabic culture is basically shaped by the country rather than the city, and it is not surprising then to find Arab poets identify their sense of loss and alienation with the terror of *The Waste Land* city. Yet this identification does not have the historical perspective of London and Paris in Eliot's poem. It is rather limited to the sinister feeling urban life invokes in those poets.

Another appealing image in Eliot's poetry is rain. In Arabic heritage, rain has a romantic association, whose poetry is still memorized by Arabs, but rain in *The Waste Land*, we know, has a different dimension altogether. It is the absence of rain rather than its celebration which finds its way in modern Arabic poetry, and this seems to be an appropriate form for the desolate mood of the Arab poets. Such negation of reality articulates the transition in the Arab sensibility from the romanticism of the thirties and forties to the realism of the fifties and sixties.

Of course the image of rain sustained is simultaneously associated with that of the waste land motif. The image of the waste land is probably more expressive in Arabic because the life of the majority of people (Arabic society is basically agricultural) is directly affected by the annual rainfall. For this reason we find the image of the waste land becoming almost a stock image.

The Waste Land has become, then, a cluster from which various images have emerged: one is the land image which seems to have inspired many Arab poems. Eliot has been known in the Arab literary scene as the poet of the waste land poetry, with all its empty and hollow reality; and Arab intelligentsia have found in Eliot's poetry an authentic expression of

the existing reality surrounding them. A leftist journal writes an
obituary for Eliot which begins as follows:

> Early this year a great poet passed away after he had spent
> seventy-seven years articulating the sad music of humanity. Life
> for him was a waste land and people were hollow-men. Because he
> sincerely wept for life and wrote its obituary, his words
> interpenetrated the conscience of modern man, and became an
> important sign post on the twentieth century. If one speaks of the
> sad feeling and alienation of the individual, of the grim reality of
> the external world, one simultaneously speaks of the poet T. S.
> Eliot. ("Great Poet" 81)[1]

A look at some titles of poems shows Arab poets' quick
response to images and motifs from Eliot's poetry. Here are
some titles by Badr Shakir Al-Sayyab: "The City of Illusion,"
"The Lost Caravan," "The River and Death," "The Soul of
Rain," "A City without Rain," "A London Night," "A Paris
Night." Ali Ahmad Said, nicknamed Adonis, entitles his collection of poems *The Ash of Resurrection* (1957). Yusuf Al-Khal,
another poet, who held the banner of innovation in modern
Arabic poetry, published a collection of poetry (1957) with the
title *Ash-River*. Khalil Hawi, another poet, published two
anthologies entitled, *From the Hell of Comedia* and *The
Wounded Thunder*.

      The appeal Arab poets find in the poetics of Eliot
can be further demonstrated from the poetry published in *Shi'r*
(Poetry), a journal devoted to the new movement in Arabic
poetry. For example, here are some of the poems which
appeared in the Spring issue of 1968: "The Tone of Alienation,"
"Diaspora," "The Disaster of Diaspora," "The Harvest of
Skulls," "In Front of the Target City."

      There is much modern Arabic poetry which, when
read, immediately recalls Eliot. We can hardly escape an association with Eliot as soon as we look at the first lines of some
poems by Salah Abdul-Sabur (Eliot's impact on him has been
fully acknowledged). These are the opening lines which appear
in his poetry collection *The Old Knight-Errant's Dreams*:

> Trees have not fruited this year
> This winter foretells me that I am dying alone

---

1. It is interesting to notice how Eliot has found his way into this journal more than once. On one
occasion Eliot is discussed along with Gorky, Orwell and other leftists, and his "Definition of Culture"
is read as a contribution to the artist's commitment to pragmatism (Mahmoud 64-71). On another
occasion Eliot is discussed as one of the group of poets who in the twenties united in the rejection of
western civilization and syntax adoption of a better reality ("C. Day-Lewis and the Crisis of the Time"
58-67). I have no reason to offer for the fact that Eliot was welcomed to a leftist review except that
Eliot was made too popular by other journals to be refused admission to a place where he doesn't
really belong.

Coming back to you my city is like making pilgrimage to a wailing wall
I leave my city, my old homeland with heavy burdens of life.

* * *

The question of popularity brings with it the reference to the man of letters who particularly promoted the name of Eliot in the Arab world. It was Rashad Rushdi, a Professor of English literature at Cairo University, and an active columnist in more than one newspaper, who claimed Eliot as the great contemporary English poet and critic. Being a favorite to the establishment, he had easy access to the mass media at the time. His lectures on Eliot would be simultaneously published in newspapers, in book form and even broadcast over the radio. Rushdi captured the spirit of the time dominated by unusual enthusiasm for innovation in modern Arabic poetry and made Eliot appear a good example for any innovative attempt. His book *What Is Literature* which includes parts on Eliot was popular enough to be considered a manifesto of New Criticism, at least among Rushdi's disciples. But Rushdi's blunt support for form and blind attack on content made him an easy target for criticism. I vividly remember the controversy over Rushdi's literary views on the pages of *Al-Masa Literary Supplement* when I was an undergraduate in Cairo. Rushdi attracted a good number of his students who would defend both their professor and mentor against traditionalist opponents and new critics.

I have shown elsewhere that Rushdi exercised a negative influence on the literary scene in the late fifties and sixties concerning the modern short story (18-20). I would like to suggest that such influence has been more negative in poetry, and that Eliot himself suffered by gaining popularity at the expense of a more effective introduction.

* * *

How can the popularity of Eliot be assessed? In his survey mentioned above, Mahir Fareed concludes that this popularity is not more than a storm in a tea cup, and that Eliot gained very little from his popular reception, and Arab poetry benefited even less from its reception of Eliot. He refers to a few people who were able to grasp Eliot and assimilate him into Arabic, but he then confirms that the impact resulting from this interplay is quite

marginal. "Our contact with Eliot," Fareed sums up, "is a failure" (192). Fareed tries to find a rationale for this situation.
Eliot's poetry, Fareed remarks, is characterized by the private
element which is related to an unusual personal experience
impossible to be rendered or even imitated by others, as is the
case with art in general. Fareed also faults Eliot's intellectual
background which contributes a great deal to the shape of his
poetry. Fareed regrets the fact that very little of Bradley, Frazer,
John the Baptist and other sources which Eliot drew upon, has
been translated into Arabic. A third reason for this failure,
Fareed thinks, lies in the difference between Arabic and Western culture where Greek, Roman and Christian components
cannot be easily assimilated into Arabic culture.

All this rationalization is acceptable on its own merit,
but it is too general to be applied only to Eliot. Fareed must
have been influenced in his evaluation more by the superficial
treatment of Eliot in Arabic (Rushdi's is one) and less by the
successful individual attempts. Before Fareed, Nizar Qabbani, a
most popular modern Arab poet, made the following assessment:

> While reviewing the influences of universal thought on us, we can-
> not neglect the Eliotic movement, which left its mark on the bulk
> of our contemporary poets. They based the legends, the religious
> and historical symbols on the association of images. In doing jus-
> tice to this movement, we must state that the results of the Eliotic
> movement in our poetry were good in general. Indeed some tal-
> ented poets had a remarkable success as they gave the contempo-
> rary Arabic poem what it lacked in the past, i.e., unity of form and
> subject . . ." (qtd. in El-Asma 671-78).

When the poetry of a great poet migrates to a different culture, the test in the process of assimilation is, I believe,
more tough for the receptive culture. It is natural that mainly
talented poets have been able to succeed in their contact with
Eliot and to survive the experience of this interaction. Poets like
Al-Sayyab, Abdul-Sabur, Jabra, Adonis, Hawi--and the list can
be longer--have greatly benefited from Eliot. Reviewers and
critics who have been engaged in evaluating the interplay
between Eliot and modern Arabic literature have been somewhat overwhelmed by the negative effect caused by the superficial treatment Eliot receives from a large number of Arab writers. At the same time the successful attempts have been
acknowledged, but with little or no critical reading of the poetry
itself, to explore the subtle transformation of Eliot into Arabic.

What I would like to say about the successful attempts in modern Arabic poetry can be better articulated by what David Moody perceptively remarks in the course of his commentary on *Ash-Wednesday*:

> So the poem is hardly at all an expression of the love-experience.
> Instead it is perfectly organized to control, distance and transform
> the feelings which persist beyond the experience. (141-42)

Poetry then is the transformation of experience by the individual talent and not the pursuit of its sources.

What is noticed about the successful attempt of those poets is the way the Eliot source is integrated into their experience. One general aspect of this practice is the localized effect which develops as a result of transformation. This means that universality in Eliot's poetry has to be localized before it acquires its own universality in Arabic poetry. Poetry may be an escape from emotions as Eliot says, but it cannot be equally an escape from a gripping reality such as the one the Arab poet found himself caught in. Hence the local Arab scene in the fifties and sixties stands as an overt pattern in the poetic experience, and this often helps to conceal (perhaps confuse) the integrated effect drawn from Eliot. For example, the image of the city versus country in modern Arabic poetry is an extended image of the hostile city in *The Waste Land* . Also a most celebrated verse from "The Rain Song" by Al-Sayyab: "Rain . . . / Rain . . . / Rain . . . / There is famine in Iraq," is a developed image of rain from *The Waste Land*. Eliot caught Arab poets at a critical time of their history: monarchies over-thrown in Eqypt and Iraq, revolutions and counter-revolutions in both countries and a state of suspense and hope for change all over the Arab world.

* * *

The impact of Eliot on modern Arab writers needs reassessment outside the noise of popularity, and based on close analysis of the text. This can show the discrepancy between the practice of reviewers and critics which often ended in making Eliot popular, and the practice of poets which, I believe, has enriched modern poetry. Such assessment can also reveal the implicit effect of this impact which, in the middle of popularity, has been overlooked by those reviewers and critics.

I would like to demonstrate this kind of impact from the text of a poem which is considered one of the great poems in modern Arabic poetry. "The Rain Song" is, to some extent, *The Waste Land* in Arabic, and studies concerning this identification are ample. Yet there is more of Eliot in it than *The Waste Land*. For example, it incorporates the renunciatory mood of "The Love Song of J. Alfred Prufrock," which is set right from the beginning of the poem:

> Your eyes are palm groves refreshed by dawn's breath
> Or terraces the moon leaves behind.
> When your eyes smile the vines flower
> And the lights dance
> Like the moon's reflections on a river
> Gently sculled at the crack of dawn
> Like stars pulsating in the depth of your eyes
> That sink in mists of grief like the sea
> Touched by the evening's hands
> And wrapped in winter warmth and autumn shiver,
> Death and birth, dark and light. (Al-Udhari 29)[2]

The shift from the romantic to the anti-romantic almost immediately after the first line is similar to that shift in "Prufrock": "When the evening is spread out against the sky / Like a patient etherized upon a table" (CPP 3).
One tradition in classical Arabic poetry is the romantic beginning of the poem in which the speaker addresses a beloved even when the poem has nothing to do with love. Whether Al-Sayyab has the tradition or Eliot on his mind, the result is the same: a movement away from romanticism where the ideal seeks realization beyond the immediate occasion of love, and this is a dominant quality of Eliot's poetry from "Prufrock" to *The Waste Land*. The eyes equated by the palm groves are nowhere in the poem related to a beloved lady, and the reference must be to the whole country, to Iraq itself. In its ambiguity the reference has something in common with that of the woman in "Prufrock." After all the darkness of evening prevails in both poems, and Al-Sayyab's "evening hands" immediately recall Eliot's "evening spreading out against the sky." On one occasion in the "Rain Song", the evening yawns and the

---

2. Subsequent references from "The Rain Song" are to this translation, which I think is superior to another translation by Issa Boullata, *Modern Arab Poets*. Yet both translations have serious flaws. Boullata, for example, misses the main part of the speaker's cry to the Gulf by suppressing "pearls." The result is that the voice and the echo end up the same, hence a focal point in the poem is lost. Al-Udhari overlooks another focus in the poem by translating the last line in the poem "It is still raining." Boullata's translation of the same line is comparatively better "And rain pours." A more accurate translation would be "And still falls the rain."

clouds / Go on pouring their loaded tears / Like a little boy raving about his mother" (29).

Like Eliot, Al-Sayyab states afterwards what he presents in images before. Thus the conclusion: "Death and birth, dark and light" (two perennial themes in Eliot) come to similarly intensify the effect.

The "Rain Song" moves around this polarity of death and birth (a polarity much more complicated in Eliot). It recalls Eliot's famous phrase "Life in death." Between death and birth stands rain in limbo, and the effective refrain of rain is intended to dramatize a major imperative of the speaker's consciousness.

The polarity of theme is further intensified by the polarity of image as we see in the shell and pearl picture. But instead of digging up the image in the history of mythology, as Eliot did, Al-Sayyab exploits the local history, in which the trade of pearls in the area was, until recently, a whole way of life; modern Arabic poetry is full of the shell versus pearl image, expressing the negation of reality. The fisherman or Sindbad coming back from a journey with shell rather than pearl is a familiar narrative frequently used by modern Arab poets.

The speaker in "The Rain Song" reiterates an outcry which obviously articulates the effect:

> I roar at the Gulf: 'Gulf,
> Giver of pearls, shells and death!'
> And the echo rings back
> In sobs:
> 'Gulf
> Giver of shells and death . . .' (30)

The discrepancy between the voice and the echo shows the tension between art and reality, art with a perspective, reality without, and the whole poem, like Eliot's poetry, expresses the "without," but with the suspended effect of the "with." The pearl envisaged in a state of suspense is only part of the total picture of rain in suspense.

What has been particularly overlooked in the various readings available about the poem is the rain's state of suspense. It is here where the focal point of this perspective in Eliot can be helpful in reading "The Rain Song." Also overlooked is the smooth transition Al-Sayyab makes from the complex imagery and mythology to the local scene and history. This is, for example, how Al-Sayyab exploits the thunder of *The Waste Land* and localizes mythology:

I can almost hear Iraq collecting and storing
Thunders and lightning on plains and mountains
And when the men snap their seal
The winds leave no trace
Of Thamud in the wadi.
I can almost hear palm trees drinking rain
Villages crying, emigrants
Struggling with oars and sails
Against Gulf storms and thunders and singing:
Rain . . .
Rain . . .
Rain . . . (30-31)

The whole movement then is singing rain (or of rain)
but not rain actualized or celebrated. The speaker singing rain is
like Prufrock speaking rather than singing of love. Storms and
thunders singing rather than making rain is in its tone in common with "the mermaids singing, each to each" (CPP 7). Both
the speaker in "The Song" and Prufrock hear singing by others
at a distance. In brief "The Rain Song" is a song without rain in
a similar way that Prufrock is a love song without love. Evidently
Al-Sayyab succeeded in his experience of reading Eliot.

APPENDIX

Song of the Rain
by Badre Al-Sayyab

Your eyes are two palm-groves at dawn
or two battlements that the moon begins to leave.
When your eyes smile, vines burst into leaf
Lights dance like moons in a river
gently stirred by the oar at dawn.
In their two caves throb the stars
They are plunged in a transparent mist of sorrow
Like the sea as evening's hands wonder over it
When Winter is warm and Autumn shivers
And there is death and birth, darkness and light
And the fulness of my soul is revived by the shuddering of grief
And by a wild ecstasy embracing Heaven
Like the ecstasy of a child who fears the Moon.
It seems the bow in the clouds drinks up the mists
which drop by drop distil in rain . . .
Children laugh in huts among the vines
and the silent bird in trees are crushed by
the song of rain . . .
Rain . . .
Rain . . .
Rain . . .

The evening yawns and the clouds still pour their heavy tears.
As a child babbles before sleep
of the mother he has not found for a year
and when he asks and asks is told
"The day after tomorrow she will come back".
She must come back.
And if friends whisper that she is there beside the hill,
Sleeping the sleep of the grave, sinking in her dust and
Drinking the rain,
He is like a grieving fisherman who draws in his knot
cursing the waters and Fate,
And scattering his song as the Moon sets.
Rain . . .
Rain . . .
Rain . . .

Do you know the sorrow which sends the rain?
And how the gutters sob as the waters flow?
And how the lonely feel desolation
Endless--like blood poured out, like the starving,
Like love, like children, like the dead, is the rain!
Your eyes appear to me with the rain.
Across the waves of the Gulf lightning speaks

the coasts of Iraq with stars and pearl-shell
As if for the dawn.
And night draws over them a veil of blood.
I cry in the Gulf "O Gulf,
O givers of pearl, and mother-of-pearl, and of destruction"
And the echo comes back,
Like a web:
"O Gulf,
O giver of mother-of-pearl and of destruction . . ."
I seem to hear Iraq hoarding the thunder,
Storing the lightning in plain and mountain.
Should men break the seal
The winds will leave no trace of Thamud in the Valley,

I almost hear the palm-trees drink the rain,
Hear the villages groan and the emigrants
Struggling with oars and sails
Against the storm winds of the Gulf and the thunder, singing:
Rain . . .
Rain . . .
Rain . . .

And in Iraq, hunger,
And the season of harvest scatters its fruits
to fill the crow and the locust
Granary and store ground.
In the mill that turns in the fields . . . with men about it.
Rain . . .
Rain . . .
Rain . . .

How many tears we shed that night of parting
And for fear of reproach we said it was the rain
Rain . . .
Rain . . .

Ever since we were young the sky
Has been cloudy in winter
And fails the rain,
And each year, as the earth grows green, we starve:
No year passes without hunger in Iraq.
Rain . . .
Rain . . .
Rain . . .

In each drop of rain
Red or yellow with the young flowers
And every tear from the hungry and naked
And every flowing drop of the blood of men
Is a smile awaiting new lips,

Or a dream glowing on the lips of the child
In tomorrow's world the youth, the giver of life!
Rain . . .
Rain . . .
Rain . . .

Iraq will grow green with the rain . . .
I call out in the Gulf, "O Gulf,
O giver of pearl and of mother-of-pearl and destruction.
And the echo comes back
Like a web
"O Gulf, O giver of mother-of-pearl and of destruction".
And the Gulf scatters its many gifts
On the sands: salt foam and mother-of-pearl
And the remains of the bones of the emigrant,
Wretched and drowned, who drinks destruction
from the bottom and abyss of the Gulf,
While in Iraq, a thousand snakes drink nectar
From flowers watered by Euphrates.
I hear the echo ringing in the Gulf,
"Rain . . .
Rain . . .
Rain . . ."

In every drop of rain
Red and yellow from the young flowers
And every tear of the hungry and the naked
And every drop that flows of the blood of men
Is a smile awaiting new lips
Or a dream glowing on the lips of the child,
In tomorrow's world the youth, the giver of life.
And still falls the rain . . .

WORKS CITED

Al-Udhari, Abdullah, trans. *Modern Poetry of the Arab World*. London: Penguin Books, 1986.

Awad, Lewis. "A Great Poet has Passed Away." *Al-Fikre Al-Mu'assir* (April 1965): 81.

Bollata, Issa. *Modern Arab Poets*. London: Heinemann, 1976.

El-Asma, Nazeer. "The Tammuz Movement and the Influence of T. S. Eliot on Badr Shakir Al-Sayyab." *Journal of the American Oriental Society* 88 (1968): 671-78.

Fareed, Mahir. "Eliot in Modern Arabic Literature." *Fusul* 1 (1981): 173-92.

Moody, A. D. *T. S. Eliot, Poet*. Cambridge: Cambridge UP, 1979.

Shaheen, Mohammad. *The Modern Arabic Short Story*. London: Macmillan, 1989.

EDWARD LOBB

CHAMBER MUSIC: ELIOT'S CLOSED ROOMS AND DIFFICULT WOMEN*

Of all T. S. Eliot's notes to *The Waste Land*, one has bedeviled criticism more than all the others combined. In explaining the *Dayadhvam* passage ("I have heard the key / Turn in the door once and turn once only" [CPP 49]) Eliot alludes to Ugolino's tower in the *Inferno* and to a passage in Bradley's *Appearance and Reality*:

> My external sensations are no less private to myself than are my thoughts or my feelings. In either case my experience falls within my own circle, a circle closed on the outside; and, with all its elements alike, every sphere is opaque to the others which surround it. . . .In brief, regarded as an existence which appears in a soul, the whole world for each is peculiar and private to that soul. (CPP 54)

In short, the prison image suggests not only the failure to "sympathize," but the impossibility of real communication between what Bradley called "finite centres of consciousness."

    The Bradley reference is unusual, however--even among Eliot's alternately whimsical and pedantic footnotes--in that it does not really clarify anything, but simply transposes the issue into more abstract and philosophical terms. As Ruth Nevo notes, "we have F. H. Bradley brought to gloss a line which is as lucid as the sun, while the truly opaque and mysterious connections and disconnections of the poem are left in fathomless obscurity" (460). Eliot's note appears to sanction philosophical explanation of his poetry, but its very superfluousness raises the question of whether such explanation does Eliot *as a poet* any real service. Given the prominence of Bradley's ideas in recent discussions of Eliot, it may be worthwhile to investigate what an image conveys when it is taken entirely on its own terms--when we use Eliot's poetry itself as the only context. If we take the

---

*This paper is a longer version of a talk given at the National Poetry Foundation's T. S. Eliot Centennial Conference, August 18-20, 1988, Orono, Maine.

image of the closed room with which we began and follow its career through Eliot's poetry, we may be able to draw some conclusions about the self-sufficiency of poetic communication.

Going back to Eliot's earliest poetry, we find that the image of the closed room tends to take two distinct forms. In the first, people are isolated in single rooms:

> With the other masquerades
> That time resumes,
> One thinks of all the hands
> That are raising dingy shades
> In a thousand furnished rooms. ("Preludes" II, CPP 12)

Prufrock has seen "lonely men in shirt-sleeves, leaning out of windows," and the speaker of "Rhapsody on a Windy Night" thinks of "female smells in shuttered rooms" (CPP 5, 15). Gerontion remembers

> Mr. Silvero
> With caressing hands, at Limoges
> Who walked all night in the next room; . . . (CPP 22)

As images of closed or isolated consciousness, these are clear in themselves, and they are reinforced, particularly in "Prufrock," by other, analogous images of isolation. The etherised patient, the sleeping fog-cat and the pair of ragged claws are wholly self-enclosed, reflecting Prufrock's sense of emotional and metaphysical confinement to the self. Gerontion's isolation is partly physical--he is blind and his other senses are failing--and partly philosophical, since, like Prufrock, he is too skeptical or too fearful to commit himself to any belief. His "decayed house"--dwelling, dynasty, body, mind--is in effect a closed room (CPP 21). In Gerontion's world, even Christ is a baby "unable to speak a word," or a mute tiger. The walls between people remain unbreached: we are already, figuratively, in Ugolino's tower, and it is easy to see why Eliot originally intended to use "Gerontion" as a sort of prologue to *The Waste Land.*

The second form of the image is slightly more complex, but still straightforward. Here the room is shared by two or more people, and conversation may actually occur, but no real communication takes place. Prufrock notes twice that

> In the room the women come and go
> Talking of Michelangelo. (CPP 4)

Why do we assume that their talk is trivial? Not because they are women, and not because we remember Yeats' later evocation of "globe-trotting Madam" disturbed by Michelangelo's frescoes "[t]ill her bowels are in a heat," but because everything else in the poem suggests the failure of communication. Prufrock and his silent companion--if he is in fact talking to someone other than himself--are also in that room, but he forestalls the companion's questions ("Oh, do not ask 'What is it?' ") and tells us that "It is impossible to say just what I mean!" (CPP 3, 6). Enclosed in his carapace of collar, necktie and morning coat, he can neither express himself nor be sure of understanding others; his great fear is that

> one, settling a pillow by her head,
> Should say: "That is not what I meant at all.
> That is not it, at all." (CPP 6)

In "Portrait of a Lady," the male speaker notes that his woman friend will

> have the scene arrange itself--as it will seem to do--
> With "I have saved this afternoon for you";
> And four wax candles in the darkened room,
> Four rings of light upon the ceiling overhead,
> An atmosphere of Juliet's tomb
> Prepared for all the things to be said, or left unsaid. (CPP 8)

The things that are said might as well be unsaid, for the male speaker is detached and self-conscious throughout. The darkened room represents both his claustrophobia and the failure of what should be shared experience. The poem traces, through four seasons, a relationship that never develops. Madame de Tornquist in "Gerontion," "in the dark room / Shifting the candles" is involved in a similar charade, and parallel scenes occur in *The Waste Land* (CPP 22). The most notable is obviously the bedroom scene in "A Game of Chess." Here a husband and wife engage in nervous, febrile conversation, but the scene is a study of two solitudes: nothing can touch the wife's neurosis or the husband's detachment. This room is echoed thematically by the typist's bed-sitter in the next section of the poem. The single room in which she lives, eats, cooks, and sleeps is a metaphor of enclosed consciousness; she is "hardly aware" of her lover after he leaves, or indeed while he is there (CPP 44). The house-agent's clerk also inhabits a private world. He misreads the typist's silence, making "a welcome of indifference," and--a final comment on his egoism--gropes blindly down the unlit stairs afterwards.

As if to reinforce the point, some of the rooms contain mirrors. In the wealthy woman's bedroom, Eliot draws attention to

> the glass
> Held up by standards wrought with fruited vines
> From which a golden Cupidon peeped out . . . . (CPP 39)

The mirror is implicitly contrasted with the pictures or tapestries in the room. The latter are unlooked-at, and consequently "withered stumps of time" (CPP 40), but they represent the past and the world, a world of action and real emotion prompted by external objects; the mirror, on the other hand, merely reflects the closed room, from which the inhabitants will escape only to "a closed car" (CPP 41). The typist, an even more extreme case, "turns and looks a moment in the glass," her self-absorption intact (CPP 44).

All of these closed-room images are consistent with the Bradley passage referred to in Eliot's note, and that note has predictably been used to summarize the theme of solipsistic consciousness in the poem and in Eliot's early work generally. Such explanations tend to be genetic: even when they do not assert explicitly that the poem is developing a philosophical idea which existed before the poem, they assume the priority of philosophical explanation by using its terminology. The implicit assertion is that the poetic complexities of a passage are "really" philosophical complexities, or that a poem dramatizes issues which are best explained in philosophical terms. Thus Harriet Davidson, after analyzing Eliot's dissertation and explaining Saussure's and Heidegger's ideas about language and epistemology, discusses *The Waste Land* largely as an enactment of hermeneutic theory.

And it may be that, of course. But if we are obliged to consider Bradley because Eliot wrote about him, we are also obliged to look at Eliot's literary criticism, and to remind ourselves that Eliot, at least until his conversion, had little use for philosophical poetry, or, in fact, for ideas of any kind in poetry. He believed that a "creation of art" should not embody a philosophy, but should "*replace* the philosophy" (SW 66). The celebrated sneer at Tennyson and Browning, who "ruminated" (SE 288), and the praise of Henry James' mind, "so fine that no idea could violate it" (Kermode 151), are in the same mold. We cannot assume, of course, that Eliot's poetic practice was perfectly in keeping with his Keatsian love of "Sensations rather than of Thoughts," but there are reasons for thinking that he did keep "thought"--non-poetic, non-incarnate thought--to a minimum.

Eliot's images are, generally, perfectly clear in themselves: the closed-room motif conveys a feeling of loneliness and intellectual isolation which is not clarified by being translated into abstract terms. If we *do* look for philosophic parallels, how-

ever, many of Eliot's dark rooms are likely to remind us of
Plato's allegory of the cave--a concrete image of limited consciousness rather than Bradley's abstract "closed circles." It is
surely significant that, in the age of gas or electric light, three of
the rooms are lit by candles:

> And four wax candles in the darkened room,
> Four rings of light upon the ceiling overhead . . .
> ("Portrait of a Lady," CPP 8)

> Madame de Tornquist, in the dark room
> Shifting the candles . . . ("Gerontion," CPP 22)

> These [odours] ascended
> In fattening the prolonged candle-flames,
> Flung their smoke into the laquearia . . .
> (*The Waste Land* 2, CPP 40)

The candles, particularly when associated with smoke and
darkness, are the equivalent of the fire in the cave in Plato's
Republic, and the rooms--if they can be reduced to ideas at all--
are more likely to represent the false or limited consciousness
discussed by Plato than Bradley's closed circles.

   An equally striking parallel occurs in Walter Pater's
study *The Renaissance*. The Eliot collection at King's College,
Cambridge, includes an annotated copy of this book, which Eliot
was given in his teens (Munby 29). In the famous--or notorious--
"Conclusion," Pater writes about objects dissolving into

> a group of impressions--colour, odour, texture--in the mind of the
> observer. And if we continue to dwell in thought on this world, not
> of objects in the solidity with which language invests them, but of
> impressions, unstable, flickering, inconsistent, which burn and are
> extinguished with our consciousness of them, it contracts still fur-
> ther; the whole scope of observation is dwarfed to the narrow
> chamber of the individual mind. Experience, already reduced to a
> swarm of impressions, is ringed round for each one of us by that
> thick wall of personality through which no real voice has ever
> pierced on its way to us, or from us to that which we can only
> conjecture to be without. Every one of those impressions is the
> impression of the individual in his isolation, each mind keeping as
> a solitary prisoner its own dream of a world. (235)

Here we have a passage which we know Eliot read; an allusion,
through the references to "flickering," "burning," etc., to Plato,
whom we also know Eliot read; and, finally, a far more concrete
metaphor of isolated consciousness than we find in Bradley. In
fact, the references in this passage to "that thick wall" and "a
solitary prisoner" suggest that not only Eliot's footnote, with

which we began, but the *Dayadhvam* passage itself may owe as much to Pater as to Dante and Bradley.

In suggesting these connections, I am not attempting to dethrone Bradley and set up Plato or Pater in his place. The whole business of influence-hunting, to which I have contributed on occasion, is necessary and often useful, but it tends to reinforce the very idea I am attacking--that Eliot's poetry is "intellectual" and deals with ideas rather than feelings. When Eliot's images are clear in themselves, or apparently derived from literary sources, philosophical explanations are supererogatory. Philosophy's traditional position as queen of the sciences, and Eliot's initial seriousness about a philosophical career, occasionally overshadow important facts: that he was primarily a poet, that poetry is not just a means of knowledge, and that when it does deal with knowledge, it does so in poetic ways.

These distinctions are acknowledged in the best recent discussion of Bradley and Eliot, Sanford Schwartz's *The Matrix of Modernism*. Schwartz's analysis of Eliot is a model of clarity and elegance, and--most importantly--it uses Eliot's dissertation not as explanation but as illustrative analogy. Eliot criticized the extremes of philosophical realism and idealism in the dissertation on Bradley; so, in a similiar way, he criticized the extremes of poetic subjectivity and photographic realism (167-68). Schwartz keeps in mind the difference between an article of belief in epistemology and a statement of values in aesthetics, and repudiates the notion that Eliot's poetry illustrates philosophic ideas. While discussing the concept of the "half-object" in the dissertation and the poetry, for example, Schwartz notes that

> We should avoid the misconception that Eliot first formulated the "half-object" and then dramatized it in his poetry. Long before he wrote his dissertation, Eliot had composed "Prufrock," "Portrait of a Lady," and several other poems that exhibit the internal-external point of view of the half-object. But ... the half-object provides us with a means of analyzing recurrent features of Eliot's verse that have been recognized but insufficiently examined. (187n)

We know, from Lyndall Gordon's excellent account of Eliot's early life, that philosophy was simply one manifestation of that interest in subject and object which informs his poetry, his criticism, and the dissertation. Philosophy was not the *fons et origo*; it was a symptom, not a cause (15-64).

If we accept the idea that Eliot's poetry is a valid form of discourse in itself, we can begin to understand how issues are addressed and finally resolved in poetic terms. The image of the closed room represents--or "replaces"--the idea of limited and possibly solipsistic knowledge: if we follow that image through Eliot's later poetry, it will show us a way out of the dilemma. But it is necessary first to look at another image associated with the rooms in Eliot's poetry, and another approach which tends to limit the intrinsic power of metaphor.

The closed rooms are usually associated with women, and the women in Eliot's earlier poetry are not--with one or two notable exceptions--an attractive lot. If we limit ourselves to the instances already referred to, we find that the women are trivial (the typist and the women who talk of Michelangelo), neurotic (the women in "Portrait of a Lady" and "A Game of Chess"), or vaguely sinister (Madame de Tornquist). There are various explanations for this assortment of loathly ladies, depending upon the poem under discussion and the critical approach taken. The women in *The Waste Land* can be seen thematically as examples of the loss of meaning and the failure of love; there are as many references to betrayed women (Dido, Cleopatra, Ophelia, etc.) as to betraying ones. But in Eliot's early poetry generally there is a clear sense of sexual unease--in Lyndall Gordon's words, "not lack of libido, but inhibition, distrust of women, and a certain physical queasiness" (75).

Gordon's work keeps psychological inference firmly in a biographical context, but psychological criticism of the poetry tends--like philosophical criticism--to claim primacy. The poetic complexities are "really" psychological complexities: thus we have Freudian critics who see Eliot's references to corridors and narrow streets as a form of conscious or unconscious sexual code. For such critics the closed room is, predictably, a vagina, and the significance of the juxtaposition of women and closed rooms is obvious. But if we look at the sexual situations in Eliot's early poetry--using "sexual" in the broadest sense--we can see that they function in a specifically literary way. We should keep in mind what Lou Andreas-Salomé told Freud: sometimes sex itself is a symbol.

The association of women with the closed-room motif suggests that they are involved in some way with the problem of knowledge, and in certain early poems of Eliot the connection is overt. In "Whispers of Immortality," for example, we are told that Webster

> knew that thought clings round dead limbs
> Tightening its lusts and luxuries.
>
> Donne, I suppose, was such another
> Who found no substitute for sense,
> To seize and clutch and penetrate;
> Expert beyond experience,
>
> He knew the anguish of the marrow
> The ague of the skeleton;
> No contact possible to flesh
> Allayed the fever of the bone. (CPP 32-33)

It is customary to read this simply as a gloss on the "dissociation of sensibility," which brought to a mysterious end the unity of intellectual and sensory perception: mourning our fall, Eliot goes on to say that

> our lot crawls between dry ribs
> To keep our metaphysics warm.

But the poem is also about knowledge generally, and it is this aspect of Eliot's use of sex that I want to look at. The metaphor is a natural one for a male poet obsessed with the prison of the self: forming a sexual or emotional connection with a woman is a means of overcoming personal isolation and is therefore a fitting symbol of overcoming intellectual isolation, solipsism, or lack of faith. Carnal knowledge is more than a dead metaphor in Eliot: "copulation" originally means "linking," and the desire to form a link--of whatever kind--is central to Eliot's early poetic *personae*, who tend to be obsessed with both women and belief. Prufrock's immediate worries are sexual and personal, and his ultimate concerns are metaphysical: many readers see the two themes as a form of ironic counterpoint--the trivial juxtaposed with the cosmic--but the two are finally aspects of the same thing.

The conjunction of sex and metaphysics is one of Eliot's links with Donne, and one of his distinctive contributions to modern poetry--a way of fully dramatizing matters of belief and escaping the trap of discursiveness. But finding a metaphor is not, of course, the same thing as finding a solution to the problem it presents. Sex is no easier than metaphysics, though it's far more popular, and Eliot's early characters routinely and naturally find that the physical act of sex is unsatisfying if it does not result in some real communion or communication. Milton speaks of the "longing to put off an unkindly solitariness by uniting another body" and the folly of doing so "without a fit

soul" (709); many of the situations in Eliot's early poetry dramatize that folly. Most of the sexual liaisons in *The Waste Land* are
physical enactments of the Thames-daughter's statement that
she can connect "[n]othing with nothing" (CPP 46).

    The problems and possibilities are well illustrated by
the wonderful central section of "Gerontion":

> After such knowledge, what forgiveness? Think now
> History has many cunning passages, contrived corridors
> And issues, deceives with whispering ambitions,
> Guides us by vanities. Think now
> She gives when our attention is distracted
> And what she gives, gives with such supple confusions
> That the giving famishes the craving. Gives too late
> What's not believed in, or if still believed,
> In memory only, reconsidered passion. Gives too soon
> Into weak hands, what's thought can be dispensed with
> Till the refusal propagates a fear. Think
> Neither fear nor courage saves us. Unnatural vices
> Are fathered by our heroism. (CPP 22)

This is one of several places in Eliot's work where the problem
of knowledge is both architectural and sexual--where images of
room and woman reinforce each other. History is a huge old
house full of secret passages, odd corridors, back stairs, priest-
holes, booby-traps; like the labyrinth which is also implied by
Eliot's language, the house is something you can't see the plan of
precisely because you're inside it. But history is also a woman
(perhaps Clio) and Eliot makes use of a whole spectrum of sexual allusion, from the ambiguous "knowledge" and "passion"
through the more overt "craving" and "supple confusions";
there are suggestions of even more exotic delights in "cunning
passages" and "unnatural vices." The metaphor is wholly appropriate, since desire, sexual or metaphysical, clouds whatever
judgment we might otherwise have; the literal level of the poem
blends seamlessly into the thematic, since Gerontion is terminally skeptical, sexually jaded, and lives in a "decayed house."

    So, while Freudian approaches may be of use in
analyzing Eliot's poetry, I think we should be wary of them--as of
philosophy--when the economy of metaphor in a poem suggests
another direction for interpretation to follow. Lou Andreas-
Salomé is a useful, and too-seldom invoked, corrective to the
Procrustean tendencies of psychoanalytic criticism.

    Since the problem of isolation has been presented in
sexual terms, the possible solution should likewise appear in
those terms; and it in fact does. The visionary moments in
Eliot's early poetry represent a way out of the prison of the self,

and these too are usually associated with women. In "La Figlia che Piange," the girl stands at the top of a stair, "her hair over her arms and her arms full of flowers," and compels the speaker's imagination, becoming a Beatrice-like figure of perfection:

> Sometimes these cogitations still amaze
> The troubled midnight and the noon's repose. (CPP 20)

In *The Waste Land*, she becomes the hyacinth girl:

> --Yet when we came back, late, from the Hyacinth garden,
> Your arms full, and your hair wet, I could not
> Speak, and my eyes failed, I was neither
> Living nor dead, and I knew nothing,
> Looking into the heart of light, the silence. (CPP 38)

As this passage suggests, however, visionary moments are not a solution in themselves: the visionary may respond inadequately to the vision, or he may fear, as Gerontion does, that his desire is producing phantoms. Conversely, the vision may not come at all--as Prufrock fears when he says of the mermaids, "I do not think that they will sing to me" (CPP 7). Lyndall Gordon notes that Eliot had experienced visionary moments and was much concerned with their validity (15, 35); but before his conversion, he could not affirm the existence of anything stable outside the self.

The conversion represents a third enticement to interpretation, this time biographical. The temptation to use our knowledge of Eliot's life is all but irresistible, but we should not give in to it until we have seen what can be accomplished by other means. If we keep in mind the two images discussed so far, we find that they persist in Eliot's later poetry and develop the earlier themes of knowledge and confinement to self. The resolution is poetically and emotionally complex, but intellectually simple: if we are confined to our individual consciousnesses, we must simply accept the fact. Thus in the first part of *Ash-Wednesday*, the abandonment of hope becomes, paradoxically, the only hope; the speaker prays to leave ratiocination behind, to forget

> These matters that with myself I too much discuss
> Too much explain. (CPP 61)

In part 3 of the poem, the speaker is confined, like many of Eliot's earlier characters, to a room--in this case a tower much like Ugolino's--but finds "strength beyond hope and despair / Climbing the third stair" (CPP 63).

Much of Eliot's later poetry describes a deliberate withdrawal to the dark world of individual consciousness--to the closed room in one or another of its forms. In *Burnt Norton* it is the enclosed, flickering world of the tube-train (another echo of Plato's cave); in *East Coker* it is "the deep lane / Shuttered with branches, dark in the afternoon" and later the darkening theater (CPP 123); in *Little Gidding* it is the cold church, "the world's end" (CPP 139). The difference between these "rooms" and the earlier ones is that these are accepted--even embraced--as the only possible area of discourse. The speaker recognizes the ultimate futility of thought, and that recognition is the key to his freedom:

> There is, it seems to us,
> At best, only a limited value
> In the knowledge derived from experience.
> The knowledge imposes a pattern, and falsifies. . . .
>
> The only wisdom we can hope to acquire
> Is the wisdom of humility: humility is endless. (CPP 125-26)

Eliot here alludes to his dissertation (published as *Knowledge and Experience in the Philosophy of F. H. Bradley*), and thereby to its skepticism about the possibility of knowledge. What is more interesting is the way in which humility--the acceptance of limitations--enables one to go beyond limitation: knowledge is limited, but humility is *endless*.

In theological terms, the recognition of our powerlessness enables us to accept grace and transcend our limitations; we cannot free ourselves by "[t]hinking of the key," but we can be freed, like St. Peter from his prison, when we acknowledge a higher power (CPP 49). Thus the enclosed and dark places in three of the *Four Quartets* become places of purgation, as in mystical literature, and lead to enlightenment; the closed rooms open into visionary experience which is not undercut by doubt. The paradoxes and resolution of the poem are familiar: the way down is the way up. My point is simply that Eliot has worked out the problem *poetically* with a beautiful economy of means, using and building on the images that appeared in his first published poems.

He also continues to use the image of woman, and makes that, too, part of his resolution of the problem of knowledge. That knowledge is represented now not by sexual connection but by the flesh itself; it is not carnal, but incarnate. The hyacinth girl makes her last appearance in *Ash-Wednesday*: transfigured, like Beatrice, but still associated with light and silence and mystical illumination--"White light folded, sheathed about her, folded" (CPP 64).

Part of our pleasure in reading a great poet lies in learning his or her vocabulary of images, and seeing how that vocabulary accumulates more and deeper meanings in the course of the poet's career. Yeats' early use of birds, trees and towers is largely conventional, even when the symbols have esoteric meanings; but when we have read through his *Collected Poems* several times, we realize that he has explored all of life through the handling of those images and a few others. We realize, too, that the knowledge required to understand his poetry is not knowledge of Irish mythology, occultism, or contempory history--useful as these prove to be--but knowledge of Yeats' own poetry. "I must leave my myths and images to explain themselves," he wrote, "as the years go by and one poem lights up another" (qtd. in Stock 236).

We would do well to read Eliot the same way. I have no quarrel, as I hope I have made clear, with analyses of Eliot's poetry which are based on philosophy, psychology, or biography. But unless these approaches are subordinated to the examination of poetic context, they are inevitably and often comically reductive. The Freudian who sees a closed room simply as a cloacal symbol is bound to miss a great deal, as is the philosopher who sees poetry primarily as enacting problems of language and discourse. Questions which are in essence extremely simple --questions like "Can I trust my knowledge of the external world?"--become complicated as philosophers discuss their implications in technical and often abstract language; they become complicated in a different and far more concrete way in poetry.

My own examination of two images of knowledge is certainly not meant to be definitive, but it is an indication of direction; and I think it is a direction that Eliot himself would find sympathetic. I have already mentioned his assertion that art should *replace* a philosophy rather than embody it, and his praise of Henry James' mind for its imperviousness to ideas. One could adduce other instances of Eliot's anti-intellectualism almost indefinitely. He maintained, for example, that he had no capacity for abstruse thought (274); that his philosophical studies left him with nothing more than a sense of three philosophers' prose styles (TCC 20-21); that, in 1964, he could no longer "pretend to understand" his dissertation (KE 10). Critics who ignore these statements would like to believe that Old Possum was just muddying the waters, as he did often enough. But if Eliot's word is not law, neither is it wholly irrelevant: if we must pay attention to his intellectual interests, we should likewise pay attention when Eliot says that he would "like an audience which could neither read nor write" or that every poet "would like to be something of a popular entertainer" (UPUC 152, 154).

Eliot was never quite that, even with the popular success of *The Cocktail Party*. But he retained throughout his career a lively sense of how poetry, like music-hall performance, was "a matter of selection and concentration" rather than abstraction and generalization (SE 457). Through a lifetime's devotion to craft, he became a part of the way we see, and has thus become popular in the most fundamental sense--more popular even than Marie Lloyd. That, I think, would please him more than all our learned commentaries.

WORKS CITED

Davidson, Harriet. *T. S. Eliot and Hermeneutics*. Baton Rouge: Louisiana State UP, 1985.

Eliot, T. S. "A Commentary." *Criterion* XI:43 (January 1932), 268-75.

Gordon, Lyndall. *Eliot's Early Years*. Oxford and New York: Oxford UP, 1977.

Kermode, Frank, ed. *Selected Prose of T. S. Eliot*. London: Faber and Faber, 1975.

Milton, John. *Complete Poems and Major Prose*, ed. Merritt Y. Hughes. New York: Odyssey, 1957.

Munby, A. N. L., ed. *Hand-List of the Literary Manuscripts in the T. S. Eliot Collection Bequeathed to King's College, Cambridge, by John Davy Hayward in 1965*. Cambridge: n.p., 1973.

Nevo, Ruth. The Waste Land: *Ur-Text of Deconstruction*. *New Literary History* XIII (1982): 453-61.

Pater, Walter. *The Renaissance: Studies in Art and Poetry*. 4th ed. 1893; rpt. London: Macmillan, 1910.

Schwartz, Sanford. *The Matrix of Modernism: Pound, Eliot and Early Twentieth-Century Thought*. Princeton: Princeton UP, 1985.

Stock, A. G. *W. B. Yeats: His Poetry and Thought*. Cambridge: Cambridge UP, 1961.

JOSEPH BENTLEY and
JEWEL SPEARS BROOKER

HOW TO READ THE END OF THE WASTE LAND*

The Waste Land ends with an extraordinary stanza that, for all
its eccentricity, seems in retrospect to sum up the whole poem's
techniques more appropriately than any other imaginable
mélange of utterances. The final lines follow a triad of interpretive exercises on the meanings that can be invented to give a retrospective voice and language to the thunder over Mount Hima-
vant. The interpretations and commentaries on *Datta, Dayadhvam*, and *Damyata* exemplify the necessarily gratuitous and
arbitrarily imaginative nature of the process of making and
understanding language. The triad of thunder words and the
notions they inspire do not provide us with an authoritative
statement of the poem's main ideas, of the poet's wisdom, or
even of some exotic guides to life, no longer common clichés
because derived from the alien cultural environment of India.
On the contrary, the thunder words provide only a reminder of
the contingency of language and the inauthenticity of interpretation.

Seen this way, the question of what the thunder said
is easily answered. The thunder said "da da da," equivalent in
English to "boom" or "kapow." Or to put it in other words, the
thunder did not say anything; it was only random noise. Certain
priests, like many literary critics, felt obliged to interpret that
noise. In the absence of meaning, they invented it. The poem's
dramatization of the way we delude ourselves into interpretation
leads directly into the notorious final stanza where we must risk
the same misplaced creativity that led Buddhist priests to insert
their own words into the sound descending from the sky.

The advantage of reading the thunder passage in this
way becomes clear when we see its effect on our understanding
of the final stanza. Its most directly important lines are:

*Most of this paper is taken from our book, *Reading* The Waste Land: *Modernism and the Limits of
Interpretation* (Amherst: U of Massachusetts P, 1990). A version was given at the National Poetry
Foundation's T. S. Eliot Centennial Conference, August 18-20, 1988, Orono, Maine.

> Shall I at least set my lands in order?

and

> These fragments I have shored against my ruins (CPP 69)

These lines signal a shift from the motifs of searching to a motif of pragmatic accommodation to circumstance. They have an effect like Candide's final answer to Pangloss: "Let us cultivate our garden." This may or may not be an allusion to Voltaire; be that as it may, there is without a doubt an analogous concluding shift of emphasis.

More important, the movement to pragmatics signals a rejection of both meaning and the varieties of guideline ideas generated by the Western interpreter(s) of the Sanskrit words. As a rejection of interpretation, the passage also suggests an abandonment of the perspectives required by the mythic method. Myth is a source of meaning, value, and order, a contrived perspective taken from Sir James George Frazer and Jessie L. Weston, which suggests transcendence to a position beyond all the positions within the world. That position is not real, because it cannot be said to exist, and is also not ideal, because it is by definition outside the possible realms of thought. All we have is the sense of movement toward an ever receding point from which to view the modern world in the poem--and the poem itself--as a unitive order. This is one reminder among many in the poem that order through perspective is only the familiar illusion of supposing that a galaxy is a single star because it is so far away that its internal diversity cannot be perceived. Here, in the final paragraph, the poem abandons the notion of perspectival order and moves toward a fragile conclusion.

To understand this point in a less abstract way, consider the opening lines.

> I sat upon the shore
> Fishing, with the arid plain behind me
> Shall I at least set my lands in order?

The speaker enacts a rejection of the quest by turning his back to the wasted land. There will be no more agonies in stony places, no more shadows, no more movements over psychic terrains of distress. His back is turned. Further, we can hardly fail to think of the speaker as some version of the Fisher King. When the impotent king of a barren land wonders--after the failure of the questing knight to arrive and prepare him for a ceremonial death to rejuvenate his realm--if he should at least set his lands in order, his message is clear beyond mistake. Now, he implies, I can only take care of myself. Kings are not metonymically one with their lands, so kings and subjects alike may go their separate ways, each responsible only for himself. If the Fisher King takes Candide's advice, his private cultivation, or setting in order, is a recognition that he is set free from the burden of being the king. From now on, it is every one for himself. Community no longer exists.

The speaker, then, moves toward a private rather than a communal order. His method involves using fragments of poetry to shore up his ruins. Removed from their contexts in various poems, and also from the contexts in which they conveyed some kind of meaning, the fragments are, from the speaker's point of view, virtually meaningless. They illustrate a position of exhaustion "after" meaning, a position of refuge not only free from surrounding ruins, but from the need to interpret, the compulsion to make sense of fragments. We must emphasize, however, that the fragments are after meaning only from the speaker's point of view. From an external position, that is, from the reader's point of view, these fragments are rich in meaning.

From the point of view of the exhausted Fisher King, the meaning of the fragments does not matter, and the order of the fragments is of no consequence. The fragments simply coexist. Thus, the fragment from *The Spanish Tragedy*, the three thunder words, and "Shantih" merely coexist with the other fragments. But from the reader's point of view, an obvious problem exists. The problem is related to the placement of the line, "These fragments I have shored against my ruins." It makes perfect sense to say "I will shore the following items against my ruins," and then go on to present an inventory of timbers, sandbags, and other props. But here the statement comes in the middle of the inventory. This is clearly more than the use of collage as an emergency procedure for preventing the collapse of ruins. Eliot's structure suggests some special complexity is at work here.

Another signal of complexity is the repetition of the word "shore." Eliot's original draft has the line, "These fragments I have spelt into my ruins," a line which alludes to the Sybil of Cumae, who prophesied by spelling messages into palm-leaves (WLF 81). Before showing the poem to Pound, Eliot revised the line, changing "spelt into" to "shored against." His original choice, actually, is fascinating. It means, for example, that the Sybil of Cumae was in the poem before Eliot put her in the epigraph and provides an argument that the Sybil is the controlling narrator. He could not have substituted "shored against" for "spelt into" thoughtlessly. And yet, he did make the substitution, causing the speaker to sit upon the shore and "shore" his fragments. Shore is thus a deliberate and striking repetition which makes a difference in the way the entire poem is read. As a noun, shore indicates the margin where land and sea meet, but as a verb, it denotes the effort to set things in order. The wordplay here has the effect of placing the process of setting things in order ("shoring") on a precarious margin (a "shore"). "Shore" and "shored against" join forces to place this final stanza squarely on a dividing line where no closure through choice of one side or the other can become a valid end of the reading process.

Eliot's purposes in this collection of concluding fragments can be clarified to some extent by looking at his manuscript. Most critics focus on Eliot's typed draft because it shows the extent to which he took Pound's advice on cutting. But the handwritten draft is much more important, because it shows crucial decisions Eliot made after the first writing but before typing it and showing it to Pound. In the handwritten draft, the line about using fragments to prevent ruin is followed only by the Sanskrit commands and benediction. But in Eliot's handwritten revision, one of the fragments, "Why then Ile fit you. Hieronymo's mad againe," is moved to its present position, *after* the statement of purpose for the fragments (WLF 89). This has the effect of positioning the statement of purpose in the midst of rather than at the end of the fragments and also of separating it from the solemn thunder words and the benediction.

This change provides a clue to what Eliot is doing in the concluding sequence. Hieronymo and his madness are plainly in conflict with the other quotations. All of the others can be interpreted in a positive way, but the reference to Hieronymo is a reference to unspeakable horror, to betrayal, revenge, madness, murder, and mutilation. Splitting it from the affirmative fragments and placing it after the statement about shoring ruins turns it into a counterstatement, a negation. If a nursery rhyme, Dante, the *Pervigilium Veneris*, and Gerard de Nerval are seen as shoring something up, *The Spanish Tragedy* can only be seen as tearing it down again. To test this possible reading, let us consider what, if anything, the fragments have in common. This project involves re-inserting the fragments backward into their contexts in the works from which they were taken, and thus backward into the realm of meaning. In this undertaking, we are doing precisely what the internal speaker, who has reached a state of passive accommodation, appears not to want. As readers, however, we must go forward. The poem gives us no other choice.

In one way or another, all of the concluding fragments have to do with song and poetry, with singing that persists through and transforms disaster. The first fragment--"London Bridge is falling down falling down falling down"--is a refrain from a children's song, a line paradoxically associated with fun and games. The line provides an example of the metamorphosis of catastrophe into innocent and mindless art. The second fragment, in Italian, is one of Eliot's favorite lines from the *Purgatorio*. It refers to Arnaut Daniel's joyous purgatorial suffering and can be translated, "Then he dived back into the refining fire." Just before he leaps, he describes himself as one who goes singing. This fragment also has to do with the transformation of suffering into music. The next line contains two fragments, both having to do with transformation, suffering and music. The first, which can be translated, "When shall I be as the swallow?" is from an ancient Latin poem and the second "O swallow swallow" is from poems by both Tennyson and Swinburne. As Eliot points out in his note, this line alludes to Philomela's rape and torture and her consequent transformation into the nightingale, a story alluded to several times in *The Waste Land*. The next fragment, from Nerval's sonnet "El Desdichado," can be translated "The prince of Aquitaine, to the ruined tower." The poem is about a disinherited prince who turns his desolation into the music of poetry. These fragments have in common the motif of singing which persists through loss and transforms disaster into art. They are followed by the statement that they are being used to shore up the ruins of the narrator, another disinherited and desolate figure trying to use remnants as building blocks for art.

A closer look at the fragments reveals that they are carefully presented in symmetrically opposed pairs. A children's song is matched--or answered--by a description of a poet hiding himself in the refining fire after urging us to be ever mindful of his pain. The symmetry appears when we see that the first fragment is a voice from earliest childhood, while the second refers to a condition after death. Further, "London Bridge is falling down falling down falling down" uses the conventions of poetic repetition and rhythm to divert attention from the song's plain meaning. Countless people know that line without it ever occurring to them that it says something horrendous. The old lullaby "Rockaby Baby in the Tree Top" is an identical example. The song goes on to sing cheerfully and soothingly about a disaster, "When the wind blows, the cradle will rock. / When the bough breaks, the cradle will fall. / Down will come baby, cradle and all." These nursery songs are part of experience before consciousness of meaning, that is, before experience is filtered through the mind, before interpretation. In symmetrical contrast, the song of the poet leaping into the purgative fire is part of experience which comes after meaning, after surrendering interpretations and indeed after having sung his final, meaning-charged song, "Now I pray you, be ever mindful of my pain." This line is as clearly after meaning--and after life--as the children's song is before meaning and awareness of catastrophe.

The second set of fragments is designed as an equivalent symmetry. In the passage from the anonymous Latin "Vigil of Venus," a poet in springtime laments that, unlike the squawking swans and the singing swallow, he cannot find his voice and cannot sing. He then asks when his spring will come, "When will I be as the swallow and my silence cease?" By contrast, the troubador from Aquitaine, province of great singers, merely stands before the ruined tower and remembers all that has been and is no more. Springtime, the beginning, is balanced by the ruined tower, the end of a tradition. The contrast between before and after meaning is continued in the single short fragment "O swallow swallow." It alludes to a poem by Tennyson in which a poet laments his inability to fly to his beloved with a song of love and instructs the swallow to go for him. It also alludes to a poem about Philomela and Procne by Swinburne, a poem in which the nightingale chides her sister, the swallow, for singing in ignorance of the grief which should make her tongue cleave to the roof of her mouth, "the small slain body, the flower-like face" of her first-born child. Instead of grieving, the swallow sings through a thousand springs and summers, and even in winter, flies south and continues her song. The Tennyson swallow is before meaning and the Swinburne swallow is after meaning. The nightingale with her consciousness of wrong and her song of grief is caught in the middle; unable to let go of meaning, she is forced continually to interpret her experience. The five fragments are poised against one another in precarious equilibrium.

Seen in these ways, the first fragments really do illustrate a shoring up process. They affirm order and art as potent answers to collapse, pain, depression, and even the dissolution of a tradition of order and art. If *The Waste Land* had ended with "These fragments I have shored against my ruins," we could have read a final message to the effect that poetry can act as a saving consolation in times of hopelessness. Matthew Arnold's statement that poetry is capable of saving us would prevail. But that is not the way the poem ends. The mocking words from *The Spanish Tragedy* intrude and destroy any notion that salvation is available through art. They negate even a temporary shoring up of ruins through art. Their placement, a deliberate choice by Eliot, clearly contradicts the implications provided by the first fragments. "Why then Ile fit you. Hieronymo's mad againe" contains its own implications about the function and possible uses of art. Hieronymo has a play performed for his enemies in order to entrap them and carry out his bloody revenge. His poetic and dramatic efforts culminate in a scene in which he avoids speech under torture by biting off his tongue and spitting it at his captors. The Philomela myth is part of the web of allusions here, for Hieronymo does to himself what King Tereus did to Philomela. The result of the first mutilation is the use of terrible wrong in the service of music, but the result of the second--Hieronymo's--is the use of poetry in the service of madness and silence.

So much for redemption through art. All solutions, all affirmations generate their formal opposites. The poem ends on the margin between secular hope and secular damnation, between order and madness. On that margin, that shored-up shore, "*Datta, Dayadhvam, Damyata*" return as mere shells of signifiers. They are stripped of their gloss, their ambitions toward being guides, like poetry, to life. The appropriate end is the repeated benediction, "Shantih shantih shantih." It is only because peace is out of the question on this precarious margin that peace must be stated. Understanding has brought us to a margin between minimal affirmation and maximal calamity, so the only peace thinkable is that which passes, transcends, understanding.

We can now take a look from the perspective of its ending at the entire poem. "These fragments I have shored against my ruins" can be understood to refer to all of *The Waste Land*, all its methods, all its directions of suggestion. Its cast of characters can be seen as fragments of a whole population, but they can also be seen as unique, isolated persons. The reading process has instructed us in how to see them, and the primary instruction is that we are not to see them in any single way that is available to us. They are at once parts of a whole and wholes in themselves. Similarly, its array of methods, techniques, and styles, along with its differing languages and variations on interpretation as action, must be seen as parts and as isolated moments of expression.

The traditional term in rhetoric that best describes the poem's method is parataxis. Simply stated, parataxis is the absence of transitions. A simple inventory of persons and perspectives is paratactic. In ordinary texts, relative importance is stated through the use of subordinating connectors, but these along with other transitions have been omitted. It seems plain that they have been omitted because they do not exist in the world. They are among the amenities demanded by language. Our medium of expression and description makes these transitions available, and convention requires their use. That medium, language, thus pushes us toward a coherence that does not exist in the world, a syntax that we desire because we want the subjects of discourse to have forms like the codes we use in stating such discourses. *The Waste Land* has succeeded in resisting the temptation to insert the coherence of language into the panoramas of myth, history, and modern urban crowds, despite its medium's pressure to do so. Like *Ulysses* and *The Cantos*, *The Waste Land* remains triumphantly paratactic, and that is the hallmark of its modernism.

LOUIS L. MARTZ

ASH-WEDNESDAY: *VOICES FOR THE VEILED SISTER*

I have been reading *Ash-Wednesday* in the edition of 1930, dedicated "To my Wife," a dedication that gives particular poignancy
to the well-known echo of Cavalcanti's lament for his separation
by exile from his beloved lady:

> Because I do not hope to turn again
> Because I do not hope
> Because I do not hope to turn
> Desiring this man's gift and that man's scope   (CPP 60)

But Shakespeare's line reads "Desiring this man's *art*." Eliot is
not limiting the lost desire to art; *gift* is a larger word: it includes
the gift of poetical creation, along with the gift of religious grace
and the gift of human love--that "power of the usual reign" that
most men and women seem to possess, even though it may be
"the infirm glory of the positive hour" or "the one veritable
transitory power" (CPP 60). For this speaker the gifts of love
and grace and poetry seem to have vanished, for he feels that he
has lost the power to "drink / There, where trees flower, and
springs flow." He has lost touch with the things of earth and
therefore feels that "place is always and only place" without the
resonance of memory and the delight of sensory response.
Therefore, he chooses to renounce "the blessèd face" that lovers
such as Cavalcanti and Dante and Petrarch saw in their beloved
Ladies. And he renounces too the voice of the beloved, along
with the voice of the prophet that had sounded so strongly as the
dominant voice of *The Waste Land* (after Pound had performed
his drastic excisions in such a way as to allow that voice to domi-
nate): the voice that cried "Son of man," like Ezekiel, the voice
that cried so insistently, "HURRY UP PLEASE ITS TIME," the voice
of "I Tiresias" who "foresuffered all / Enacted on this same
divan or bed," the voices of Buddha and Augustine, the voice
that, like St. Paul, addresses "Gentile or Jew" and warns,
"Consider Phlebas, who was once handsome and tall as you,"
and finally, transcending all, the voice of the Thunder, com-

manding, "Da / *Datta*", "Da / *Dayadhvam*", "Da / *Damyata*"
(CPP 41, 44, 47, 49).

All these powerful voices are renounced in this dry
voice of penitence and self-analysis:

> And I pray that I may forget
> These matters that with myself I too much discuss
> Too much explain   (CPP 61)

What those matters have been, at their worst, we may see by
reading the excised Fresca passage of *The Waste Land*, or the
truly horrifying "Ode: To you particularly, and to all the Vols-
cians, Great hurt and mischief"--a poem of sexual self-laceration
that appeared only in *Ara Vos Prec* (1920). *Ash-Wednesday* is, in
part, an act of contrition and amendment for such thoughts as
these.

> Because I do not hope to turn again
> Let these words answer
> For what is done, not to be done again
> May the judgement not be too heavy upon us

--upon *us*. In this context the prayer does not sound general: it is
intimate, personal, *us*, the two of us. But at the close of this section the prayer becomes more general, echoing the liturgy of the
Virgin:

> Pray for us sinners now and at the hour of our death
> Pray for us now and at the hour of our death.

One may wonder why Eliot, recently converted to the
Church of England, should so insistently in this poem echo the
Roman liturgy rather than the Book of Common Prayer. But
this choice is not ecclesiastical: it is thematic and poetical, a part
of the decorum created by the love-poetry of Cavalcanti, Dante,
and Petrarch. One may think of Petrarch's words in the final
poem of his sequence to his beloved, a hymn to the Virgin:

> Tre dolci et cari nomi ài in te raccolti,
> madre, figluola et sposa
> donna del Re ché nostri lacci à sciolti
> et fatto 'l mondo libero et felice. . . .

> You have gathered into yourself three sweet names: mother,
> daughter, and bride, O glorious Virgin, Lady of that King who has
> loosed our bonds and made the world free and happy. . . . (578-79)

donna del Re. The Lady now addressed in the first word of the
next poem in Eliot's sequence is primarily the Lady of this King
--but of course she includes, after the manner of the *dolce stil*

nuovo, the beloved earthly lady, transfigured. It is to this composite Lady, then, that the "dissembled" speaker tells here, indeed, celebrates here, the story of his redemption. For the three white leopards are the agents of grace who bring to the speaker the message of God, as it came to despairing Elijah "under a juniper-tree," and as it came, in a different way, to Adam and Eve after the Fall "in the cool of the day" (CPP 61). What he hears now is a voice that he has just renounced--the voice of the prophet Ezekiel, repeating the words of the Lord that came to him in the valley of dry bones: "God said / Shall these bones live? shall these / Bones live? / .... And God said / Prophesy to the wind"--words that evoke the redemptive message of Ezekiel (CPP 61-62):

> Prophesy unto the wind, prophesy, son of man, and say to the wind, Thus saith the Lord God; Come from the four winds, O breath, and breathe upon these slain, that they may live. So I prophesied as he commanded me, and the breath came into them, and they lived, and stood up upon their feet, an exceeding great army. (Ezek. 37.9-10)

Eliot's lines, however, continue with words that imply a state of doubt: "Prophesy to the wind, to the wind only for only / The wind will listen" (CPP 62). But the bones seem to know more, for they now sing ("chirping") a long litany to the "Lady of silences":

> Terminate torment
> Of love unsatisfied
> The greater torment
> Of love satisfied . . .
> Grace to the Mother
> For the Garden
> Where all love ends.

The conclusion of this section alludes to the later words of Ezekiel: "This is the land which ye / Shall divide by lot" (see Ezek. 47.22). The desert setting may seem to give an ironical twist to the prophet's words as Eliot adds: "This is the land. We have our inheritance" (CPP 63). Yet this conclusion is subtly optimistic, for the words from the forty-seventh chapter of Ezekiel are preceded by the long and lyrical description of the bountiful and fertilizing river:

> And by the river upon the bank thereof, on this side and on that side, shall grow all trees for meat, whose leaf shall not fade, neither shall the fruit thereof be consumed: it shall bring forth new fruit according to his months, because their waters they issued out

> of the sanctuary: and the fruit thereof shall be for meat, and the
> leaf thereof for medicine. (Ezek. 47.12)

The witty word-play on "dissembled" and "burden," the "bright-
ness" and singing of the bones, the bland, serene enumeration of
what might have been the macabre details of physical disintegra-
tion--all combine to support the optimistic tone. These bones
will live and the desert will bloom like a garden. It is a land of
promise.

The second poem in the sequence thus foretells the
goal and progress of the entire group--an interpretation helped
by the title and epigraph that Eliot gave this section at its separate publication in 1927: "Salutation. *e vo significando.*" The epigraph points to the passage in the twenty-fourth canto of the
Purgatorio where Dante acknowledges himself as author of *le
nove rime* beginning "Donne ch'avete intelletto d'amore"--
"Ladies that have understanding of love" (261). This is the
opening line of the canzone (19) that marks the turning-point of
the *Vita Nuova*: the turning away from sickly yearnings of the
physical self for the physical lady, and a turning toward the celebration of her redeeming virtue, her heavenly quality:

> My lady is desired in highest Heaven.
>   Now let me tell you something of her power.
>   . . . if she finds one worthy to behold her,
>   that man will feel her power for salvation
>   when she accords to him her salutation
>   [ché li avvien, ciò che li dona, in salute]
>   which humbles him till he forgets all wrongs. (32-33)

In the *Purgatorio* Dante tacitly accepts and explains the newness
of *le nove rime* by saying: "I am one who, when Love inspires me,
takes note, and goes setting it forth [*vo significando*] after the
fashion which he [Love] dictates within me." One may wish that
Eliot had preserved the early heading for this second section,
since it implies that, for the speaker, a turning point is being celebrated, a turning that, as with Dante, marks the regeneration of
the poetic voice and the regeneration of the self.

Section 2, in its proleptic action, thus intermingles
past, present, and future: memory, present resolution, and the
recovery to come. Section 3 is almost wholly memory: of temptations and distractions overcome, especially the distractions
offered by sensuous landscape, sensuous music, and sexual love:

> Blown hair is sweet, brown hair over the mouth blown,
> Lilac and brown hair;
> Distraction, music of the flute, stops and steps of the mind over the
>   third stair,

> Fading, fading; strength beyond hope and despair
> Climbing the third stair. (CPP 63)

These are distractions overcome by the faith demonstrated in the closing lines that echo again the Roman liturgy, with the words of the faithful centurion to Christ (Matt. 8.5-10):

> Lord, I am not worthy
> Lord, I am not worthy
>
> but speak the word only. (CPP 63)

The speaker no longer renounces the desire to hear the voice: he prays for the healing word to be spoken.

In section 4 the healing word comes, mysteriously, "The token of the word unheard, unspoken." It is unspoken by the Lady

> Who walked between the violet and the violet
> Who walked between
> The various ranks of varied green
> Going in white and blue, in Mary's colour, . . .
> Who then made strong the fountains and made fresh the springs
> (CPP 64)

Religious and poetic inspiration are mingled in the presence of this Lady who, like another Beatrice or Laura, wears "[W]hite light folded, sheathed about her, folded."

> The new years walk, restoring . . .
> With a new verse the ancient rhyme. Redeem
> The time. (CPP 64)

It seems inevitable that one should be mindful ("*Sovegna vos*") that in the fifth chapter of Ephesians, where St. Paul speaks of "Redeeming the time, because the days are evil," these words are followed by the verses traditionally taken as a justification for writing religious poetry: "be filled with the Spirit; Speaking to yourselves in psalms and hymns and spiritual songs, singing and making melody in your heart to the Lord." And then this passage is immediately followed by Paul's lengthy advice about the proper relationship between husbands and wives. Not only does he give the now (and perhaps then) unpopular advice: "Wives, submit yourselves unto your own husbands, as unto the Lord;" he follows this with the much longer and much more eloquent advice: "Husbands, love your wives, even as Christ also loved the church. . . . So ought men to love their wives as their own bodies. He that loveth his wife loveth himself." In a poem dedicated "To my Wife" I do not see how this context can be forgotten.

But if we hear these marginal grace-notes, what do they mean? The "new verse" (*le nove rime*) of religious song is a way of redeeming the time when a failure in love threatens the vital center of being. The speaker here is seeking, in Stevens' terms, the One of Fictive Music who can give back the imagination that he spurned and craves. By following in the mode of ancient rhyme where the "*bella donna*" became the "Lady of all grace," the speaker here has found a way of creating what modern theory would call a "textual self," a fictional self that can transcend the absence of the beloved, as Cavalcanti did at the close of his Ballata, when he cried out to his poem (in Ezra Pound's translation):

> O smothered voice and weak that tak'st the road
> Out from the weeping heart and dolorous,
> Go, crying out my shatter'd mind's alarm,
> Forth with my soul and this song piteous
> Until thou find a lady of such charm,
> So sweetly intelligent
> That e'en thy sorrow is spent. (123)

A complex of all these things is happening here, for now the veiled lady, fictive image of the higher dream, gives her silent word that seems to be the sign of acceptance, understanding, forgiveness, and renewal:

> The silent sister veiled in white and blue
> Between the yews, behind the garden god,
> Whose flute is breathless, bent her head and signed but spoke no word
>
> But the fountain sprang up and the bird sang down
> Redeem the time, redeem the dream
> The token of the word unheard, unspoken. . . . (CPP 64)

I find no problem in moving out from the final words of this part, "And after this our exile," into the chatter and the clatter of the whirling world in section 5. For the speaker's exile from the things of earth has ended. Redeem the time because the days are evil. Such concern for the evils of the world, for those who walk in darkness, is a normal movement in the religious life: from contemplation to action, or the thought of action. It is a sign of returning health, returning wholeness. Section 5 is a prayer for all of humanity, not only for the self. The voice of the prophet, "O my people, what have I done unto thee," returns to still for a moment the whirl and the clatter of modern rhyming.

And so, finally, in section 6, comes the reluctant recognition that things of the world, things of the flesh, things of the earth are not necessarily distractions:

> Although I do not hope to turn again
> Although I do not hope
> Although I do not hope to turn   (CPP 66)

the self is already turning, has been turning since the second section dramatized the song of the bones. And now, although he feels it is a backward step, a sign of weakness, and "though I do not wish to wish these things,"

> From the wide window towards the granite shore
> The white sails still fly seaward, seaward flying
> Unbroken wings

This is imagery of release: the wide window looks out towards the granite shore (of New England) and beyond the shore he sees the sails in liberated action, flying seaward. And soon his heart rejoices in what he had thought were "the lost lilac and the lost sea voices"

> And the weak spirit quickens to rebel
> For the bent golden-rod and the lost sea smell
> Quickens to recover
> The cry of quail and the whirling plover

The whirling plover is part of the unstilled world that "whirled / About the centre of the silent Word" in the previous section; but now the rhyming is not a senseless clatter. This is not weakness, it is not rebellion, it is a natural movement in which the redeemed spirit quickens to recover its love of human life. The speaker misapprehends the action of grace upon his whole being, thinks these revived responses to the things of earth are "empty forms between the ivory gates" of a false dream-world-- nevertheless the process of recovery continues: "And smell renews the salt savour of the sandy earth."

All this is very close to the feeling and attitude conveyed by Dante at the end of the twenty-fourth canto of his *Purgatorio*:

> And as, heralding the dawn, the breeze of May stirs and smells sweet, all impregnate with grass and with flowers, such a wind I felt strike full on my brow, and right well I felt the pinions move, which wafted ambrosial fragrance to my senses; and I heard say, "Blessed are they who are so illumined by grace that the love of taste kindles not too great desire in their breasts, and who hunger always so far as is just." (267)

The senses, then, have their just and proper place in human experience. So Eliot concludes:

> And even among these rocks
> Sister, mother
> And spirit of the river, spirit of the sea,
> Suffer me not to be separated
>
> And let my cry come unto Thee. (CPP 67)

By thus truncating the traditional cry, "Suffer me not to be separated from thee," Eliot has created a peculiar effect--a plea not to be separated from the love of woman, not to be separated from love of the river and the sea and the lilac, the golden-rod, the cry of quail, the sea smell, the salt savor of the sandy earth: all the things and beings of earth that make the whole man live and make poetry possible.

But in one respect, at least, the plea could not be answered. In 1936 Eliot removed the dedication to this poem. But we can, and we should, restore it.

WORKS CITED

Dante. *Dante's Vita Nuova*. Trans. Mark Musa. Bloomington: Indiana UP, 1973.
_____. *The Divine Comedy*. Trans. Charles S. Singleton. Princeton: Princeton UP, 1970-75.
Petrarch, Francesco. *Petrarch's Lyric Poems*. Trans. Robert M. Durling. Cambridge: Harvard UP, 1976.
Pound, Ezra. *Translations*. New York: New Directions, 1963.

BARBARA EVERETT

EAST COKER: *THE VILLAGE OF THE HEART**

Two things stand out in Eliot's *East Coker*. One is the intensity with which the image of an English village is created. The other is the energy with which that image is dispelled. The relation between these two things is neither accidental nor willful, but a part of the meaning of the poem: a part even of the poem's title, though it may sound merely topographical. Eliot called his poem *East Coker*, which we now know to be the name of the village in Somerset from which his seventeenth-century ancestor had emigrated to America; almost three hundred years later, on an August afternoon in the later 1930s, Eliot himself visited it.

In this naming of his poem he was following a pattern set five years earlier, when he had given to a poem the name of a house in Gloucestershire, *Burnt Norton*, similarly visited by the poet and a friend. And both these titles are as simple and assured as if the poet were alluding to places all travelled people knew; as indeed many people do know of them now, since Eliot wrote of them. But when the poems first appeared, the places were of an obscurity almost ideal. Every one of them might as well have been where the poet gravely locates Little Gidding, "behind the pig-sty" (CPP 139). The titles are in fact almost a way of saying that the places where people truly meet-- as people do meet in reading a poem--are the places where they find out what it is they do not know. They meet in a sense of limits, an acknowledgment of ends--as the dead in a country churchyard may be found on "old stones that cannot be deciphered" (CPP 129).

A character in *The Family Reunion*, the play that is Eliot's last major work before *East Coker* (and he wrote it just after visiting the real East Coker) says, "Meeting is for strangers," which perhaps means something like, "Maps are for aliens"; in much the same way, place-name titles in modernist

*This article was first delivered as a B.B.C. Third Programme broadcast in 1982. We are grateful for the B.B.C.'s permission to publish it.

poems may sometimes only sign-post a sad or ironic sense, bringing poet and reader together, of just where we are *not* (CPP 279).

The Family Reunion is about the fact that a young Englishman has to come home after long absence to his family's country house to find out just why he cannot stay there: why it would be wrong for him to inherit again the wrong past there, to marry again the wrong dream there, or to become again the wrong person there. The title of *The Family Reunion* is para-doxical, because it is less about a reunion than about an exodus: Harry comes home to find out how to depart. Similarly *East Coker* is about a homecoming; and also about how to see a dream-place clearly enough to be able to leave it, though that is not the same as failing to care for it.

If you are reading *East Coker*, you haven't gone far in it before you come across a

> deep lane
> Shuttered with branches, dark in the afternoon,
> Where you lean against a bank while a van passes,
> And the deep lane insists on the direction
> Into the village, in the electric heat
> Hypnotised. In a warm haze the sultry light
> Is absorbed, not refracted, by grey stone.
> The dahlias sleep in the empty silence.
> Wait for the early owl. (CPP 123)

The poem then imagines the fields outside the village on mid-summer-eve, with the courting couples going through the ancient ceremony, as they did in Tudor times, of leaping through the flames of midsummer-eve bonfires: images that fade with the light of dawn, as the in fact long dead and gone lovers crum-ble in the earth that holds them. Later on in the poem it is said that the sea--the estranging, isolating sea--has swallowed the houses, and the hill covered the dancers. At the end of the poem there is the glimpse of "old stones that cannot be deciphered," as it might be in the churchyard of *East Coker* (CPP 129). And that is all we ever see of the village of East Coker. And yet the image of it in the poem named after the place in Somerset has an enormous, spell-binding potency hardly to be explained by geographical associations. Eliot himself explains the power of the image he has called up in terms of enchantment, of magic presences true "[i]f you do not come too close" (CPP 123).

One way of preserving a proper distance, of finding that detachment from experience which the poet seems to be asking for here, is to stress to oneself how little in fact one sees of East Coker in the poem. Not only do we not stay there: we hardly do more than *arrive* at the village. Turning aside before we see more than light absorbed by stone, and late summer flowers floating on "empty silence" as if on water that is not there (CPP 123), we encounter a poetry not so much of East Coker as of arriving there--indeed a poetry simply of arriving, of coming this way (as Eliot says later),

> Taking any route, starting from anywhere,
> At any time or at any season, . . . (CPP 139)

The French Symbolists invented a "poetry of departures"; Eliot's is a poetry of arrivals, of beginnings. But this is so, in a special sense. The poem's *East Coker*, the poet's image of a village, stirs us deeply because it is a precise image of the place we think we want to get to, and particularly of the place we want to get back to, a beginning and an end: an image of *home*. Eliot has set down a quasi-topographical outline of a lane turning into an English village street; and this brief passage, as if it might be a photograph caught in late summer afternoon sunlight, has the power to make a reader find the place long lived in, known once intimately, and missed ever after leaving. And this is because in describing a direction, Eliot describes inward direction--the human longing to move, to arrive, to be securely "there."

He discovers in short in a recollected experience the lineaments of profound and even naked human feeling; and this is why the entry into East Coker, in the poem, is the beginning of a dream. Light "falls," the lane is "shuttered," you "lean," the lane "insists," "hypnotised" "in the electric heat"; light is "absorbed," dahlias "sleep," and we wait for that most local of dangerous birds, the owl, to glide exhilaratingly over on silent wings (CPP 123). It must be obvious that the landscape we travel through here is to some extent a *paysage moralisé*, or that--to put it another way--the poet's analysis of the human hunger for some "long home" discovers as one of its components something very like the simple experience of falling in love. It is still often assumed that Eliot is a cold poet, who has little to say of love. But *Burnt Norton* and *East Coker* are two of the most distinguished of modern love poems. Their subtle intimations of romantic and erotic experience are--it is true--haunted and melancholy; but most of the best English love poetry is sad.

In *Burnt Norton* love is the most private of experiences; a haunting in a secret garden outside a shuttered house whose owner is unknown and insignificant; and the obscure style of the poem intensifies this reticence. But for love in *East Coker* the poet finds the image of a village set in a whole historic past. There is a clear difference between the medium of *Burnt Norton* and that of *East Coker*, a difference not wholly explained by the mere fact that writing plays for actors has taught Eliot a more extroverted speech. Five years have surely brought other and greater changes in helping to do what Dryden called "moving the sleeping images of things towards the light." For though *East Coker* is still a reflective and essentially solitary work, its address is all the same perceptibly more public, its style clearer, tougher, more humorous. *East Coker* was written in 1940, towards the end of the first winter of the Second World War, during that early period of pause and uncertainty before the Battle of Britain began. It was the eruption of war, frustrating the poet's hope of continuing his career as a stage dramatist, that made him turn back to the poem with which he had closed his 1935 collection, the finely inward and barely articulate *Burnt Norton*, and begin another on the same pattern. Eliot has recorded the profound crisis and shock the coming of a second world war brought to him, as to other men: but that crisis and shock had evidently a creative side that is visible in the poem he began to write then--and not only in it but in the two further *Quartets* which the writing of *East Coker* generated.

   To put it simply, the real threat of England's defeat, and the possibility that civilised Europe would now be overthrown, seems to have brought a peculiar clarification to all Eliot's more inward struggles. All his life he had been in some sense involved with a belief in "lost causes," a belief in the savingness, as it were, of not winning as the world wins. Now suddenly England itself, at this stage of the war helplessly unarmed and hopelessly outnumbered, seemed liable to become a rather actual lost cause. And this fact seems to have brought a peculiar new pressure of the public into Eliot's formerly private poetry: a kind of release and definition and decision, a sense of being at last free from solitude, in company.

   The poet says of his garden in *Burnt Norton*, "But I cannot say where"--and means it (CPP 119). The village in *East Coker*, though a dream, has decidedly more substance--indeed the whole poem has a new substance, a kind of solid earthy radiance. It is to the point that the poet's own ashes have now, by his own direction, found their way to what another poet, the Biblical Ecclesiastes, calls their "long home" in the church at East Coker. For despite all its strong distinctions and ironies, this could be called Eliot's most "English" poem. Even its literary sources are especially English (where the dominant influences of

Burnt Norton are, in my opinion, French, and of *The Dry Salvages*, American). But to Blake and Clough in *East Coker* we might I think add the voice of Eliot's friend and almost protégé, Auden, the leading English poet of his generation: for it is to Auden's invention of what he called "the village of the heart" that Eliot is indebted for his iconography of *East Coker*, and especially to the play Auden wrote with Isherwood, *The Dog Beneath the Skin*: "We would show you at first an English village: You shall choose its location, / Wherever your heart directs you most longingly to look; you are loving towards it ..." (Auden 191). Auden himself is perhaps only mediating what appears to be a great theme in English writing in the 1920s and 30s, the dream of what might be called ironically (as ironically or questioningly as it was often treated by the more sophisticated writers)--the dream of "England, Home and Beauty."

But this friendly debt to English writers--who had, of course, learned from Eliot in their turn--is only a technical manifestation of what more vitally existed within Eliot himself. The deep but questioning relationship with England, the whole stirred and critical analysis of the sense of "patria," of "Home," of what precisely such loyalty consisted in--this is an issue of peculiar importance to the poet of *East Coker*, and consequently to the *Quartets* that followed it. Eliot said very little publicly about his family background or early years, but one thing he did stress was his family's unrootedness in America, their never quite belonging either in the industrial Southwest or on the Eastern seaboard. This sense of unrootedness cannot have been diminished by the poet's own half-accidental translation to England when he married and, caught by the First World War, began to make his home here; and the final dissolution of that bitterly unhappy marriage must have left Eliot, from the mid-1930s on, something of an authority on dislocation. It is interesting that the third quartet reaches back in memories to those East Coast holidays spent in childhood with his family; and that the other three quartets all take their titles and primary images from places merely visited, and complex moments of happiness briefly experienced, on those weekends after his work in London when friends and acquaintances seem to have offered the wandering poet hospitality in his homelessness.

Near the end of *East Coker* Eliot recalls the "evening under lamplight" in a domestic, probably childhood context (CPP 129): and the image is borrowed, I think, from the first stanza of Baudelaire's great poem, "Le Voyage," which contrasts the splendor and scale of this world in the "lamplight" of a child's hopes as he pours over maps and picture-books, with its diminution in the adult eyes of memory:

> Ah! que le monde est grand à la clarté des lampes!
> Aux yeux de souvenir que le monde est petit!

Both experience and principle fuse to make Eliot subject his "village of the heart" to a fierce scrutiny, so that it becomes at once nobly and newly substantial, *and* also a shadow, a dream to be awoken from. To Baudelaire, death is the only end to journeys; we love *East Coker*, so the Christian poet of the *Quartets* argues, precisely because we have what St. Paul called "no continuing city." Home is a place to leave; "[h]ome is where one starts from" (CPP 129); the truest loyalty, the truest attachment contains (in the language of the last quartet) its own "detachment" and "indifference" (CPP 142). This results in the peculiar nature of *East Coker* itself, where a profound romantic depth and nostalgia go hand in hand with a continuous and exhilarating energy of attack, a kind of continual moral comedy of effective dispersal. Every "beginning" is an end, every "end" a beginning.

With the start of the second section the poet impassively translates the whole vision of East Coker, the universal hunger for the secure enchantment of the past, into something like the coming of late love to a senile romantic, converts that sentimentality into a dead rhetoric and calmly dismisses *that* as "not very satisfactory"--as indeed it is not (CPP 125). With the third he gathers up this fusion of worldly love, success and rhetoric--houses "rising and falling"--into a great dance of death, "They all go into the dark" (CPP 126)--and then collapses that as well:

> You say I am repeating
> Something I have said before. (CPP 127)

And collapses that:

> I shall say it again.

And that:

> Shall I say it again?

In the fourth and fifth, every cause for thinking that there is any depth in the idea that "we are sound substantial flesh and blood" (CPP 128) is (in the words of "Marina") "become unsubstantial, reduced," collapsed, capsized--even in the end of the illusion that there is such a thing as "art" itself (CPP 72). There is only one

fight to recover what has been lost
And found and lost again and again: and now, under conditions
That seem unpropitious. (CPP 128)

It is in fact this process of absolute undermining which gives the poem, dark and quiet as it is, its curious exhilarating energy, as of a procedure of spiritual trampolining. The great art (it seems to say) is to find balance where the ground is from every angle unstable; and balance is really just the knack of learning to fall well, and of knowing when one is down. "Humility is endless" (CPP 126). In short all these technical gymnastics, brilliant as they are, all these continual changes of style and substance that make reading the poem like a process of falling through a kaleidoscope, make sense because they subserve an evident and even simple human meaning, a learning to lose in order to find. Not the main object of this losing and finding, but something incidental to it, is the discovery of the sense of some real poetic self--some more largely human self. Almost the best moment, for me, in the poem, and one of the best in all Eliot's work, is the steady shock of surprise as at the beginning of the last movement a quiet voice suddenly says: "So here I am . . ." (CPP 128). The "I" thus finds itself at last, "in the middle" of "[t]wenty years largely wasted, the years of *l'entre deux guerres*--. . . ."

Between two wars: and the power of the poem-- which is in many ways my favorite among the *Quartets*--lies in its quiet existence "between wars": the extraordinary equipoise it holds between warring opposites, as the destruction of the image is the creation of the fidelity. And yet these opposites are also reconciled from the beginning. The creation of the "village of the heart" lies within exact limits of self-knowledge: it is the village and the lane which are "hypnotised," and not the traveller. And similarly what is in theory "destruction" has in Eliot an extreme potency, a creativeness. Four of the best lines that Eliot ever wrote describe the coming of the dawn that takes away the dream of East Coker; and this dissolution at the end of the poem's first movement contains in itself an enormous enfranchisement, an awakening that prophesies a deeper human need than security, and even opens the poem's end to the beginning of the next quartet:

Dawn points, and another day
Prepares for heat and silence. Out at sea the dawn wind
Wrinkles and slides. I am here
Or there, or elsewhere. In my beginning. (CPP 124)

WORKS CITED

Auden, W. H., Christopher Isherwood. *The Dog Beneath the Skin*. Princeton:
    Princeton UP, 1988. *Plays and Other Dramatic Writings by W. H. Auden*.
    Ed. Edward Mendelson.

CLEO McNELLY KEARNS

DOCTRINE AND WISDOM IN FOUR QUARTETS

No modern poet is so anthologized in collections of devotional and religious verse as T. S. Eliot, and no poet would have been more ambivalent about this mode of reception. This response is not one Eliot actively solicited for his work, nor one to which his poetry is always as conveniently suited as it may appear. The ambiguity ancient and well-preserved monuments represent, at once occasions of living worship and testaments to a desire to fetishize as past what we cannot quite assent to as present, often attends as well a devotional use of Eliot's work. Hence his poems function uneasily, if at all, as a kind of modern day simulacrum of the kind of traditional religious and inspirational art to which they are so often compared.

Eliot was, I would argue, fully aware of this slight disjuncture between his poetry and that of other, less secular, cultures and times. Rather than waste energy in deploring it, however, he made of it part of the substance of his reflections. He thus contributed far more than a mere lesson in nostalgia to the religious sensibility of his time. The poems of his Christian period are in this respect at once devotional and modern not only in the literary, but in the religious senses of the term. While clearly designed to evoke more than a merely aesthetic reponse, they are at the same time fully reflective of that essential relativizing and reformulating of Christian tradition which stemmed, at the end of the nineteenth century and the beginning of the twentieth, from a greater knowledge of other faiths, from Biblical criticism, and from the rise of science. (The term *modern* in this context refers, of course, specifically, to the efforts in and around the Roman Catholic church to open its teaching to the insights of the new Biblical scholarship. Baron von Hügel, whose thought so attracted and repelled Yeats, was perhaps its best-known Roman Catholic exponent, one of the few moderates to survive the repressive reaction. Eliot himself sometimes made use of the term in this sense. See for instance his syllabus for a

course of lectures given to adult students in London reprinted in
A. D. Moody's *T. S. Eliot, Poet* [124].)

Some such modern stance was widely felt, in Eliot's
day, to be the necessary consequence, both for Roman Catholics
and for Protestants, of three major factors: the rediscovery of
other, notably Eastern, religious and spiritual traditions; the
entirely new view of Christian history and of Biblical truth
required by the development of the Higher Criticism in Germany, with its emphasis on the role of changing interpretation in
constituting the Christian community; and the need to formulate
a non-defensive and intellectually respectable response to the
growing prestige of science. Eliot's interest in all of these fields
of inquiry is evident from his graduate school papers and from
the numerous reviews he wrote for the *International Journal of
Ethics* and other learned periodicals in his early years, reviews
which touched often on the issues raised for religious faith by
science, psychology, anthropology and sociology, as well as by
philosophy and comparative religion.

Eliot judged a good deal of the liberal response to
these challenges a mere attenuation of Christian truth, a
method, as he said of Royce's efforts in this direction, of the last
resuscitation of the dead. He was, however, by no means oblivi-
ous to or dismissive of modern tendencies in religion, and later
his position in church politics and dogmatic disputes did not
always place him on the conservative end of the spectrum. Con-
tra Yeats, he did, of course, regard belief in such doctrines as
the incarnation as touchstones of Christian faith, but he also
wrestled again and again with the precise terms on which these
doctrines could be affirmed in an intellectually responsible way.
Similarly with a number of the issues which confronted and
changed church life and even church policy in his times, he tried
to be responsive both to the Catholic tradition and to the new
forms of knowledge which required the shattering and refound-
ing of that tradition from a more sophisticated point of view.
Eliot's middle and later work reflects throughout this wrestle
with words and meanings, as well as a tension between doctrinal
formulations which demand assent or denial and those more diffuse and subtle, but by no means less powerful, appeals which
require a transformation of emotion and will. Throughout, he
attempted to hold skepticism not in abeyance but in solution,
until it could be dissolved and recrystallized, again and again,
into belief.

To some extent, this modern approach to religious
certainty cohabits, not always smoothly, with Eliot's own devo-

tional temperament and his deep assimilation of the inspirational and spiritual writing of other cultures and of the past. We can see him brooding over the resulting problems and contradictions in a small preface he wrote for an anthology of devotional writing by Tagore's son-in-law, N. Gangulee. Here Eliot wished to establish a certain hierarchy in ways of reading, whereby a devotional, as opposed to philosophical and aesthetic, response to a text is distinctly a higher enterprise, one in which differences of religious tradition and even discursive belief are transcended; though it is only in relation to these that the transcendence has meaning. Nevertheless, he did not want simply to ignore questions of doctrinal difference at the discursive level or pretend that these might simply be reduced to some lowest common denominator or perennial philosophy. Nor did he wish to ignore all the complex motivations for reading that psychology and to some extent sociology and history had taught him were implicated in the reception of any text. His summary of these problems has an Eliotic suavity and grace that conceal as well as reveal the profundity and wisdom of his own consideration of these issues. In devotional reading, he says:

> We have to abandon some of our usual motives for reading. We must surrender the love of Power--whether over others, or over ourselves, or over the material world. We must abandon even the love of Knowledge . . . what these writers aim at, in their various idioms, in whatever language or in terms of whatever religion, is the Love of God. They gave their lives to this, and their destination is not one which we can reach any quicker than they did or without the same tireless activity and tireless passivity. (Gangulee x)

And yet, Eliot concludes, we must not, on the other hand, assume that doctrinal distinctions do not matter, for it was "only in relation to his own religion that the insights of any of these [devotional writers] had significance to him" at all (13).

   We must note that the austerity and totality of response Eliot calls for in this preface reside in the activity of reading, rather than in any position affirmed within the text itself, and thus cannot be completely identified with the discursive content of the work considered independently of that response. Eliot thus establishes the force and validity of a way of reading which is open at once to the learned and the unlearned, and which depends on the attention and involvement of the whole self in the act of reading, not simply on the intellectual assent of the reasoning or logical part of the mind. This devotional attention does not finesse but surpasses the issues of doctrine and belief, making use of them as ladders, not as goals. It also insists on unmasking, through introspection and self-mastery, that will to power that lurks under the guise of the will to truth (and to doctrinal correctness) and even under the more apparently innocent aspect of the will to beauty.

Eliot's remarks on the question of the Christian relation to other faiths, particularly Eastern ones, spell out a kind of program for *Four Quartets*:

> Some readers, attracted by the occult, think only Asiatic literature has religious understanding. Others distrust mysticism and stay narrowly Christian. For both it is salutary to learn that the Truth is not occult, and that it is not wholly confined on the one hand to their own religious tradition, or on the other hand to an alien culture and religion which they regard with superstitious awe. (Gangulee 11)

The Dry Salvages may be read as a concerted effort to instill this salutary lesson by means of a poetic juxtaposition of Christian devotion as classically understood and the devotion of the *Bhagavad Gita*.

There is, however, a certain problem when this celebration of devotional reading is brought into relation with a modern sensibility, whether we think of the modern as an aesthetic or a religious category. In the first place, as Eliot clearly points out, the ultimate proof of a devotional text lies in its reading not its writing. This reception is, however, in the final analysis outside the writer's control. Issues of craft and technique in the text itself, issues so foregrounded in the modern tradition, will then have only a proximate relevance. Secondly, if the hallmark of devotion is simplicity and totality of response, the hallmark of modernity is complexity and qualification, and the two do not always easily coincide. How affirm a deep, non-discursive truth requiring the full attention and assent of the whole reading self and at the same time insist that the reader bear in mind the relativism of its presentation, the presence around it of other, sometime opposing, traditions and points of view, the dangers of a will to power underlying its will to truth, the crucial dimension of historicity which conditions it, the ever-present possibility of unconscious psychological motivations which may subvert and even pervert its intended meaning, and the dependence of the whole effort on a highly sophisticated and continually changing tradition of interpretation? The two can only be brought together by a supreme effort, one which may well end less in a full yet multi-dimensional reading than in a kind of double-think or squint.

While there is perhaps no ultimate solution to this problem, at least part of the responsibility for the overcoming of which rests with the reader alone, it is still arguable that certain texts are better designed to evoke the kind of response that Eliot wanted for his work than others. As he matured, Eliot came to see the advantages in this respect of what he called *wisdom*, a term which implies both a stance toward experience and a way of writing. As a rhetorical mode, wisdom discourse has certain characteristics Eliot found appealing. First, it depends heavily not on discursive or doctrinal formulation, but on proverb or aphorism for its effect, thus making use of popular expressions, oral formulae, and communal tradition, and by-passing, often usefully, certain issues of dogma and rational belief. Secondly, it is often anonymous or pseudonymous, sometimes by attribution to some speaker with a ritual function, a Solomon, or a David, sometimes by association with a persona, Sophia, or the Shekinah, for example. Wisdom writing is thus "impersonal" in Eliot's sense, being divorced as much as possible from the accidents of particular characters or a particular ethos or political/social situation.

Finally, the wisdom tradition allows for wide, even, from a logical point of view, mutually exclusive stances toward experience and belief, ranging from the deepest and most logocentric affirmations--of, for instance, a transcendental Signifier, a God present in and above the entire universe and in language itself--to some of the most radical deconstructive gestures--as for instance the repeated insistence that notions such as God and direct linguistic revelation are worse, in their feebleness, than the silence in which skepticism and mystery are one. Hence, in the wisdom tradition of the Bible, such lines as "the fool has said in his heart, 'there is no God' " may be less contradicted than thrown into deeper relief by other, darker sayings such as "vanity of vanities, all is vanity saith the Preacher." In general, wisdom writing finds no need to reconcile, at least in discursive terms, such apparently divergent positions, allowing context, sensibility, and intuition to invoke them in ways that subvert, without ever entirely cancelling, one another. To this end it tries to maintain a certain rhetoric of universality, which is not the same as a perennial philosophy or a reduction to a set of common propositions, though it is often weakly misread in that way.

The rhetoric and stance of the wisdom tradition often helped Eliot reconcile the conflicting demands of modernity and devotion. Of the advantages of this tradition for poetry he was himself entirely aware. In his late essay on Goethe, an essay he almost decided to call "A Discourse in Praise of Wisdom," Eliot explains that wisdom writing, for him, means writing that bases its appeal on something "deeper than ... logical propositions" and so does not always require assent or denial at the propositional level to be effective. "Of revealed religions, and of philosophical systems, we must believe that one is right and the others wrong," he maintains, "but wisdom is *logos xunos*, the same for all men everywhere" (OPP 264). It is at once simple, profound, and open in the ecumenical sense that the modern movement was to develop as it sought to come to grips with the respect and reverence due to other faiths.

In terms of Eliot's own work, the reference to *logos xunos*, common or open wisdom, takes us to Heraclitus and one of the epigraphs to *Burnt Norton*. This epigraph may be translated loosely--though Eliot does not translate it at all--as "wisdom is actually common property, but people treat it as if it were a special preserve." When it comes to the expression of this quality of wisdom, Eliot goes on in his Goethe essay, all language is inadequate but probably the language of poetry is least so. He concludes this essay, which itself makes a good gloss on several passages in *Four Quartets*, with an extended quotation from Ecclesiastes which pairs the Greek pre-Socratic philosopher with the Hebrew sage, and captures very well the self-evident, open, universalist simplicity of this poetic mode:

> Wisdom shall praise herself,
> And shall glory in the midst of her people.
> In the congregation of the Most High shall she open her mouth,
> And triumph before His power. (OPP 257)

These and similar models of wisdom and a wisdom mode of discourse informed, I think, much of Eliot's later verse, *Four Quartets* in particular, and helped him to write a relativized, self-conscious and complex kind of religious poetry, open to the existence of other faiths and experiences and "modern" in the sense I have tried to specify, and yet a poetry susceptible as well to devotional reading, and capable of evoking and supporting great simplicity as well as great complexity of response.

Eliot's use of the wisdom tradition to by-pass deliberately questions of dogmatic truth and doctrinal assent in *Four Quartets*, even when he himself had arrived at a provisional set of religious beliefs, is much in line not only with the modern movement in religion, but with the philosophical position he had worked out in *Knowledge and Experience*, his dissertation on F. H. Bradley for Harvard, many years before. In this work, skepticism and belief are not opposed to one another but represented as different points along a continuum of response, any absolute claims of either being subverted *a priori* by its dependence on the other. The question of belief in this case is not so much posed for a yes or no as relativized from the beginning. Such a mobile view of discursive truth is, needless to say, by no means a disadvantage when it comes to the writing of poetry. Indeed it allows and encourages that dialectic of "surrender and recovery," identification and detachment, Eliot himself understood the appropriation of poetic texts to entail. Hence "poetry" may be both distinguished from and inhabited by "belief" in very complex ways, with neither entirely privileged over the other.

This wisdom tradition, however, was not without its dangers for a poet like Eliot. To take only one facet of the problem, "simple wisdom" can very easily look more like platitude than insight, more like sentiment than feeling, more like the ridiculous then the sublime. A quarter turn from its lofty perspectives and one gets hot air rather than inspiration, Polonius rather than the Preacher, Goethe as didact rather than Goethe as sage. We need think only of Whitman at his worst to be reminded of the pitfalls here. Secondly, there is the danger of sentimentality, compromise and appeasement, what Eliot called the "false wisdom" of old age. Here the sharpness of the agonies of youth, the moment in the hyacinth garden or at the top of the stair, are not so much transcended as repressed, and desire is pacified rather than transformed by genuine purgation. Finally, there is the danger of conflation of opposing doctrines and positions, of what Eliot called the "luxury of confounding" as opposed to the "task of combining" different doctrines and points of view (rev. Wolf 426).

In *Four Quartets* Eliot seeks to avoid these pitfalls by insisting that the cost of wisdom is "not less than everything" (CPP 145). "Everything" here must, I think, be seen to include much doctrinal and pious certainty often associated with these poems. 'That old-time religion' is simply not celebrated here, not even in the service of "a further union, a deeper communion" (CPP 129). Among the certainties which, for Eliot, must be sacrificed are a naive and uncritical belief in the immortality of what we like to think of as the individual self or soul, an unqualified affirmation of Christian belief as superior to other beliefs in all respects, and an easy expectation that all pain and suffering will be taken care of either by a simple passage of time or by some system of rewards and punishments after death. These are excess baggage that Eliot's brief but intense sojourn in the mazes of Buddhism and later intense practice of Christian meditation further persuaded him must be jettisoned. That his call to a more rigorous faith has been so often misread and misunderstood is only one of the multiple ironies that have always attended the reception of his work.

We can see this more rigorous formulation of the tradition, a formulation at once modern and yet infused with the immediacy of an active devotional practice, at work throughout *Four Quartets*. These four linked poems, while accessible on the surface, are by no means as genial and instantly affirmative of traditional Christian truths and pieties as they might at first appear. If they do offer pious consolations, those consolations are of a peculiarly radical sort, and the cure may be worse than the disease. Consider, for instance, *East Coker*, the second of the quartets. This is the one first prompted, as A. D. Moody has pointed out, by the shock to Eliot's sometimes complacent neutralism in politics occasioned by the advance of the Second World War, and in particular by Chamberlain's placation of Hitler at Munich. Here Eliot writes of the first step toward wisdom, which is to be able to recognize its counterfeits. "What was to be the value," he asks, "of the long looked forward to, / Long hoped for calm, the autumnal serenity / And the wisdom of age? / Had they deceived us / Or deceived themselves, the quiet-voiced elders, / Bequeathing us merely a receipt for deceit?/ The serenity only a deliberate hebetude, / The wisdom only the knowledge of dead secrets / Useless in the darkness into which they peered / Or from which they turned their eyes" (CPP 125). A few lines later there follows one of those aphorisms with which Eliot tried repeatedly to capture the tone and function of the wisdom tradition, aphorisms so finely turned that they seem cited from long tradition already present in the language rather than composed: "We are only undeceived / Of that which, deceiving, could no longer harm."

This section of *East Coker* ends by insisting that the only real wisdom is the wisdom of humility, but the movement of the poem is off and away from this somewhat dead center, which is rather weak at this point, as if Eliot were telling, not showing, preaching, not evoking. Whatever may be premature about the wisdom of *East Coker*, however, is amply destabilized and thrown into question in the great third quartet, *The Dry Salvages*. Here begins a long engaged confrontation with all that makes wisdom seem at times so weak: the savagery of experience, including the experience of holiness, its roots in pain, and the multiple ironies of suffering generated by its extension over time. The problem of this quartet is to peer into that darkness from which the old men of Munich turned their eyes, but to do so without either bitterness or rhetoric or excess.

The techniques Eliot begins to develop here include again the aphorism, the use of a deceptively conversational, ruminative and apparently relaxed style for extremely frightening, catastrophic and subversive insights, the sudden shift from a voice of speculation, as if you were listening to some old friend muse, somewhat disjointedly, over a glass of brandy at the club, to a voice of absolute authority in which the sum of the starkest truths of the poem are delivered. Hence you have "It seems, as one becomes older . . . " (CPP 132)--ah, yes, now we know exactly what to expect, the vapid reminiscences of a sweet old man. What, though, do we get? Well, some of this, to be sure, but as the passage unwinds, we "come to discover" that "the moments of agony . . . are likewise permanent / With such permanence as time has" (CPP 133). Furthermore, since true wisdom is often corrosive as well as salutary, we are then reminded that we "appreciate this better" in the "agony of others" than in our own. This is surely not the wisdom of hebetude or senility or even conventional Christian piety; indeed it rises at times to a dry realism, a sharpness, which is redeemed from misanthropy only by accuracy of insight. One finds this kind of writing elsewhere only in the French tradition, in La Rochefoucauld or Montaigne. Or think about this one: "You cannot face it steadily, but this thing is sure, / That time is no healer: the patient is no longer there" (CPP 134). Easy notions of cheap redemption and ready personal immortality, the false wisdom of the 'long view' and the 'long run,' do not easily survive this quartet. They are part of that cost of "not less than everything" to which the last lines of *Little Gidding* refer, and for which they are an important preparation (CPP 145).

Little Gidding itself opens with a rather brilliant *tour de force* in Eliot's old metaphysical style. It sounds a bit like the opening of *The Waste Land*, a poem no one has accused of being too sunny. "Midwinter spring is its own season" answers neatly to "April is the cruelest month" (CPP 138, 37). Here we are back again at the beginning, where desire and death are reborn at one and the same moment, leading, it might seem, to the same sterile repetitions, the same hell of necessity without end. We almost expect to meet Tiresias again, that great waste land figure of partial wisdom at its most bleak and most impotent, unable either to break the deadlock of the past or to imagine a different future. In a way, in fact, we *do* meet Tiresias here again, or something like him, for this poem, like *The Waste Land*, like the first of Pound's cantos, begins with an invocation of the spirits of the dead as found in the Odyssey and in Virgil, an invocation out of which Tiresias' is, traditionally, the first voice that rises. It is possible to read the following three stanzas of part 2, the lyrics of death by air, earth, and fire, as placed, as it were, in the mouth of Tiresias, the great steady observer of inevitable human futility from Eliot's earlier work.

To continue in this vein, it is perfectly possible, as well, to add to the long list of compound features of the uncanny ghost or figure the speaker encounters in part 2 those of Tiresias, especially in his capacity as harbinger of what awaits us after death. The message isn't particularly pleasant. "Let me disclose," the ghostly double proposes, "the gifts reserved for age / To set a crown upon your lifetime's effort. / First, the cold friction of expiring sense / Without enchantment, offering no promise / But bitter tastelessness of shadow fruit ... / Second, the conscious impotence of rage / At human folly, and the laceration / Of laughter at what ceases to amuse" (CPP 141, 142). And as if this were not enough, "last, the rending pain of re-enactment / Of all that you have done and been; the shame / Of motives late revealed, and the awareness / Of things ill done and done to others' harm / Which once you took for exercise of virtue." Surely this is an echo of that walk "among the lowest of the dead" that showed an earlier version of Tiresias those automatons of empty sex and failed humanity, the "typist home at teatime" and the "young man carbuncular," who are also, as *The Waste Land* makes ineluctably clear, earlier versions of ourselves (CPP 44). Then indeed, to cut back to *Little Gidding* again, one might say with Eliot, that "fools' approval stings, and honor stains" (CPP 142). Humility here is less a rather pompous and pedantic virtue, as it can seem in *East Coker*, than a rigorous exercise in confrontation with the self, one in which no dark stone is left unturned.

If this is wisdom, some may prefer folly, or prefer at least *The Waste Land*'s passionate drive, right to the breaking point of the mind, to be free of this endless circle of self-interested, self-reflexive and self-deluded motivations. Here, however, given his commitment to what he calls *logos xunos*, open wisdom, Eliot cannot turn directly either to Sanskrit or Latin, Italian or Provençal, to find words which will convey both the simplicity of the solution to this problem and its absolute freshness and surprise. Nor can he rely automatically, in the way that many of even his best critics presume he does, on a simple last minute 'save' by tradition or history. If he is to draw on the resources of his culture, he must do so in a way that has authority and originality, as well as congruence with the past, and that changes the direction of his culture even as it summons up its strength. Otherwise, he will simply be rehearsing dead wisdom instead of rediscovering the wisdom of the dead.

His solution at the thematic level is to draw into the poem not the energy of his culture's great victories, but the profundity of its major losses. We do indeed hear the voice of that great sister of wisdom Julian of Norwich, but are reminded that her "all shall be well" emerged from a context of "incandescent terror" generated by extreme mental and physical pain. The reference to a "king at nightfall" (CPP 143) is likewise no exercise in partisanship or nostalgia for a time when one could be "classicist in letters, Anglican in religion and monarchist in politics" without sounding ridiculous, but a reminder of failure counter-balancing the equal and opposite failure of that king's political enemy, the poet who dies "blind and quiet" a few lines later. Likewise, there is no easy recourse to a notion of one's work or one's political struggle living after one by way of consolation. Action as well as contemplation here reach their end, where every gesture of transcendence is "a step to the block, to the fire, down the sea's throat / Or to an illegible stone" (CPP 144).

So what we have here, then, at the height of the war, precisely, in fact, as the battle of El Alemein is turning the tide in favor of the Allies and preserving the world for nuclear holocaust, is not a hymn to the glories of Western religion and culture but an epitaph for their end, at least as exclusive and self-evident goods. True wisdom lies, for Eliot, not in a false reaffirmation of traditional religious values but in a recognition of the essential conditioning of even the best of their representations by time and relativity. Paradoxically, however, only tradition can reveal its own ephemera; only history its own emptiness. As Gertrude Stein put it, "all that history teaches is--history teaches." Perhaps one's life had to have exactly the curve of Eliot's, coming of age when Western culture was first tearing itself to shreds and then coming to middle age as it did so again, to yield precisely this kind of bitter wisdom. " 'Vanity of vanities, all is vanity,' saith the preacher."

The wisdom tradition, however, though based on just such paradoxes as these, ultimately requires celebration and simplicity, and comes to fruition only in these modes. But "[a]fter such knowledge, what forgiveness?" How was Eliot to

find, to reaffirm, to induct into his poem these qualities of simplicity and joy? The answer, I would argue, lay in a renunciation
not only of personal identity as conceived and cherished by the
ego, but of the weight of a certain poetic and cultural capital as
well. At the end of *Four Quartets* both tradition and the individual talent are sent to the block, down the sea's throat, to an
illegible stone, are sent, that is, toward the vanishing point on
the horizon of culture where many peoples, religions, value-sys-
tems are, in defiance of the wars that divide them, made one.

  This renunciation, this vanishing point, cannot, however, for Eliot, be allowed to collapse into poetic or intellectual
abdication, or into denial of that difference against which alone
it has significance. There must be simplicity, but not oversimpli-
fication, ease but not laxity, repose but not a false peace. Eliot's
solution to this problem in the last stanza of *Little Gidding* is a
lesson in mastery of craft; it involves a highly studied combination of great levelness and decorum of diction, extreme syntactic
and grammatical complexity, and a use of imagery as remarkable for its economy as for its power. The diction itself is telling,
fulfilling the mandate announced earlier in the poem for a discourse where "every word is at home, / Taking its place to support the others, / The word neither diffident nor ostentatious"
(CPP 144). The syntax, however, departs from this decorum,
beginning with a phrase floating in white space

> With the drawing of this Love and the voice of this Calling
> (CPP 145)

after which we almost hear a Poundian "so that": Then comes a
straightforward sentence, or so it seems, but one which takes off
again into an unfixed relative clause, "When the last of earth left
to discover," and having in the end, if examined carefully, no
established main subject or verb. These syntactic indetermina-
cies are suddenly interrupted by "quick now, here, now always"
before flowing on again to their end in the final sentence. Even
this sentence, however, takes its syntactical core and deep structure from a devotional text of the past, Julian of Norwich's "All
shall be well and all manner of thing shall be well," a core which
Eliot carefully surrounds by his own conditional and qualifying
clauses.

  In that final sentence, the images which close the
poem, the fire and the rose, are common to many traditions,
occult and exoteric alike, from Buddhism's Fire Sermon to the
gnostic traditions of the Rosicrucians or the Persian and later
the Sufi celebrations of the traditional Middle Eastern flower of

mystic love. There is, however, a sense here of these associations dropping away, along with a number of the doctrinal distinctions which cluster around them, so that the close becomes less a set of allusions than λόγος ξυνός , open wisdom. This wisdom is accessible indeed, but with an accessibility "costing not less than everything" (CPP 145). Part of that cost is the certainty of Christian pieties often taken for granted as part of the poem but actually asserted there, if at all, only as intensely modern, highly relativized and provisional truths. Having paid that price, moreover, the poem does not rest on its laurels, but asks for more: the sacrifice and purgation not only of idiosyncrasy and personality in Eliot's old sense, but also of pseudo-devotional sentimentality and unearned consolation as well. The "tireless passivity and tireless activity" required to give this poem the kind of reading it deserves are, then, not to be exhausted in one sitting, or even across a lifetime's renewed consideration, nor are they confined, as we are coming to learn, to one culture alone.

WORKS CITED

Costello, Harry T. *Josiah Royce's Seminar, 1913-1914: As Recorded in the Note-books of Harry T. Costello*. Ed. Grover Smith. New Brunswick: Rutgers UP, 1963.

Eliot, T. S. Preface. *Thoughts for Meditation: A Way to Recovery from Within*. By N. Gangulee. London: Faber and Faber, 1951. 11-14.

_____. Rev. of *The Philosophy of Nietzsche* by A. Wolf. *International Journal of Ethics* 26 (Apr. 1916) 426-27.

Moody, A. D. *Thomas Stearns Eliot: Poet*. Cambridge: Cambridge UP, 1979.

JAMES E. MILLER, JR.

FOUR QUARTETS *AND* AN *"ACUTE PERSONAL REMINISCENCE"*

PROLOGUE

In 1977, I published a book entitled *T. S. Eliot's Personal Waste Land: Exorcism of the Demons*. The gestation period for that book was a prolonged one, the last stage of which began with the publication of the long-lost manuscripts of *The Waste Land* in 1971, edited by Valerie Eliot. The more I read and re-read the original version of the famous poem, the more I became convinced that the poem was indeed a personal poem, as Eliot himself in later life repeatedly claimed.

A footnote I chanced upon while reading the 1971 Robert Sencourt biography of Eliot led me to an essay on *The Waste Land* that I had somehow missed. This essay by a Canadian critic, John Peter, had appeared under the title "A New Interpretation of *The Waste Land*," in *Essays in Criticism* in 1952, and was a detailed reading of *The Waste Land* as a kind of modern *In Memoriam*, in which the central consciousness--not identified as Eliot's--is grieving for the loss of a friend and comrade through death by drowning. This was a quite persuasive reading, and was offered in the most tentative and gentle terms imaginable. What I discovered, to my astonishment, was that not all copies of that particular issue of *Essays in Criticism* contained the John Peter essay--because the magazine had been legally forced to omit the essay in the middle of publication. The suit had been brought by solicitors acting on behalf of T. S. Eliot. The story of this 1952 suppression is told by John Peter in a postscript at the end of a republication of his essay in a 1969 issue of *Essays in Criticism*. Recall that Eliot died in 1965, thus making republication possible without risk of violating the complicated British libel laws.

In the postscript John Peter reveals for the first time the background of the action Eliot took against Peter's interpretation. Eliot's solicitors informed Peter that Eliot read Peter's essay "with amazement and disgust," and that it was "absurd" and "completely erroneous" (Peter 173, qtd. in Miller 13). Keep in mind that Peter had not identified the protagonist of the poem as Eliot. This angry poet denouncing an interpretation of *The Waste Land* is the same poet who would say in a 1959 interview that he "wasn't even bothering" whether he "understood what he was saying" in *The Waste Land* (qtd. in Miller 13). Whereas his 1952 suppressed essay interpreted the poem in relation to assumptions about a central consciousness, Peter's 1969 postscript ventured to identify the central consciousness as Eliot's. And it postulated that the dead friend for whom Eliot grieved was Jean Verdenal, to whom Eliot dedicated his first book, *Prufrock and Other Observations* (1917) with a quotation from Dante's *Purgatorio* (21, 133-36), which reads in translation: "You are able to understand the quantity of love that warms me toward you / When I forget our emptiness / Treating shades as if they were solid." This dedication reveals that Verdenal died in 1915 in the Dardanelles.

  In my research on Jean Verdenal, filled with a number of adventures I must omit here, I assembled the following account of the friendship based on the facts or plausible conjecture from the facts (see Miller 17-32). At the age of 22, Eliot went to Paris and found living in his pension a charming young Frenchman less than two years younger who was studying medicine and who wrote poetry. Loneliness impelled Eliot into close friendship. It would have been natural for the two to travel in Italy and Germany during the summer and it is likely that Eliot attempted to renew--perhaps did renew--their relationship in 1914 on Eliot's return to Paris. World War I forced Eliot's departure from Germany to England in 1914, and led to Verdenal's entering the French forces as a medical officer. Caught up in the blundering campaign to take the Dardanelles in 1915, he was one of the countless young Frenchmen, Englishmen, and Australians who were lost in the waters of the Strait or the mud of Gallipoli peninsula beginning with the landings of April 24, 1915. Verdenal's service record reveals that he was "killed by the enemy on the 2nd May 1915 in the Dardanelles ... while dressing a wounded man on the field of battle" (qtd. in Miller 21). Eliot would have heard of his death later in May, or at the latest in early June, and his dismay and anguish may well have impelled him into a hasty marriage to Vivienne Haigh-Wood on June 26 that was largely meaningless except as an irrational response to his bitter loss. The marriage turned out to be catastrophic and Eliot appeared grateful, only some six months after the marriage, when the well-known womanizer Bertrand Russell took Vivienne off on a seaside holiday alone. But as Vivienne's mental health deteriorated, perhaps in part through the frustrations of her marriage, T. S. Eliot's health began to deteriorate and his ability to write poetry to decline. The critical point was reached in 1921, when he found his only refuge from a breakdown was to take leave from his job as a bank clerk at Lloyd's Bank, consult a nerve specialist, or psychiatrist, in Lausanne, Switzerland, and write a long poem which had been under contemplation for some time. After accumulating a sheaf of manuscripts entitled "He Do the Police in Different Voices," he turned them over in Paris to Ezra Pound, who revised by cutting the poem drastically and who helped Eliot publish the poem in 1922--the title changed to *The Waste Land*.

Using this sketch as a base, filled in with some detail, I offered in my book an extended reading of the original *The Waste Land*, exploiting to the full the availability of the richly revealing manuscripts that John Peter had not had at hand when he wrote his essay back in 1952 and his postscript in 1969. *The Waste Land* as Eliot originally wrote it, I demonstrated, does not make an objective statement of social criticism about the world become waste land. Rather, it is a dramatization of an individual consciousness in a precarious state living "his life again in every detail of desire, temptation, and surrender" (words from the original epigraph from Conrad's *Heart of Darkness*) as he works his way to that "supreme moment of complete knowledge" out of the Thunder's voice (at the end of "What the Thunder Said"). The details of that life are consonant with the details of Eliot's, with particular emphasis on the loss of the beloved Verdenal and the following disastrous marriage to Vivienne. The knowledge the thunder brings is self-knowledge summoned from the self's depths. The final vision of the protagonist is a vision of the self broken and shattered, shoring some literary-intellectual fragments against his "ruins." The waste land lies within.

What I wish to do now is explore the ways in which the biographical and psychological materials that shaped *The Waste Land* continued to haunt Eliot's imagination and became important in the writing and revising of *Four Quartets* some two decades later.

*　　*　　*

In contrast with *The Waste Land*, which was put together (assembled and written) when Eliot was suffering a breakdown and seeking help from a psychiatrist in Lausanne, Switzerland, in 1921, the *Four Quartets* grew into a long poem over an extended period of time, beginning in 1935 with some passages left over from Eliot's play, *Murder in the Cathedral*, and the poem was not finished until 1941, with publication in 1943. During this period Eliot (born in 1888) was 47-54 years old. The *Four Quartets* was to be his last serious poetic work; the remainder of his career was to be devoted largely to the writing of plays. With the publication of the manuscripts of the *Four Quartets* in 1978, edited by Helen Gardner, we now know that Eliot consulted closely with his friend John Hayward in the revision of the poem. Hayward's role was in a way similar to Pound's role in the revision and publication of *The Waste Land*. But Hayward saw a far more nearly finished manuscript than did Pound, and his relation with Eliot in the 1930s and 40s was quite different from Pound's relationship in the early 1920s: Eliot was master to Hayward, while Pound was master to Eliot.

It is helpful to recall some of the biographical details of Eliot's life before turning to some particular and revealing details that I wish to focus on in *Four Quartets*. Eliot's disastrous marriage to Vivienne Haigh-Wood in June, 1915, which was (as I speculated in my book) precipitated by the death of Eliot's young French friend and pension-mate in early May of 1915 on the shores of Gallipoli, was finally resolved in a permanent separation in 1933. It was then that Eliot arranged, after his departure to lecture in America, for his solicitors to inform Vivienne Eliot that he would never return to her. It was the following year, 1934, that Eliot made his only other public reference to Jean Verdenal (the first being his expression of love in the earlier dedication of *Prufrock and Other Observations* to Verdenal; see my account of the gradual emergence of this dedication and epigraph in Eliot's books from 1917 to 1925 [qtd. in Miller 17-18]). The 1934 reference was in the middle of a *Criterion* review of a book about the Paris of 1910-11, the time Eliot was living in the pension with Verdenal. In the review Eliot exclaimed, as though moved by emotions welling up from deep within, apropos of nothing in the substance of the book under review: "I am willing to admit that my own retrospect is touched by a sentimental sunset, the memory of a friend coming across the Luxembourg Gardens in the late afternoon, waving a branch of lilac, a friend who was later (so far as I could find out) to be mixed with the mud of Gallipoli" (qtd. in Miller 19). It was in 1935 (according to Helen Gardner) that John Hayward suggested to Eliot that "they should set up house together." Eliot was not ready for such an arrangement, but his friendship with Hayward was such that beginning some time before World War II he began to send the parts of *Four Quartets* to him for his reaction and comments and suggested revisions. When *Four Quartets* was published in 1943, Eliot singled out John Hayward in a prefatory note of thanks for "general criticism and specific suggestions during the composition of these poems."

Since John Hayward was important in the composition of *Four Quartets*, it might be useful to glance a bit more sharply at his background and relationship with Eliot. The most thoroughly factual account is found in the first chapter of Helen Gardner's edition of the *Four Quartets* manuscripts (5-12). Born in 1905 (and thus some 17 years younger than Eliot), John Hayward suffered from boyhood from a "muscular dystrophy" that caused the muscles gradually to wither. The disease did not prevent him from receiving an excellent education in which he cultivated his passionate interest in languages and literature. He met Eliot in 1927, at age 22, and they became close friends by 1930. When Eliot returned from America in 1933, permanently separated from Vivienne, Hayward was one of a group of male friends with whom Eliot found regular companionship. We have already noted that by the time of the composition of *Four Quartets*, Hayward was the friend to whom Eliot turned for advice on revision (indeed, the Gardner edition of the manuscripts relies substantially on drafts preserved by Hayward and lengthy correspondence between him and Eliot). Having turned down Hayward's invitation to live with him in 1935, Eliot accepted another invitation in 1946, by which time Hayward's deteriorating health caused his confinement to a wheelchair. They took an apartment in Chelsea, and shared it for eleven years, until 1957. At the beginning of this period, Hayward was 41 years old, Eliot 58. The apartment at 19 Carlyle Mansions, Cheyne Walk, became a gathering place where Hayward could, without the awkwardness of going out, indulge his passion for literary discussion and gossip. There is reason to believe that Eliot found greater peace in this domestic arrangement than he had ever found in his life with Vivienne, who had died in 1947.

John Hayward's letters and papers relating to Eliot were deposited at Kings College, Cambridge, and will not be available for study until 2000. Helen Gardner had access to them for her edition of the *Four Quartets* manuscripts, but her account of Hayward's relationship with Eliot in her short biographical sketch, though factually informative, remains discreetly silent in areas where many questions arise. The two Eliot biographies that analyze the relationship are somewhat at variance. Robert Sencourt, in his *T. S. Eliot: A Memoir* writes: "[F]ar from their companionship being a mere arrangement of convenience, or the gregarious impulse of two lonely and aging men, it was a deep communion of interests in which each side contributed fruitfully to the other" (205-06; see also 203-05, 212-15). T. S. Matthews, in *Great Tom: Notes Toward the Definition of T. S. Eliot*, drawing a portrait of "not an altogether estimable character," dwells on Hayward's "sharp tongue" and caustic wit, and indicates that one of his early targets was Valerie Fletcher, Eliot's young secretary. The implication is that Hayward had some kind of premonition that Valerie might one day "lure Eliot from their flat, and even the enchantment of friendship" (see Matthews 155-61). Hayward's intuition, it turned out, was justified. Eliot's domestic arrangement with him came to an abrupt end in January of 1957, when Eliot (68) secretly married Valerie Fletcher (29).

Both biographies dwell at some length on the way Eliot handled this break with Hayward, and both point out the similarity to the break with Vivienne some 24 years before. Sencourt says that Eliot quietly slipped his belongings out of the apartment and did not inform Hayward until after the secret marriage--and then by phone--that he would not be returning. Matthews presents a number of accounts. One is the "official version," and perhaps the most untrustworthy, told by the widow Valerie, that Eliot informed Hayward about the marriage some two days before it was to take place and that Hayward took the news "extremely well." Hayward apparently spread several versions of the separation story, according to Matthews, one being that reported by Sencourt. But all of Hayward's versions suggest duplicity and even betrayal on Eliot's part. Whatever the case, the separation brought about by Eliot's marriage caused a rupture in the friendship that the embittered Hayward found impossible to overcome. Eliot died in 1965, and Hayward died a few months later in the same year, without resolution of their old quarrel.

Many of the details I have outlined here cannot, of course, have direct relevance for *Four Quartets*, but neither can they be dismissed as irrelevant for psychoanalytic-oriented readers interested in probing beneath the surface of literary texts for those aspects of personality that reveal the essence of an individual and his life. I take these details as indirectly supportive of the speculative interpretations I have presented in *T. S. Eliot's Personal Waste Land*, and I would like now to trace what I take to be some of the continuities between that early poetry and Eliot's last substantial work of poetry, *Four Quartets*.

My discussion of *Four Quartets* will focus on the last of the four parts, *Little Gidding*, and within *Little Gidding* on the lines devoted to the "familiar compound ghost" in section 2 (CPP 140). In my book, written before the manuscripts were published, I suggested that Jean Verdenal figured importantly in these lines. With the availability of the manuscripts, it becomes possible to explore my suggestion in greater depth than previously. We learn from the manuscripts that Eliot had more difficulty in writing *Little Gidding* than with any other of the parts of *Four Quartets*. And we learn further that he had his greatest problems with the lines on the "familiar compound ghost." As Helen Gardner remarks, "This passage gave Eliot more trouble than any other section of the poem" (171). The reasons for the difficulty are certainly complex, but one cause, I want to suggest, has to do with these connections I want to draw with the earlier poetry.

But before pursuing these connections, I believe it useful to remember the nature of the "compound ghost" passage. In "What Dante Means to Me" (1950), Eliot described his difficulties in writing the lines imitating (without rhyme) Dante's *terza rima* of the *Divine Comedy*: "It was not simply that I was limited to the Dantesque type of imagery, simile and figure of speech. It was chiefly that in this very bare and austere style, in which every word has to be 'functional', the slightest vagueness or imprecision is immediately noticeable" (TCC 128). Eliot referred to the *Little Gidding* passage as "a hallucinated scene after an air-raid." The passage opens:

> In the uncertain hour before the morning
>   Near the ending of interminable night
>   At the recurrent end of the unending
> After the dark dove with the flickering tongue
>   Had passed below the horizon of his homing
>   While the dead leaves still rattled on like tin
> Over the asphalt where no other sound was
>   Between three districts whence the smoke arose
>   I met one walking, loitering and hurried
> As if blown towards me like the metal leaves
>   Before the urban dawn wind unresisting.
>   And as I fixed upon the down-turned face
> That pointed scrutiny with which we challenge
>   The first-met stranger in the waning dusk

> I caught the sudden look of some dead master
> Whom I had known, forgotten, half recalled
> Both one and many; in the brown baked features
> The eyes of a familar compound ghost
> Both intimate and unidentifiable. (CPP 140)

The relatively straight narrative of these lines begins to blur in subsequent ones, as the hallucinatory elements multiply and come to the fore:

> So I assumed a double part, and cried
> And heard another's voice cry: 'What! are *you* here?'
> Although we were not. I was still the same,
> Knowing myself yet being someone other--
> And he a face still forming; yet the words sufficed
> To compel the recognition they preceded.
> And so, compliant to the common wind,
> Too strange to each other for misunderstanding,
> In concord at this intersection time
> Of meeting nowhere, no before and after,
> We trod the pavement in a dead patrol. (CPP 141)

We may be assured that the mixture of reality and unreality here is intentional, and we may observe, too, that Eliot achieved a kind of vagueness in spite of the inhibitions he thought imposed by Dante's form.

Now with these lines fresh in our minds, approximately the first half of this celebrated passage, I want to turn to those connections between the early poetry and this part of *Four Quartets*. I long ago developed a feeling or intuition that three of Eliot's works contained passages and lines hovering close to the sources of a personal anguish so acute as to be barely containable beneath the surface of the poems. The three works are "The Love Song of J. Alfred Prufrock," *The Waste Land*, and the "familiar compound ghost" passage of *Four Quartets*' *Little Gidding*. And it was only recently I noticed that a recurring allusion in key positions in these three works (or in manuscript drafts of them) might perhaps relate to my feelings in connecting them. The allusion is to Dante's canto 26 of the *Purgatorio*, the canto describing Dante's encounter with the bands of sodomites and the hermaphroditic lustful; at the end of the canto, in lines that inspired Eliot's fascination, Arnaut Daniel, a Provençal poet, emerges from the fire, identifies himself, asks that Dante be mindful of his pain, and then returns to the refining or purifying fire from which he came. As Eliot scholars have often observed, Eliot used phrases from this canto for titles in various of his poems and books in addition to the allusions in the poems mentioned above. Back in 1926, I. A. Richards observed: "There is

Canto XXVI of the *Purgatorio* to be studied--the relevance of the close of that canto to the whole of Mr. Eliot's work must be insisted upon. It illuminates his persistent concern with sex, the problem of our generation, as religion was the problem of the last" (292). In 1933, in *The Use of Poetry and the Use of Criticism*, Eliot "went out of his way" (as John Peter observed in 1969 [170]) to compliment Richards: "I readily admit the importance of canto 26, and it was shrewd of Mr. Richards to notice it; but in his contrast of sex and religion he makes a distinction which is too subtle for me to grasp" (UPUC 126-27).

We might take Eliot's comments as a confession of his "persistent concern with sex" in his poetry; moreover, his acknowledgment of the central importance to his work of that notorious canto 26 (*Purgatorio*), with its roving bands of sodomites and hermaphroditic lustful, would seem to suggest that the kind of sex with which he is concerned is not what might be called "natural" heterosexuality, but rather sex identified in Dante as unnatural. Had Eliot wanted to evoke heterosexuality, there were famous and moving passages in Dante that would have worked well for him--as, for example, the Paolo and Francesca encounter in canto 5 of the *Inferno*. It is time now to turn to the three Eliot passages in which *Purgatorio*'s canto 26 strikingly figures.

First is the manuscript version of "The Love Song of J. Alfred Prufrock." This version appears in the *Notebook* now in the New York Public Library's Berg Collection (see Gallup 1240). Accompanying this manuscript is the date July-August, 1911--identifying this version with the end of Eliot's year in Paris, after he has come to know Jean Verdenal. The present title of the poem is accompanied by a subtitle, "Prufrock among the Women." And the epigraph, instead of the present one we know (which is taken from *Inferno*, canto 27, and has no sexual context or reference) consists of the last two lines of the favorite canto 26 of *Purgatorio* (with Arnaut Daniel finishing his speech and returning to his redemptive punishment):

". . . be mindful in your time of my pain."
Then he dived back into the fire that refines them. (see Gallup 1240)

This epigraph is far more revelatory of Prufrock's nature than the one ultimately substituted for it on publication. And indeed, had this original epigraph remained the epigraph of the poem, with its evocation of the context of its source, it is likely that we would have read the poem in a radically different way, identifying Prufrock with Arnaut Daniel and the sins of the sodomites and hermaphroditic lustful of canto 26--thus making clear his difficulties in relationship with women (the deleted subtitle, "Prufrock among the Women," suggesting that Prufrock's natural habitat was with men, where most likely he did not suffer the same difficulties he suffers in relating to women).

In an aside in my book on Eliot's *The Waste Land*, I took note of Eliot's revelation that the "you" of Prufrock's opening line ("Let us go then you and I") refers not to the reluctant inner self of Prufrock, but rather to (as Eliot himself put it) "merely some friend or companion, presumably of the male sex, whom the speaker is at the moment addressing" (qtd. in Miller 52). And I speculated that, given Eliot's involvement with Jean Verdenal at the time "Prufrock" was written, that the "you and I" may well at some level have been based on Eliot himself and his friend Verdenal (the dedicatee, remember, of the later "Prufrock" volume).

The second key appearance of the canto 26 lines comes, of course, at the end of "What the Thunder Said," the concluding section of *The Waste Land*. I have shown in my book how the manuscript versions of this section of *The Waste Land* clearly reveal what the published version conceals, that the "awful daring of a moment's surrender" (CPP 49), traditionally interpreted as involving the male speaker with a woman, in actuality involves him with another man:

> DATTA. ~~we brother~~, what have we given?
>   blood shaking ~~within~~
> My friend, my ~~blood/friend, beating in~~ my heart,
> The awful daring of a moment's surrender
>   never
> Which an age of prudence ca~~nnot~~ retract-- . . . (WLF 77)

These lines from the manuscript version come near the end of *The Waste Land*, and represent the climactic moment of insight by the protagonist in the poem, precipitated by the voice of the Thunder. Shortly after this passage, the protagonist become Fisher King (in mythology his impotence has caused the lands to be barren) attempts to shore a number of literary and philosophical fragments against his ruins. The first fragment summoned to mind is the last line from *Purgatorio*'s canto 26: "Poi s'ascose nel fuoco che gli affina" (Then he [Arnaut Daniel] dived back into the fire that refines them [WLF 81]).[1] Thus the Fisher King of *The Waste Land* becomes at a critical moment in the poem identified with Arnaut Daniel, suggesting that the

---

1. Eliot incorrectly remembers the actual line which is "Poi s'ascose nel foco che li affina" (Sinclair 342).

cause of his impotence is, like Prufrock's, related to the drives
and obsessions of those described by Dante in the bands of
sodomites and hermaphroditic lustful of *Purgatorio*'s canto 26
(see Miller 126-35).
. The third key allusion to these Dantean lines comes
near the end of the "familiar compound ghost" passage in part
II of *Little Gidding*. The reference comes at the conclusion of the
speech made by the "compound ghost" to the poet as they walk
their "dead patrol" during a night in World War II London:

> From wrong to wrong the exasperated spirit
> Proceeds, unless restored by that refining fire
> Where you must move in measure, like a dancer. (CPP 142)

In this instance, the allusion does not appear in the earliest surviving draft of the passage, but was added as part of Eliot's
deliberate effort to change the Inferno-like nature of the scene
to something more clearly "Purgatorial." But though the familiar canto 26 of *Purgatorio* did not figure in the early version of
the "compound ghost" passage, canto 15 of Dante's *Inferno* did:
in the first version, when the poet meets the "compound ghost,"
he hails him as the writer and poet Ser Brunetto of the sodomite
band in that canto. The early version reads:

> And I, becoming other and many, cried
> And heard my voice: "Are you here, Ser Brunetto?"
> Although we were not. I was always dead,
>   Always revived, and always something other,
>   And he a face changing: yet the words sufficed
> For recognition where was no acquaintance
>   And no identity, blown by one airless wind . . . .
>   (qtd. in Gardner 228)

In an intermediate draft of the lines, Eliot deleted specific reference to Ser Brunetto, and in a note John Hayward asked him
why. By the time of this exchange, considerable revision of the
entire "compound ghost" passage had taken place, making it
more and more possible to identify--or misidentify--the figure as
William Butler Yeats. Eliot replied to Hayward: "The first
[reason for deleting Ser Brunetto] is that the visionary figure has
now become somewhat more definite and will no doubt be identified by some readers with Yeats though I do not mean anything so precise as that. However, I do not wish to take the
responsibility of putting Yeats or anybody else into Hell and I do
not want to impute to him the particular vice which took
Brunetto there. Secondly, although the reference to that canto is
intended to be explicit, I wished the effect of the whole to be

Purgatorial which is much more appropriate" (qtd. in Gardner 176).

Eliot's reply suggests the kind of confusion of meaning and purpose that gave him so much difficulty in writing and revising this section of *Four Quartets*. What is perhaps most revealing in Eliot's comment is that he was quite sensitive to the sexual implications of his Dante allusions, indeed sensitive enough to delete or diminish one so that he will not seem to have maligned Yeats (and of course the compound ghost is not *really* Yeats) by imputing "to him the particular vice which took Brunetto there," by which, of course, Eliot means sodomy. Eliot adds, curiously, that his "reference to that Canto is intended to be explicit." John Hayward might have responded to this remark by asking for a reason: none is given or hinted. But we can only conclude from the remark that Eliot is saying that he indeed had wanted to invoke the particular vice of Brunetto and of canto 15 (*Inferno*) in his portrayal of his "familiar compound ghost." We seem at this point to be approaching a contradiction. Eliot's original intent for the lines was to quote canto 15 with the specific purpose of invoking its context of homosexuality. But in revising the lines to suggest Yeats (but not to mean anything so precise as Yeats), the allusion to canto 15 must be muted. The irony, of course, is that enough of the allusion to canto 15 was left in the finished version that readers readily identified the specific episode and its context that Eliot thought important for his purposes. And the details that might have called forth the name of Yeats were blurred enough to feed a continuing critical controversy as to the identity of the compound ghost. Thus by retaining allusions to canto 15 of the *Inferno* and by adding in revision the allusion to canto 26 of *Purgatorio* (discussed above), Eliot appears to have increased, not diminished, the sexual suggestiveness of the passage with specific overtones of sodomy and homosexuality. Eliot's comment to John Hayward that his reference to canto 15 of the *Inferno* had been intended to be explicit merely confirms that allusions in Eliot's poetry must always be taken seriously as a part of intended meaning. After all, Eliot was the modern poet who developed the technique of allusion as a major poetic resource for the poet.

The earliest surviving draft of *Little Gidding* appears in Appendix A of Helen Gardner's edition of the *Four Quartets* manuscripts, together with John Hayward's letter of criticism, with its concentration not on the larger movements or over-all coherence of the poetry but on what he called "niggling details," particularly sounds, unintentional repetitions, etc. (qtd. in Gardner 235). A part of Eliot's reply to this letter is quoted by Helen Gardner in a chapter of her book devoted to the sources of *Four Quartets*. Eliot's comment provides in an almost casual tone one of the deepest insights we have as to Eliot's obscure purposes in the "familiar compound ghost" lines. He wrote to Hayward that he had been "particularly unhappy about Part II," and believed that it required "some sharpening of personal poignancy" (qtd. in Gardner 67). And he added: "The defect of the whole poem, I feel, is the lack of some acute personal reminiscence (never to be explicated, of course, but to give power from well below the surface) and I can *perhaps* supply this in Part II." The language Eliot uses here is most interesting and perhaps revealing and we should linger over it to be sure we catch its implications. This poet long known for his "impersonal theory" of poetry is unhappy over lines that are flat because they apparently need "some sharpening of personal poignancy." And the problem with the whole of *Little Gidding* is that it lacks "some acute personal reminiscence," which might in revision be supplied in part 2--the "familiar compound ghost" passage. *Acute personal reminiscence*: each of these words has its own resonance--*acute*, anguishing or lacerating; *personal*, involving the poet's innermost feelings; *reminiscence*, a remembrance of things past, of one's youth when passions were fresh and intense. Place this resonant phrase next to Eliot's insistent and privately affirmed allusions to Dante's two cantos, evoking their bands of sodomites and hermaphroditic lustful in the persons of Ser Brunetto from the *Inferno* and Arnaut Daniel from the *Purgatorio*, and we are brought back, inevitably, I believe, to that year in Paris, 1910-11, and the relationship vital to Eliot's imagination, the friendship with Jean Verdenal. It is fair to speculate, I think, that Eliot is being partially but not entirely open with John Hayward in what he says; he has already in the early draft of part 2 of *Little Gidding* embodied fragments of his "acute personal reminiscence" in the figure of the "familiar compound ghost," but he has held back, has not provided enough--not even enough for someone as close as John Hayward--to sense its presence (Hayward's letter does not reveal the kind of heightened response to part 2 that Eliot clearly felt the passage should elicit).

   Eliot's full remark to Hayward, we should now recall, runs thus: "The defect of the whole poem, I feel, is the lack of some acute personal reminscence (never to be explicated, of course, but to give power from well below the surface) and I can *perhaps* supply this in Part II." There is self-assurance in the tone here, as though the speaker *knows* from experience. Of course if my reading of *The Waste Land* has some measure of truth, Eliot *knows* from his experience in the writing of that poem that an "acute personal reminiscence" can give a poem a "power from well below the surface," even when it remains unexplicated. We might assume that in finishing *The Waste Land* in 1921 in the middle of his breakdown (or, as Eliot called it, an "aboulie and emotional derangement" [WLF xxii]), Eliot had barely sensed in the subconscious, or intuited, what he states now with great confidence as established theory: that the embedded personal reminscence in a poem can supply power from beneath the surface without ever being fully understood or delineated. It is possible that such power is most intensely present when it enters the sub-surface levels of the poem unconsciously or intuitively. And thus we might conjecture that Eliot's great difficulty with the writing of *Little Gidding*, and with the "familiar compound ghost" passage of part 2 in particular, came because he was trying intellectually to follow a well-articulated theory instead of abandoning himself emotionally to the engrossing, obsessive memories of the personal experience. Whatever the case, Eliot's comment to Hayward appears to justify the belief that Eliot did include in his poetry, "well below the surface," fragments of an "acute personal experience." His slightly nervous aside--"never to be explicated"--need not detain us here. As I have previously observed, Eliot at times seems to be dropping along the way so many clues as to the nature of the sub-surface currents of his poetry that he seems to want the very explication he here bars or dismisses (160-65).

There seems to be a contradiction in Eliot's pledge in revising part 2 of *Little Gidding* to somehow include that critically missing "acute personal reminiscence," and his actual practice in the revision of increasingly linking the "familiar compound ghost" with William Butler Yeats, in a role that appears to bear no personal involvement with Eliot. We might conclude that Eliot wanted to provide a surface (the Yeatsian hints) that tantalized with its multiple possibilities of explication while providing below the surface that reminiscence whose power would be felt but whose meaning would never be explicated. Even so, the question persists: why Yeats? We may find some of the answers to the question in an essay on Yeats which Eliot was preparing at a time when he was also working hard on *Four Quartets*, to be delivered in Dublin in 1940. It is an essay abundantly full of personal reference.

Eliot paid homage in his lecture *not* to the young Yeats but to the Yeats of middle age, pointing out how unusual it was for a poet to sustain the power of his poetry into later life. He said: "[I]t is my experience that towards middle age a man has three choices: to stop writing altogether, to repeat himself with perhaps an increasing skill of virtuosity, or by taking thought to adapt himself to middle age and find a different way of working" (OPP 297). We need only recall that *Four Quartets* was to be Eliot's last major poetic effort, to realize that Eliot has his own career in mind as much as Yeats'. He added: "That a poet should develop at all, that he should find something new to say, and say it equally well, in middle age, has always something miraculous about it" (OPP 298).

What is missing in Yeats' early poetry, Eliot pointed out, is the personal: "Now among all the poems in Yeats' earlier volumes I find only in a line here or there, that sense of a unique personality which makes one sit up in excitement and eagerness to learn more about the author's mind and feelings. The intensity of Yeats' own emotional experience hardly appears" (OPP 298-99). Here Eliot seems to find the missing ingredient in Yeats' poetry precisely the same as that missing ingredient he would shortly after detect in his own *Little Gidding*. And in anticipation of the critic's charge of inconsistency, Eliot adds:

> I have, in early essays, extolled what I called impersonality in art, and it may seem that, in giving as a reason for the superiority of Yeats' later work the greater expression of personality in it, I am contradicting myself. It may be that I expressed myself badly, or that I had only an adolescent grasp of that idea--as I can never bear to re-read my own prose writings, I am willing to leave the point unsettled--but I think now, at least, the truth of the matter is as follows. There are two forms of impersonality: that which is natural to the mere skilful craftsman, and that which is more and more achieved by the maturing artist. The first is that of what I have called the 'anthology piece,' of a lyric by Lovelace or Suckling, or of Campion, a finer poet than either. The second impersonality is that of the poet who, out of intense and personal experience, is able to express a general truth; retaining all the particularity of his experience, to make of it a general symbol. (OPP 299)

Yeats, Eliot says, was the first kind of poet when young, and became a great poet of the second kind as he developed. And it is, of course, a poet of this second kind that we have observed Eliot himself trying to become in his revision of *Four Quartets*. Although he remained silent on the matter, Eliot's very silence underscores his assumption that he thought his own early poetry contained that personal intensity that Yeats' early poetry lacked.

As an example of Yeats' excellent later poetry, Eliot quotes the following lines (the poem is entitled "The Spur"):

You think it horrible that lust and rage
Should dance attendance² upon my old age;
They were not such a plague when I was young;
What else have I to spur me into song? (OPP 302)

Eliot's comment reveals as much about himself as about Yeats:

> These lines are very impressive and not very pleasant, and the
> sentiment has recently been criticized by an English critic whom I
> generally respect. But I think he misread them. I do not read them
> as a personal confession of a man who differed from other men,
> but of a man who was essentially the same as most other men; the
> only difference is in the greater clarity, honesty and vigour. To
> what honest man, old enough, can these sentiments be entirely
> alien? They can be subdued and disciplined by religion, but who
> can say that they are dead? Only those to whom the maxim of La
> Rochefoucauld applies: "Quand les vices nous quittent, nous nous
> flattons de la créance que c'est nous qui les quittons." The tragedy
> of Yeats' epigram is all in the last line.

That last line, "What else have I [other than lust and rage] to
spur me into song?", might well sum up Eliot's dilemma in
working to revise the "familiar compound ghost" passage, seeking to infuse beneath the surface of the poem that "acute personal reminiscence" that had already before spurred him into
the writing of *The Waste Land*. But the astonishing revelation in
Eliot's comment is the quickness with which he identifies the
feelings of "lust and rage" dancing "attendance upon" old age as
in effect a universal feeling: "To what honest man, old enough,
can these sentiments be entirely alien?" In identifying with
Yeats through these lines, which in turn carry him back to his
youthful Paris days and an experience of intense "personal
poignancy," Eliot here perhaps provides the answer as to why,
later, in revising the "compound ghost" passage of *Four Quartets*
he will decide to combine a clearly suggestive but meticulously
inexplicit portrait of Yeats together with a sub-surface "acute
personal reminiscence," in the hope of providing the ambiguity
and the intensity he thought the passage needed.

     The portrait of Yeats, inasmuch as it emerges in the
"familiar compound ghost" lines, is only partial, not to say
vague. The significant details appear in the first half of the
ghost's long speech, mainly retrospective:

> 'I am not eager to rehearse
> My thought and theory which you have forgotten.
> These things have served their purpose: let them be.
> So with your own, and pray they be forgiven

---

2. Eliot misquotes this word, which was "attention," in Yeats (309).

By others, as I pray you to forgive
Both bad and good. Last season's fruit is eaten
And the fullfed beast shall kick the empty pail.
For last year's words belong to last year's language
And next year's words await another voice.
But, as the passage now presents no hindrance
To the spirit unappeased and peregrine
Between two worlds become much like each other,
So I find words I never thought to speak
In streets I never thought I should revisit
When I left my body on a distant shore. (CPP 141)

We have already seen that Eliot did not want the specific Dantean allusion in earlier lines, with its implication of sexual inversion, to apply to Yeats. And we might in addition observe that when the ghost says "I left my body on a distant shore," the detail could apply to both Yeats and Jean Verdenal (Yeats buried originally in Roquebrune, overlooking the coast of France, Verdenal in the "mud of Gallipoli"). Eliot himself, when reading critics who identified the ghost as a specific person, exclaimed in wonder: "But why the phrase 'compound ghost' 'Both one and many' should still leave people convinced that the stranger was one particular person, I don't understand" (qtd. in ftn. Gardner 67, 77). If we take hints from Eliot's 1940 essay on Yeats, we might assume that Yeats is dimly shadowed forth in order to evoke his poetry of old age affirming eloquently the persistence of lust and rage.

The next passage in the ghost's speech, indeed, echoes many of the sentiments of Yeats' later poetry:

Let me disclose the gifts reserved for age
To set a crown upon your lifetime's effort.
First, the cold friction of expiring sense
Without enchantment, offering no promise
But bitter tastelessness of shadow fruit
As body and soul begin to fall asunder.
Second, the conscious impotence of rage
At human folly, and the laceration
Of laughter at what ceases to amuse,
And last, the rending pain of re-enactment
Of all that you have done, and been; the shame
Of motives late revealed, and the awareness
Of things ill done and done to others' harm
Which once you took for exercise of virtue.
Then fools' approval stings, and honour stains.
From wrong to wrong the exasperated spirit
Proceeds, unless restored by that refining fire
Where you must move in measure, like a dance. (CPP 141-42)

The prophecy is a bleak one, and has the ring of authenticity. But though the sentiments are, in part, Yeatsian, the voice is more clearly Eliotic. As we recall that the speaker has earlier, on encountering the ghost, "assumed a double part," is both himself and yet "someone other," we might fairly conclude that the prophecy wells up from within, and is honest self-knowledge as to what the future will bring.

The ambiguity of the source of the prophecy should remind us of a similar ambiguity in *The Waste Land*, when the thunder speaks at the end of part 5. There each of the thunder's three sounds is translated by the protagonist into the wisdom of self-knowledge, a kind of honest confrontation with things as they are in the most personal sense, all somehow obscurely related to "the awful daring of a moment's surrender," which I read as related to Jean Verdenal. The direct confrontation with personal reality, brought about by the thunder, brings a kind of release from the previous paralysis: the poet is able now to begin shoring against his ruins, albeit all he has to shore are the scattered fragments with which he is left, one of the fragments Dante's line about Arnaut Daniel diving back into the refining fire. Similarly, in *Four Quartets'* "compound ghost" passage, the poet soberly confronts three aspects of the personal reality of old age, the "cold friction of expiring sense," "conscious impotence of rage at human folly," and the "rending pain of re-enactment" of all that he has done and been. There are no fragments to shore against his ruins, but only the awareness that he will proceed, an "exasperated spirit," from "wrong to wrong,"--until he reaches that same refining fire awaiting *The Waste Land's* protagonist. These two moments of intensity in these two remarkable poems, although separated by some two decades, suggest a continuity of feeling and being astonishing in their endurance. They are uniquely similar in that they seem to import voices--thunder, ghost--from outside the poems' protagonists for prophetic pronouncement; but these voices turn out to be voices from the deepest levels of the protagonists themselves. The wisdom proffered about life in the two moments changes or deepens with the age of the poet and his protagonists, but the wisdom of the necessity of the refining fire, the rite of purification, remains unchanged.

After the "compound ghost's" long speech, the scene is drawn quickly to a close:

> The day was breaking. In the disfigured street
> He left me, with a kind of valediction,
> And faded on the blowing of the horn.

Like all proper ghosts, this one fades with the day, but not before saying his farewell to the poet. And this farewell seems to me to take on that dimension of the personal that Eliot said he would try to inject on the sub-surface level as he revised. If the ghost may, in some obscure way, be identified as Jean Verdenal (but of course not limited to him), then this farewell in a "disfigured street" is a personal farewell to a memory that has haunted the poet for a long time through some of his greatest poetic moments, as in "Prufrock" and *The Waste Land*. It is also a farewell to poetry inasmuch as this "acute personal reminiscence" has been summoned as a source for poetic passion for the last time; it has been exhausted as a poetic resource. Perhaps this is one of the major reasons that Eliot exclaimed, in his 1950 lecture in "What Dante Means to Me," "This section of . . . [the] poem [on the "compound ghost"] cost me far more time and trouble and vexation than any passage of the same length that I have ever written" (TCC 129). Eliot, in sorting through those options listed in his lecture on Yeats, chose not to stop writing altogether, and he chose *not* to repeat himself, but he did choose to "adapt himself to middle age and find a different way of working"--in drama and prose. Unlike Yeats' early poetry, Eliot's early poetry contained, as he was well aware, the intensity of the poet's "own emotional experience." Eliot's satisfaction at that awareness is vividly implicit in the Yeats essay. It is that self-awareness that enables Eliot to appreciate so lavishly Yeats' old age poetry, which contains that intensity of the personal that Eliot's later poetry lacked. Thus the farewell in *Four Quartets* is poignant indeed, as it represents Eliot's acknowledgment to himself that he will turn to a "different way of working." It is his farewell to the ghost of Verdenal; it is his farewell to poetry.

WORKS CITED

Dante. *The Divine Comedy.* Ed. John D. Sinclair. New York: Oxford UP, 1978.

Eliot, T. S. *On Poetry and Poets.* New York: The Noonday Press, Farrar, Straus, & Giroux, 1957.

_____. "What Dante Means to Me." *To Criticize the Critic.* New York: Farrar, Straus & Giroux, 1965. 128-29.

Gallup, Donald. "The 'Lost' Manuscripts of T. S. Eliot." *Times Literary Supplement* 7 Nov. 1968: 1240.

Gardner, Helen, ed. *The Composition of Four Quartets.* New York: Oxford UP, 1978.

Matthews, T. S. *Great Tom: Notes Towards the Definition of T. S. Eliot.* New York: Harper & Row, Pub., 1974.

Miller, James E., Jr. *T. S. Eliot's Personal Waste Land: Exorcism of the Demons*.
    Chicago: U of Chicago P, 1977.
Peter, John. "*The Waste Land* Reinterpreted: Postscript (1969)." *Essays in Criti-*
    cism 19 (Apr. 1969): 170.
Richards, I. A. *Principles of Literary Criticism*. 2nd ed. New York: Harcourt,
    Brace and Co., 1948.
Sencourt, Robert. *T. S. Eliot: A Memoir*. New York: Dodd, Mead & Co., 1971.
Yeats, William Butler. *The Collected Poems of William Butler Yeats*. New York:
    Macmillan, 1976.

RICHARD BADENHAUSEN

"WHEN THE POET SPEAKS ONLY FOR HIMSELF": THE CHORUS AS 'FIRST VOICE' IN MURDER IN THE CATHEDRAL*

In *The Idiom of Drama*, Thomas Van Laan explains that the chief limitation of the dramatic medium is "the absence of a single expressive voice" (viii). When T. S. Eliot turned to writing drama in mid-career, this feature, more than any other, troubled him. Eliot's early fondness for the dramatic monologue and his frequent dependence in poems on single controlling protagonists like Prufrock, Gerontion, and Tiresias, complicated the playwright's task when he was faced with creating numerous voices for a theatrical medium.

Consequently, in his first full-length play, *Murder in the Cathedral*, Eliot employed a chorus (the Women of Canterbury), a device that came as close as dramatically possible to a single expressive voice. As he polished his dramatic skills in later plays, Eliot no longer had to depend on the chorus as an authorial mouthpiece--by *The Cocktail Party* he had abandoned the chorus for good. But in 1935 Eliot was still struggling to discover the proper voice for his characters. He was also continually troubled by the difference between composing poetry and writing for the stage, so much so that in 1953 he tried to resolve the problem once and for all by establishing, in "The Three Voices of Poetry," appropriate voices for the poet talking to himself, speaking to an audience, and writing for a dramatic character:

> The first voice is the voice of the poet talking to himself--or to nobody. The second is the voice of the poet addressing an audience, whether large or small. The third is the voice of the poet when he attempts to create a dramatic character speaking in verse; when he is saying, not what he would say in his own person, but only what he can say within the limits of one imaginary character addressing another imaginary character. (OPP 96)

---

*This essay is a longer version of a paper given at the National Poetry Foundation's T. S. Eliot Centennial Conference, August 18-20, 1988, Orono, Maine.

Whereas Eliot could maintain that in a poem he wrote for his "own voice ... [to achieve] the equivalent in words for that much of what I have felt," the prospect of this intimate voice appearing on stage before a public audience proved disconcerting (Hall 62). As one who frequently expressed embarrassment when confronted by pronouncements made in his critical writing,[1] Eliot found it just as difficult to face his personal voice ("the voice of the poet talking to himself") when it surfaced in the plays. Eliot used the "Three Voices" essay to divorce that private voice from that of his dramatic creations. Yet the Chorus in *Murder in the Cathedral* actually speaks lines which expose Eliot's so-called 'first voice' (the poet speaking to himself), recalls early Eliotic speakers (such as Prufrock, Gerontion, and Tiresias), and reveals the familiar concerns, fears, and obsessions of the poet.[2] In fact, the choral device served as a perfect transition from the poetry to the drama because it allowed Eliot to develop the third voice through characters like Becket, the Priests, and the Knights, while still exercising the first voice in the lines of the Chorus. As *Murder in the Cathedral* evolved, Eliot recognized this more personal voice surfacing in the lines of the Chorus. In addition to the later defenses in the prose, the dramatist responded to this threatening voice by constructing a strictly ordered framework within the play (a technique which had succeeded in the poetry), especially through the instruments of setting, dramatic structure, and versification, in an attempt to control this energy.

Although Eliot enjoyed advancing a theory which distinguished among three voices, the system does not apply to much of his own poetry and drama. We need only recall that Eliot originally wrote the first fifteen lines of *Burnt Norton* (published in 1936, one year after the first production of *Murder in the Cathedral*) as a speech for the Second Priest, to understand the poet's confusion of voices (Gardner, *The Composition of* Four Quartets 39). In *Murder in the Cathedral* the Chorus' speech beginning "There is no rest in the house" was originally written only in first person singular pronouns (CPP 193). But in preparing the fourth edition--a text which contains the prefatory note: "certain further rearrangements and deletions have been made, which have been found advisable by experiment in the

---

1. In "Goethe as Sage," he confesses that "I have always found the re-reading of my own prose writings too painful a task," while in "The Music of Poetry," he claims "I can never re-read any of my own prose writings without acute embarrassment: I shirk the task." Both passages appear in OPP (256, 17). See also OPP 299.
2. Thus I cannot agree completely with David Jones' assessment of the Chorus as an independent character speaking in the third voice which "required Eliot to make an imaginative identification," in *The Plays of T. S. Eliot* 48.

course of production"--Eliot changed one line to read "And the earth presses up against our feet," from the original ". . . presses up beneath *my* feet."[3] In 1953, Eliot was still struggling to understand his difficulty in discovering the proper voice for the Chorus: "for a chorus of women of Canterbury," he writes, "I had to make some effort to identify myself with these women, instead of merely identifying them with myself" (OPP 99). Eliot recognized, in retrospect, his tendency to employ the Chorus as a mouthpiece for his own voice--at least initially, he had failed to accomplish his stated goal of "identify[ing] myself with these women."

Other observations by Eliot suggest that he felt particularly comfortable with the Chorus in his first play, and therefore might have assigned its members his more personal poetry. Two decades after having employed the device in *The Rock*, performed in 1934, Eliot confessed that the members of the Chorus, at some stages in the pageant, "were speaking *for me*, not uttering words that really represented any supposed character of their own" (OPP 99). In a discussion of *The Rock*, E. Martin Browne (who played the Fourth Tempter in the Canterbury production of *Murder in the Cathedral*) confirmed that the choral device comforted Eliot:

> this use of a liturgical hymn . . . gave him a sense of security. It is a characteristic manifestation of the combination in his temperament of adventurousness and caution, and of his need to feel himself launching his flights from a pad of classic structure. (26)

Likewise, in a letter written to Rupert Doone (who produced *Sweeney Agonistes* in 1934) dated 25 July 1934, Eliot mentions that "if I write the play I have in mind, it would require a chorus, and my recent experience warns me that choruses need long and arduous training" (39). His insistence upon using a chorus, even before agreeing to write a play (which Browne presumes was *Murder in the Cathedral*), suggests its appeal to Eliot. Likewise this early conception of the chorus--Eliot's handwritten notes to *Murder in the Cathedral* show that the chorus was far more developed than the other characters in the early stages of composition[4]--encouraged the poet to compose choral passages in the 'first voice' and separated the Women of Canterbury from

---

3. The third edition of *Murder in the Cathedral* with autograph revisions throughout (used by Eliot to prepare the fourth edition) is held at the Harry Ransom Humanities Research Center at the University of Texas and is designated A29d(1) in Alexander Sackton's catalogue *The T. S. Eliot Collection of The University of Texas at Austin* (Austin: Humanities Research Center, 1975), hereafter referred to as Sackton. The quotation appears on p. 40, italics added.
4. See Browne 40-55, on the relatively early conception of choral passages in Eliot's manuscript notes, now held at the Houghton Library.

the other dramatic creations. He shows a similar devotion to the chorus during the composition of *The Family Reunion*, for Browne tells us that the Chorus' lines were essentially complete by the first draft and that they remained "unaffected by alterations made to that end . . . they must have been one of the clearest features in Eliot's first conception" (93). In another essay, Eliot explains that "it is easier for a poet to write choral verse than to write dramatic dialogue. It is more like the kind of writing which he has already mastered" ("The Aims of Poetic Drama" 11). Here Eliot comes as close as he ever would to identifying the Chorus with his early 'first voice' poetry. But the poet later wondered about the value of admitting that connection, for he dropped the above confession from "Poetry and Drama," the revised version of "The Aims of Poetic Drama."

   If we think of the Chorus as a single character speaking in the first person singular, then we may align it with the many "I"-figures in a line of Eliotic speakers which includes Prufrock, Gerontion, and Tiresias. The nominative singular personal pronoun is employed in *Murder in the Cathedral* when the choral unit breaks up to allow for speeches by single members of the group. Though such breaks are given only in the published text of the film version of the play and not in earlier editions of the play, the initial production of *Murder in the Cathedral* at Canterbury established the tradition of allotting various portions of text to individual speakers or groups within the Chorus.[5] Some critics have gone so far as trying to identify individual personalities within the choral group, though I think this attaches a dimension to the Chorus that is supported neither by the play nor by the Chorus' lines. Browne comes closer to Eliot's conception of the Chorus when he identifies "threads of character" that recur in choral passages.[6] The "I" usually sur-

---

5. Individual choral parts are noted in T. S. Eliot and George Hoellering, *The Film of* Murder in the Cathedral. In *The Making of T. S. Eliot's Plays*, Browne discusses the "Chorus in Performance" in the initial production (80-89). Likewise, prompt copies of *Murder in the Cathedral* held in the Harry Ransom Humanities Research Center at the University of Texas at Austin and in the Houghton Library at Harvard show the various assignments of each woman in the Chorus. Their names are written in pencil in the margins of the text next to their respective lines.

6. In "Voices in the Cathedral: The Chorus in Eliot's *Murder in the Cathedral*," William J. McGill traces three individual dramatic voices, "each stressing a particular dimension of the choral function" (293). Browne's phrase, "threads of character," which he adapts from Elsie Fogerty's description of the original production (she directed the choruses for *The Rock* and *Murder in the Cathedral*), is more convincing. These "threads of character," he remarks in *The Making of T. S. Eliot's Plays*, are "expressed in recurring lines of a certain mood: a mood of bitterness, a mood of unquenchable optimism, a mood of practical common sense, a mood of fearfulness" (86).

   A prompt copy of *Murder in the Cathedral* for a production at the Poet's Theatre of Harvard (19-24 March 1937), now held by the Houghton Library, has a page entitled "characterizations" which designates each woman's characteristics during the opening choral ode. The "Second Woman" is "resigned, accepting," while the "Fifth Woman" is "earthy, strong." Presumably the women retained these personalities throughout the performance. While these traits were appointed to each character during rehearsals, their lines do little to reinforce the particular qualities.

faces at particularly climatic and imaginative moments when the speaker acts as a representative spokesperson for the group by expressing fear of external events that threaten to bring about change, always a painful experience in Eliot's poetic world. For example, one member fears a "disturbance of the quiet seasons" (CPP 176), while another dreads the coming of the murderers: "I have smelt them, the death-bringers" (CPP 207).

Individuality within the Chorus emerges most often during moments when the imagination exerts itself, thus aligning the Women of Canterbury with earlier 'first voice' speakers. Their voice expresses a tension in the play like that which numerous critics have identified in the poetry, among them George Bornstein, who recognizes "the conflict between the fear and fostering of explosive powers within the psyche often associated with imagination" (xii), and David Spurr, who understands Eliot's poetry as revealing

> a consciousness whose emotional intensity derives from an aware-ness of its own inner divisions; its strength lies in its refusal to allow the controlling power of the intellect or the controlling form of the poem to annihilate the dark impulses of horror and ecstasy. (xix-xx)

By embracing the 'first voice', Eliot's most intimate and personal voice, the Chorus joins the voices of Prufrock, Gerontion, and Tiresias (or, as Eliot explains, those voices that express "the equivalent in words for that much of what I have felt"), as a dramatic version of a character who exposes the psychic strife in the poet's mind (Hall 62).

In his non-dramatic poetry, Eliot attempts to control this psychic conflict by constructing a firm external order for his poems.[7] The search for a supporting structure continues in *Murder in the Cathedral*, which is carefully shaped so that its events parallel the ritual of the Mass.[8] Thomas' Christmas morning homily appears in the same location that we would find the tra-ditional sermon. Near the conclusion, a choir sings a *Dies Irae* and a *Te Deum* in the background, reaffirming the Mass struc-ture. As early as 1928, Eliot suggests that

> the consummation of the drama, the perfect and ideal drama, is to be found in the ceremony of the Mass . . . drama springs from reli-gious liturgy, and . . . it cannot afford to depart far from religious

---

7. See Bornstein on how Eliot "sought to snare the eruptions in a framework of order" (xii).
8. Many critics have noted this affinity. Particularly insightful studies which trace the developments of the play in terms of the Mass structure are Robert W. Ayers, *"Murder in the Cathedral*: A 'Liturgy Less Divine'," and John P. Cutts, "Evidence for Ambivalence of Motives in *Murder in the Cathedral*."

> liturgy. . . . The Mass is a small drama, having all the unities. (SE 35)

He understood it as the task of poetic drama to provide some assemblage of order to the chaos of everyday reality. While defining the ideal poetic drama in "Poetry and Drama" (1951), Eliot pauses to explain that

> it is ultimately the function of art, in imposing a credible order upon ordinary reality, and thereby eliciting some perception of an order *in* reality, to bring us to a condition of serenity, stillness, and reconciliation. (OPP 94)

Even the setting for the original production of the play--the Chapter House at Canterbury--provided Eliot with an external framework of order within which to work and allowed him, as he recognized, to "exploit . . . the special advantages of such a setting" (Eliot and Hoellering ix). The setting functioned as an ordering device which kept the Chorus from losing itself entirely in disturbing, chaotic imaginings, such as the outburst at the end of part 1, when the women experience visions of flying animals "swing[ing] and wing[ing] through the dark air" (CPP 196).

      The inclination to break out of the established Christian framework surfaces, most notably, in the Chorus' tendency toward hysterical and violent rhetoric (often with sexual undertones) and, less overtly, in the fragmentation of the choral unit which allows individual female speakers to employ the "I" during imaginative moments.[9] As the Priests attempt to drag Thomas to vespers and thus protect him from the murderous Knights, the Chorus' graphically horrific language undercuts the unusually regular stanzaic form as well as the ordered Latin hymn sung in the distance:

> Numb the hand and dry the eyelid,
> Still the horror, but more horror
> Than when tearing in the belly.
>
> Still the horror, but more horror
> Than when twisting in 'the fingers,
> Than when splitting in the skull. (CPP 210)

Or, as the second Latin hymn, the *Te Deum*, reaffirms a Christian order towards the conclusion, the Chorus moves into a description of Becket's shrine and then abruptly displaces time and space by referring to *future* visitors' desecration of the shrine in the *present tense*: "There is holy ground, and the sanc-

---

9. See, for example, the choral passage cited below in note 14.

tity shall not depart from it / Though armies trample over it, though sightseers come with guide-books looking over it" (CPP 221). Even the title of the play, *Murder in the Cathedral*, suggests the inherent tension between a lurking violence and the Christian framework.[10] The use of two such disparate nouns as "murder" and "cathedral" embodies perfectly the tension between the classical elements (chorus, fate, murder) and the Christian qualities (Mass, salvation, sainthood) of the play. This conflict within a title recalls "The Love Song of J. Alfred Prufrock," in which the emotional, lyrical connotations of "Love Song" disagree with those of the formal, conventional "J. Alfred Prufrock," foreshadowing a basic dichotomy in the poem between emotion and restraint.

Such tensions, both structural and thematic, and present in many Eliotic speakers, reveal themselves most often in the language of the Chorus. Recognizing direct similarities in the type of tensions which surface in both the speakers of earlier poems and the voice of the Chorus allows us to situate the Chorus in the line of Eliot's 'first voice' poetic speakers. We may first identify the Chorus with earlier speakers both through its status as witness of events and through its tendency to reflect the overall mood of the action. Eliot understood the traditional functions of the Greek chorus, which included the representation of public temperament, viewing the action on stage and, when its members did not act, commenting upon the dramatic situation or offering advice and warning.[11] In the play's opening lines, the Chorus tells us: "Some presage of an act / Which our eyes are compelled to witness, has forced our feet / Towards the cathedral. We are forced to bear witness. . . . For us, the poor, there is no action, / But only to wait and to witness" (CPP 175, 177). These lines fulfill one of the basic functions of the chorus, that of exposition at the start of a drama: the women have been forced into action by the approach of Archbishop Thomas Becket, who has returned after a seven year absence. The play opens as if all action has been suspended during Thomas' sabbatical. Only his return can restart the still point of Time's wheel. By identifying Becket as an external authority that compels them to act, the Chorus affiliates itself with speakers like

---

10. As Lionel Pike notes, "the cathedral is traditionally a place of sanctuary, not of danger. This element of conflict is introduced immediately as the play begins: . . . 'there is no safety in the cathedral'." See his "Liturgy and Time: *Murder in the Cathedral*" 281.

11. Van Laan's *The Idiom of Drama* contains an insightful discussion of the chorus in Greek Tragedy (17-22). He notes that the chorus is a particularly good tool for a dramatist who wishes to manipulate plot, characters, and spectators of a play. He also makes an interesting comparison between the "impersonal voice" of the chorus and the "omniscient narrative voice of prose fiction" (21), a connection which sheds further light on the Chorus as 'first voice'.

Prufrock and Gerontion, both of whom also encounter difficulties with agency and will. Most of the Chorus' movements transpire as *responses*, as reactions to the coming of an outside, foreign presence, like Becket, who arrives "with applause . . . with rejoicing . . . but . . . bringing death into Canterbury" (CPP 180), or the entrance of the Knights, the "death-bringers" (CPP 207). Both force the Women of Canterbury to confront issues unrelated to their usual domestic experience, and the resultant challenge brings with it a sharp and disturbing pain. Because the play contains numerous such encounters, the Chorus' role as witness to and reflector of the many disturbances emerges as an agonizing one.

This inclination to wait and to witness surfaces repeatedly in Prufrock's voice and is reinforced by his many fantasies, usually imagined in tentative conditionals. Even Prufrock's visions emphasize stasis and connect visual witnessing with fixity, as when he wonders:

> And I have known the eyes already, known them all--
> The eyes that fix you in a formulated phrase,
> And when I am formulated, sprawling on a pin,
> When I am pinned and wriggling on the wall,
> Then how should I begin
> To spit out all the butt-ends of my days and ways? (CPP 5)

More importantly, though, the poem's events are determined by Prufrock's mind, for it is the controlling agent of the poem. As I argue elsewhere, manuscript evidence suggests that the choral passages functioned in a similar way, as an organizing principle in *Murder in the Cathedral* (Badenhausen 33-38). In "Gerontion," a waiting figure foreshadows the Chorus' "but only to wait and to witness" (CPP 177). The poem opens in a similar manner to *Murder in the Cathedral*, with the old man, responding to the action of another (a boy), waiting for seasonal change: "Here I am, an old man in a dry month, / Being read to by a boy, waiting for rain" (CPP 21). The Chorus delivers its version at the very start of the play: "Here let us stand, close by the cathedral. Here let us wait. . . . The New Year waits, breathes, waits, whispers in darkness" (CPP 175). One substantial difference, however, is Gerontion's longing for an external event which will initiate personal movement or growth. His vocabulary suggests a personal stasis that is destructive, as when he imagines, "when I / Stiffen in a rented house" (CPP 22). Unlike the Chorus, which undergoes a collective transformation and realization due to external events (even though its members are terrified of the change), by the end of "Gerontion," besides not moving physically, the speaker has not achieved psychological or spiritual growth. He laments, "Tenants of the house, / Thoughts of a dry brain in a dry season"--the rainstorm has yet to arrive (CPP 23).

In Tiresias we have the speaker who most resembles the Chorus, especially in his ability to witness events and react to them. Eliot's note explaining the role of Tiresias (though appended after *The Waste Land* was essentially complete) could apply, with few qualifications, to the Women of Canterbury:

> Tiresias, although a mere spectator and not indeed a 'character', is yet the most important personage in the poem, uniting all the rest ... so all the women are one woman, and the two sexes meet in Tiresias. What Tiresias *sees*, in fact, is the substance of the poem. (CPP 52)

We need take only one more step to arrive at "reflecting in their emotion the significance of the action," Eliot's definition of the role of the Chorus (OPP 86). What the Chorus sees is, in large part, the substance of the play. The Women of Canterbury embody both the masculine and feminine principles, as Tiresias does, for they confess: "we acknowledge ourselves as type of the common man, / Of the men and women who shut the door and sit by the fire" (CPP 221). Likewise, Eliot's comment that Tiresias unites "all the rest ... so all the women are one woman" foreshadows the make-up of the later choral unit. In its watching, waiting, and reacting the Chorus is the natural successor to Tiresias.

Because they wait and witness, and are disturbed by movement outside their households, the Women of Canterbury dread external intrusions like Thomas' homecoming. This fear reveals itself in the Chorus' strong resistance to change and its continual search for quiet anonymity:

> And we are content if we are left alone.
> We try to keep our households in order;
> ....
> Preferring to pass unobserved.
> ....
> We do not wish anything to happen.
> Seven years we have lived quietly,
> Succeeded in avoiding notice. (CPP 176, 180)

Because the impending arrival of the Archbishop threatens to disturb this calm, the Chorus expresses its dissatisfaction in a shocking use of the imperative: "Leave us to perish in quiet" (CPP 180). Besides fearing human intrusion, the Chorus is alarmed by seasonal change; hence its description of the passing of the seasons emerges in typically violent language:

> Now I fear the disturbance of the quiet seasons:
> Winter shall come bringing death from the sea,
> Ruinous spring shall beat at our doors,
> Root and shoot shall eat our eyes and our ears,
> Disastrous summer burn up the beds of our streams
> And the poor shall wait for another decaying October. (CPP 176)

As usual during these charged moments, the Chorus breaks up into single speakers who employ the "I," thus strengthening the presence of Eliot's 'first voice'.

Like the Women of Canterbury, the 'first voice' speaker in "Gerontion" resists growth and rejects the renewal traditionally offered in spring. Even though the poem opens with Gerontion "waiting for rain," renewal never takes place and his quest fails--he remains a figure of stasis. The old man speaks of a "depraved May," employing an adjective which undercuts the traditional associations of spring as a time of youth, future growth, and rebirth (associations which Eliot calls up earlier in the same line with "the juvescence of the year"), and instead characterizes the season as corrupt (CPP 21). When discussing the change from one year to the next, Gerontion employs menacing images which indicate the potential for violence and pain in seasonal cycles: "The tiger springs in the new year. Us he devours" (CPP 22). The Chorus also perceives the new year as threatening, and it embraces similar language in describing the potentially harmful change; like an animal lurking in the shadows, "the New Year waits, breathes, waits, whispers in darkness" (CPP 175).

In *The Waste Land*, Eliot writes for a voice that most resembles the Chorus in its fear of growth and renewal usually associated with spring. In the well-known opening lines of his poem, Eliot's use of unexpected adjectives ("cruellest," "dead," "Dull") and bitter tone undercuts our expectations from the start in a passage seemingly about spring: "April is the cruellest month, breeding / Lilacs out of the dead land, mixing / Memory and desire, stirring / Dull roots with spring rain" (CPP 37). The attention to the detail of the stirring roots and the incessant upward pressure anticipates the language in choral passages which portray growth in spring, and even foreshadows the agony of rebirth as understood by Mary in *The Family Reunion*, when she chants: "The cold spring now is the time / For the ache in the moving root / The agony in the dark / The slow flow throbbing the trunk / The pain of the breaking bud" (CPP 251).

I am not alone in presuming that the Chorus' lines make up the best poetry in the play.[12] Contrary to Eliot's assertions in "The Three Voices of Poetry"--that you cannot afford to "give him (or her) all the 'poetry' to speak" (OPP 100)--the women of the Chorus *do* have most of the good 'poetry', a further reason why we may identify them more readily with Eliot's 'first voice'. In fact, in "The Future of Poetic Drama" (1938), Eliot identifies many of the best lines of a first draft as 'his' poetry:

> I find that in my first draft of a play there are passages which seem to me first-rate, and they are likely to be the ones that I have to remove. They may be plums, but if so it is right that plums should be pulled out; they are poetry, *but they are my poetry and not that of my character who speaks them.* (4, italics added)

My argument has suggested that Eliot did not pull out quite all the plums. It is also telling that Eliot finds first drafts especially pleasing and particularly personal (the two seem to go together), for as noted earlier, the choral passages for *Murder in the Cathedral* were completed earlier than the other lines and through the many editions of the play were left mostly unchanged.[13] Likewise, the choral passages composed early in the evolution of *The Family Reunion* changed little in subsequent drafts.

Finally, the Chorus tends to embrace thematic concerns that often arise in Eliot's 'first voice' poetry, such as the spatialization of the poetic world by locating energy downward and inward and situating restraint upward and outward;[14] the

---

12. In *"Murder in the Cathedral*: The Limits of Drama," Murray Krieger observes of the Chorus: "their poetry constitutes the finest passages in the play" (81); and Helen Gardner argues, "the real drama of the play is to be found in fact where its greatest poetry lies--in the Choruses" (Gardner, *The Art of T. S. Eliot* 136). Others however have not been as enthusiastic. Hugh Kenner writes of the lines, "they remain a poetic embarrassment" (285). Likewise, in *T. S. Eliot: A Study in Character and Style*, Ronald Bush speaks of Eliot's "groping use of the Chorus in *The Rock* and *Murder in the Cathedral*" (169).

13. The text Eliot used to prepare a fourth edition (A29d[1] in Sackton) shows that of the nine major choral passages in *Murder in the Cathedral* six were left untouched, one contains a change in punctuation, one contains a single word change, and one has two words altered. Relative to the rest of the text, the Chorus' lines are remarkable for their few modifications.

14. See Bornstein, who identifies in Eliot's poetry, "the tendency of romantic imagery to locate sources of power downward and within, rather than upward and outward. . . . [the] familiar cluster of vitality from below" (133-34), and Spurr, who acknowledges that Eliot "characteristically locates the origins of inspiration downward and inward" (24-25). An example of this tendency in the plays occurs in part 2 of *Murder in the Cathedral*. As the Knights approach Thomas before murdering him, various choral members engage in a frantic chant dominated by imagery of a spatialized world:

> Flirted with the passage of the kite, I have
> > plunged with the kite and cowered with the
> > wren.
> . . . .
> I have smelt
> Corruption in the dish, incense in the latrine, the
> > sewer in the incense . . . I have seen
> Rings of light coiling downwards, descending
> To the horror of the ape.
> . . . .
> What is woven in the councils of princes

undercurrent of violence which often surfaces during imaginatively charged moments or during sexual encounters; the fear of
reality especially when that reality threatens to suffocate the
character; and a reliance on animal imagery during climactic
moments. Those thematic parallels suggest the type of dramatic
moments which most often contain hints of the 'first voice'. And
in most cases, these moments involve the Chorus mouthing lines
which are unusually personal ("my poetry and not that of my
character who speaks them") in a language distinct from that of
the other characters.

In the end, Eliot's Chorus proves a strong representative of the poetic 'first voice'; its concerns and obsessions
recall similar fears in early Eliotic speakers. Eliot's apprehen-
siveness over writing in a new medium dictated the use of a
form which allowed for both expression of the familiar 'first
voice' and experimentation with the 'third voice'. The Chorus
satisfied this need and made *Murder in the Cathedral* the perfect
bridge between Eliot's early poetry and his verse drama. It is less
surprising, then, that the poet grafted a passage from *Murder in
the Cathedral* into *Burnt Norton*. I have paid particular attention
to choral passages which recall early poems because it reinforces
my argument that the 'first voice' remains prominent in the
dramatic poetry. The Chorus differs from earlier speakers only
in its change in spiritual state at the conclusion of *Murder in the
Cathedral*. In response to Thomas' death, the women embrace
the possibility of spiritual rebirth; and they no longer fear the
change of the seasons because they now view time in terms of a
Christian cycle. By the end of the play they speak in a lyrical and
peaceful voice when discussing subjects which had previously
brought discontent and pain: "Even in us the voices of seasons,
the snuffle of winter, the song of spring, the drone of summer,
the voices of beasts and of birds, praise Thee" (CPP 221). Eliot's
religious conversion obviously dictates an ending different from
the unfulfilled concluding moments of the early poems. We do
find, however, that Eliot's technique to achieve closure recalls
similar tactics employed in the poetry. In *Murder in the Cathedral*, the Chorus, through its prayer, brings the action to a close
with an allusion to the Mass structure, thus reestablishing the
original ordering framework of the play: "Lord, have mercy

Is woven also in our veins, our brains,
Is woven like a pattern of living worms
In the guts of the women of Canterbury. (CPP 207-8)
  The presence of the "I" is particularly strong in the early part of the imaginative vision. As the
movement down and in occurs, the Chorus loses control of its language until the graphic image of the
patterned cloth of worms collapses the progression down and in with horrific finality.

upon us. / Christ, have mercy upon us" (CPP 221). More than a decade earlier, Eliot had reached for allusion in a desperate search for order at the end of *The Waste Land*. Though in that case the framework was not exclusively religious:

> These fragments I have shored against my ruins
> Why then Ile fit you. Hieronymo's mad againe.
> Datta. Dayadhvam. Damyata.
>   Shantih   shantih   shantih (CPP 50)

The circumstances have changed, but the technique remains strikingly similar. It really should not surprise us to discover that Eliot composed the choral speeches largely in that voice which he knew and understood best--the 'first voice'. The prose pieces which attempt to dissociate Eliot from the voice of the Chorus (and other characters) reveal a poet employing a defensive tactic to protect himself from a poetic creativity that thrives on tension. Despite Eliot's wishful assertion of "the difference, the abyss, between writing for the first and for the third voice" (OPP 102), the Chorus of *Murder in the Cathedral* was the product of a playwright who had yet to shake his intense attraction to the poetic 'first voice'.

WORKS CITED

Ayers, Robert W. "Murder in the Cathedral: A 'Liturgy Less Divine'." *Texas Studies in Literature and Language* 20 (1978): 579-98.

Badenhausen, Richard. "The Double Voices of T. S. Eliot: Divisions in Dramatic Theory and Practice." Diss. University of Michigan, Ann Arbor, 1989.

Bornstein, George. *Transformations of Romanticism in Yeats, Eliot, and Stevens*. Chicago: U of Chicago P, 1976.

Browne, E. Martin. *The Making of T. S. Eliot's Plays*. Cambridge: Cambridge UP, 1969.

Bush, Ronald. *T. S. Eliot: A Study in Character and Style*. New York: Oxford UP, 1984.

Cutts, John P. "Evidence for Ambivalence of Motives in *Murder in the Cathedral*." *Comparative Drama* 8 (1974): 199-210.

Eliot, T. S. "The Aims of Poetic Drama." *Adam: international review* 200 (Nov. 1949): 10-16.

_____. "The Art of Poetry I: T. S. Eliot." With Donald Hall. *The Paris Review* 6.21 (Spring-Summer 1959): 47-70.

_____. "The Future of Poetic Drama." *Drama* 17 (Oct. 1938): 3-5.

_____. *Murder in the Cathedral*. 3rd ed. with autograph revisions. London: Faber and Faber, 1937. Humanities Research Center, University of Texas, Austin.

_____. *Murder in the Cathedral*. Prompt copy for first production at Mercury Theater, 1935. With autograph corrections. Humanities Research Center, University of Texas, Austin.

_____. *Murder in the Cathedral*. Prompt copy for production at Poet's Theatre of Harvard University, 1937. Houghton Library, Harvard University.

Eliot, T. S., and George Hoellering. *The Film of* Murder in the Cathedral. New York: Harcourt, Brace and Company, 1952.

Gardner, Helen. *The Art of T. S. Eliot*. London: The Cresset Press, 1949.

_____. *The Composition of* Four Quartets. London: Faber and Faber, 1978.

Jones, David E. *The Plays of T. S. Eliot*. London: Routledge and Kegan Paul, 1960.

Kenner, Hugh. *The Invisible Poet: T. S. Eliot*. New York: Ivan Obolensky, 1959.

Krieger, Murray. "*Murder in the Cathedral*: The Limits of Drama." *The Shaken Realist*. Ed. Melvin J. Friedman and John B. Vickering. Baton Rouge: Louisiana State UP, 1970. 72-99.

McGill, William J. "Voices in the Cathedral: The Chorus in Eliot's *Murder in the Cathedral*." *Modern Drama* 23 (Sept. 1980): 292-96.

Pike, Lionel. "Liturgy and Time in Counterpoint: A View of T. S. Eliot's *Murder in the Cathedral*." *Modern Drama* 23 (1980): 277-91.

Sackton, Alexander, comp. *The T. S. Eliot Collection of the University of Texas at Austin*. Austin: Humanities Research Center, 1975.

Spurr, David. *Conflicts in Consciousness: T. S. Eliot's Poetry and Criticism*. Chicago: U of Illinois P, 1984.

Van Laan, Thomas. *The Idiom of Drama*. Ithaca: Cornell UP, 1970.

W. B. WORTHEN

MURDER IN THE CATHEDRAL
AND THE WORK OF ACTING

> The working-man who went to the music-hall
> and saw Marie Lloyd and joined in the cho-
> rus was himself performing part of the work
> of acting; he was engaged in that collabora-
> tion of the audience with the artist which is
> necessary in all art and most obviously in
> dramatic art.
>
>   --"London Letter," *Dial* (December 1922)

> The working man who went to the music-hall
> and saw Marie Lloyd and joined in the cho-
> rus was himself performing part of the act;
> he was engaged in that collaboration of the
> audience with the artist which is necessary in
> all art and most obviously in dramatic art.
>
>   --"In Memoriam: Marie Lloyd," *The
>   Criterion* (January 1923)

Announcing a commitment to a popular, collaborative, even
entertaining form of theater, T. S. Eliot's famous obituary for
Marie Lloyd provides a familiar point of repair from the austeri-
ties usually associated with "poetic drama." But Eliot tinkered
with his *Dial* "London Letter" when preparing it for publication
the following month in *The Criterion*, introducing a number of
small changes in wording and emphasis. In both texts, Eliot
mourns the loss of Marie Lloyd, and marks in the passing of this
"expressive figure" the decline of music-hall, and the more general demise of theater as a social institution. And both versions
similarly describe the theater's function in society: through performance, the theater provides an expressive form for the audience it serves. Having given "artistic expression and dignity" to
the life of "the lower classes," the music-hall emblematizes the
waning of a truly popular art of theater. The middle classes, with
no "independent virtues as a class which might give them as a
conscious class any dignity," have nothing to express through the
sociable arts of the stage; their characteristic mode is the soli-

tary and "listless apathy" of the cinema spectator ("London Letter," Dec. 1922, 662). Indeed, it's at this point--characterizing
the audience--that Eliot seems to have hesitated: is the working
man who joins in the chorus constituted by the event, as a "part
of the act"; or does he create and determine the meaning of the
event, perform "the work of acting"? The revision in phrasing is
subtle, but it traces the dialectic that the elaborate rhetoric of
theater claims as an identity: the difference between the fictive
"action" of the drama, and the present activity of performance
that presents (and represents) it.[1] As rhetoric, theatricality identifies both its subject matter--the drama--and its performing
subjects--actors and audience. The spectator of cinema can
"receive, without giving," but the theater both identifies a role
for the audience as "part of the act," and provides the means to
render it significant, dramatic. Like the music-hall, theater
enables the audience to identify themselves in and through "the
work of acting."

　　　To consider the theatrical semiosis of Eliot's "poetic
drama," we might first consider the possibility of a poetic *theater*, how our understanding of poetic drama can be reconceived
within the signifying practice of a poetic stage. The terms themselves are distracting. I don't mean "poetry *in* the theater," the
kind of rhythmic recitation associated with the performance of
Yeats' early plays, or--a greater evasion--the so-called "poetry *of*
the theater," the imagistic, visual "poetry" of the *mise-en-scène*.
Poetic *theater* theorizes the precise situation of the verse text in
relation to its production on the stage, the ordering of its realization, representation, even retextualization in the signifying
forms of enactment (see Berger). To consider poetic drama as
an instrument of the poetic theater is to interrogate both the
suasive idiom that produces the poetic text as dramatic performance, and that identifies the "audience" as a site of interpretation, a collaborator in the event. Eliot recognized the relationship between the "rhetoric" of the dramatic text and the
ambiguous, displaced involvement of the spectator. "A speech in
a play should never appear to be intended to move us as it might
conceivably move other characters in the play, for it is essential
that we should preserve our position of spectators, and observe
always from the outside though with complete understanding"
(" 'Rhetoric' and Poetic Drama," SE 28). In a larger sense,
though, dramatic production necessarily calls for a "rhetoric" of
the *mise-en-scène*, a rhetoric which has eluded theorists of poetic

---

1. On "action" and activity, see Beckerman.

drama, in part because it has been conceived exclusively as a function of the text, of the poetic *word*. Yet to adapt a phrase of Kenneth Burke's, *theatrical* "persuasion is affected by the character of the scene in which it takes place and of the agents to whom it is addressed"; theatrical "rhetoric" relates the drama, through the complement of activity that stages it, to an identifiable audience (62).[2] The production "identifies" the dramatic text with and through the act of its staging; in so doing, the production "identifies" its audience as well, claims certain acts of observation, attention, interpretation as legitimate activity /"action" for its spectators. Although we may "preserve our position of spectators" outside the drama, we are nonetheless cast, so to speak, among the "*other* characters *in* the play" of theater.

The rhetoric of a given theatrical mode--realistic, poetic, symbolic, political--frames dramatic meaning by claiming a specific relationship between the drama, its staging, and the audience. How the verbal order of the drama is identified--staged *as* poetry, so to speak--depends on how it is identified with/through the activities that stage it: as characterizing acting, elocution, lyrical song, and so on. Modern poetic drama usually opens from a repudiation of dramatic realism--"the world of Ibsen and the world of Tchehov [sic]"--and its performance rhetoric emerges most clearly in this contrast ("The Possibility of a Poetic Drama," SW 69). The rhetoric of poetic theater challenges the formalities of stage realism, but only incidentally on verbal grounds. For the rhetoric of realism privileges the visual coherence of the theatrical/dramatic *scene* rather than the verbal order of the absent text, the authority of the *word*. Indeed, the scenic of emphasis of realism is usually described not as rhetoric, but as a function of the theater's "evolution," its technological determination of dramatic forms. As an early historian of the modern drama, Brander Matthews, describes it:

> In the course of the middle half of the nineteenth century the actual stage underwent a transformation. It was so amply lighted first by gas and then by electricity, that the actor had no longer to go down to the footlights to let his changing expression be seen. The parallel wings and borders by means of which interiors had been crudely indicated were abolisht and the compact box-set enabled the stage-director to suggest more satisfactorily an actual

---

2. It should be clear that I am using "identification" in Burke's rhetorical sense here (see 20-29). I don't mean to suggest that this identification--especially that between actor and "character"--is necessarily psychological in orientation, implying the kind of vicarious experience we usually mean when we say an actor or an audience "identifies" with a particular dramatic character (certain production styles --those influenced by American versions of "the Method"--may, of course, "identify" actor and character in this way.)

> room. The apron was cut away; and the curtain rose and fell in a
> picture-frame. The characters of the play were thereafter elements
> in a picture, which had a characteristic background, and which
> might be furnisht with the most realistic elaboration. The former
> intimacy of the actor with the spectators, due to his close proxim-
> ity, disappeared speedily; and with this intimacy there disappeared
> also its concomitant, the soliloquy addrest by a character to the
> audience for the sole purpose of supplying information. The
> drama immediately became more pictorial; it could rely more cer-
> tainly upon gesture; it could renounce the aid of purely rhetorical
> oratory; it could dispense with description; and it insisted that the
> performer should subdue himself to those new conditions and to
> be on his guard lest he should "get out of the picture." (236-37)

Despite its pretensions as history, Matthews' outline evokes the
rhetoric of realism, for verisimilitude emerges as the effect of a
specific signifying practice. This effect is sustained by a characteristic structure of identifications that relate the text, the *mise-
en-scène*, the performers, and the audience: an aggressively prosaic language, impoverished of soliloquy, oratory, or even
description; a commitment to pictorial coherence and integration, usually based on the frame of the box-set; an underplayed,
behavioristic performance style, urgently differentiated from
"acting," staginess, and again integrated with the material world
of the set; and, finally, the exclusion of the audience from the
field of signification. The defining moment of realism is this era-
sure of the productive activity of the theater--the "work of acting"--as a legitimate "part of the act," as an inseparable part of
our interpretation of the dramatic event. Seated in the dark,
"shut out" from the dramatic performance by the boundary of
the fourth wall, the audience is assigned a "listless apathy" in the
guise of ostensible freedom; like the photographer's camera, the
relations that govern the "realistic" image are held to be transparent, not complicit in the knowledge they produce.[3] In such a
theater, the text's production on the stage is determined not by
the features of its language, its "poetry," but by its function in
the stage scene. Speaking, acting, movement, and gesture will all
be used to assimilate the dramatic text to the scenic ensemble--
the stage picture--and to the theatrical (and ideological) apparatus that produces it as "realistic."

---

3. To allegorize Eliot's remarks in "John Marston," the "doubleness in the action, as if it took place on
two planes at once" that distinguishes "poetic drama from prosaic drama" might be attributed both to
the thematic "pattern behind the pattern" that emerges from the ordering of the text, but also to the
dialectics of theatrical signification. For in the audience, we are "living at once on the plane that we
know"--the immediacy of theatrical experience--"and on some other plane of reality from which we
are shut out"--the plane of the fictive drama (EE 173, 177).

Poetic drama only begins to attack the rhetoric of realism when it resituates the text in the *mise-en-scène*, refiguring the authority of the word over/in/through the various forms of signification that identify the drama, the spectacle, and the audience. As Eliot suggests, whether "we use prose or verse on the stage, they are both but means to an end," an end realized only after the texture of language has been represented in the languages of its staging ("Poetry and Drama," SP 132). Although verse, prose, and poetry may have a thematic function in the drama--as they do in, say, *1 Henry IV*--the significance of "language" in performance emerges in the relation between the verbal order and the means of its production on the stage--gesture, movement, intonation, characterization, acting style, and so on. While Eliot often claimed privileged access to an unconscious, inarticulate, primitive, or even ritualistic "depth" of meaning for "poetry" in the theater, his remarks tend to dramatize this interdependence of textual and performative signification, and in a surprising way. Introducing S. L. Bethell's *Shakespeare and the Popular Dramatic Tradition*, for instance, Eliot thematizes the role of language in both poetic and realistic drama:

> A verse play is not a play done into verse, but a different kind of play: in a way more realistic than "naturalistic drama," because, instead of clothing nature in poetry, it should remove the surface of things, expose the underneath, or the inside, of the natural surface appearance. It may allow the characters to behave inconsistently, but only with respect to a deeper consistency. It may use any device to show their real feelings and volitions, instead of just what, in actual life, they would normally profess or be conscious of; it must reveal, underneath the vacillating or infirm character, the indomitable unconscious will; and underneath the resolute purpose of the planning animal, the victim of circumstance and the doomed or sanctified being. [11]

The "deeper consistency" that Eliot conceives here as a function of the verse becomes in performance an effect of acting, of histrionic characterization, and is exemplary of one of the most familiar projects of modern stage realism. The dramatic exposure of a threatened, "buried life" not only describes the action of plays from *Rosmersholm* to *The Iceman Cometh* and beyond, it also describes the characteristic process of modern realistic performance, an experience that actors from Stanislavski onward have been trained to make palpable, dramatic, interpretable as *acting*. The verse of Eliot's later plays, then, much like the allusive language of Ibsen, Strindberg, or O'Neill, is subject to the scenic coherence privileged by the rhetoric of realistic theater. *The Family Reunion, The Cocktail Party, The Confidential Clerk,* and *The Elder Statesman* all demand the "ritual of appearances" characteristic of the *scene* of realistic theater (Kenner 280); employ the conventions of realistic characterization, "whereby the characters are living on two levels, one of normal, self-suppressing, polite, Forsytish behaviour, the other of self-revelation to the audience" (Brown 376); and deploy the "well-made plot" that foregrounds "the impression of efficient and causal interconnection" typical of realistic dramatic action (Goldman, "Fear in the Way" 162, 163). Although these plays mark the limitations of realism, they do so by reifying the determining order of its rhetoric. Realistic performance identifies dramatic language as subordinate to the representational codes of staging, "causal" plotting, and Romantic characterization; this rhetorical order is, in part, responsible for the sense that the texts of Eliot's later plays--whether in prose, verse, or poetry--operate much like the texts of Chekhov or Pinter, depending on the realistic procedures they invoke, parody, or subvert.[4] They are, in this sense, realistic plays "done into verse."

In experimental forays like *Sweeney Agonistes* and *Murder in the Cathedral,* on the other hand, Eliot shrewdly takes up the lead opened by Yeats' "plays for dancers." Speaking on the BBC in 1936, Eliot not only attributed "the revival of poetic drama in our time" to Yeats, but also cited Yeats' transformation of stage performance: "We have begun to see that the actor is more important than the scenery, that the verse should be spoken as verse and not as prose, and that the actor should be in an intimacy of relation to the audience which had for a long time been the secret of the music-hall comedian" ("The Need for Poetic Drama" 994). Eliot strikes several of Yeats' characteristic themes here--the withdrawal of acting style from the scenic requirements of realism, and the privileging of "speech" (as opposed to "acting") as the text's principal mode of theatrical representation--while replacing Yeats' preference for an aristocratic intimacy between spectacle and spectator with the more

---

4. On "vitality" in modern dramatic characterization, see Goldman, "The Ghost of Joy." Indeed, critics of Eliot's drama have increasingly come to conceive Eliot's later drama as a problematic form of realism, rather than as a distinct mode of "poetic drama"; as Katharine Worth suggests, "Eliot's central characters suffer from a troubling sense of division between their real selves and their acted selves. 'Real' self is a concept that still has force in his drama--here he separates from successors like Pinter-- but the performing self is very much in the foreground, uneasily conscious of its liability to be taken over by the 'speechless self,' the mute, tough one" (*Revolutions* 55-56). Finally, the relationship between poetic drama and what was once termed "theater of the absurd" seems increasingly prominent, as Eliot and Yeats are seen in some respects to open ground for Pinter and Beckett; see Worth, *The Irish Drama of Europe,* and Spanos, " 'Wanna Go Home, Baby?': *Sweeney Agonistes* as Drama of the Absurd."

exuberant figure of the music-hall (see Yeats, "The Play, the Player, and the Scene").[5] As Eliot may have recognized when reviewing the Pound-Fenollosa *Noh, or Accomplishment*, the Noh and poetic theater share a similar "peculiarity": "The peculiarity of the Noh is that the focus of interest, and centre of construction, is the scene *on the stage*" (103). In place of a "substitute for reality," poetic theater offers a specifically theatrical event, one that negotiates the signification of "poetry" through the physical, immediate, and personalizing forms of the stage.[6]

Nonetheless, the semiosis of Eliot's poetic theater remains elusive, possibly because Eliot--unlike Yeats--kept more detached from production itself, distant from the roles of director, dramaturge, and acting coach that might have invited him to engage more directly the problem of the poetic text's reproduction as theater. The familiar thematics of Eliot's dramatic criticism provide only indirect help here. Eliot's urging of a "native popular drama" nearer "to Shakespeare than to Ibsen or Chekhov," his attraction to a "mordant, ferocious, and personal" native theater like music-hall ("London Letter," June 1921:687), his "Rome, Cambridge, and Harley Street" reading of ritual: Eliot's writing about such events tends to identify the effects of performance, without clarifying how such effects are produced ("The Ballet" 442).[7] Indeed, to frame Eliot's plays as dramatized

---

5. Yeats' "dance plays" demonstrate a hard-won reconception of the relationship between text and performance. In his early plays, *The Shadowy Waters* for instance, Yeats emphasizes the authorizing function of the word in "poetic drama" by subordinating other theatrical enunciators--acting, gesture, movement, lighting, scene design--to "speech." In the dance plays, however, Yeats extends and complicates the representation of the poetic text in the languages of the stage. The dance plays tend to interrupt the hierarchy of text-to-performance and word-to-speech characteristic of "poetic" and symbolic drama; their rhetoric distributes the text among the languages of its articulation--speech, song, acting, dance--rather than assimilating them to the privileged mode "speech" alone. See Worthen, "The Discipline of the Theatrical Sense."

6. Even the sordid contemporary scene of *Sweeney Agonistes*, as Eliot wrote to Hallie Flanagan for her Vassar production of the play, "should be stylized as in the Noh drama--see Ezra Pound's book and Yeats' preface and notes to *The Hawk's Well*," a stylization that is specifically directed toward suspending the realistic subordination of language to character, character to scene: "Characters *ought* to wear masks; the ones wearing old masks ought to give the impression of being young persons (as actors) and vice versa. Diction should not have too much expression. I had intended the whole play to be accompanied by light drum taps to accentuate the beats (esp. the chorus, which ought to have a noise like a street drill)" (Flanagan 83).

7. For a sampling of Eliot's many comments integrating ritual, performance, the popular arts, and modern drama, see Eliot's response to the Russian ballet: "The later ballet is more sophisticated, but also more simplified, and simplifies more; and what is needed of art is a simplification of current life into something rich and strange. This simplification neither Congreve nor Mr. Shaw attained; and however brilliant their comedies, they are a divagation from art" ("London Letter," August 1921:214); his finding of Frazer in *Le Sacre du Printemps*, "The spirit of the music was modern, and the spirit of the ballet was primitive ceremony" ("London Letter," October 1921:453); the "tropical exuberance" of the "curious Freudian-social-mystical-rationalistic-higher-critical interpretation of the Classics and what used to be called the Scriptures" ("Euripides and Professor Murray," SE 49); various allusions to Chaplin as an anomaly, whose "egregious merit . . . is that he has escaped in his own way from the realism of the cinema and invented a *rhythm*" ("Dramatis Personae" 306); as well as the various remarks on Frazer, and on the relationship between modern art and its "primitive purposes" (Rev. "The Growth of Civilisation" 491) that pepper Eliot's writing throughout the 1920s.

Frazer is to risk consigning them to the realm of lost ritual and
forgotten theater, where poetic drama becomes simply a
"conscious, 'pretty' piece of archeology" ("The Ballet" 443).
Instead, we might look briefly at Eliot's incidental remarks on
the "work of acting" as theatrical signification, on acting as a
means of representing the dramatic text on the stage.[8]

   Although Eliot opposed the "utter rout of the actor
profession," the attempt of the poetic theater to " 'get around'
the actor, to envelop him in masks, to set up a few 'conventions'
for him to stumble over, or even to develop little breeds of
actors for some special Art drama," Eliot's sense of the actor's
subordination to the text of poetic drama is markedly influenced
by the vogue of such "refined automatons" ("The Possibility of a
Poetic Drama," SW 69). The automata of Yeats, Craig, and
Maeterlinck (whether human or mechanical) are useful to
"poetic" drama, in that they privilege "speech," the depersonalized delivery of the words, as the actor's mode of "presenting"
the text. In this view, the characteristic instabilities of perfor-
mance--the absent text decenters the authority of the actor's
self-presence, a presence that nonetheless prevents the actor
from fully inhabiting, presenting the text--are suspended, for the
text is said to be made present by the speaking voice, neither
supplemented nor displaced by the distracting claims of the
actor's "personality." The automaton submits his presentation
fully to the ordering of the text, as its designs inscribe themselves in his bodily posture (statuesque), movements
(restrained), and vocalization (rhythmic speech).

   For this reason, the theory of "poetic" or "symbolic"
performance usually opens with an assault not only on realistic
acting, but also on actors themselves. As Arthur Symons suggests in "An Apology for Puppets":

> The living actor, even when he condescends to subordinate himself
> to the requirements of pantomime, has always what he is proud to
> call his temperament; in other words, so much personal caprice,
> which for the most part means wilful misunderstanding; and in
> seeing his acting you have to consider this intrusive little personal-
> ity of his as well as the author's. (3)

Marking the poetic drama's characteristic effort to displace the
interfering "little personality" of the actor, to produce an
unmediated communion between author, text, and audience,
Symons anticipates Eliot's account of the "struggle, more or less
unconscious, between the creator and the interpreter" ("The

---

8. For an excellent reading of how Eliot's emphasis on ritual and music-hall has preempted the recognition of other contexts of his drama, see Everett.

Possibility of a Poetic Drama," SW 69). Despite repeated denials--"I do not by any means intend the actor to be an automaton, nor would I admit that the human actor can be replaced by a marionette"--Eliot's theater traverses the terrain opened by the theorists of "poetic" performances ("Four Elizabethan Dramatists," SE 96). Drawing on the choreography/performance paradigm of ballet, Eliot imagines a theater in which "only that is left to the actor which is properly the actor's part. The general movements are set for him. There are only limited movements that he can make, only a limited degree of emotion that he can express. He is not called upon for his personality." In this sense, "a true acting play is surely a play which does not depend upon the actor for anything but acting" (SE 95).[9] Although Eliot echoes Yeats here, his program for performance rightly draws its inspiration from his own poetics as well. Finding that the "chaos of the modern stage is a chaos of styles of acting as much as of types of play" ("Dramatis Personae" 304), Eliot refigures the expressive dialectics of "Tradition and the Individual Talent," calling for a mode of enactment that is "not the expression of personality, but an escape from personality" (SE 10). Eliot finds a promising representation of this mode in the dancer Leonid Massine, "the greatest actor whom we have in London. Massine, the most completely unhuman, impersonal, abstract, belongs to the future stage" ("Dramatis Personae" 305). Like the marionettes, such a dancer is "a conventional being, a being which exists only in and for the work of art which is the ballet" ("Four Elizabethan Dramatists" SE 95). But in the theater, Massine's performance emulates the catalytic mind of the poet; subordinating his person to convention, his performance creates a "personality" that becomes the audience's point of interpretation, its focus for reading the spectacle. Moreover, Massine's performance clarifies the function of "personality" in the theater: "Any one who has observed one of the great dancers of the Russian school will have observed that the man or the woman whom we admire is a being who exists only during the performances, that it is a personality, a vital flame which appears from nowhere, disappears into nothing and is complete and sufficient in its appearance." Neither Massine, the "character" he performs, nor the attentive audience escape from personality--this isn't marionette theater, after all--but neither do they perform "themselves." Instead, the performance constructs fictive *personae* which articulate the experience of the

---

9. The essay was first published in *The Criterion* 2 (1924): 115-23.

theater, and, of course, the experience of the self, of the "personality" both displaced and represented. The production of the poetic theater, in contrast to the realistic effacement of the audience, works to figure and thematize the audience's performance, to enable both actor and audience to become "part of the act," to discover a "vital flame" enabled precisely by the artifice of performance itself, their mutual "work of acting."

*   *   *

As poetic theater, *Murder in the Cathedral* participates in the dialectic between "the act" and "the work of acting," organizing the fictive "personalities" of the theater--actor, character, spectator--as the expression of the "poetic" formalities of the text. For *Murder in the Cathedral* is a play *about* its audience, who, like the play's protagonist and like the choral audience onstage, come to know that "action is suffering / And suffering action" (*Murder in the Cathedral*, CP 17). As theater, the audience's engagement in suffering or acting is partly signalled by changes in the mode of the text--choral ode, verse dialogue, the Knights' prose, for instance--or, more precisely, by changes both in the text and in the enunciation it requires, as choral speaking, individualized acting, or soapbox oratory. The complex thematics of Eliot's drama--the role of Thomas' will in the spectacle of martyrdom--have been frequently, often brilliantly described; here, I want to describe the relation between the form of the text and four forms of its performance: the characterization of the Chorus, the verse dialogue of the Priests and the Tempters, the sermon, and the Knights' apology.[10] For at such moments, the rhetoric of Eliot's theater becomes visible, and we can examine the relationship between the text and its production as the "vital flame" of personality at the intersection of acting and suffering-- that of the dramatic characters, and also of the "other characters" (actors, audience) who share the playing.

Given the vaudevillian cast of "different voices" that speak his earlier poetry (and given Eliot's talent for self-dramatization), it's surprising to find Eliot searching for a *"neutral"* verse style for his play, claiming that "a poet writing for the first time for the stage, is much more at home in choral verse than in dramatic dialogue" ("Poetry and Drama," SP 139, 140).[11] Choral

10. See especially Gardner, Fergusson, and Krieger.
11. See Ackroyd for various accounts of Eliot's offstage performances, particularly a suspicion--noted by the Sitwells, Virginia Woolf, and others--that he wore a faintly greenish makeup (136); he also provides Edmund Wilson's description of Eliot as a "completely artificial, or, rather, self-invented char-

delivery seems to retain the privileged function conventionally assigned to the text by poetic drama, producing the text as a generalized "speech," a verbal order relatively dissociated from the personalizing effect of histrionic characterization, of "acting." But Eliot's Chorus is neither a marionette nor an automaton, and Eliot's characterization of the Chorus renders its relation both to the poetic text and to the audience oddly problematic. For Eliot's Chorus performs a dual function, both as a "character" in the drama, and as a "character" in the theater, delivering the poetic text to the offstage spectators. As a representation of the offstage audience, playing the Chorus requires a specifically histrionic--personalizing, characterizing, physicalizing--engagement of the text: "*Here* let us *stand, close* by the cathedral. *Here* let us *wait.* / Are we *drawn* by the danger?" (CP 11, italics added). As actors have recognized, the Chorus must be conceived as a group of individual performers, a body of roles requiring individuation.[12] In this sense, the Chorus becomes a character in the drama, a real community composed of " 'individual threads of character' " as Elsie Fogerty put it (Browne 86), not the "amorphous protoplasm" of Eliot's "bourgeoisie" ("London Letter," December 1922:662). Although the Chorus is composed of "excited and sometimes hysterical women," it refers more broadly to the range of their society, the laborers, merchants, and others who inhabit it, and so represent the "character" of Eliot's theater audience in general ("Poetry and Drama," SP 140). In other words, *Murder in the Cathedral* develops the paradigm of *Sweeney Agonistes*, in which Eliot tried to develop "an understanding between this protagonist and a small number of the audience, while the rest of the audience would share the responses of the other characters in the play" (UPUC 147).[13] Placed as a spectator of the action, "forced to bear witness" in a role in which "there is no action," the Chorus' characterization shapes our initial "understanding" of the drama, in part by representing our activity within the dramatic action (CP 11-12). Like the Chorus, "we are content if we are left alone"; the action both of the drama and of the theater work to prevent such solitude (CP 11).

acter" (199). By "different voices," I have in mind the draft title for the first section of *The Waste Land*--"He do the Police in Different Voices"--subsequently jettisoned; see WLF. Of course, Eliot might have been the first to claim that "From one point of view, the poet aspires to the condition of the music-hall comedian" (UPUC 22).

12. Hallie Flanagan, for instance, describes the almost-Stanislavskian preparation of her students for the Chorus: "Individual actors built up their own characters, not only from the play, but from a study of the lives of women who had known 'oppression and torture, destitution, disease.' They pored over *These Are Our Lives, Have You Seen Their Faces,* and the drawings of Käthe Kollwitz" (129).

13. The Chorus might be taken to represent Eliot's ideal audience, insofar as its members are "capable of receiving meanings at different depths" (Eagleton 281).

As Eliot recognized, the modern theater requires "that we should preserve our position of spectators, and observe always from the outside though with complete understanding" (" 'Rhetoric' and Poetic Drama," SE 28). But the characterization of the Chorus begins to blur the relation between inside and outside, suffering and acting, witnessing and performing. For the Chorus' performance not only represents a fictive character in the drama, it articulates the immediate theatrical continuity between stage and audience. The Chorus' text is the most insistently "poetic" text in the play. Its formal structure, density of imagery, range of reference, contextualizing function in the drama, remoteness from realistic stage language, and, obviously, the fact that it is produced *as* a chorus, tend to prevent a complete subordination of the language to characterization. The Chorus' liminal oscillation between the dramatic fiction and the present audience is signalled by one of the persistent challenges of *Murder in the Cathedral* in production: striking a just balance between the Chorus as "character" and as "speaker" of poetic verse.[14] Characterizing the Chorus tends to insert it into the drama, and so to call into play familiar strategies of character interpretation--the search for motivation, for psychological integration, for social continuity, and so on. Articulating the text as speech forces the dramatic "character" into the background, and identifies the Chorus principally as a cast of performers. This dialectic--"women of Canterbury" or Chorus--is itself emblematic of the theater audience's situation, and is responsible for an ongoing difficulty of the play's reception. Robert Speaight, while complimenting Elsie Fogerty's training of the original Canterbury Chorus, thought the women "remained middle-class young women from South Kensington. Nothing more remote from the medieval poor could have been imagined" ("With Becket" 184). Helen Gardner assigns a similar dissatisfaction to the Chorus' costumes: "The power of the poetry triumphs over the curious costumes in which the 'poor women of Canterbury' are usually draped. They are made to look like young ladies who, for a charade, have done the best they could with a set of slightly old-fashioned artistic bedspreads" (138n). And Martin Esslin reports of the 1972 Royal Shakespeare Company production, "In this case the seven ladies of Canterbury sound as though they were reciting poems of T. S. Eliot which they had just learnt

14. Victor Turner's discussions of "liminal" and "liminoid" genres, and how meanings are generated "at the interfaces between established cultural subsystems," are now familiar (*From Ritual to Theatre* 41). His study of Becket's confrontation with the king at the Council of Northampton provides an interesting alternative to Eliot's "ritual" construction in *Murder in the Cathedral*. See *Dramas, Fields, and Metaphors* 60-97.

by heart. Their voices are far too middle class, their intonations far too Third Programme to make them believable medieval paupers of Canterbury" (45).[15] This is not merely a technical flaw in individual productions, but a problem engrained in the rhetoric that produces the text as theater. For Eliot's writing of the Chorus' part seems to require this instability, this dissonance. In this sense, our inability to assimilate the Chorus fully into the drama is neither a failure of imagination on our part, nor necessarily a failure of the production. Instead, much as the Chorus' represented emotions--fear, attraction--articulate our reactions in the audience, so the performance of the Chorus provides an index to the dialectics of our own enactment. Like the Chorus, to become fully complicit in the drama we must be assigned--and perform--a characterizing role, a fictive "personality" constructed as part of the spectacle, part of the act. In "the design of God," martyrdom is "never an accident" and never "the effect of a man's will"; Eliot's logos, the "poetic" design represented on the stage, similarly represents its audience at the intersection where accident and will are undecidable (CP 33). The dialectics that produce the Chorus in the theater--expressed as character, constructed by the text--will, in a manner of speaking, come to shape our own performance if we are to enter into the play at all.[16]

    The acting of the verse text of Becket, the Priests, and the Tempters presents somewhat different problems, for we expect these texts to be more completely identified through the rhetoric of characterization. Yet the First Priest's opening line-- "Seven years and the summer is over" (CP 12)--repeats an earlier choral line, a technique Eliot uses effectively throughout the play, most notably when the Fourth Tempter repeats Thomas' opening lines as his final temptation. Although each Priest is played by an individual actor, their roles are provided with relatively little definition; the Priests seem more like voices echoing a text than "characters" in the conventional sense, as may be implied by Eliot's decision to revise Thomas' advisers Herbert of Bosham and John, Dean of Salisbury out of the play (Browne 41-42). Although they share the Chorus' incriminating attitude-- "We do not wish anything to happen" (CP 15)--the Priests provide an instance of Eliot's *"operatic"* characterization, in which

---

15. On Elsie Fogerty's work with the Chorus, and her seminal role in the development of speech training in modern British acting, see Cole.

16. Herbert Howarth, in his indispensable "notes" on Eliot, suggests the collaborative relationship between the Chorus and the audience when he remarks that Eliot's play elicits the dignity of the women of Canterbury in much the same fashion that Marie Lloyd elicits the dignity of her working class audience. See Howarth 305.

"[l]ines are assigned, not in the interest of a particular character, but in keeping with the function of the speakers in the movement and music of the whole" (Rehak 47).[17] Insofar as they become even mildly individuated only when they engage the Chorus, it might be said that "character" emerges in the play only agonistically, only through conflict with others, or, as in the case of Thomas, with internalized others. Eliot's rhetoric of characterization seems to privilege this conflict, by assigning to the Tempters--as he will assign to the Knights--more clearly characterized roles than those assigned to the Priests (see Whitaker 147). Unlike the Priests, each of the Tempters has a distinct verse style, and a distinct speaking style as well. Each also accords with, and so dramatizes, one of Thomas' past roles: "Old Tom, gay Tom," the "master of policy," the "rough straightforward Englishman" (CP 18, 20, 22). By subordinating the text of the Tempters' speeches more fully to the lineaments of stage characterization, Eliot's play emphasizes the reality of Thomas' internal struggle. And by articulating this conflict through the rhetoric of realistic character, Eliot seems to claim that such expressionistic, inner struggle has a greater reality, is more dramatic, than the external relations between characters-- between Thomas and the Priests, for instance.[18]

"From this it follows that a mixture of prose and verse in the same play is generally to be avoided: each transition makes the auditor aware, with a jolt, of the medium. It is, we may say, justifiable when the author wishes to produce this jolt: when, that is, he wishes to transport the audience violently from one plane of reality to another" ("Poetry and Drama," SP 133). The first such "jolt" provided by the play is Thomas' sermon; the sermon also "jolts" the performance "medium" at this point as well, the relative distance maintained between the verse text and the "personality" of the performers throughout part 1. The sermon's prose entails a recalibration of the relationship between actor, text, and audience. As Robert Speaight recognized, the sermon is "theatrically speaking, the *pièce de résistance* of the play," as any text that allows the actor to play to the audience usually is ("With Becket" 186). The play's central theatrical conspiracy--to stage the audience's complicity in Thomas' murder--develops a new sharpness here, for the sermon provides the actor with the

---

17. Denis Donoghue makes a similar point when he remarks, "In the case of *Murder in the Cathedral* the words seem to operate almost apart from the character and situation they are designed to serve" (87).
18. In somewhat different terms, the "reality" of this struggle might also be emphasized by the fact that Eliot read the voice-over of the Fourth Tempter's lines in the film version of *Murder in the Cathedral* (Hoellering 83).

opportunity to bring a different kind of characterization to bear both on Thomas and on his audience. The sermon enacts the expected scene of Thomas' preaching to his flock on Christmas morning; it also provides a kind of thematic center for the play as well, Thomas' oblique defense both of his own behavior and of the status of martyrdom. In the design of the performance, this is also the moment where the "intrusive little personality" of the actor exerts its most palpable influence, in that the sermon provides an opportunity to *act* for the audience (rather than, say, to be acted upon by the Tempters), to produce Thomas for us through the inescapable lineaments of a stage personality. As an acting text, the sermon provides a release from Becket's passivity, from a role that can seem "more of a figure than a part" especially in part 1 (Speaight, "Interpreting Becket" 71). Moreover, the realism of the text invites both the actor and the audience to conceive Thomas through the interpretive conventions of realistic characterization, with the privileging of "motive," cause, and origin that such interpretation entails. These are, of course, precisely the issues that realistic acting consigns to the "subtext," and so renders ambiguous, even undecidable. While the Chorus' performance represents us within the drama, Thomas' "realistic" performance stages us in the *scene* of the drama itself; this was, of course, most evident in the play's first production at the Canterbury chapter house. In a sense, we engage Thomas' sermon in something closer to the unprotected immediacy of our offstage lives. The effect of this is, I think, necessarily to foreground Thomas' rhetoric as rhetoric. Thomas' attempt to convince us that the "true martyr is he who has become the instrument of God" is articulated through the actor's self-presentation, his necessary effort to persuade himself of the theatrical reality of the moment, in order to persuade us to accept the provisional reality of his characterization of Thomas (CP 33). Oddly enough, then, by situating the text of Thomas' sermon within the performance rhetoric of realistic characterization, Eliot invites us to interpret Thomas in the way we interpret character in realistic drama, and perhaps in the way we interpret "character" in the prosaic drama of our lives--by indirection, through the suspicion that motives are always falsified by their enactment. Is Thomas *"cheering himself up,"* as Eliot said of Othello, "adopting an *aesthetic* rather than a moral attitude, dramatising himself against his environment" ("Shakespeare and the Stoicism of Seneca," SE 111)? As in realistic theater more generally, we can never know, because neither Thomas nor the actor who plays him can say.

Ronald Peacock thought that a poetic drama provides "a breakaway from poetry conceived too exclusively as the
expression of the sentient anarchic individual, and a return to
the wider conception of it as a presentation of human actions
with their reverberations in human society" (5). But the drama
becomes "an instrument of community" in performance, and
Eliot's uses of prose and verse tend to operate differently in this
regard. The verse--the versified dialogue of the Priests, for
example--tends to establish a theatrical continuity between the
performers and the audience; the prose tends to establish a continuity between the dramatic characters and a represented audience. The Chorus--whose characterized verse mediates between
these positions--precisely emblematizes our situation by the text,
for we are rendered as continuous with the sometimes conflicting demands of the drama and of the performance. This
dichotomy in the ways in which the "vital flame" of the audience's personality is constructed in performance is confirmed
and extended by the Knights' apology. The Knights' direct
address was, as George Hoellering reports, Eliot's "main reason
for writing the play" (83), and despite the tang of Shaw's *Saint
Joan*, the Knights produce a very un-Shavian spectacle.[19] Shaw's
Fabian gradualism is, of course, opposed to the figural simul-
taneity that Eliot claims between the events of history, their rep-

---

19. The sense in which the Knights' address forges a real community--i.e., one of diverse opinion--is
perhaps suggested by another anecdote of Hoellering's: "When, towards the end of the play, we came
to the speeches in which the three Knights justify themselves before the crowd, the sound recordist
suddenly turned round to Mr Eliot and, completely forgetting his control switches, said excitedly,
'Aren't they right, sir. What do you think?' Mr Eliot, needless to say, was highly amused" (82-83).
Eliot's allusion to the possible "influence of *St. Joan*" ("Poetry and Drama," SP 141) is striking in view
both of his distaste for *Saint Joan*, and for its author: "Yet his Joan of Arc is perhaps the greatest sacri-
lege of all Joans: for instead of the saint or the strumpet of the legends to which he objects, he has
turned her into a great middle-class reformer, and her place is a little higher than Mrs. Pankhurst. If
Mr. Shaw is an artist, he may contemplate his work with ecstasy." Throughout the 1920s, Eliot uses
Shaw to emblematize aspects of literature he wants to consign to the past. Commenting (as "Crites")
on Shaw and *Saint Joan* for *The Criterion*, Eliot argues that "*St. Joan* seems to illustrate Mr. Shaw's
mind more clearly than anything he has written before. No one can grasp more firmly an idea which
he does not maintain, or expound it with more cogency, than Mr. Shaw. He manipulates every idea so
brilliantly that he blinds us when we attempt to look for the ideas *with which he works*. And the ideas
with which he works, are they more than the residue of the great Victorian labours of Darwin, and
Huxley, and Cobden?" ("A Commentary," *The Criterion* 3 [1924]: 4-5). As part of his effort to locate
Shaw as an "Edwardian" ("London Letter," October 1921:454), Eliot continually hammers several
themes: Shaw's immaturity: "Mr. Shaw reveals himself as the artist whose development was checked at
puberty" ("The Idea of a Literary Review" 6); his dangerous seductiveness as mountebank: "Hence
the danger, with his 'St. Joan,' of his deluding the numberless crowd of sentimentally religious people
who are incapable of following any argument to a conclusion. Such people will be misled until they
can be made to understand that the potent ju-ju of the Life Force is a gross superstition; and that (in
particular) Mr. Shaw's 'St. Joan' is one of the most superstitious of the effigies which have been
erected to that remarkable woman" (Rev. of *Mr. Shaw and 'The Maid'* 389); and Shaw's inability to
grasp the contemporary mind, or at least the mind that Eliot was attempting to frame with these
essays. This last hesitation is apparent even in Eliot's grudging praise for Shaw's Nobel award: "We
have often attacked, and shall probably attack often again, Mr. Bernard Shaw and the world of his creation; but we cannot demur to the attribution to him of the Nobel Prize," especially since the prize's
function is "merely to seal a verdict already given by success and notoriety" ("A Commentary," *The
Criterion* 5 [1927]: 3-4). In the attribution of the unsigned commentaries to Eliot, I have followed
Gallup.

resentation as drama, and the drama's presentation on the contemporary stage (Spanos, *The Christian Tradition* 89-90; on *figurae*, see 28 and *passim*). Beyond that, though, we may well feel that the Knights' function less to educate us than to offend us. For inasmuch as "modern blasphemy is merely a department of bad form" (Eliot, "Personality and Demonic Possession" 94), the Knights performance seems designed to forge a precisely "blasphemous" relationship between the Knights and the audience, "the leering inference that we ought to be mouthing the lines of prose with the Knights" (Krieger 357). This identification again arises through the relationship between the design of the text and the conventions of the realistic stage. For unlike the formal language of Thomas' sermon, the Knights' text is composed in a recognizably colloquial, even contemporary idiom, one that may indeed require a more relaxed, physically nonchalant gestural style of the performer. Engaging us through our own moral platitudes ("we had taken on a pretty stiff job," "it does go against the grain to kill an Archbishop," "if we seemed a bit rowdy," "I am awfully sorry about it," "personally I had a tremendous admiration for him" [CP 49]), the Knights again establish a continuity between dramatic character and theater spectator: by speaking our language, the Knights claim "consubstantiality" with the moral order that guides our everyday lives. To play our part, to "witness" the dramatic representation of martyrdom, we must reject this identification. The play produces an ironic relation between our performance as "spectators" and the performance of our lives outside the theater.

Without in any way trivializing the significance of martyrdom, I would like to suggest that the process of Eliot's theater is designed, in part, to provide a kind of simulation, not of martyrdom, but of the spiritual education necessary for a modern faith.[20] Like the Chorus, perhaps, we want to have a "theatrical" relationship to events like martyrdom, to see them

---

20. Indeed, it might be hard to emulate Eliot's own irony on this score, located most evidently in the play's title. Many critics have commented on Eliot's debt to detective fiction in *Murder in the Cathedral*, and Grover Smith even locates the source of the exchange between Becket and the Second Tempter in Doyle's Sherlock Holmes story, "The Musgrave Ritual" (194). Some, of course, found this suggestion somewhat appalling in view of the play's subject, as did F. O. Matthiessen: "the play--the title of which, with its unfortunately smart suggestion of a detective story I have done my best to avoid" (328). Eliot, on the other hand, found that the title--suggested by Henzie Raeburn (Mrs. E. Martin Browne)--"with its sardonic implications, had a contemporary quality which would induce in an audience an attitude favourable to the acceptance of the ironies, particularly in the Knights' apology, as a natural part of the play" (Browne 55-56). Indeed, the spectatorial role is, in Eliot's view, what characterizes the function of the reader of detective fiction as opposed to mysteries: "In the detective story nothing should happen: the crime has already been committed, and the rest of the tale consists in the collection, selection and combination of evidence. In a mystery tale the reader is led from fresh adventure to fresh adventure" ("Recent Detective Fiction" 360).

without having to witness them, without having to be trans-
formed--if not transfigured--by them. Watching *Murder in the
Cathedral*, we are urged briefly to forsake our other parts for the
role of the audience, a demanding part which requires our direct
engagement in the "work of acting" if we are to comprehend the
play's designs on us. In this tiny figure is inscribed not only the
sign of the greater revolution that the play dramatizes--Thomas'
performance of the "design of God" (CP 33)--but also the suggestion, again in little, of what witnessing such an act might
entail for us. This is, it seems to me, partly the burden of the
final chorus, the prayer that asks forgiveness both for the Chorus and for the contemporary audience, the "sightseers come
with guide-books" (CP 53-54). The prayer depends precisely
upon the "personalities" Eliot has evoked throughout the performance, for as the audience is invited to assume a specific
identification with the drama--to authorize the possibility of
martyrdom by rejecting the explanation of the Knights--the Chorus undergoes a transformation. Presenting Eliot's verse
(foregrounded as such through the collocation of the *Te Deum*),
the Chorus is converted into a community of our contemporaries, coextensive with the community we have, through the
rhetoric of the play's production, become.

"I see myself emerging / From my spectral existence
into something like reality": like Lord Claverton in *The Elder
Statesman*, the audience of *Murder in the Cathedral* emerges
from a ghostly absence, into a "real" relation to the events of the
stage (CP 341). I have come some way from the rhetoric of
poetic theater, and I would like to return to it for a moment as a
way of suggesting the place of *Murder in the Cathedral* in the
development of modern theatricality. In a review of the play
published in Eliot's *Criterion* in 1936, Michael Sayers posed the
question of the play's permanence in these terms: "It may occasion a revolution in popular thought and theatre through subsequent imitations, and by its direct influence similar to that
brought about by the comedies of Shaw. Or it may go down to
the popular limbo as one of the curiosities of a moribund theatre" (655). Although the experimental rhetoric of *Murder in the
Cathedral* is "too incisive, too original, too mordant" to be
ignored, Eliot's play has indeed slipped into the limbo of "poetic
drama," or possibly someplace worse. Yeats may be a more
original dramatist--certainly Yeats has a more sure sense of the
stage--but in some respects *Murder in the Cathedral* undertakes a
more radical displacement of the authority of the text than
Yeats' plays do, precisely because Eliot contaminates the

"poetic" spectacle, not with prose as such, but with prose that is inscribed by the dynamics of realistic stage production, realistic acting. In this sense, *Murder in the Cathedral*--perhaps like *Sweeney Agonistes*--destabilizes the poetic text's authority over the constitution of meaning, and acknowledges--requires, in fact--the retextualization of "poetry" in the various, competing codes of stage performance. In this regard, Eliot's poetic theater not only challenges the semiosis of realism, it might be said partly to challenge the privileged status of the word in the semiosis of poetic theater as well. Finally, Eliot's dramaturgy strategically designs the spectator's performance as essential to the meaning of the theatrical event; Yeats preconceives his aristocratic audience, while Eliot produces a form for the audience's "collaboration." Eliot's attention to the spectator, his attempt to inscribe the spectator's performance in the play's design, to provide a theatrical "escape" from the habitual "personality" with which we confront the world at large, may point surprisingly enough in a different direction, toward a theatrical rhetoric more overtly engaged in the production of the audience as "subject"--the rhetoric of political theater. For like poetry, the rhetoric of poetic theater "may effect revolutions in sensibility such as are periodically needed; may help to break up the conventional modes of perception and valuation which are perpetually forming, and make people see the world afresh, or some new part of it" (UPUC 149).

WORKS CITED

Ackroyd, Peter. *T. S. Eliot: A Life*. New York: Simon and Schuster, 1984.

Beckerman, Bernard. *Dynamics of Drama*. New York: Drama Book Specialists, 1979.

Berger, Harry, Jr. "Bodies and Texts." *Representations* 17 (Winter 1987): 144-66.

Braybrooke, Neville, ed. *T. S. Eliot: A Symposium for His Seventieth Birthday*. 1958. New York: Books for Libraries P, 1968.

Brown, Ivor. Rev. of *The Family Reunion*. Grant 375-77.

Browne, E. Martin. *The Making of T. S. Eliot's Plays*. Cambridge: Cambridge UP, 1969.

Burke, Kenneth. *A Rhetoric of Motives*. 1950. Berkeley: U of California P, 1969.

Cole, Marion. *Fogie*. London: Peter Davies, 1967.

Donoghue, Denis. *The Third Voice: Modern British and American Verse Drama*. Princeton: Princeton UP, 1959.

Eagleton, Terry. "Eliot and a Common Culture." *Eliot in Perspective*. Ed. Graham Martin. London: Macmillan; New York: Humanities P, 1970.

Eliot, T. S. "The Ballet." *The Criterion* 3 (1925): 441-43.

_____. "The Beating of a Drum." *Nation and Atheneum* 6 October 1923: 11-12.

_____. "A Commentary." *The Criterion* 3 (1924): 1-5.

_____. "A Commentary." *The Criterion* 5 (1927): 1-6.

_____. "Dramatis Personae." *The Criterion* 1 (1923): 303-306.

_____. Rev. of *The Growth of Civilisation* and *The Origin of Magic and Religion*, by W. J. Perry. *The Criterion* 2 (1924): 489-91.

_____. "The Idea of a Literary Review." *The Criterion* 4 (1926): 1-6.

_____. "In Memoriam: Marie Lloyd." *The Criterion* 1 (1923): 192-95.

_____. Introduction. *Shakespeare and the Popular Dramatic Tradition*. By S. L. Bethell. London: Staples, 1944. n.p.

_____. "John Marston." *Elizabethan Essays*. London: Faber & Faber, 1934. 177-95.

_____. "London Letter." *Dial* 70 (June 1921): 686-91.

_____. "London Letter." *Dial* 71 (August 1921): 213-17.

_____. "London Letter." *Dial* 71 (October 1921): 452-55.

_____. "London Letter." *Dial* 73 (December 1922): 659-63.

_____. Rev. of *Mr. Shaw and 'The Maid'* by the Rt. Hon. J. M. Robertson. *The Criterion* 4 (1926): 388-89.

_____. "The Need for Poetic Drama." *The Listener* 25 November 1936: 994-95.

_____. Rev. of *Noh, or Accomplishment*, by Ernest Fenollosa and Ezra Pound. *Egoist* 4.7 (August 1917): 102-103.

_____. "Personality and Demonic Possession." *Virginia Quarterly Review* 10 (1934): 94-103.

_____. "Recent Detective Fiction." *The Criterion* 5 (1927): 359-62.

Esslin, Martin. Rev. of *Murder in the Cathedral*. *Plays and Players* 229 (October 1972): 44-45.

Everett, Barbara. "The New Style of *Sweeney Agonistes*." *Yearbook of English Studies* 14 (1984): 243-63.

Fergusson, Francis. *The Idea of a Theater*. Princeton: Princeton UP, 1949.

Flanagan, Hallie. *Dynamo*. New York: Duell, Sloan and Pearce, 1943.

Gallup, Donald. *T. S. Eliot: A Bibliography*. New York: Harcourt, Brace and World, 1969.

Gardner, Helen. *The Art of T. S. Eliot*. 1949. London: Cresset P, 1961.

Goldman, Michael. "Fear in the Way: The Design of Eliot's Drama." *Eliot in His Time*. Ed. A. Walton Litz. Princeton: Princeton UP, 1973. 155-80.

_____. "The Ghost of Joy: Reflections on Romanticism and the Forms of Modern Drama." *Romantic and Modern: Revaluations of Literary Tradition*. Ed. George Bornstein. Pittsburgh: U of Pittsburgh P, 1977. 58-68.

Grant, Michael, ed. *T. S. Eliot: The Critical Heritage*. London and Boston: Routledge & Kegan Paul, 1982.

Hoellering, George. "Filming *Murder in the Cathedral*." Braybrooke 81-84.

Howarth, Herbert. *Notes on Some Figures Behind T. S. Eliot*. Boston: Houghton Mifflin, 1964.

Kenner, Hugh. *The Invisible Poet: T. S. Eliot*. London: W. H. Allen, 1960.

Krieger, Murray. *The Classic Vision: The Retreat from Extremity in Modern Literature*. Baltimore and London: The Johns Hopkins UP, 1971.

Matthews, Brander. *The Principles of Playmaking and Other Discussions of the Drama*. New York: Charles Scribner's Sons, 1919.

Matthiessen, F. O. Rev. of *Murder in the Cathedral*. Grant 324-28.

Peacock, Ronald. *The Poet in the Theatre*. New York: Harcourt, Brace, 1946.

Rehak, Louise Rouse. "On the Use of Martyrs: Tennyson and Eliot on Thomas Becket." *University of Toronto Quarterly* 33 (1963-64): 43-60.

Sayers, Michael. "A Year in Theatre." *The Criterion* 15 (1936): 648-62.

Smith, Grover, Jr. *T. S. Eliot's Poetry and Plays*. 1956. Chicago: U of Chicago P, 1958.

Spanos, William V. *The Christian Tradition in Modern British Verse Drama: The Poetics of Sacramental Time*. New Brunswick: Rutgers UP, 1967.

_____. " 'Wanna Go Home, Baby?': *Sweeney Agonistes* as Drama of the Absurd." PMLA 85 (1970): 8-20

Speaight, Robert. "Interpreting Becket and Other Parts." Braybrooke 70-78.

_____. "With Becket in *Murder in the Cathedral*." Tate 182-93.

Symons, Arthur. "An Apology for Puppets." *Plays, Acting and Music: A Book of Theory*. New York: Dutton, 1909. 3-8.

Tate, Allen, ed. *T. S. Eliot: The Man and His Work*. New York: Delacorte, 1966.

Turner, Victor. *Dramas, Fields, and Metaphors: Symbolic Action in Human Society*. Ithaca and London: Cornell UP, 1974.

_____. *From Ritual to Theatre: The Human Seriousness of Play*. New York: Performing Arts Journal Publications, 1982.

Whitaker, Thomas R. *Fields of Play in Modern Drama*. Princeton: Princeton UP, 1977.

Worth, Katharine. *The Irish Drama of Europe from Yeats to Beckett*. London: Athlone, 1978.

_____. *Revolutions in Modern English Drama*. London: G. Bell, 1972.

Worthen, W. B. "The Discipline of the Theatrical Sense: *At the Hawk's Well* and the Rhetoric of the Stage." *Modern Drama* 30 (1987): 90-103.

Yeats, W. B. "The Play, the Player, and the Scene." *Explorations*. New York: Macmillan, 1962. 164-180.

"A DISTINCTIVE ACTIVITY OF THE CIVILIZED MIND": ELIOT'S CRITICISM

J. P. RIQUELME

AESTHETIC VALUES AND PROCESSES IN ELIOT, ARNOLD, AND THE ROMANTICS

T. S. Eliot has come to be understood by some critics, especially ones antagonistic to Modernism, as a self-conscious Modernist writer whose self-reflexive works tend to express in highly conscious, controlled, analytical ways negative attitudes toward many of the literary and cultural conventions of his day.[1] In his prose and in his poetry he is, without question, often highly critical of his nineteenth-century poetic predecessors, especially the English Romantics. As Eliot bluntly remarks in *The Sacred Wood*, "the only cure for Romanticism is to analyse it" (31), and analyze it he does in a variety of works that have often been taken to be primarily analytical. In fact, however, the analytical elements are regularly conjoined with countervailing elements that are at least as important, elements that cannot be described as self-conscious, controlled, or negative. Often these countervailing elements emerge most clearly in passages of the prose and the poetry in which Eliot attempts to represent processes of aesthetic creation.

Those passages frequently work in divergent ways simultaneously to differentiate Eliot from his Romantic predecessors and to align him with them. Through complex stylistic strategies Eliot is able to distance himself clearly from certain Romantic attitudes by relying on or evoking other Romantic positions. One of the passages from the criticism presenting aesthetic processes focuses on what Eliot calls "the auditory imagination." It holds a climactic position at the end of the antepenultimate lecture in *The Use of Poetry and the Use of Criticism* (1933), a series of lectures Eliot gave at Harvard in 1932-33. In that lecture, Eliot criticizes Arnold at some length for holding attitudes derived from the Romantics that limit the ways in which poetry can be written and read. The critique of Arnold's

---

1. There is, of course, no critical consensus concerning "Modernism." Many commentators, however, emphasize, "an unremitting self-consciousness" in describing "the sceptical modernist intelligence" (see Faulkner 18-19).

Romanticism is at the heart of the series. As part of his commentary on Romanticism, however, Eliot describes at various
points alternative attitudes that he can accept. The "auditory
imagination," which is among these, turns out to be an alternative to Arnold's implicit and explicit views about aesthetic creation that also takes issue with Wordsworth and Coleridge by
invoking and employing other Romantic positions. An equally
important and vivid passage concerning aesthetic creation
occurs in *Little Gidding* 2 in the Dantesque encounter with the
"familiar compound ghost." In his essays, Eliot regularly uses
the Metaphysical poets and Dante to pose contrasts for Romantic ideas and procedures. In *Little Gidding*, however, during the
curious and compelling presentation of the act of writing as a
ventriloquial doubling that is a fusion as well, the figures of the
poet and the poet's predecessors, including not only Dante but
also Shelley, merge. The merger takes place through a form of
remembering that is one version of the "returning . . . and
bringing something back" effected by the "auditory imagination"
(UPUC 111). Like that returning, the merger has little to do
with the logical processes of consciousness and cannot be
explained with reference to them.

       Eliot goes about analyzing Romanticism in one way
in the introduction to *The Use of Poetry* and in the lecture on
Wordsworth and Coleridge by juxtaposing and comparing the
well-known Romantic distinction between Imagination and
Fancy from the *Biographia Literaria* with earlier comments
about poetic creation from Dryden's *Preface to Annus Mirabilis*
(UPUC 18-19, 67-71). Part of Eliot's originality in the discussion
is his refusal to accept without examination central Romantic
formulations. The unusual character of Eliot's skepticism can be
gauged by noting that in Pater's essay on Wordsworth, an essay
Eliot cites in "Arnold and Pater" (1930), Pater mentions the distinction at the outset. But he does so with apparent full acceptance of it, and he praises Wordsworth for having worked with it
so thoroughly and successfully (37-63). It is this sort of immediate, unquestioning acceptance by an earlier generation of inter-
preters that Eliot rejects in his skeptical procedures. Eliot particularly stresses that in order to maintain the Romantic distinction between Imagination and Fancy, memory as a common, but
ill-defined, attribute of both has to be ignored. On the other
hand, after discussing the distinction in the lecture on
Wordsworth and Coleridge, Eliot quotes admiringly two other
passages from the *Biographia Literaria*, one about the possibility
of combining opposites, the other about musical delight (UPUC

71). In his later statement about the "auditory imagination" at the end of the Arnold lecture, Eliot emphasizes its character as a process of retrieval, that is, a form of memory, but he also returns to these other motifs, combining and transforming them for his own purposes. In so doing Eliot emphasizes his affinity with Coleridge, as he does as well at the end of the final lecture. Eliot suggests this affinity, however, while taking a distinctly different course and only after a skeptical scrutinizing unlike anything undertaken by Pater or Arnold with regard to the Romantics.

One aspect of that different course is Eliot's challenging of the Romantic distinction between Imagination and Fancy as a distinction between creative and critical faculties of mind leading to a negative attitude toward criticism and analytical thinking in general. That negative attitude, which Eliot finds in Arnold, is connected for him to a large misunderstanding of the poet's position and the function of poetry in society. Eliot identifies the "important moment for the appearance of criticism" as "the time when poetry ceases to be the expression of the mind of a whole people" (UPUC 12). For Eliot, criticism emerges prominently when consensus in a society deteriorates; at the same time, poetry as a group-oriented activity ceases to be possible. In his introduction, Eliot cites Dryden, for Arnold and the Romantics a poet of mere Fancy, as an example of a poet turning to criticism who is writing for "something like an intellectual aristocracy" rather than "for the whole people" (UPUC 13, 12). Concerned to define his own contemporary situation by contrast, Eliot suggests that the position of the modern poet is considerably different from and more difficult than Dryden's. Not only is there no intellectual group sufficient to provide a viable audience, but a repressive false consciousness attempts to limit in advance what the writer can undertake: "when power is in the hands of a class so democratised that whilst still a class it represents itself to be the whole nation; when the only alternatives seem to be to talk to a coterie or to soliloquise, the difficulties of the poet and the necessity of criticism become greater" (UPUC 13). The necessity is greater because the innovative poet's beleaguered situation forces the asking of fundamental questions about the purpose, audience, and technical strategies of poetry (UPUC 21). The fact that these questions have to be asked, however, does not mean that creative faculties have been displaced by critical faculties that are somehow not appropriate in the process of creation. And it does not mean that the questioning must be limited to "criticism" as distinct from something more valuable called "poetry."

The questions can arise both in what we conventionally think of as criticism and in poetry that has been critical. They are unavoidable questions for a poet who claims, as Eliot does, that " 'the use of poetry' " is "to give pleasure," that is, to be read and "enjoyed by as large and various a number of people as possible" (UPUC 22). Eliot's attitude can be understood as part of his stance against Arnold, who, according to Eliot, by treating poetry as instrumental, undermines the possibility that poetry will be read carefully. Eliot suggests quite reasonably that it is unlikely any poet would deliberately restrict his audience through his choices of style and subject-matter but that instead, a poet may well be "incapable of altering his wares to suit a prevailing taste" (UPUC 22). This category of poet, to which Eliot clearly relegates himself, is "vitally interested in the *use* of poetry" (UPUC 23). Such a vital interest may emerge, as in these lectures, in critical work focusing on the functions of poetry, but it also emerges in "extremely critical" modern poetry, which, like its prose counterpart, is full of questions about poetry's uses as well as some tentative answers (UPUC 20). If poetry turns out to be critical, of course, the Arnoldean distinction in value between criticism and poetry becomes untenable. By emphasizing the critical character of modern poetry at the end of the first lecture, Eliot is preparing for the more explicit, detailed discussion of Arnold and the communication theory of poetry in the sixth.

In that discussion Eliot presses his disagreement with Arnold about criticism and poetry further by asserting that Arnold's "own poetry is decidedly critical" (UPUC 103). From the Arnoldean perspective the statement is disparaging, but from Eliot's it is not. With this assertion Eliot manages at once to counter Arnold's differentiation between poetry and criticism and to praise him on a basis Arnold would himself have eschewed.[2] The praise is real in a way that is obviously lacking when Arnold, using a related but harsher rhetorical strategy, ironically praises the works of Dryden and Pope as "classics of our prose." Eliot's positive meaning is especially clear when he calls *Heine's Grave* "very fine criticism" and "a kind of criticism which is justified because it could not be made in prose" (UPUC 103). Eliot is not here denying that there are differences

---

2. Eliot is responding to the implications of Arnold's well-known 1864 lecture at Oxford on "The Function of Criticism at the Present Time," as had Oscar Wilde a generation earlier in *Intentions* (1891), especially in "The Critic as Artist."

between prose and poetry, but he does deny that criticism can or should be limited to just the one form or the other.

It is clear that by *critical* Eliot does not mean merely "logically analytical" or "aesthetically self-reflexive" when he goes a step further in linking poetry and criticism by asserting that they are essentially similar in at least one crucial respect when they are of high quality. This judgment of quality is based specifically on a criterion that crosses the putative, and for Eliot artificial, boundaries of genre. The criterion involves the dissolving of the unified self rather than the exercise of logical thinking. The shared factor is the author's adopting the persona of the writer criticized. Whether in poetry or in prose, that adoption of a mask can result in criticism of high quality, for "the critic assumes, in a way, the personality of the author whom he criticises, and through this personality is able to speak with his own voice" (UPUC 104). This statement suggests that an odd kind of doubling, mediation, and fusion takes place in writing, whether prose or poetry, that can be applauded as *critical*. In this sort of writing, the author achieves a distinctive style that cannot be distinguished wholly from the mask of the earlier writer. At the end of the lecture, when Eliot dons a Coleridgean mask, he gives us stylistically an example of the process he here identifies, a process that is far from being *critical* in the sense of being wholly logical and analytical. It appears rather to be a merger as well as a separation into parts. He gives a more extended stylistic instance of the process in *Little Gidding* 2.

Eliot provides at this point in *The Use of Poetry* one way for understanding his comment earlier that Wordsworth would not recognize himself in Arnold's version, for he says there is as much Arnold in that version as there is Wordsworth. He goes even further, however, in a way that echoes Yeats, when he claims that the author criticized, the role assumed, may be "as far as possible the antithesis" of the writer's own, "a personality which has actualized all that has been suppressed in himself; we can sometimes arrive at a very satisfactory intimacy with our anti-masks" (UPUC 104). Though more extreme, this comment resembles the earlier one concerning Arnold's poetry as critical, for it works in different ways to blame and to praise simultaneously. On the one hand, the general statement can be taken to refer specifically to Arnold and Wordsworth. In that case, Eliot is suggesting that Arnold's reading is considerably off the mark, since there is so much Arnold in a commentary on an author who is his antithesis. On the other hand, Eliot also praises Arnold for succeeding in a task that Arnold's basic con-

ception of poetry would have ruled out, a task that is in fact
wholly opposed to Arnold's understanding of poetic reception.
From Eliot's perspective, instead of having experienced in an
unmediated fashion Wordsworth's virtually unalloyed feelings
through the essentially transparent vehicle of poetry, Arnold has
constructed a mediation and experienced a doubling that enable
him to speak not exactly with Wordsworth's voice but with what
has become his own. In other words, he has been enabled to
write what *he* can express, and that should not be confused with
Wordsworth. Writing and reading, poetry and criticism have
become thoroughly imbricated in one another in this decidedly
unArnoldean reading of Arnold.

When Eliot mentions the satisfaction of adopting the
mask of an antithetical writer, he seems to be referring to the
process of doubling, mediation, and fusion that results in new
style and new meaning. If we understand the relationship with
this other, alternative self also with reference to Eliot's comments earlier in the lecture concerning the joy of writing, the
process involves the dissolution of the self. After commenting
that in his criticism Arnold is "little concerned with poetry from
the maker's point of view," Eliot suggests "that the writing of
poetry brought [Arnold] little of that excitement, that joyful loss
of self in the workmanship of art, that intense and transitory
relief which comes at the moment of completion and is the chief
reward of creative work" (UPUC 100). The writer's satisfaction
in producing a new style by means of a persona is the unlikely
and also unsustainable experience of giving up the secure, habitual sense of self. Eliot evokes that experience in various ways in
his own poetry, especially in *Four Quartets*, but he finds little
evidence of this risky, even terrifying, but joyful process in
Arnold.

In a more contemporary parlance, the kind of relief
and reward Eliot mentions would be *jouissance*. The possibility
of achieving *jouissance*, as well as the process by which it occurs,
arises again, albeit implicitly, in the passage on the "auditory
imagination." What Eliot describes there is related to Julia Kristeva's concept of the *semiotic* (by which she means, generally
speaking, the instinctually rhythmical) as a transforming element
existing within, as well as before the *symbolic*, her term for the
ordered, codified language system. "The first echolalias of
infants" is, for Kristeva, an instance of the semiotic, which she
claims "functions in all adult discourses as a supplementary register" as well (216). Poetic language enables *jouissance* when the
semiotic disrupts the symbolic by setting in process "a heteroge-

neous dynamic" (218). This dynamic "operates on a clearly definable linguistic level" through semantic and syntactical ambiguities and difficulties (219).[3] Such difficulties are regular features of Eliot's writing. In his work, however, the dynamic also takes the form of a historical echolalia through multiple, proliferating, and ultimately indeterminate echoes of past writing.

Jouissance is clearly different from the joy Arnold discerns and praises in Wordsworth. Central to Eliot's lecture on Arnold is a commentary on Arnold's essay on Wordsworth, in which Eliot identifies various indications of a general orientation toward poetry that Eliot strongly objects to. He objects because of what it leads to in the case of Walter Pater. He objects because it interferes with the taking of poetic language seriously. He objects because it treats poetry as instrumental, as the vehicle for communicating joy in Arnold's sense of that word. But before resuming his argument against the communication theory of poetry, already begun in the introductory lecture, Eliot presents his mixed feelings about Arnold by making clear how highly he esteems his work.

He ranks Arnold, for instance, along with Dryden and Johnson, as a critic who has performed the monumental and necessary task of reviewing and readjusting for his generation the poetic canon "as well as human frailty will allow" (UPUC 101). This is the task, described here as "not one of revolution" (UPUC 100), Eliot has outlined in one way in the introduction as the experienced reader's "reorganisation" of the poetic canon. It involves the finding of "a new pattern of poetry arranging itself in consequence" of the encounter with something new in contemporary writing (UPUC 9). His comments suggest that this is a task of revision and preservation primarily, not of elimination. Eliot implies in this regard that Wordsworth, who was a revolutionary rather than a reformer (UPUC 16), was perhaps engaged in a different kind of project, about which Eliot is skeptical. The skepticism is based on an attitude toward language Eliot expresses in *Four Quartets*, often in the fifth sections: the impossibility of ever achieving a successful revolution, that is, a permanent break with convention. Wordsworth may have thought he was achieving something absolutely and permanently different from earlier poets, but in Eliot's view Words-

---

3. The quotations are taken from Julia Kristeva's essay, "The Speaking Subject," in which she provides a brief overview of how the disrupting of the symbolic by the semiotic proceeds in poetic language. There is a much lengthier account focusing on nineteenth-century French poetry in her *La Révolution du langage poétique. L'Avant-garde à la fin du XIXe siècle: Lautréamont et Mallarmé*, available in English translation as *Revolution in Poetic Language*.

worth's "own language was as capable of artificiality, and no more capable of naturalness, than that of Pope--as Byron felt, and as Coleridge candidly pointed out." Eliot's use here of the Romantics in relation to themselves indicates a recurring aspect of his approach to them, one that helps do away with the notion that Romanticism was a monolithic movement, the elements of which can easily, once and for all, be codified and systematically accepted or rejected.

Understood in light of Eliot's own commitment to rearranging the order of poets and poems as a work of preservation, his objection to the distinction between Imagination and Fancy is based in part on the way it had been used to create hierarchical, and ultimately exclusionary, categories of poetry. For him, the terms are untenable if they are merely labels for good and bad writing, labels that carry value judgments that cannot be justified based on those terms (UPUC 69). Among the aspects of Arnold's work Eliot objects to most is his accepting the Romantic exclusionary tendency by feeling "called upon to set the poets in rank" according to their relative greatness (UPUC 109). In this regard, Eliot complains about the distinction Arnold makes, clearly based on the Romantic one, between genuine poetry " 'conceived and composed in the soul' " and " 'the poetry of Dryden, Pope and all their school . . . conceived and composed in their wits' " (UPUC 110). Eliot's campaign to define and re-establish the importance of Metaphysical poetry and of wit is part of his attempt to counter this exclusionary aspect of the Arnoldean Romantic heritage.

In attempting to do that so persistently and stringently, Eliot regularly runs the risk of encouraging by the harshness of his criticism the downgrading and even the exclusion of the writers he chides. His sometimes astonishing lack of tact in his formulations has earned him the reputation for being churlish, as for instance in his reference near the beginning of the Arnold lecture to "the riff-raff of the early part of the century" (UPUC 97). Presumably he means Keats and Shelley, the subjects of the preceding lecture. Toward the end of the Arnold lecture, Eliot comments on the unlikelihood that a critic who is also a good reader can actually remain true to inflexible, exclusionary principles while trying "to set the poets in rank" according to their supposed greatness. Inevitably, such a critic will render judgments that do not conform to the principles. Eliot's severity shows him beset by the opposite difficulty of occasionally displacing close readings by judgments that are exclusionary, though Eliot's avowed principles are not. What Eliot calls "human frailty" plays its role in the lapses. Despite these lapses, Eliot generally works against exclusion by frequently citing elements in the work of earlier writers that he can praise. He does that even, as in the case of Arnold, when there are extreme differences in perspective on basic issues about poetry. And he does it with the Romantics when he echoes them in some of his most intense passages. The very procedure of close reading, in so far as it is an attempt to specify Arnold's views, does Arnold the justice of assuming his statements should be examined seriously. As Eliot says near the beginning of the lecture, "the definition of limitation may be at the same time a precision of the writer's excellences." For Eliot, many of Arnold's excellences and his limitations are most evident in the essay on Wordsworth.

Eliot identifies in Arnold's responses to Wordsworth Arnold's most direct expressions of what poetry meant to him. Although Eliot's rejecting these general attitudes toward poetry has been taken to be a wholesale rejection of the Romantics, it is more precisely a disagreement with Arnold. Central to Eliot's critique is his objection to Arnold's explanation of Wordsworth's greatness: "Wordsworth's poetry is great because of the extraordinary power with which Wordsworth feels the joy offered to us in nature, the joy offered to us in the simple primary affections and duties; and because of the extraordinary power with which, in case after case, he shows us this joy, and renders it so as to make us share it" (qtd. in UPUC 107). Given Eliot's thorough questioning of this statement, if Arnold's description of Wordsworth is correct, Eliot is here criticizing Wordsworth as well. Rather than arguing for its accuracy, however, Eliot has implied earlier that Arnold's version of Wordsworth, while influential, is suspect.

Eliot finds Arnold's means of measuring Wordsworth's greatness unconvincing because its maxim cannot be generalized. He stresses the dependence of Arnold's criteria on what the author has felt when he asks "whether Wordsworth would be a less great poet, if he felt with extraordinary power the horror offered to us in nature, and the boredom and sense of restriction in the simple, primary affections and duties" (UPUC 108). By putting his question in this way, Eliot effectively shows the exclusionary bias of Arnold's judgment, which relies on the poet's responding positively to certain aspects of nature and human relations. Eliot implies that a writer need not share those feelings in order to produce good work. He implies as well that Wordsworth himself might have experienced feelings that are strongly antithetical to the ones Arnold describes and still gone on to write poetry applauding nature, affections, and duties. The judgment about the writer as poet needs to be separated from the writer's feelings. Eliot questions as well the origin and character of *joy* as Arnold uses that word by countering it sharply with the words "horror," "boredom," and "restriction" (UPUC 98). While most of Eliot's remarks earlier in the lecture are less stark, as we have seen, Eliot has already provided some alternative ways to understand the kinds of satisfaction, delight, or enjoyment that reading and writing may involve. And he suggested at the start of the lecture that Arnold was generally unable to admit and put the fact of human suffering to use. Although Eliot finds "unrest, loneliness and dissatisfaction" in Arnold's best poems, as a critic Arnold is too willing to find delusive comfort in "the 'consolatory' power of Wordsworth's poetry" (UPUC 99).

Arnold errs primarily according to Eliot by "putting the emphasis upon the poet's feelings, instead of upon the poetry" (UPUC 108), within a communication theory of poetry, a theory that identifies "the poet as teacher, leader, or priest" (UPUC 107). While Eliot does not deny that communication occurs between reader and writer, he refuses to characterize poetry as "primarily the vehicle of communication" that is, merely instrumental (UPUC 108). Poetry for Eliot is no transparent medium whose purpose is to show the poet's exhilaration and "to make us share it," as Arnold puts it. Eliot has already redefined poetic communication in his introduction by arguing that the experience to be communicated in poetry "may only exist ... in the expression of it" (UPUC 21): "The poem's existence is somewhere between the writer and the reader; it has reality which is not simply the reality of what the writer is trying to 'express,' or of his experience of writing it, or of the experience of the reader or of the writer as reader." By rejecting Arnold's assumptions about poetry's communicative function and about what it should communicate, Eliot suggests the constricting limits of Arnold's attitudes, which he finds still dominant over half a century later. Those attitudes tend to prevent alternatives from even being formulated, much less pursued. In response to Arnold's distinction between genuine poetry and poetry of the wits and to his claim that the " 'difference between the two kinds of poetry is immense,' " Eliot counters that "there are not two kinds of poetry, but many kinds; and the difference here is no more immense than that between the kind of Shakespeare and the kind of Arnold" (UPUC 110). Eliot is clearly arguing that these many kinds need all to be recognized as genuine, that is, as poetry.

Toward the end of his remarks on Arnold, Eliot suggests a way to make that recognition possible by emphasizing style as fundamental to understanding poetry. Eliot provides an alternative to focusing on the writer by avoiding Arnold's failure to deal with the language of poetry. He questions whether Arnold "was highly sensitive to the musical qualities of verse" and asserts that Arnold "never emphasizes this virtue of poetic style, this fundamental, in his criticism" (UPUC 111). In stressing the role of the ear in the experience of reading and writing poetry, Eliot distances himself explicitly from Arnold's apparent critical deafness and implicitly from the Romantic "visionary gleam." He does so in a prominent and arresting way when he characterizes the "auditory imagination" at some length and in a heightened style. The passage occurs at a climactic moment in *The Use of Poetry and the Use of Criticism*, close to the end of the lecture on Arnold:

> What I call the 'auditory imagination' is the feeling for syllable and rhythm, penetrating far below the conscious levels of thought and feeling, invigorating every word; sinking to the most primitive and forgotten, returning to the origin and bringing something back, seeking the beginning and the end. It works through meanings, certainly, or not without meanings in the ordinary sense, and fuses the old and obliterated and the trite, the current, and the new and surprising, the most ancient and the most civilised mentality. (UPUC 111)

The lecture and perhaps the entire series reaches its moment of highest intensity and greatest stylistic complexity and compression in this brief passage, in which sound, syntax, and sense combine to fuse opposites and evoke multiplicities by creating parallels and contrasts simultaneously. In the first sentence, the series of present participial constructions (penetrating, invigorating, sinking, returning and bringing back, seeking) linked through grammatical parallelism and rime have the appearance of being versions of one another that seem meant to clarify what the auditory imagination might be. But the explanation is itself in need of elucidation, since nearly every participial phrase is double and antithetical, either because there are two participles linked by a coordinating conjunction, as in "returning . . . and bringing" back, or because the participles are linked to two nouns: "thought and feeling," "the most primitive and forgotten," "the beginning and the end." Returning and bringing back, both of which involve a return, are normally not semanti-

cally antithetical, but in this context they refer to travelling in
opposing directions since the place returned *to* is also the place
something is brought back *from*. The coordinated nouns also
generally participate in a similar structure of simultaneous connection and sharp difference. Thought and feeling are linked in
the passage since both are aspects of consciousness, but normally they would be understood in contrast to one another. The
more usual semantic contrast, like the more usual semantic similarity of returning and bringing back, is evoked by the sentence's language at the same time that language is used to
reverse the usual relationship. Likewise, "beginning" and "end"
are clearly opposites, but here as alpha and omega they refer to
the common goal being sought.

So much simultaneous linking and differentiating in
a single sentence tends to engender a sense of a slippage, or an
overlap, or a transformational process among its elements
rather than maintaining the clarity and distinctness of logical
relations. The slippage or transformation involves something
apparently clear and distinct turning out to be merged with its
ostensible opposite or else apparently similar things turning out
to be also quite different. One conceptual implication of this
anomalous stylistic complexity seems to be that the kind of
imagination Eliot calls "auditory" requires for its description an
internally transforming discourse involving multiple connections
and differentiations among elements that cannot be wholly separated from one another. Through this style, which embodies
both harmony and dissonances, similarities and difference, Eliot
is countering aspects of both Arnoldean and Romantic versions
of poetic creation. For Eliot, the imaginative, creative process is
one that can never be adequately presented in conventional ref-
erential language that identifies it as primarily one thing or
another, that defines it as distinct from other mental processes
or faculties, including especially memory. It requires instead a
language that announces its difference from whatever we may
provisionally think it is, even from the language used to describe
it. Eliot asserts that the "auditory imagination" bears a relationship to language, in fact in one manifestation it is that relationship or "feeling for" aspects of language embodied in the musical qualities of literary styles, which would be a kind of memory
incarnate. Eliot's statement works through language, or not
without language in the ordinary sense, to suggest that the
imagination stands always in at least two places, for it is perpetually in the process of becoming what it is not. What it is not

includes both language and meaning, the necessary concomitants and traces of poetic creation.

One general difference between Eliot's view and the Arnoldean and Romantic positions is that for him imagination is not in service to expressing the poet's feelings and making them available to the reader. Eliot stresses the difference by his repetition of the word "feeling" twice in the sentence. In its second appearance, in the phrase "conscious levels of thought and feeling," the word refers to the kind of conscious, personalized mental phenomenon Eliot objects to in Romantic descriptions of aesthetic creation, especially Wordsworth's well-known attempt in the "Preface to *Lyrical Ballads*." The first appearance of the word in the phrase, "the feeling for syllable and rhythm," establishes an antithetical meaning, for this feeling is specifically the means for "penetrating far below" conscious "feeling." Rather than being related to emotion, as in the Romantics, and by contrast with the lack of musical sense Eliot finds in Arnold, this "feeling for syllable and rhythm" is an intuitive, musical sense of fit, such as that a composer might possess. But the phrase "feeling for" something carries a more physical, less self-assured meaning in so far as it suggests groping for something in an attempt to get hold of it. The one word, then, carries both mental and physical connotations, but ones that differ sharply from emotions as mental states and from feeling, such as the feeling of pain, as the registering of physical sensation. This particular combination of mental and physical carries forward the double implication of the phrase "auditory imagination," which suggests a physical perceiving in the act of hearing that is also an active mental process. In this context both aspects of the phrase apply primarily to the material, linguistic, rhythmical components of poetry as part of Eliot's focus on language in poetry rather than on the communicating of the author's experience.

The physical meaning of "feeling for" as a kind of seeking would not be so clearly suggested without the series of participial constructions that follow in the sentence. They have the effect of stressing the participial aspect of the word *feeling*, which as a verbal noun can have either a relatively static meaning or one that suggests an active process. Imagination, a faculty of mind, is to be understood in Eliot's evocation as a process and not just as a static mode of apprehension. Eliot, of course, prevents us from reading "feeling" as a present participle rather than a gerund by preceding it with the definite article. But the word's status as a noun is affected by the participles to come, in part because of the connection through rhyming, since these participles stress an active process with directions and goals. The participles modify grammatically and describe semantically "the feeling" but they are also a version of what this "feeling for" is. The stylistic direction Eliot's writing takes here aligns it with aspects of Yeats' later poetry. For example, at the beginning of the final stanza of "Among School Children," we learn that "[l]abour is blossoming or dancing." The participles are what labor *is* and they are what it is doing. This is a blossoming or dancing labor, one that comes into blossom or is able to dance under certain conditions, but it is also a labor identical to blossoming or dancing. Eliot produces briefly in prose a conceptually similar style that tells us both what the auditory imagination *is*, an intuitive recognition or knowledge, and what, in its feeling for the objects that can incarnate that intuition, it is *doing*: penetrating, invigorating, sinking, returning, bringing back, and, ultimately, seeking.

The second sentence proceeds differently from the first, but it too expresses doubling and fusion. Eliot makes one double movement explicit when he initially indicates how this imagination works, then modifies and partially retracts the description: "through meanings ... or not without them." Its products are not meaningless, but the meanings are distinctly secondary. The imagination works with them apparently because it cannot do without them. The sentence's compound predicate suggests that the process going on has at least two components, the working through language and the fusing of disparate elements. Had Eliot chosen a different structure for the sentence, the two might have been simply merged. He could, for instance, have asserted more straightforwardly that by working through meanings it creates a fusion. But instead by saying separately, though in a compound verb, that it does two things, the first of which is instantly retracted, Eliot suggests that the fusion effected is independent of the meanings as ordinarily understood. In order to create the simultaneous antithesis and parallelism, Eliot has to set sense and grammar partly at odds with one another by virtually eliminating the logical parallelism normally indicated by "and" in a compound predicate. He achieves this partial effacing of the usual logical implications by treating the sentence as a temporal structure, whose meaning builds and changes as the reader experiences a sequence of modifications. The resulting diverging and merging involve a kind of meaning, if that word can even still be used, in which apparent opposites turn out, as in the earlier sentence, not to be entirely distinct or in which things that we might think are related, such as working through meanings and fusing in this sentence, turn out to be distinct. Stylistically, the sentences make that meaning available as performance. The outcome of penetrating far below conscious levels includes the amalgamating of the elements the imagination sinks to, "the most primitive and forgotten," or as the second sentence has it "the old and obliterated" and "the most ancient," with their opposites, "the current," "the new," "and the most civilised." The familiar and the strange, "the trite" and the "surprising," perhaps even meanings, in the new sense, and fusion, merge.

By emphasizing fusion and overlap Eliot counters the nineteenth-century tendency, as in the Romantic distinction between Imagination and Fancy and in Arnold's disparaging of criticism by comparison with poetry, to draw sharp boundaries between faculties of mind where he feel divisions cannot be coherently made. Eliot proposes a conception of creativity in which neither Wordsworthian feeling nor the Coleridgean distinction plays an important role, and he does so employing a style sufficiently intense to put Arnold's separation of criticism and poetry into question. Eliot's own skepticism about absolute distinctions, however, keeps him from distancing himself entirely from the Romantics. In this regard, by linking his view with attitudes the Romantics expressed as well as distinguishing it from Romantic attitudes, Eliot attempts to capture in his statement's literary historical implications the very amalgamating and the antithetically double qualities he is describing. He attempts this unlikely feat of standing in two places at once by building his evocation of the auditory imagination, with its large deviations from Romantic conventions, around Coleridgean elements. As I have already mentioned, he even includes the relevant passages from Coleridge two lectures earlier so that there will be no mistake about the affinity. The one focuses on the amalgamating of " 'opposite or discordant qualities' " as a sign of the imagination, and the other deals with the " 'sense of musical delight' " (UPUC 71). Eliot fuses the one with the other in describing the workings of the auditory imagination.

Despite this unambiguous connection there is, of course, no denying the stylistic and conceptual differences between Eliot's positions and Arnold's, Wordsworth's, or Coleridge's. But it is equally true and at least as significant that Eliot constructs part of his critique of Arnold out of elements the Romantics, too, recognized as important. His complexly mixed attitude toward these nineteenth-century precursors with whom he frequently disagrees so substantially includes, like his description of the imagination, simultaneous connection and sharp difference. In the lecture, Eliot expresses implicitly that his difference from Arnold is also a difference between Coleridge and Arnold. With the help of Coleridge as persona, Eliot is able to realize that difference stylistically by speaking with his own voice. In the midst of and as part of his quarrel with Arnold, Eliot returns to the Romantics and brings something important back with him. He works through the Romantics, or not without them, in pursuing his description of writing and reading as acts of memory.

Eliot works in a related way in presenting a parable about aesthetic processes in the meeting between the anonymous poetic "I" and the anonymous "familiar compound ghost" in the "disfigured" street of *Little Gidding* 2. A remarkable aspect of Eliot's development as a poet emerges in this section, and in *Four Quartets* as a whole, for his persistent evocation of something centrally at work in poetry different from personality, and especially different from personal feeling and a personal voice, does not prevent him from producing styles that create as well as undermine the impression of voices. The character and the effects of style, scene, and action in this section of *Little Gidding* pose problems of description as great as those faced by the reader of Eliot's earlier poetry and prose, though of a different kind. As in many of Eliot's earlier poems, opposites are juxtaposed or commingled in various ways. But the language is not syntactically tortuous, as in "Rhapsody on a Windy Night," nor filled with the radical stylistic contrasts of *The Waste Land*. Because the peculiarities are less obvious than in the earlier poems, it is possible to take the language as representative of a voice, as some critics have done, including Robert Langbaum in *The Poetry of Experience* (94). The language, however, is not presented as a personal voice, though it is the poet's utterance in the same way that Joyce's portrayal of Stephen Dedalus is a portrayal of the artist in general and not just one artist. It is not the voice of the writer of this poem, but of a more general persona who can be understood as representing the character of the poet. While the depersonalizing is related to the undermining of prosopopoeia in Eliot's earlier poetry, it is generated in a different way and carries some new implications.

Stylistically, the poem encourages us to think of "I" in the passage in terms similar to those used to describe the ghost, who also speaks as an anonymous "I." Like the ghost, the initial "I" is familiar but not identifiable as a person, including the writer of the text, in part because there is no clear evidence provided within the poem to identify the voice. As critics have regularly pointed out, there are references that link the passage to Eliot's own experiences in London during the Second World War, but that connection is not made explicit in the poem. The frequent changes in style from passage to passage in *Four Quartets* as a whole make it difficult to argue that any of the styles and the *I*'s in the poem, or all of them, are to be taken as spoken *in propria persona* by any identifiable person. If we do so argue, then by *person* and *I* we have in mind something different from the stable source of a recognizably continuous and coherent discourse normally associated with self and voice.

Even leaving aside the rest of the poem, with its frequent shifting of styles, as a determining context for interpreting the passage, several considerations within the passage tend to prevent our understanding the language as an instance of the poet's emerging to speak *in propria persona*. This is so even though the passage is in some ways an exceptional one within *Four Quartets* because of its length and its apparently readily accessible character; it is, for example, one of the longest (seventy-one lines) and seemingly most self-contained of the entire poem, to the extent that it is sometimes excerpted from the poem in anthologies. The considerations complicating the impression of unity and accessibility are mainly matters of the language's multiply allusive qualities.[4] The numerous critical attempts to identify the "familiar compound ghost" with a particular poet are one indication of the allusive multiplicity. In this regard, the poem includes elements that lead the critical logic of determinate readings, including autobiographical ones, to undermine itself because of the numerous identifications. The attempt to identify the ghost is the critical counterpart of casting Eliot in the role of poetic speaker. But there is such an abundance of evidence concerning so many poets who might be the ghost that the endeavor to limit the choice only makes clearer that the sources and implications of the language are multiple. This is especially the case since the passage presents the initial "I" taking on the role of the ghost. When that "I" becomes another "I" whose identity is multiple, the character of the poet as Eliot presents it is close to the all-inclusiveness Stephen Dedalus argues for in the "Scylla and Charybdis" episode of *Ulysses*. The artist for Stephen, as for Eliot, is "all in all," an actor in his own play visited by a ghost who is himself.

---

4. In his early study of Eliot's work, Grover Smith attempts to trace allusions in his writing, including in *Little Gidding* (*T. S. Eliot's Poetry and Plays: A Study in Sources and Meaning* 286-96), as have many critics since. A. D. Moody, for instance, provides an exemplary list of some of the poets alluded to in *Little Gidding* 2 in *Thomas Stearns Eliot: Poet* (252).

Often the passage provides reasonable evidence for
the identifications of the ghost. Yeats, who died only a few years
before the writing of the poem, is, as Richard Ellmann suggested
in *Eminent Domain*, one likely candidate, given, among other
details, the visionary situation, the dialogue form, the comments
about old age, and the images of fire and dancing (94-95). But
Eliot has included so many allusions to other poets that this
identification is no more convincing than several others. And it
does not account for the presence of such lines as the Shake-
spearean sounding "Then fools' approval stings, and honour
stains" (CPP 142, l. 143). Through the style Eliot puts the reader
in a situation like that of the poet character, who encounters
something "intimate" but also "unidentifiable," something
"familiar" but "compound" and ghostly, not singular and tangible. The figure remains for the reader and for the living poet
character "a face still forming," a bundle of characteristics in a
continual process of shifting that never crystallizes into definitive features, though there is no lack of recognizable details. The
face still forming suggests that something is in the process of
being produced, that it is still coming into being. The process of
production rather than a specific poetic personality is the focus
of the passage.

One of the clearest allusions in the ghost's speech is
a reference to Mallarmé and the effort "to purify the dialect of
the tribe" (CPP 141, l. 127), an effort that might also reasonably
be identified with Romantic efforts to change poetic language,
including Wordsworth's. But the statements that follow concerning "the gifts reserved for age" are antithetical to the positive aspects of being older that Wordsworth writes about, for
instance in the "Immortality Ode," despite his idealizing of
childhood. And they are far different from the Victorian version
of this Wordsworthian optimism about age in Browning's
"Rabbi ben Ezra." Like some of Eliot's earlier poems, these
statements compose a kind of "Mortality Ode" that calls up past
poets and their poems largely by contrast. On the one hand, the
statements allude to Yeats' railing against old age in many
poems, but on the other, the ghost's remarks that precede them
encourage us to identify the origin by antithesis. Since the ghost
tells us that what he says is not what he would have said when
alive, the attempt to identify him becomes complicated beyond
possibility. He speaks from an insight he never imagined before
death:

> But, as the passage now presents no hindrance
>   To the spirit unappeased and peregrine

> Between two worlds become much like each other,
> So I find words I never thought to speak
> In streets I never thought I should revisit
> When I left my body on a distant shore. (CPP 141, ll. 120-25)

Not only do we encounter multiple allusions to various poets and their works, but according to these lines, we can reason by contrast in identifying the ghostly "I" with a poet who wrote quite differently. The lines could conceivably be taken to mean simply that the ghost never thought he would be able to speak these words in the streets he left behind. But they also suggest that the words are ones he never thought of rather than ones that had occurred to him he might speak. Even the way this ambiguity arises contributes to the complications of identifying the speaker, because it links the ghost's way of speaking with Yeats' often highly ambiguous poetic phrasing, as in the final stanza of "In Memory of Major Robert Gregory." While stylistically the lines point again to Yeats, semantically they encourage other possibilities.

The all-inclusive, protean quality of the poet and the poetic process that emerges through the highly allusive character of the style in *Little Gidding* gives some new implications to poetic strategies Eliot developed much earlier. The allusiveness there and in other portions of *Four Quartets* is an extreme extrapolation and transformation of the styles of allusion in Eliot's early poetry. As in his earlier verse, Eliot alludes to Romantic traditions and modifies them, sometimes, as in *The Waste Land*, by combining those allusions with others from a different historical period. In *Four Quartets*, the Romantic traditions are still being called up, as are the language and meanings of other eras, but now there are so many allusions that it is difficult to separate one reference from another. There are, of course, proliferating allusions in *The Waste Land* as well, but not such an impression of merging and mingling as in the later poem. Whereas the multiple allusions in *The Waste Land* tend to fragment the discourse and dissolve the impression of a voice, in *Four Quartets*, the merging of them gives that impression while simultaneously indicating its composed and mediated rather than spontaneous and unmediated character. As in *The Waste Land*, the effect is comparable to that of montage or collage, but in *Little Gidding* it is closer to some techniques of Cubist and late Impressionist painting. The voice is like the Cubist presentation of a human head made up of various geometrical shapes. We recognize the human image but also the shapes, which are not natural but instead call attention to their made character.

Or, as in paintings by Seurat and Van Gogh that employ techniques of *pointillisme*, a human face is clearly suggested, but so
are the points of color used to create the illusion, depending on
the light and on the distance from which the painting is viewed.
In a related way, Eliot's style in *Little Gidding* projects a voice
but also allusions, which are not elements of voice but of writing,
that contribute in essential ways to the style.

But these analogies are not completely satisfactory
because of the differences of medium and because they overem-
phasize self-conscious, controlled, aesthetic self-reflexivity. The
elements of poetic language contributing to the illusion of voice
in *Little Gidding* are not just aspects of techniques that work
more or less mechanically, though linguistic techniques do obviously play their role. The elements have historical implications
because they allude to earlier literary texts. When the reader
recognizes an allusion, or several, or merely the fact that an
indeterminate echoing is taking place, something more than a
self-consciousness about the poem's artifice is suggested. That
something more involves multiple, variable historical and
semantic linkages between the language used by the contemporary writer of the poem and the language used by other poets in
the past. These linkages are various and not completely determinate because the highly allusive quality of the style in *Four
Quartets* suggests an aleatory process at work as well as the necessarily historically embedded character of poetic language and
the historical element in poetic creation.

The effects and implications of Eliot's language and
the process it evokes are too complex to support entirely the
assertion critics regularly make that in *Little Gidding* 2 "we can
discern the dead poets, Eliot's chosen ancestors" (Moody 252).
Eliot did clearly choose to echo some of the poets readers recognize in his lines, but he could not possibly have consciously
chosen to refer to all the poets readers find traces of in the
poem. The producing of this sort of writing, like the reading of
it, involves aspects of mental processes other than *choice* and
intention. The poet no more chooses all the echoes than does
the reader choose to recognize or not to recognize them. The
echoes have instead chosen the poet and the reader to produce
them through writing and reading. By means of the echolalia of
allusion, Eliot's writing generates as well as represents a
labyrinthine, aleatory experience in which the ordinary conventions of understanding give way briefly to transforming alternatives. This is clearly not the sort of echolalia Kristeva mentions
with regard to infants but instead one that transforms the ele-

ments of language pertinent to knowing by including them in a discourse in process of doing or producing. The historical echolalia of poetic production and response involves reverberations through an indeterminate space that existed before the particular instance of writing or reading, a space that poetic language enables us to explore and reconfigure through echoes we discover ourselves producing.

For Eliot poetry writing is historical; it involves the reconstruction or interpretation of the past by the present as well as the partial, inevitable construction of the present by its historical antecedents. This double relationship of simultaneous movement forward and backward in reciprocal exchange is represented and enacted by the dialogue as a mutual exchange between the living poet and the dead one that is also a one-sided exchange. As we heard the ghost assert already, he is involved in a "passage" "[b]etween two worlds become much like each other." The ambiguity of the word "passage" in a text focusing on a ghost and poetry writing suggests that the passage of the spirit and the passage in the poem are the event, fact, and literary product of a process of interaction that puts into words something new, something the ghost "never thought to speak." That process of interaction is simultaneously mental and historical, and its product is not entirely determinate. The process involves both the past speaking through the mediation of the living poet and the living poet producing new words that mediate for the past.

The peculiar ventriloquism of writing results in a dialogue of one. This singular dialogue arises through the curious doubling of the poet in response to the visitation, a doubling that has to be discounted in critical attempts to provide a precise, limiting identity for the ghost and the poet. That doubling, clearly presented in the following lines, is at the heart of Eliot's evocation of aesthetic creation in *Little Gidding*:

> So I assumed a double part, and cried
>   And heard another's voice cry: 'What! are *you* here?'
> Although we were not. I was still the same,
>   Knowing myself yet being someone other—
>   And he a face still forming; yet the words sufficed
> To compel the recognition they preceded.
>   And so, compliant to the common wind,
>   Too strange to each other for misunderstanding,
> In concord at this intersection time
>   Of meeting nowhere, no before and after,
>   We trod the pavement in a dead patrol. (CPP 141, ll. 97-107)

Though presented matter-of-factly without hyperbole, the details of the meeting and the response are radically at odds with any imaginable determinate scene in which the roles in the dialogue are clearly divided. Those details contribute not to a representation of a meeting and an exchange in the ordinary senses but to the representation of a doubling that occurs within consciousness when the act of writing turns the singular self into something multiple, the familiar into the strange, the strange into the recognizable, the living and the dead into one another, and normal temporal sequence into preposterous reversals. These kinds of doubling and transforming are not only mentioned or implied in this brief statement but also exemplified in an extended way in the entire passage concerning the ghost.

As an evocation of the process of composition, in which the writer assumes "a double part," cries out, but hears "another's voice," the dialogue of one between the living poet and the ghostly representative of dead ones constitutes one version of the harmony of dissonances in Eliot's late poetry. In that harmony, things that are "strange to each other" are also "[i]n concord" because the poet can be "still the same" and yet "someone other." And words precede and produce meaning rather than merely communicating knowledge that is independent of language; that is, the voice refers to *you* in a way that suggests recognition, but it is the words that "compel the recognition they preceded." The problem of interpretation this statement poses is a general one in the encounter, because it is not clear who recognizes whom. Because of the announced doubling, the question " 'What! are *you* here?' " both emanates from and is directed toward the living poet who has assumed the part of the ghost as well as keeping his own. His words may compel the ghost to recognize him, or they may compel him to recognize the ghost. Or else the ghost's words result in that latter recognition. The situation prevents the question "who speaks?" from ever being answered in an uncomplicated way. However strongly the allusions in the passage may point to a determinate source in literary history for the ghost's voice, the source is always a multitude represented by the living poet who has assumed a double part, produced language that seems someone else's, and belatedly recognized some of the sources that have contributed to what is now the poet's own voice.

The merged identity of living poet and ghost involves the associating of the poet with all those other poets of the past alluded to in various ways in the ghost's speech. But that dispersal of the poet's self through identification with a multitude occurs in the context of the whole in this section of *Little Gidding* and not just in the dialogue of one. The poet character has already been cast in multiple roles, is already a compound, though seemingly familiar, before the exchange with the ghost gives the multiplicity some extra twists. That multiplicity depends in part on the allusive quality of the verse form. The presentation of the section in an English version of terza rima insures that it will be understood in relation to Dante's *Divine Comedy*, in which the poet character as pilgrim speaks with various figures, including dead poets. In Eliot's poem, the living poet takes the role of Dante as pilgrim and poet, and that role-taking provides a frame for understanding the encounter with the ghost. But the exchange with the ghost as dialogue of one and representation of poetic processes also provides in its turn a framework for understanding such taking on of poetic roles. It does so by suggesting how poetry, including the very passage in which it occurs, is produced.

Considered within that internally generated framework, the poet's writing in terza rima involves crying out in "another's voice" in the process of having contact with a ghostly precursor who becomes recognizable only after the the living poet's discovery of having spoken with a different voice. As the ghost maintains, however, what the poet speaks is not what the dead poet would have "thought to speak." It is instead a passage in which the two worlds of the living and the dead intermingle by means of a doubling in consciousness that produces surprising results. The results are surprising because they correspond neither to what the past has said nor to what the living poet may have intended. The two worlds of bombed London and Dante's underworld become figures for one another, just as the *I*'s of living and dead poets represent one another. The suggested interaction stands for the process of aesthetic creation, which involves the effacing of normal reality and the uncanny visitation of the dead. In this realm of doubling and reversals, however, it is the dead poet who visits the world of the living turned inferno rather than the living poet who descends to visit the dead, though the living poet is clearly involved figuratively in a descent. The complicated relationship of frame to dialogue, both involving multiple allusions, encourages various descriptions of what is taking place, all however suggesting the doubling of poetic roles in a process of historical feedback that is so complex as to become hyperbolic and vertiginous. The ghost of a past poet, Dante, visits the living poet, who discovers himself having spoken in Dante's style, in which he presents a poet, himself become Dantesque, encountering the ghost of a dead poet whose voice he assumes and for whom he speaks, simultaneously reenacting and representing the act he is already in the process of accomplishing, the assuming and transforming of past poetic styles.

The dizzying implications of the encounter create an interpretative situation for the reader like the one that arises at the end of "Tradition and the Individual Talent" when the process of writing is also presented in terms of repetitions and reversals, chiasmus within chiasmus. As in much of Eliot's earlier poetry, the style suggests a depersonalizing that is at odds with the Romantic convention of a personal voice. Rather than being the expression of a self, the voice is instead a composition that decomposes individuality. It is something written, in which various styles are presented in their historically sedimented and mutually modifying relationships, not in a controlled way, but in a way that suggests a proliferation of continually interacting perspectives. Despite the clearly unromantic quality of the style in the presentation of itself as a group voice, as even a kind of chorus, the composition includes some prominent allusions to Romantic writing. These are not just of the negative sort, as in the reversal of Wordsworth's optimism about old age, nor do they occur only in the ghost's speech. Perhaps the most positive and important of these allusions involves Shelley, one of the Romantics about whose writing Eliot complained most strongly. Despite those protests, Shelley is clearly among the past poets called up in *Little Gidding*, not just as one among many possible identifications for the "familiar compound ghost" but as a writer who provided a model for the entire section. When Eliot presents the poet's surprise at recognizing another poet whose voice he had already assumed, he may have been registering, among other things, the surprise he himself felt at recognizing Shelley as well as Dante to be one of the primary sources for the encounter. He would have known that readers of *Little Gidding* 2 would associate his rewriting of Dante with the other well-known attempt to write terza rima in English, Shelley's *The Triumph of Life*, in which the speaker has an obscure, visionary encounter with a dead master.

Little Gidding 2 stands at the end of a lengthy, complicated development in Eliot's styles of writing and in their implications concerning the writing process and the relationship of the present to the past. It is among his last attempts in nondramatic verse, and among his most successful, to achieve a modern style of wit inspired by the Metaphysicals in which dissonance is also a kind of harmony. As in the description of the "auditory imagination," the implications of that style, as it unfolds in Eliot's career, require that the Romantics be recognized rather than excluded. The end of that unfolding in *Little Gidding* is clearly not a total rejection of the English Romantics, for one of the results is a strange and unexpected poetic concord in a homage to Dante that is also a homage to Shelley.

WORKS CITED

Ellmann, Richard. *Eminent Domain: Yeats Among Wilde, Joyce, Pound, Eliot and Auden*. New York: Oxford UP, 1967.

Faulkner, Peter. *Modernism*. London & New York: Methuen, 1977.

Kristeva, Julia. *Revolution in Poetic Language*. New York: Columbia UP, 1984.

_____. "The Speaking Subject." *On Signs*. Ed. Marshall Blonsky. Baltimore: Johns Hopkins UP, 1985. 210-20.

Langbaum, Robert. *The Poetry of Experience: The Dramatic Monologue in Modern Literary Tradition*. 1957. New York: Norton, 1963

Moody, A. D. *Thomas Stearns Eliot: Poet*. Cambridge, England: Cambridge UP, 1979.

Pater, Walter. "Wordsworth" 1874. *Appreciations. With an Essay on Style*. 1889. London: MacMillan & Co., 1931. 37-63.

Smith, Grover. *T. S. Eliot's Poetry and Plays: A Study in Sources and Meanings*. 1950. Chicago: University of Chicago Press, 1965. 286-96.

JEWEL SPEARS BROOKER

*T. S. ELIOT AND THE REVOLT AGAINST DUALISM: HIS DISSERTATION ON F. H. BRADLEY IN ITS INTELLECTUAL CONTEXT**

In 1915 and 1916, T. S. Eliot wrote a Ph.D. dissertation on the epistemology of F. H. Bradley. Some critics, such as Hugh Kenner, believe that Bradley is important only for flavor. "Bradley has an attractive mind, though he has perhaps nothing to tell us. He is an experience, like the taste of nectarines or the style of Henry James" (*The Invisible Poet* 63). Eliot himself commented on the relationship on several occasions, and in every instance downplayed its importance. Once, however, when writing about Bradley in an unself-conscious way, focusing on Bradley's general significance for an audience which knew nothing of his own connection to Bradley, he let slip what I take to be the truest account of his debt. In an obituary article written in 1924 for the *Criterion*, Eliot said that for the few who will surrender patient years to the study of his meaning, Bradley's "writings perform that mysterious and complete operation which transmutes not one department of thought only, but the whole intellectual and emotional tone of their being. To them, in the living generation, the news of his death has brought an intimate and private grief" (9). Eliot claims that Bradley's style is "the finest philosophic style in our language, [one] in which acute intellect and passionate feeling preserve a classic balance." By the time Eliot finished his dissertation in 1916, he had surrendered those patient years. Those who know of his lifelong struggle to nurture both intellect and feeling and to preserve them in classic balance will find the tribute moving and convincing.

But what of the dissertation? Did the patient years surrendered to following Bradley's meaning make a difference in Eliot's poetry and his literary criticism? In several articles written between 1979 and 1986, I maintained that Bradley pro-

*This paper is a revision of a speech given at Duke University on February 15, 1988, and a talk given at the National Poetry Foundation's T. S. Eliot Centennial Conference, August 18-20, 1988, Orono, Maine.

foundly influenced both the shape and the content of Eliot's
work, and in *Reading* The Waste Land: *Modernism and the Limits of Interpretation* (1990), Joseph Bentley and I demonstrate
through a close reading of *The Waste Land* that an awareness of
Bradley's ideas can be enormously helpful in understanding
Eliot's contribution to modernism. Several recent critics have
also focused on the relevance of Eliot's early work on Bradley.
Sanford Schwartz, for example, clearly demonstrates in *The
Matrix of Modernism* (1985) that an awareness of Eliot's early
philosophical studies, especially of his work on Bradley's epistemology, is immediately helpful in understanding Eliot's criticism and his position in the modernist revolution.

The context into which I would like to put Eliot's dissertation is what, in a leading article in September 1926, the
Times Literary Supplement called "The Dethronement of
Descartes." The writer described the last three hundred years in
Western philosophy as a development of Cartesianism, and went
on to claim that Descartes and the great physicist-philosophers
of the seventeenth century had been dethroned by the physicists
and philosophers of the early twentieth, ushering in a new dispensation in intellectual history. Eliot, an occasional contributor
to and regular reader of the *TLS*, had made the same point
some eight months earlier in his Clark Lectures at Trinity College, Cambridge. After quoting a passage from *Meditations* (the
6th), he asserts that Descartes' crude reasoning is behind the
pseudo-science of epistemology which has haunted the Western
mind for the last three centuries (Clark Lectures 2). Eliot's focus
is on poetry, the *TLS* writer's focus is on philosophy, but both
are focused on the twentieth century's rebellion against the
seventeenth, and both identify the deposed monarch as
Descartes. A few years earlier, in 1921, Eliot had reviewed Grierson's *Metaphysical Lyrics and Poems of the Seventeenth Century*, a review included in *Selected Essays* under the title "The
Metaphysical Poets." His dispensational analysis of English
poetry in that review is explicitly based on the realization that in
the seventeenth century, something "happened to the mind of
England." That something was the triumph of dualistic thinking,
a triumph which produced, to use Eliot's phrase, "a dissociation
of sensibility":

> The poets of the seventeenth century . . . possessed a mechanism
> of sensibility which could devour any kind of experience. . . . In the
> seventeenth century a dissociation of sensibility set in, from which
> we have never recovered. (SE 247)

Mind and matter, thought and feeling, subject and object, fell apart; poets thought and felt by starts and fits. In phrases now famous, Eliot claims that before Descartes took over the Western mind, poets could feel their thoughts and think their feelings. They could feel their thoughts as immediately as the odor of a rose.

A brilliant account of the dethronement of Descartes is given in A. O. Lovejoy's *Revolt Against Dualism* (1929). Lovejoy argues that Western thought has been dominated for three centuries by the assumptions of Descartes, Locke, and Newton. These geniuses all believed that the subject and the object were separable, that objectivity was possible and even necessary for understanding the world. Lovejoy argues that early twentieth-century philosophers joined in an attempt to escape from this epistemological dualism of subject and object, and also from the parallel psychophysical dualism of mind and matter. The realization that subject and object are connected in a systematic way and that mind and body are aspects of a single world is in effect a dethronement of Descartes. Lovejoy's argument, articulated in 1929, anticipates the work of such intellectual historians as Thomas Kuhn, Gerald Holton, and Jacob Bronowski. His thesis, like theirs, is helpful in approaching modern thinkers in many fields. Most of the makers of the twentieth-century mind, figures as diverse as Freud, Heisenberg, Picasso, Royce, and Eliot have in common an about-face on the subject-object question and the mind-matter question; they all try to discredit the dualism which arbitrarily splits the world into pieces. Bertrand Russell and the Neo-Realists refuse to give up the subject-object distinction, but they too join in rejecting the division of the world into mind and matter.

Russell is, of course, important in Eliot's own revolt against dualism. He was Eliot's teacher at Harvard and his benefactor in the early London years. In the fall of 1915, while Eliot was writing his dissertation on Bradley, he and his bride moved in with Russell. Russell was at this time specifically involved in trying to overcome the distinction between mind and matter, maintaining, for example, that sense-data are the ultimate constituents of matter; on the other hand, he was strenuously holding to the dualism of subject and object. Russell's general point of view at this time is preserved in *Mysticism and Logic*, a book which Eliot reviewed; in the process displaying an in-depth knowledge of Russell's work. There can be no doubt that Eliot learned much from Russell; at the same time, there can be no doubt of the early and fundamental dissent, already clearly evident in the dissertation. In chapter 4, he critiques Russell's realism, and concludes by rejecting Russell's dualism: "the curious dualism of Mr. Russell ... which has much in common with obvious, though I can hardly think correct, interpretations of Plato, will not hold good of a world which is always partially in time, but never wholly in time, with respect to any of its elements" (KE 101). For a detailed and slightly different account of Eliot's indebtedness to Russell, I recommend Richard Shusterman's *T. S. Eliot and the Philosophy of Criticism* (1988). Shusterman's valuable discussion of the philosophical underpinnings of Eliot's literary criticism makes much of Russell and the Neo-Realists. By all accounts, of course, Eliot's situation in late 1915 was extraordinary. He was a close student of both Bradley and Russell; he had studied with Bradley's friend and disciple Harold Joachim and with Russell himself. And now, while writing a dissertation explaining and in general defending Bradley against Russell, Eliot found himself face to face with Russell across the breakfast table. Moreover, as the husband of a fragile wife to whom both (each in his own way) were devoted, Eliot must have found life to be a kaleidoscope of brilliant and fluctuating patterns.

The subject of this paper, however, is not Russell, but Bradley, one generation older, living in seclusion at Oxford, and generally considered as the greatest living philosopher. Bradley was a trailblazer in intellectual history, with insights anticipating and paralleling those of Heisenberg in physics and Picasso in painting. He was an unflinching leader in the revolt against dualism; and from the beginning of his career, he was a radical skeptic who rejected the notion that there is such a thing as objectivity or objective truth. Like all idealists, he believed that everything is connected to everything else in a systematic way, and that everything is part of a single all-encompassing whole. He believed, consequently, that every perspective is partial and incomplete and thus, to use his terminology, an appearance.

Bradley is labelled an idealist, and often a "Neo-Hegelian," labels that are true in a sense but to the casually informed, very misleading. He began his work with one foot in German Idealism, but the other firmly planted on the ground, the ground being British Empiricism. His distinction is that he forged these two traditions into a synthesis, a synthesis preserving the intellectual and the experiential--in Eliot's words, intellect and feeling. Bradley believed, with Hegel, that reality is an all-encompassing unity, but he disagreed with Hegel's first principle, that is, with the notion that the real is of the nature of thought, that it is intellectual--to use a Hegelian vocabulary, that the real is the rational. "It may come from a failure in my meta-physics, or from a weakness of the flesh ... but the notion that existence could be the same as understanding strikes as cold and ghost-like as the dreariest materialism" (*Principles of Logic* 2: 591).

Bradley believed that the real *includes* the intellec-tual, but like Locke and the British empiricists, he believed that everything begins and ends in experience. As Eliot correctly stated in his 1927 review of *Ethical Studies*, "Bradley is thor-oughly empirical, much more empirical than the philosophies that he opposed" (SE 403). The philosophers he opposed, of course, lived in a world dominated by Newton and Descartes, and to them, experience consisted of a subject who does the experiencing, and an object, which is experienced; to them, experience has two parts, mind and matter. Bradley retained their commitment to experience, but dropped their dualism. Like Wordsworth, he believed that the universe is a living whole, that mind and matter, subject and object, are parts of a single whole. Bradley changed subject and object from nouns to adjec-tives, from things-in-themselves to the subjective and objective aspects of experience.

Bradley's empiricism is of the essence in under-standing his work. It is best to think of him not as an idealist, but as an idealist-empiricist, as much a part of British Empiricism as of German Idealism. In keeping with his Lockean roots, Bradley claims that "Everything is experience," and also that "experience is one." "There is but one Reality," he insists, "and its being consists in experience. In this one whole all appear-ances come together" (*Appearance and Reality* 457, 455). Now we are compelled by language to think of experience as "my" experience, or as some other person's experience. To the extent that we think of it in this way, we are missing Bradley's point and lapsing into dualism. He is not speaking of experience as something which is experienced by an experiencer, but as some-thing which simply is, as a complex encompassing experiencer and experienced. The absolute is experience, and it systemati-cally includes everything that exists or can be imagined to exist. We can, with minimal distortion, think of Bradley's Absolute as a complete inventory of all experiences that have ever existed or will ever exist. This means, of course, that his Absolute itself does not yet exist in its completeness, and will do so only in that moment when all experience is finished and comprehended. In that moment, it will also cease to exist.

The revolt against dualism is immediately helpful in understanding *Appearance and Reality* (2nd ed., 1897), the main Bradleyean text behind Eliot's dissertation. Bradley's field here is metaphysics, which he defines on his first page as "the attempt to know reality as against mere appearance." For unsuspecting literary critics, this definition will be congruous with a common literary theme, the opposition between appearance and reality, such as one finds in the plays of Shakespeare, or the poems of Dickinson. But let us, briefly, take a closer look. Bradley's book is divided into two parts, one on appearance and one on reality. The first is a devastating attack on traditional ways of attempting to understand truth or first principles. Thinking by its very nature divides reality into this and that, into temporal and spatial, into body and soul, into mind and matter, into subject and object. All of these divisions collapse under scrutiny into self-contradiction. The second part of Bradley's book is called "Reality," and for the casual reader, it will promise Bradley's alternative to appearance. But instead of an alternative, the reader finds instead the disconcerting suggestion that appearance and reality are not opposites at all. An appearance is reality in any less than a comprehensive aspect. Bradley's reality is not an abstraction lying behind the appearances in the external world. "The Absolute *is* its appearances, it really is all and every one of them,"--not all totalled together, but all unified (*Appearance and Reality* 486).

Eliot's dissertation springs to life when it is understood in the context of the revolt against dualism. His purpose is to explain and to some extent to defend Bradley's epistemology. Now epistemology, the investigation of how we know what we know, is by definition dualistic. It involves a systematic analysis of subjects and objects and their relations. The central Bradleyean truth, however, is that the world is one, that reality is one, that dualism always leads to self-contradiction, and in fact, Bradley argues that there can be no such thing as epistemology, and Eliot agrees with him. The epistemology that Bradley and Eliot reject is the activity of that name fathered by Descartes and nurtured by Kant. Ten years later, in the Clark Lectures, long after Eliot had abandoned philosophy as a career, he speaks scornfully of epistemology as a pseudo-science. But in the dissertation, he says he is trying to elucidate and criticize Bradley's "theory of knowledge." At any rate, we must insist, as Lovejoy does, that knowing is part of being human, and that a denial that one has a theory of knowing is a clear indication that one is theorizing about knowledge. Eliot's dissertation, then, is the attempt of a man who does not believe in epistemology to explain the epistemology of a man who denies that epistemology exists.

The opening chapter is Eliot's attempt to get behind the dualism implicit in his subject by grounding Bradley's theory of knowledge in something which is not dualistic. He does this, first, by making the case for Bradley's all-encompassing empiricism. "Reality, . . . the ultimate criterion which gives meaning to our judgments . . . is our experience" (KE 32). He proceeds by positing "immediate experience" as a pre-dualistic unity, as a pre-cognitional condition, arguing that epistemology can only begin after we have fallen away from this unity. We are forced, Eliot says, "in building up our theory of knowledge, to postulate something given upon which knowledge is founded" (KE 17). That something given, "immediate experience" is a knowing-and-being-in-one which precedes subjects and objects (KE 16). Epistemology or the speculation on subjects and objects, experiencers and experienced, follows and builds upon "immediate experience."

The first chapter also argues that knowing is self-transcendent, that it reaches beyond itself and is taken up in a larger unity. He thus situates "epistemology" in the realm of "appearance," in the dualistic realm of relations. "Thinking" emerges from and moves toward feeling or experience, and in his own analysis of subjects and objects, Eliot is always careful to indicate his awareness that his activity is sandwiched between the beginning and the end. His conclusion in the last paragraph of chapter one is: "We are led to the conception of an all-inclusive experience outside of which nothing shall fall. If anyone object that mere experience at the beginning and complete experience at the end are hypothetical limits, I can say not a word in refutation for this would be just the reverse side of what opinions I hold" (KE 31).

The second chapter of Eliot's dissertation takes up the question of what Lovejoy calls psychophysical dualism, or as the chapter title puts it, the "Distinction of Real and Ideal." The point of the chapter is that such distinctions are invalid, mainly because the real and the ideal are dependent on each other for existence. They are systematically intertwined in such a way that if one appears the other does, and if one dissolves, the other cannot survive. Eliot admits that immediate experience falls apart of itself into subjects and objects, mind and matter, but insists that this dualism is "tentative and provisional, a moment in a process" (KE 32). The process, ever repeated, never ending, is the movement from the unity of immediate experience to the unity of transcendent experience. Distinctions such as real and ideal are relative and depend on focusing on one part from one point of view, a process which automatically generates an opposite, an other-than. Epistemology, the study of subjects and objects, then, can only be carried on from some relative and shifting point of view.

The next chapters of the dissertation are deconstructions of two approaches to knowledge, that of the psychologist, who thinks in terms of mental content and external reality (mind and matter), and that of the epistemologist, who thinks in terms of subjects and objects. Eliot critiques the psychologist by adopting the stance or point of view of the epistemologist, and then shifting his point of view, he critiques the epistemologist by adopting the point of view of the psychologist. He critiques idealism from the point of view of realism, and vice versa. His point is that neither is right, that both are relative, that either can be reduced to its so-called opposite. Eliot's philosophical skepticism and his dialectical rhetoric make it possible to find statements which support opposite points of view, statements which contradict each other. This will not disturb those who understand his method and his position, stated at the opening of his last chapter, that every theory depends on adopting some point of view, and that every point of view is no more than one point of view. The fact is that any epistemology can be undermined fatally simply by shifting one's point of view. Standing on Bradley's argument, Eliot concludes: "no [valid] definition can anywhere be found to throw the mental on one side and the physical on the other. . . . The difference between the mental and the real, or . . . the personal and the objective, is one of practical convenience and varies at every moment" (KE 84). We divide the world into mental and physical, but "the mental resolves into a curious and intricate mechanism, and the physical reveals itself as a mental construct" (KE 154). Both Bradley and Eliot are attempting to show that all thinking is relational, that any truth can be dissolved into its opposite, and that since thinking takes place in a space between mere experience and complete experience, it can only proceed from one limited point of view or another. Thinking is always relative, always tentative, never final.

In the last chapter of his dissertation, Eliot drops the dialectical method and summarizes his own conclusions. He objects to a number of points from Bradley's *Principles of Logic*, but as he confesses, he is in substantial agreement with *Appear-*

ance and Reality. He specifically affirms the following Bradleyean positions:

1. Reality is experience. His own words: "From first to last Reality is experience" (KE 165).

2. Reality is one. To quote Eliot: "We are forced to the assumption that truth is one, and to the assumption that reality is one" (KE 168).

3. Reality is all-comprehensive. The clearest one-sentence statement of this is in his first chapter: "We are led to the conception of an all-inclusive experience outside of which nothing shall fall" (KE 31).

4. Reality is systematic. For it to include everything and still be one thing, it *must* be systematic. This simply means that everything is connected to everything else, and that any "new fact" which comes into being instantly becomes part of something bigger than itself, part of a system of reality. Eliot's words: "Facts are not merely found in the world and laid together like bricks, but every fact has in a sense its place prepared for it before it arrives, and without the implication of a system in which it belongs the fact is not a fact at all" (KE 60).

5. All relations are internal. Eliot says that he is compelled to accept Bradley's doctrine of the internality of relations (KE 153). The compulsion comes from logic. If everything is a systematic part of one thing, then all relations or connections are between fragments or parts and relations are inside the all-comprehensive totality. This is important in part because it means that nothing has its meaning alone, that no action is isolated in its significance. Any change or adjustment or development in any one part changes the whole. In the opposite doctrine, the one Eliot denies, entities are complete in themselves. Thus relations which connect them are external to each entity, and moreover, changes in any one entity affect only that one entity.

6. Finally, Eliot says he is also compelled to accept the idea of degrees of truth, degrees of reality (KE 153). "The only real truth is the whole truth," he says (KE 163), but the fact that no one can know the whole truth does not mean no one can know truth. Partial truth is truth, to a degree. He maintains that everything, including falsehoods, errors, and hallucinations, is part of

reality. Eliot illustrates this by discussing the reality status of the bear which a frightened child "thinks it sees" in its bedroom. "It is . . . not altogether true or altogether false to say that the child sees a bear." The doctrine of degrees of truth allows him to accept both the bear in the nursery and the bear in the woods as real without requiring him to agree that they have the same status in truth and reality (KE 115-16). Or, to take an example which forms part of Eliot's argument with Russell, references to the "present king of France" are and are not references to something which exists. The doctrine of degrees of reality permits him to distinguish the "present king of France" from the present king of a country like England which still has a monarch. Both are real, though not in the same way (KE 127ff.). All imaginable truth, then, is partial, although some truths are fuller than other truths.

These principles are everywhere evident in Eliot's literary and social criticism, and also in his account of history. No doctrine is more important than that of wholeness, no word more ubiquitous in his prose. In talking about other writers, for example, he insists that the plays of Shakespeare are one play, the novels of James one novel, that none of these works have meaning alone, that all are *systematically* connected. Otherwise, of course, he could not consider many plays as *one* play, many novels as *one* novel. All six of the points I have just outlined are prominent features of Eliot's doctrine of tradition and the individual talent. Tradition involves the historical sense, which

> compels a man to write not merely with his own generation in his bones, but with a feeling that the whole of the literature of Europe from Homer and within it the whole of the literature of his own country has a simultaneous existence and composes a simultaneous order. (SE 4)

Eliot's description of the relation between artists within the tradition and between the tradition and individual artists provides a textbook example of the doctrines of the internality of relations and the systematic nature of the whole.

> No poet, no artist of any art, has his complete meaning alone. . . . you . . . must set him, for contrast and comparison, among the dead. . . . The necessity that he shall conform . . . is not onesided; what happens when a new work of art is created is something that happens simultaneously to all the works of art which preceded it. The existing monuments form an ideal order among themselves, which is modified by the introduction of the new . . . work of art among them. The existing order is complete before the new work

> arrives; for order to persist after the supervention of novelty, the *whole* existing order must be ... altered; and so the relations, proportions, values of each work of art toward the whole are readjusted. ... Whoever has approved this idea of order ... will not find it preposterous that the past should be altered by the present as much as the present is directed by the past. (SE 4-5)

What keeps this from being preposterous is the doctrine of internal relations. If every artist is related within an organic and systematic whole, then any alteration in any part changes both every other part and the whole itself, just as any change of any part of my body affects not just that part but other parts and also me as a whole person. Thus we can say that the *Divine Comedy* alters *The Waste Land*, but we can also say that *The Waste Land* alters both the *Divine Comedy* and the tradition of which both are a part. These notions about organic wholes and systems of art are repeated in the opening paragraphs of "The Function of Criticism."

These ideas are also helpful in reading Eliot's poetry. "Gerontion" and the so-called "quatrain poems" were written on the heels of the dissertation, and the principles which Eliot accepted from Bradley's philosophy are everywhere apparent. To take "Gerontion" as an example: One of its major subjects is history, and Eliot brings in everything from the war between the Greeks and the Persians at Thermopylae several centuries before Christ to the First World War and the treaty at Versailles in 1919, the very year he was writing the poem. Not only does he bring in everything, he forces the reader to see that everything is systematically connected, that all relations are internal, fragment to fragment, both within history and within the poem, and he compels the reader to connect these whirling fragments into a unity. His use of allusion and juxtaposition, his collapse of time and space, his comprehensiveness and complexity--all of these and more are in my view inseparable from Bradley's ideas. Other complicated influences are included, of course. Frazer is there, and so are Théophile Gautier, Ezra Pound, and others. But Bradley is my subject, and Bradley is of the essence. As I argued in a 1979 article in *English Literary History* ("The Structure of Eliot's 'Gerontion' "), the structure of the poem is based on the Bradleyean principle of the systematic nature of truth, on self-transcendence of parts always leading toward greater, more inclusive wholes. The last lines of the poem--"Tenants of the house, / Thoughts of a dry brain in a dry season"--provide the major structural clue (CPP 23). Eliot has composed the poem as a complex of houses within houses within houses, all decayed, all crumbling. Gerontion's dry thoughts are contained in his dry brain which is contained in his desiccated body which is contained in his crumbling house in his rocky yard in war-torn Europe in Western civilization over thousands of years, and all of these are contained in a whirling cosmos. Both the content and the form of the poem illustrate Bradleyean principles.

The epistemology, or theory of knowing, outlined and in its major points defended in Eliot's dissertation, rests upon the metaphysics. All knowledge, Bradley argues, begins and ends in experience. Knowing occurs in three stages which are also three levels of experience. The first and most foundational is "immediate experience," the second is "relational experience," and the most comprehensive is "transcendent experience." Immediate experience is experience which has not been mediated through the mind; it is a knowing and feeling and being in one which is prior to the development of logical or temporal or spatial categories. The first chapter of Eliot's dissertation, "On our Knowledge of Immediate Experience," is a review of an essay by Bradley which has the same title. The point of both is to postulate a starting point for knowledge, a foundation upon which knowledge can be built and to which it can return. Eliot defines this doctrine by quoting Bradley. Immediate experience is

> first, the general condition before distinctions and relations have been developed, and where as yet neither subject nor object exists. And . . . second . . . anything which is present at any stage of mental life, in so far as that is only present and simply is. (KE 16)

Bradley also says:

> We in short have experience in which there is no distinction between my awareness and that of which it is aware. There is an immediate feeling, a knowing and being in one, with which knowledge begins; and, though this in a manner is transcended, it nevertheless remains throughout as the present foundation of my known world. And if you remove this direct sense of my momentary contents and being, you bring down the whole of consciousness in one common wreck. For it is in the end ruin to divide experience into something on one side experienced as an object, and on the other side something not experienced at all. (*Essays on Truth and Reality* 159-60)

As an example of immediate experience, Eliot describes the viewing of a painting in which the viewer is so absorbed that he has no consciousness of self or subject, on the one side, and painting or object, on the other. This directly experienced non-relational many-in-one is not the viewer's experience, for he as subject and the painting as object do not yet exist. When he becomes aware of "his" experience and of the painting as other than himself, then immediate experience has dissolved into the realm of relations, of self and not-self (KE 20). *Four Quartets* contains several references to immediate experience, for example, the "music heard so deeply / That it is not heard at all" (*Dry Salvages*, CPP 136).

It is the nature of immediate experience to fall apart. It breaks up because mind, existing heretofore as an undifferentiated part of feeling or experience, suddenly assumes dominance. Consciously, the intellect begins to structure and organize the elements which, like itself, had been undiscriminated in immediate experience. Reality can no longer be apprehended directly, as a unity, but must be approached through the tortuous streets of thought, in terms of relations. Relational experience is the level of our conscious everyday life, of the thinker and the thought, of the self and the not-self, of the knower and the known, of mind and matter, of the here and there, of the now and then, etc. All of these necessarily dualistic concepts are abstractions from reality; all are unreal. This is the level of all analytical thinking, of all philosophy, including epistemology, and this level is the major subject of Eliot's dissertation, which is in simplest terms an analysis of the nature of objects. This level is unavoidable, for to quote Eliot, "[t]he only way in which we can handle reality intellectually is to turn it into objects, and the justification of this operation is that the world we live in has been built in this way" (KE 159).

Immediate experience can be known only through reflection and intuition after it has dissolved. Time does not exist in immediate experience, but immediate experience does exist in time, for it does not last. In the following lines from *Burnt Norton*, Eliot describes relational experience, the level in which we are not fully conscious because our consciousness is primarily intellectual and reductive.

> Time past and time future
> Allow but a little consciousness.
> To be conscious is not to be in time
> But only in time can the moment in the rose-garden,
> The moment in the arbour where the rain beat,
> The moment in the draughty church at smokefall
> Be remembered; involved with past and future.
> Only through time time is conquered. (CPP 119-20)

If immediate experience were all that we had, in a paradoxical way, we would not even have it, for it is only in time that we can remember immediate experience and thereby in a sense begin to conquer time.

There is, in Bradley's view, a third level, a transcendent experience, which permits a return of sorts to the wholeness and unity of immediate experience. Immediate experience exists before relations, but transcendent experience exists after or above relations. Immediate experience dissolves of itself into relational experience, but relational experience resists resolution into the higher monistic experience. The villain is the discursive intellect, and the transcendence of relations such as self and other or space and time becomes largely a matter of reforming the discursive intellect from a servant of division and fragmentation to a partner in the achievement of wholeness. Whereas immediate experience is characterized by a *knowing* and feeling in one which comes before intellection, transcendent experience is characterized by a *thinking* and feeling in one which comes after and which is achieved through intellection.

This idea of transcendent experience can also be readily illustrated from *Four Quartets*, which in a number of passages reads like Bradley versified. The following lines are from *Dry Salvages* 2:

> We had the experience but missed the meaning,
> And approach to the meaning restores the experience
> In a different form, beyond any meaning
> We can assign to happiness. (CPP 133)

We had the immediate experience, say, the moment in the draughty church at smokefall, but because in immediate experience we simply exist as part of a larger unity, we are not conscious of meaning. But in relational experience, when we remember and reflect, we can approach the meaning in such a way that it will be restored in a more complex and comprehensive form. That form will be transcendent experience, and it will take us beyond the level where we are aware of assigning meanings to happiness.

The idea of transcendent experience runs throughout Eliot's literary and religious criticism. The famous notion of the unified sensibility in the essay on "The Metaphysical Poets" is one of his numerous uses of transcendent experience. A number of critics have said that when Eliot refers to "a direct sensuous apprehension of thought, or a recreation of thought into feeling" (SE 246), he is referring to immediate experience. But it is clear from his terminology that he is describing transcendent experience. One of Bradley's favorite terms for transcendent experience is "felt thought." This is precisely the language that Eliot uses to distinguish between the poets of the seventeenth and the nineteenth centuries. This is a unity that comes after thought, not before it. It is a complex of feeling and thinking in one.

There is no doubt that Eliot shared this general view of relational experience as enclosed in an envelope of undiscriminated felt nonrelational totality. He says so in plain words at the end of the first chapter of his dissertation. To Eliot, then, as to Bradley, immediate experience at the beginning, that is, before (yet including) intellectual consciousness, and transcendent experience at the end, that is, after (yet including) intellectual consciousness, are not mere hypothetical limits to the comprehended dualistic sphere we are calling relational experience. Together, they constitute the reality which makes possible our construction of the relational world, the everyday world of appearances.

In conclusion, I would like to point to several pervasive principles in Eliot's work which have direct parallels in Bradley's philosophy:

1. Analytical thinking shatters the unity between knowing and feeling by breaking reality into thinking subject and object of thought. Thinking is intrinsically limited, in part because it can only proceed from one thinking subject, from one point of view, at a time. This means that the movement towards truth involves not only development of one point of view, but migration from one interpretation to another, occupation of as many perspectives as possible. A main principle associated with greater degrees of truth and reality is comprehensiveness, so the more comprehensive, the more true. These matters are evident everywhere in Eliot, but nowhere more than in the multiplicity or plurality of point of view in his poetry. In *The Waste Land*, for example, Eliot attempts to speak through many voices, from many points of view, from many times and places, all at once.

2. Language is necessarily and profoundly reductive; moreover, its grammar and syntax skew prepositions. Over and over in his dissertation, Eliot says that "when we try to press an exact meaning ... we find language forcing untenable theories upon us" (KE 129-30). In the first chapter, he speaks of the "embarrassment" to our theories created by the fact that we have to reduce them to words. He constantly shows an awareness of being caught in the language trap. For example, he says, "In describing immediate experience we must use terms which offer a surreptitious suggestion of subject or object" (KE 22).

This suspicion of language is everywhere in his work. Prufrock is terrified by language, and Sweeney moans "I gotta use words when I talk to you" (CPP 84). And at the heart of each of the quartets, we find an "intolerable wrestle / With words and meaning" (CPP 125). In *East Coker*, for example, Eliot refers to twenty years of

> Trying to learn to use words, and every attempt
> Is a wholly new start, and a different kind of failure
> Because one has only learnt to get the better of words
> For the thing one no longer has to say, or the way in which
> One is no longer disposed to say it. And so each venture
> Is a new beginning, a raid on the inarticulate
> With shabby equipment always deteriorating
> In the general mess of imprecision of feeling,
> Undisciplined squads of emotion. (CPP 128)

3. Eliot's rhetoric, the way he develops his discussions, is deeply indebted to Bradley's epistemology, in which feeling is transcended in thought and then both are transcended in "felt thought" or "thought feeling" or "transcendent experience." Bradley typically focuses on opposites, deconstructs both of them, and then reclaims them in a new and unified form. Think briefly of Eliot's opposition of tradition and the individual talent and his inclusion of both in a greater tradition. Or of his opposition of romanticism and classicism, and his inclusion of both in a more comprehensive framework. The ghost of Hegel hovers here, of course, but this dialectical imagination goes beyond Hegel, especially in its emphasis on experience.

4. As Eliot himself said, his prose style is modelled on Bradley's. The combination of humility and irony, of feeling and intelligence, which characterizes Bradley's writings is a hallmark of Eliot's. Both the humility and the irony are genuine: both, in fact, are necessary results of the epistemology. They come from the double awareness that one has glimpsed some light and that one can only work in the dark; from the compulsion to refute error coupled with the consciousness that one's own work is bound to be in error; from an awareness that one is making a raid on the absolute with shabby equipment always deteriorating. One of the disarming aspects of Bradley's rhetoric is that he generally concludes by calling his own theories into doubt. Thus in the *Ethical Studies*, he shows that Kant's formalism and John Stuart Mill's utilitarianism are deeply flawed ethical theories. He then presents his own ethical theory based on the idea that society is a moral organism. He concludes, however, by arguing

the insufficiency of all ethical theories, including the one he has just proposed. Being ethical and formulating ethical theories, he claims, are worlds apart, not because an ethical philosopher might be himself unethical, but because being anything and analyzing it are inconsistent activities.

Each of the positions I have mentioned represents a conscious and strenuous effort to overcome dualism. I am not suggesting that Eliot was dependent upon Bradley for these insights. The revolt against dualism, as Lovejoy and others have documented, was in the air in the early part of the century; moreover, Eliot had already mounted his own revolt against dualism in his poems of 1909-11. It must be noted, however, that Eliot found in Bradley an elegant and convincing argument against every type of dualism, and that he surrendered several patient years to a sympathetic reading of Bradley's work. In spite of the closest personal and intellectual involvement with a formidable Neo-Realist (Russell), he explicitly endorsed many of Bradley's ideas in his dissertation, ideas which remained to color all of his subsequent work, including *Four Quartets*.

WORKS CITED

Bradley, F. H. *Appearance and Reality* 2nd ed. (1897). Oxford: Clarendon Press, 1978.

_____. *Essays on Truth and Reality* (1914). Oxford: Clarendon Press, 1950. 159-60.

_____. *Principles of Logic Vol 2.* (1883). London: Oxford UP, 1928.

Brooker, Jewel Spears. "The Structure of Eliot's 'Gerontion'." *English Literary History* 46 (1979): 314-40.

"The Dethronement of Descartes." *Times Literary Supplement* 9 Sept. 1926: 1-2.

Eliot, T. S. "Obituary for F. H. Bradley." *Criterion* III, 1924: 9.

Kenner, Hugh. *The Invisible Poet.* New York: McDowell, Oblensky, 1959.

SANFORD SCHWARTZ

BEYOND THE "OBJECTIVE CORRELATIVE": ELIOT AND THE OBJECTIFICATION OF EMOTION

Of the many memorable phrases and formulations in Eliot's essays, few have made a more lasting impression than his famous reference to the "objective correlative," which first appeared in "Hamlet and his Problems" (1919): "The only way of expressing emotion in the form of art is by finding an 'objective correlative'; in other words, a set of objects, a situation, a chain of events which shall be the formula of that *particular* emotion; such that when the external facts, which must terminate in sensory experience, are given, the emotion is immediately evoked" (SW 100). For many years this statement served as a touchstone of poetic Modernism, or more precisely, of Modernism as interpreted and codified by the New Criticism. In the forties and fifties it was widely assumed that Eliot's pronouncement epitomized a major transformation from the Romantic poetics of authorial self-expression--the "spontaneous overflow of powerful feelings"--to a new Classical poetics based on impersonality, objectivity, and detachment. In recent decades, however, we have grown more sensitive to the once submerged continuities between Romanticism and Modernism, and are now alert to the many passages in which the promoter of the "impersonal theory of poetry" (SW 53) actually identifies literature with the expression of personal emotion.[1] But as a result of this shift in perspective, which was motivated in part by a desire to debunk the movement that Eliot was thought to represent, we now prefer to accuse Eliot of incoherence rather than assume that his seemingly incompatible statements conceal an underlying consistency of thought. Thus the revisionist view of Modernism has uncovered a previously neglected stratum of Eliot's works, but given its polemical origins and aims, it has prevented us from appreciating the systematic network in which

---

1. See, for instance, his various essays on Elizabethan and Jacobean dramatists, which assume that "what every poet starts from is his own emotions" (SE 117) and emphasize the "personal emotion" (SE 180) that underlies the dramatic action.

the deceptively casual and seemingly inconsistent terms of his literary criticism are firmly embedded. It is the purpose of this essay to lay out this network of terms and relations, which is articulated in Eliot's doctoral dissertation and endures through all the major changes in his career. As we shall see, the dissertation displays the same dialectical relationship between emotions and objects, feelings and thought, that informs the "objective correlative," "dissociation of sensibility," and other crucial terms of his literary essays.[2] Moreover, it will become increasingly apparent that Eliot's philosophical and critical works transpose into conceptual terms the same emotional conflicts that are expressed more directly in the poetry, while the poetry reveals the essential core of feelings that are idealized, and partially sanctioned, in the discursive writings.

I

Eliot's doctoral dissertation, "Experience and the Objects of Knowledge in the Philosophy of F. H. Bradley," was completed in April 1916 and concluded more than a half-decade of graduate study in philosophy.[3] In this work, which goes well beyond the mere exegesis of Bradley it is often taken to be, Eliot maps out the relationship between emotion and objectification that would soon appear in his literary criticism. The thesis begins with a discussion of Bradley's notion of "immediate experience," or "feeling." At the outset Eliot warns us that "immediate experience" is not something that takes place in the mind of a subject distinguishable from the world of external objects. For Bradley, "immediate experience" refers not to a form of consciousness, but rather to that original totality from which we subsequently derive the very distinction between consciousness and world, internal feelings and external objects.[4] This original "unity and continuity of feeling and objectivity" is lost in everyday life, where we assume that there is a natural and fixed division between subjective and objective domains (KE 115). But according to Bradley, the divide between subject and object is

---

2. It is unfortunate that Eliot's dissertation was not published until long after a restrictive and somewhat misleading interpretation had been affixed to his critical dicta. When the thesis finally appeared in 1964, it did little to rectify the situation, in part because the existing interpretation was firmly in place, and in part because of the intractable nature of the thesis itself.

3. The dissertation was published under the title *Knowledge and Experience in the Philosophy of F. H. Bradley*. I discuss the thesis and its implications at greater length in *The Matrix of Modernism: Pound, Eliot, and Early Twentieth-Century Thought* ch. 4.

4. We must get used to Eliot's slippery use of the term "feeling." At certain times, "feeling" is synonymous with "immediate experience" and designates that which precedes the division into subject and object; at other times, it refers to the purely subjective state that results from the same division.

always conventional and transient, and the boundary between them, as Eliot puts it, "is always a question for partial and practical interests to decide" (KE 21). Hence the relationship between the mental and the physical, emotion and things, is more fluid than we ordinarily assume. Even in practical life, where "feelings and things are torn apart," phenomena such as optical illusions and hallucinations still provide evidence of the "continuous transition by which feeling becomes object and object becomes feeling" (KE 25).

After he dissolves the rigid boundary between consciousness and external reality, Eliot begins to analyze those sciences that rely on a clear-cut distinction between them. First he considers psychology, which rests on the assumption that consciousness, or "mental content," can be detached from its objects and made the focus of an independent science. Then he turns to epistemology, which commits the opposite error "of assuming that there is a real world outside of our knowledge and asking how we may know it" (KE 109). Psychology is akin to philosophical idealism, which begins with consciousness and then tries to show how it constitutes our knowledge of the external world. Epistemology, on the other hand, is like philosophical realism, which privileges external reality and then examines the way it is represented in consciousness. While each pair elevates one side of experience and makes the other dependent upon it, Eliot appeals to the original unity of "immediate experience" and refuses to grant priority either to mind or world: "That objects are dependent upon consciousness, or consciousness upon objects, we most resolutely deny" (KE 29-30). His strategy is to show both the psychologist and epistemologist that the separate domains of each may be reduced entirely to the terms of the other: "Consciousness, we shall find, is reducible to relations between objects, and objects we shall find to be reducible to relations between different states of consciousness; and neither point of view is more nearly ultimate than the other" (KE 30). In other words, Eliot attacks psychology by assuming the standpoint of the epistemologist, and then unravels epistemology by assuming the standpoint of the psychologist. Claiming that neither side is entirely right, he curbs the excesses of one by adopting the position of the other.

This dialectical strategy has momentous implications for Eliot's literary criticism, which analyzes works of art in terms of subject/object relations and repeatedly offsets the tendency to privilege one side of experience by reasserting the significance of the other. Eliot's well-known critique of Romanticism, for instance, is directed not only to reified subjectivity, as is commonly believed, but also to the opposite extreme: "Romanticism stands for *excess* in any direction. Its splits up into two directions: escape from the world of fact, and devotion to brute fact. The two great currents of the nineteenth century-- vague emotionality and the apotheosis of science (realism) alike spring from Rousseau."[5] Eliot struggled against both of these currents--the "vague emotionality" of Romantic poetry and the "devotion to brute fact" in fiction and drama--and his early criti- cal essays may be regarded as an attempt to overcome these antithetical extremes of nineteenth-century culture.

Eliot's analysis of psychology paves the way for his approach to "vague emotionality" in poetry. In the dissertation he challenges the psychologist's assumption that we can isolate consciousness from the objects of which it is aware. Once we subtract the object from the "mental content," he argues, the psychologist has nothing left to study. Adopting a stance that owes less to Bradley than to realists such as Meinong and Rus- sell, Eliot contends that from one point of view the mind is "nothing more than the system of objects which appears before it."[6] The same argument appears in Eliot's literary essays: just as he responds to the psychologist and idealist by declaring that consciousness "is reducible to relations between objects" (KE 30), Eliot offsets the "vague emotionality" of Romantic poetry by reaffirming objective presentation and claiming that all emo- tions can be rendered through their correlative objects. In his essay on Swinburne (1920), he attacks the late Romantic ten- dency to evoke emotion through language that is devoid of pre- cise objective reference: "[Swinburne] uses the most general word, because his emotion is never particular, never in direct line of vision, never focused. . . . It is, in fact, the word that gives him the thrill, not the object" (SW 147-48). A year later he com- pared the verbal "mistiness" of William Morris to the "bright, hard precision" of Andrew Marvell, arguing that "the emotion of Morris is not more refined or more spiritual; it is merely more vague: if anyone doubts whether the more refined or spiri- tual emotion can be precise, he should study the treatment of the varieties of discarnate emotion in the *Paradiso*" (SE 258). Here as elsewhere, Eliot invokes the example of Dante to show

---

5. From a syllabus prepared for a university extension course in 1916. See Ronald Schuchard, "T. S. Eliot as an Extension Lecturer, 1916-1919" 165. Eliot's statement on Romanticism bears the imprint of his Harvard mentor, Irving Babbitt, but the latter's division of nineteenth-century culture into extremes of emotional and scientific naturalism merges easily into Bradley's dialectic.

6. From an unpublished student essay on the theory of objects, probably written at Oxford and now at Houghton Library. The quotation expresses succinctly the point made in the dissertation.

that it is possible to render objectively even the most rarified states of human emotion, and that "language in a healthy state presents the object, is so close to the object that the two are identified" (SW 149).[7]

Mere objectification, however, is no guarantee of artistic success. In "Reflections on Contemporary Poetry" (1917), Eliot examines the difficulties of two groups of poets-- one British, the other American--who attempt to escape from "rhetoric" by turning to the presentation of objects. The Georgian poets follow Wordsworth into the tendency to dwell upon trivial objects; they present the object "for its own sake, not because of association with passions specifically human" (118). The unnamed Americans have a somewhat different problem: they fix upon the incidental features of an object, "letting these in turn fasten upon the attention to such an extent as to replace the emotion which gave them their importance." Distancing himself from both groups, Eliot turns to the poetry of John Donne, in which "the feeling and the material symbol preserve exactly their proper proportions":

> When my grave is broke up again . . .
>   And he that digs it, spies
> A bracelet of bright hair about the bone. . . .

Lesser poets might have erred in one of two opposing directions: some would have become absorbed in the hair as a material object and forgotten the emotional association that originally made it significant; others would have succumbed to the temptation to "endow the hair with ghostly or moralistic meaning." In other words, Eliot is suggesting that imaginary objects may slide in the direction of either pure reference or pure meaning, and it takes a superior poet to strike the right balance between them. Thus it is not enough simply to commit oneself to objective presentation: "vague emotionality" may be eliminated by returning to the object, but the latter may itself suffer from excessive objectivity on one side or from emotional overload on the other.

The same concern with objectification also accounts for the celebrated reference to the "objective correlative." In his

---

7. A similar critique of "vague emotionality" is directed to nineteenth-century philosophical idealism. Just as Swinburne expresses emotion with no precise object, Hegelian idealism has aggravated "the tendency of words to become indefinite emotions" (SW 9). Unlike Aristotle, who "looked solely and steadfastly at the object" (SW 11), Hegel became "the most prodigious exponent of emotional systematization, dealing with his emotions as if they were definite objects which had aroused those emotions (SW 9). As a result of this aspiration to make language express the priority of emotions over objects, mind over external reality, philosophy like poetry succumbed to a pernicious "verbalism" that dissociates words from precise objects.

critique of psychology, Eliot discusses Bradley's argument that emotion (in this case pleasure) "is always partially objective: the emotion is really part of the object, and is ultimately just as objective" (KE 80). The wording of his next remark--"when the object, or complex of objects, is recalled, the pleasure is recalled in the same way"--anticipates the literary dictum that would appear several years later: "The only way of expressing emotion in the form of art is by finding an 'objective correlative'; in other words, a set of objects, a situation, a chain of events which shall be the formula of that *particular* emotion; such that when the external facts, which must terminate in sensory experience, are given, the emotion is immediately evoked" (SW 100). The similarities between these statements reveal the unmistakable influence of Bradley, who taught Eliot that subjective phenomena are always partially objective. And yet, paradoxically, it was Bradley's philosophical opponents--the "new realists," including Moore and Russell in England and Meinong and Husserl on the Continent--who encouraged Eliot to go a step further and consider mental life in terms of the objects to which it is directed. Meinong's theory of objects is especially prominent in Eliot's student essays and in his doctoral dissertation. One of Eliot's classmates records that in May 1914 Eliot read a paper on Meinong to Josiah Royce's seminar, and in the discussion that followed, he claimed that emotion is as external as any other object of perception: "In my theory there is something outside-- e.g., beauty is outside, and distressed world, etc." (Costello 176). Eliot argues the same point in his thesis, where he demonstrates that all subjective phenomena--emotions, sensations, fantasies, and the like--are reducible to the objects to which they are directed. Moreover, the very term *"objektive Korrelat"* appears in Husserl's *Logical Investigations* (1900), which Eliot was reading in 1914, and with his extensive training in philosophy Eliot was aware that Husserl's attempt to shift the study of mind from psychic sensations to intentional objects--"consciousness is consciousness *of* something"--was directed at the same excessive subjectivity that Eliot discerned in Romantic poetry. Thus, from his exposure to Meinong, Husserl, and an expanding company of Anglo-American realists, Eliot became accustomed to the idea that emotions are reducible to their correlative objects, and the lessons he learned from these turn-of-the-century philosophers were soon applied to the problems of artistic expression.

As significant as it was to his critical project, Eliot's insistence on the objectification of emotion must be seen in relation to its dialectical counterpart--the equally forceful critique of excessive objectivity--which began with the analysis of epistemology in his doctoral dissertation. While the psychologist assumes that we can dissociate consciousness from its objects, the epistemologist assumes that there is an objective reality independent of the subjects who perceive it. Eliot responds to the epistemologist by shifting to the opposite side of the subject/object divide. Whereas he had previously established that consciousness is reducible to its objects, he now demonstrates that external objects are "reducible to relations between different states of consciousness" (KE 30). In his view, the so-called "real world" is actually constituted by a community of subjects in the process of social interaction: "We come to interpret our own experience as the attention to a world of objects, as we feel obscurely an identity between the experiences of other centres and our own. And it is this identity which gradually shapes itself into the external world.... Thus in adjusting our behaviour to that of others and in co-operating with them we come to intend an identical world" (KE 143). In other words, it is we who have shaped the reality we regard as external to ourselves. In the process of social exchange, we gradually divide immediate experience into a shared but fixed distinction between subjective and objective realms, elevating the latter to the status of an independent reality and relegating the former to "the debris of our own slight structure" (KE 118).

Eliot later applied this critique of objectivism to fiction and drama that simply mirrors the everyday "real world." In his literary essays, he repeatedly expresses dissatisfaction with artistic "realism," which "ends its course in the desert of exact likeness to the reality which is perceived by the most commonplace mind" (SE 93). If poets like Swinburne and Morris "escape from the world of fact" into "vague emotionality," many of their contemporaries run to the objectivist extreme of "devotion to brute fact." Eliot maintains that art should not mirror ordinary reality but "create a new world" ("London" 216), a world that proceeds from "an emotional source" and possesses an intrinsic logic of its own (SW 119). In a revealing phrase, he maintains that the artist must "intensify the world to his emotions" (SW 102); that is to say, the artist must draw upon the depths of personal feeling in order to transform the familiar world into the new world of art. If reified subjectivity is offset by turning emotions into objects, reified objectivity is overcome by exploiting the creative potential of human emotion.[8]

---

8. If in *Hamlet* Shakespeare was struggling with an emotion he could not objectify into art, Philip Massinger generally suffered from the opposite problem--the lack of authentic personal emotion--and

Departing too far from objective reference can be hazardous, however, and the artist must strive to establish a delicate balance between subjective "meaning" and objective "reference":

> Can we, in reading a novel, simply assume the characters and the situations? On the contrary, I seem to find that we either accept them as real ... or consider them as *meanings*, as a criticism of reality from the author's point of view. Actually, I think that if we did not vacillate between these two extremes (one of which alone would give the 'photographic' novel and the other the arid 'pièce à thèse') a novel would mean very little to us. (KE 123)

While "photographic" realism goes astray by presenting a world no different from everyday reality, the "pièce à thèse" errs by presenting no distinctive world at all, merely a "criticism of reality from the author's point of view." The successful novel avoids either extreme, maintaining a productive tension between "reference" and "meaning." In this respect it has something in common with the poetry of Donne, whose "bracelet of bright hair about the bone" avoids the temptation either to fixate on the realistic details of the object or to overwhelm the object "with ghostly or moralistic meaning."

Eliot's approach to excessive objectivity also informs another aspect of his literary essays. In his thesis he charges that the epistemologist not only assumes that there is a single "real world" but also believes that it is the principal task of the intellect to identify and represent that world. Similarly, in his critical writings Eliot assails the artist whose intellect is directed less to his own personal emotions and sensations than to current knowledge of external reality. This orientation produces the "dissociation of sensibility" that Eliot found in poetry since the time of Donne: "Tennyson and Browning are poets, and they think; but they do not feel their thought as immediately as the odour of a rose. A thought to Donne was an experience; it modified his sensibility. ... In the seventeenth century a dissociation of sensibility set in, from which we have never recovered" (SE 247). The thoughts and feelings of the Metaphysicals were in harmony, but their successors "thought and felt by fits, unbalanced" (SE 248). If Swinburne relies too heavily on emotion with no precise object, Tennyson trades in abstract ideas that

---

remained too much a creature of convention to achieve "the transformation of a personality into a personal work of art": "... his personality hardly exists. He did not, out of his own personality, build a world of art" (SW 139). The same contrast may be found in their characters. While Hamlet is unable to objectify emotion, the characters in Massinger's plays are marked by "the disappearance of all personal and real emotions" (SW 133): "When Massinger's ladies resist temptation they do not appear to undergo any important emotion; they merely know what is expected of them" (SW 134).

have no foundation in personal feelings. In Jules Laforgue, his own early mentor who possessed an instinctive urge to reintegrate the two sides of experience, Eliot could detect a wobble in both directions: "there are unassimilated fragments of metaphysics and, on the other hand, of sentiments floating about" ("Observations" 70). Deprived by his age of a coherent structure that unites emotions and intellect, Laforgue was engaged in "a continuous war between the feelings implied by his ideas, and the ideas implied by his feelings" (Clark).

Thus it is clear from his philosophical works that Eliot the critic was campaigning on two fronts simultaneously. His critique of "vague emotionality" in poetry was complemented by an attack on "devotion to brute fact" in literary realism and on the modern dissociation of intellect and feeling. For Eliot, the presentation of objects severed from emotion is as undesirable as the expression of emotion detached from objects, and both are the effects of the same reification of experience into subjective and objective extremes. As we shall see, the sense of a rigidly bifurcated universe is also expressed in Eliot's early poetry, which portrays a seemingly irreconcilable conflict between emotion and object, feeling and thought, in the very attempt to overcome the opposition between them.

II

Well before he completed his dissertation Eliot was composing poems that display a relationship between emotion and objectivity similar to that which appears in his philosophical and literary prose. This relationship, however, is articulated not conceptually but dramatically in the conflict between Eliot's poetic personae and the external world they encounter. Moreover, the poems emphasize not the "unity and continuity of feeling and objectivity" (KE 115), as does the dissertation, but rather a sharp division into subjective and objective realms. And unlike the literary essays, which treat this division as a problem to be overcome, the poetry renders the separation between subject and object, feelings and things, as an inescapable condition of human experience. Thus the poetry manifests somewhat more directly and concretely the personal struggles that are idealized and expressed abstractly in the prose, while the prose itself provides us with an appropriate network of terms and relations through which to analyze the poetry.

Eliot's early personae may be approached by comparing them to the literary characters he examines in his essays.
In " 'Rhetoric' and Poetic Drama" (1919), for example, he
praises Rostand's Cyrano de Bergerac for possessing a rare
ability to objectify, or dramatize, his emotions.[9] Cyrano takes
conscious delight in his talent for "the expression of the emotion" (SW 84), which lends him "a gusto . . . uncommon on the
modern stage" (SW 83). A few months later Eliot diagnosed
Hamlet's problem as a failure to objectify emotion: "Hamlet
(the man) is dominated by an emotion which is inexpressible,
because it is in *excess* of the facts as they appear" (SW 101).
Hamlet's antics express neither madness nor mere dissimula-
tion; they are rather "a form of emotional relief" from feelings
that have no adequate object and cannot be objectified in action
(SW 102). Hence the emotion "which he cannot understand . . .
cannot objectify" remains "to poison life and obstruct action"
(SW 101). These and other examples offer a guide to the personae of Eliot's own verse, who tend to have more in common
with Hamlet than with Cyrano. In many early poems we find a
virtually unbridgeable gap between the affective life of the persona (always a male) and the external world in which he
ambivalently participates. These self-conscious personae are
detached from the surrounding world and annoyed by the emotional demands it seems to make upon them. Conversely, they
possess emotions that have no outlet in action and therefore
attach themselves to imaginary objects, most of which express
the longing to flee from the burdens of everyday life. This bifurcation between subject and object, however, represents only one
extreme of a broad spectrum of available options. At the other
extreme, Eliot envisions a state in which feelings and objects are
in perfect harmony: the moment of sudden repose when the
emotions settle upon a fully adequate object, or the instant of
rapture when the usual barriers between one person and
another begin to melt away.[10] Such moments are rare in the desolate world of Eliot's early verse, but they establish the other
end of a scale that runs from the state of total alienation at one
extreme to a state of full communion at the other, and at various
points along this scale we can locate many of the figures in
Eliot's poetry.

---

9. The original title was "Whether Rostand Had Something About Him," *Athenaeum* 665. The new
title first appeared the following year in *The Sacred Wood*.
10. Eliot finds this state in the love scenes of *Romeo and Juliet*, where Shakespeare "shows his lovers
melting into incoherent unconsciousness of their isolated selves, shows the human soul in the process
of forgetting itself" (SW 83).

Typically the early verse displays a vast rift between the affective life of the persona and the external world that confronts him. In the published poems as well as the unpublished notebooks, we often find an observer who walks through decaying city streets and registers the sights, sounds, and smells to which he is unable to offer an adequate emotional response.[11] The recognition that the scene should elicit his pity only underscores the troubled awareness of his own indifference. Symptomatic of these poems is the manner in which the observer apprehends other people, who are merely an extension of the urban debris and appear not as whole persons but as parts of bodies--"feet that press / To early coffee-stands" and "hands / That are raising dingy shades" (CPP 12). From this vantage point, in which human activities are reduced to empty "masquerades / That time resumes," there is no essential difference between "men and bits of paper" (CPP 120). The feelings that do arise are associated primarily with annoyance or anger over the power of external objects to bombard the sensorium and compel the observer to fasten his attention upon them. This is especially true in more intimate settings, where sensory impressions lure the persona into "digressions"--"Is it perfume from a dress / That makes me so digress?" (CPP 5)--and perpetually threaten his "self-possession." Hence the stream of sensations is at once "inconsequential" and "intolerable," inconsequential because it is devoid of significance and intolerable because it nevertheless maintains an irresistible hold over the observer's awareness.

In certain cases it is easy to identify with the emotional anemia of Eliot's personae, since their psychic state seems justified by the depravity of the world they observe. In other cases, however, it is difficult to know whether the source of alienation lies in the external world itself or in the persona's own emotional inadequacies. Eliot's speakers often display a compelling need to protect themselves from emotional involvement with the outer world and especially from intimate relations with other persons. At the end of "Preludes," for instance, the emergence of sympathetic feeling immediately provokes a sharp recoil:

> I am moved by fancies that are curled
> Around these images, and cling:
> The notion of some infinitely gentle
> Infinitely suffering thing.

---

11. The unpublished notebooks are located in the Berg Collection of the New York Public Library.

> Wipe your hand across your mouth, and laugh;
> The worlds revolve like ancient women
> Gathering fuel in vacant lots. (CPP 13)

This retreat from emotion (often marked by a laugh or a smile) characterizes many poems in which the persona is called upon to elicit emotions he does not possess or, for whatever reason, is compelled to resist. In "Portrait of a Lady" we may be inclined to share the persona's discomfort over the woman's entreaties, but we also begin to suspect that the young man may be incapable of the kind of emotion that is demanded of him. It is noteworthy that the persona attempts to preserve his "self-possession" by adhering strictly to conventional behavior, using his polite smile to ward off the lady's solicitations and protect himself from the acquisition, or even the simulation, of unwanted emotion. Such responses, which are accompanied by a large dose of self-ridicule, are characteristic of Eliot's personae, but the defensive reaction against the claims of emotion can be so powerful that it produces a violent urge to destroy the agent who disturbs one's "self-possession." This urge is expressed in the pervasive misogyny that runs throughout the poetry and occasionally erupts into sadistic sarcasm or outright violence.[12]

Eliot frequently places his personae in romantic situations that call for a display of emotions that they either do not have or cannot express. Since the persona himself is usually "confused" about his feelings, it is often difficult to tell whether the problem lies in the affections themselves or in the process of translating them into action. Eliot admired Cyrano de Bergerac for his ability to objectify passion, but his own personae remain passive spectators to their own conventional behavior or resort like Hamlet to the self-deprecating buffoonery that expresses their emotional confusion. The speaker in "Conversation Galante," for example, engages in a kind of antic behavior that subverts the romantic role he is expected to play:

> I observe: "Our sentimental friend the moon!
> Or possibly (fantastic, I confess)
> It may be Prester John's balloon
> Or an old battered lantern hung aloft
> To light poor travellers to their distress."
>   She then: "How you digress!" (CPP 19)

---

12. The more blatant manifestations of this syndrome appear in the unpublished "Love Song of St. Sebastian" (a variation on Browning's "Porphyria's Lover"), *Sweeney Agonistes*--"Any man has to, needs to, wants to / Once in a lifetime, do a girl in" (CPP 83)--and *The Family Reunion*, in which we learn that Harry has pushed his wife (or desired to push her) over the side of a ship.

Such personae regard "the usual debate / Of love" as an empty masquerade, and consider themselves inept and somewhat ridiculous actors upon the social stage (PEY 23). Even when they desire to approach the other person, they act like performers of a role that many others have played before. They maintain a heightened if not exaggerated awareness of the gap between emotion and its externalization, and feel as if any objectification in speech or action forces both parties into conventional postures that inevitably belie the emotions that they are meant to express. Since those emotions are in any case beset by crippling doubts, the persona's sense of a hopeless split between internal emotion and external gesture provides a convenient rationalization for his own inaction.

While the outer world makes claims upon the affections, the persona often harbors emotions that find no outlet in the social world. These emotions are projected onto imaginary objects--Prufrock's "pair of ragged claws" (CPP 5) or his vision of "the mermaids singing, each to each" (CPP 7)--which express a wish to be released from the painful ordeal of everyday life. Here the persona's feelings are objectified in surreal images, "as if a magic lantern threw the nerves in patterns on a screen" (CPP 6). Like Prufrock's "yellow fog that rubs its back upon the window-panes" (CPP 4), the inanimate landscape comes alive to reveal the "thousand sordid images / Of which your soul was constituted" (CPP 12). In the unpublished "Prufrock's Pervigilium," the evening rises up to haunt the troubled persona, who sees the houses leaning over to point an accusing finger at him and feels the midnight darkness enter and gradually permeate his room. A similar animation of inanimates occurs in "Morning at the Window":

> The brown waves of fog toss up to me
> Twisted faces from the bottom of the street,
> And tear from a passer-by with muddy skirts
> An aimless smile that hovers in the air
> And vanishes along the level of the roofs. (CPP 16)

If the city street is usually the scene of objects devoid of any emotional significance, in this case it is imaginatively transfigured to become the correlative of personal emotions. The persona's passions are transformed into poetry (which arises from the artist's capacity "to intensify the world to his emotions"), though in most instances the process of objectification brings little relief or satisfaction to the suffering agent.

Eliot's early poems point beyond the everyday world not only in their surreal landscapes but also in their evocation of a reality that transcends the plane of ordinary existence. Many of the poems that depict the misery and vacuity of ordinary life conclude with apocalyptic images that lead us to "the doorstep of the Absolute" (PEY 26). To be sure, these images are usually presented ironically and serve not to affirm a higher reality but to remind us of the distance between the ideal and the real. Nevertheless, their very appearance suggests the presence of emotions that could never be satisfied by everyday life in this world. As Eliot makes clear in his later works, these emotions are objectified only in a spiritual realm that has become the object of actual belief. But most of the early personae are hardly aware that they are suffering from a "passionate dissatisfaction with human life unless a spiritual explanation could be found" (SE 360). Those like Gerontion who possess such awareness seem to share their author's failure to believe in the only possible source of redemption, and therefore remain trapped within the intolerable maze of sensual experience. Unable to realize their emotions through belief in a transcendent world, they are reduced to mere disaffection with the inadequate objects of this world.[13]

We find then a profound disequilibrium between emotion and object in Eliot's early poetry. On the one hand, there is the objective world that appears bereft of meaning but makes emotional demands that elicit only resentment and despair. On the other hand, there are feelings that cannot be externalized in ordinary life and are projected onto imaginary objects. Only in rare instances do we find emotion and object in harmony. In the unpublished manuscripts these moments are identified with a sudden sense of repose, or stillness, when the mind seems content to rest upon the object it beholds. But these are the exceptions that prove the rule, and for the most part the poetry enacts the jarring conflict between internal and external realms--emotions that cannot be objectified in everyday life, and a world that has the power to consume the attention even of those who wish to escape it.

It is instructive to compare Eliot's personae to his vision of the poems in which they appear. In his critical essays, Eliot speaks of the artist's ability to objectify emotions and to bring into existence the "new combinations," or "new world," embodied in the work of art (SW 54; "new world" in "London" 216). In his poetry, on the other hand, he creates personae who

---

13. Speaking of Dante's Hell, Eliot states that "it is part of damnation to experience desires that we can no longer gratify" (SW 166). Dante's characters are punished in the afterlife for acting on their carnal passions, while Eliot's suffer in this life for their inability to realize their spiritual passions. For both groups, Hell is the possession of emotions that cannot be objectified.

are caught between their disaffection with the existing world and the inability to fasten the emotions unequivocally upon the objects of a higher world. These personae often exhibit the artist's capacity for "amalgamating disparate experience" (SE 247) and display the "wit"--"a recognition, implicit in the expression of every experience, of other kinds of experience which are possible" (SE 262)--that distinguishes them from mere creatures of convention. But at the same time this capacity offers them little more than painful awareness of their own lamentable condition. To a certain extent they can transmute their sufferings into art, but this process brings them neither relief nor redemption from the burdens of temporal existence. In other words, while Eliot's artist objectifies his emotions into a new world, his personae are reduced simply to disenchantment with the old world. If these personae are in some way representative of their creator, we may then regard the early poetry as an expression of the conflict between the desire to escape from the painful ordeal of existence, a desire that is only partially relieved by turning passion into poetry, and the tragic inability to affirm what for Eliot was the only authentic means of deliverance.

III

The 1920s brought about many changes in Eliot's writings. With his acceptance of Christianity came the search for a new poetic style that could address the theme of spiritual pilgrimage in a manner suitable both to the distinctive conditions of modernity and to the enduring traditions of the Church. A similar change occurred in his critical orientation, which turned in his words from "the problem of the integrity of poetry" to that of "the relation of poetry to the spiritual and social life of its time and of other times" (SW viii). Related to each of these developments is a shift in literary allegiance from John Donne and the Metaphysicals--"Donne is a poet . . . perhaps even a great poet, of chaos" (Clark)--to Dante and the great Thomistic synthesis upon which he and his contemporaries could draw. Donne's ingenious capacity for "amalgamating disparate experience" (SE 247), so evident in the elliptical style that inspired Eliot's early work, gives way to Dante's use of "clear visual images" (SE 204) that provide the sensuous equivalent to a coherent system of thought. But despite all these changes, there is a remarkable continuity in Eliot's approach to the poetic enterprise. The interaction between emotion and object, feeling and thought, continues to play a prominent and perhaps even an even more conspicuous role in his works. We find the same emphasis upon the objectification of emotion, even though Eliot is now more concerned with objects that enable us to "apprehend sensuously the various states and stages of blessedness" (SE 226). We also find the other side of Eliot's dialectic, first in his creation of dramatic works that reveal the power of spiritual emotion to transfigure conventional reality, and secondly in his search for poetic resources that express the feelings which accompany religious belief--that is to say, the subjective correlative to the propositions accepted by the intellect.

As he explored the implications of his new outlook, Eliot became increasingly sensitive to the various shades of human emotion and to the consequences of failing to distinguish between them. The religious poets of the age of Donne, for instance, manifest "that fusion or confusion of feeling of human and divine, that transposition of human sentiment to divine objects which characterizes the religious verse of the sixteenth and seventeenth centuries, in contrast to that of the thirteenth century, in which the distinctions of feeling towards human objects and divine objects are preserved" ("Burning Babe" 508). In a similar manner, Eliot's approach to the Romantics shifted from the "vague emotionality" of their poetic language to the loss of faith that led them to transfer spiritual emotion to the sphere of human relations: "in much romantic poetry the sadness is due to the exploitation of the fact that no human relations are adequate to human desires, but also to the disbelief in any further object for human desires than that which, being human, fails to satisfy them" (SE 379). In attributing this phenomenon to poets such as Baudelaire, Eliot was also casting a retrospective glance at his own early poetry, where the persona's emotions fail to find adequate expression in the social world and project themselves without conviction to a realm beyond it.

The positive side of this critique was an attempt to find objects that could render precisely "the varieties of discarnate emotion" (SE 258). In this endeavor Eliot's guiding light was Dante, who possessed an insurpassable capacity for visualizing the most rarified spiritual states: "Nowhere in poetry has experience so remote from ordinary experience been expressed so concretely. . . . One can feel only awe at the power of the master who could thus at every moment realize the inapprehensible in visual images" (SE 227-28). Dante also provided a model for objectification in the sense that his feelings find their realization in a coherent system of thought. He dwells in a universe in which "the personal to oneself is fused and completed in the impersonal and general, not extinguished, but enriched, expanded, developed, and more itself by becoming more something not itself" ("Poetry and Propaganda" 599). In addition to Dante, another stream of influence came from poets such as St.-John Perse and Mallarmé, whose poetic images went beyond the powers of purely visual imagination and "était une expansion de leur sensibilité *au-delà des limites du monde normal,* une découverte de nouveaux objects propres à susciter de nouvelles émotions" ("an expansion of their sensibility beyond the limits of the ordinary world, a discovery of new objects suitable to evoke new emotions") ("Note sur Mallarmé et Poe" 525).[14] Interpreting these poets in light of his own theory of emotion and objectification, Eliot found their often inscrutable but felicitous images a fertile source of inspiration as he struggled to give voice to the "unread vision in the higher dream" (CPP 64).

While his approach to the objectification of emotion underwent some subtle modifications, Eliot's approach to excessive objectivity was also adapted to the interests that emerged in the twenties. Although he continued to stress the artist's need "to intensify the world to his emotions" (SW 102), he began around the middle of the decade to focus upon a phenomenon he found in authors such as Shakespeare, Chapman, and Marston and described as "a kind of doubleness in the action, as if it took place on two planes at once" (EE 173). At the same time as we follow the dramatic action on the stage we also seem to be "following another train of thought, listening to other voices, feeling with other senses; and acting out another scene than that visible upon the stage" (Clark). In his late romances, for example, Shakespeare constructs a distinctive world in which the characters and actions seem to point beyond themselves to the spiritual emotions of which they are the sensuous embodiment:

> The personages in *Cymbeline, The Winter's Tale, The Tempest,* and *Pericles* are the work of a writer who has finally seen *through* the dramatic action of men into a spiritual action which transcends it. . . . Dramatic action, in the ordinary sense, is inadequate for making these emotions perceptible. Shakespeare tends, therefore, to simplify his characters, to make them vehicles for conveying something of which they are unaware. . . . Something is exhibited of which we have only rare glimpses in our daily life. ("Shakespeare as Poet"; qtd. in Bush 165-66).

---

14. On the influence of Mallarmé and Perse, see Ronald Bush, especially 123-29, 173-79. Bush is one of the few critics who has attended closely to Eliot's remarks on the objectification of emotion and made admirable use of them to analyze the poetry.

Without abandoning tangible events and actions, these plays infuse the dramatic world with a spiritual emotion that intensifies ordinary reality and ultimately raises it to a condition of blessedness.

This attempt to heighten reality is also apparent in Eliot's own dramatic works, all of which turn on the conflict between characters who possess a special type of emotion and those who represent the world of ordinary existence. In the earlier plays--*Sweeney Agonistes, Murder in the Cathedral*, and *The Family Reunion*--the individuals who bear these deeper feelings stand apart from everyday reality and simultaneously threaten to overturn it. Unlike the personae of Eliot's early poetry, these characters are able to objectify their passions in speech or action and thereby challenge the settled ways of those around them. In the later plays, including *The Cocktail Party, The Confidential Clerk*, and *The Elder Statesman*, such characters appear as spiritual guardians who intervene in the lives of others and bring them to greater self-awareness. These last plays, which aspire to the condition of Shakespeare's late romances, represent a decisive movement away from the irreconcilable conflicts of the early poetry by portraying a lost world that is ultimately redeemed by love. They come progressively closer to showing us the objective "real world" transfigured by the power of spiritual emotion.

As we have seen, Eliot's critique of objectivism was directed not only to fictional realism but also to the dissociation of intellect and feeling. Here too the focus of attention shifted slightly as Eliot became absorbed with the problem of expressing the emotions correlative to doctrinal beliefs, or what he called "the emotional equivalent of thought" (SE 115). Dante was again his primary inspiration, but Eliot also found what he was looking for in less celebrated writers, such as the early seventeenth-century jurist and poet, Sir John Davies, who "had that strange gift, so rarely bestowed, for turning thought into feeling" (OPP 153). A similar claim is made for Lancelot Andrewes, whose sermons possess the right proportion between feeling and thought, and in this respect may be distinguished from the sermons of John Donne. According to Eliot, Donne's sermons "are a 'means of self-expression.' He is constantly finding an object which shall be adequate to his feelings; Andrewes is wholly absorbed in the object and therefore responds with the adequate emotions" (SE 309). In other words, Donne finds objective correlatives to his own emotion, but the emotion itself proceeds from his "personality" and not directly from the object of contemplation. Andrewes, by contrast, provides the subjective correlative to the doctrines accepted by the intellect: "Andrewes's emotion is purely contemplative; it is not personal, it is wholly evoked by the object of contemplation, to which it is wholly adequate; his emotion wholly contained in and explained by its object" (SE 308-09). Such analyses not only reveal the kind of discriminations that arose from Eliot's unique orientation but also tell us something about his own evolving concerns as poet. As he searched for a new poetic voice, Eliot wanted to avoid the projection of purely human emotion, which he found in Donne, Crashaw, and others, as well as the mere versification of doctrine that all too often passes for religious poetry. Instead, he sought to render the precise emotional equivalent to religious beliefs, that is, "not the assertion that something is true, but the making that truth more fully real to us . . . the creation of a sensuous embodiment . . . the Word Flesh" ("Poetry and Propaganda" 601). To this end he would mobilize the emotive resources of language, especially the incantatory effects of rhythm and the power of sensuous images, to convey to us *"what it feels like* to hold certain beliefs" ("Social Function of Poetry" 154).

The most extensive statement of Eliot's developing aesthetic appears in his unpublished Clark Lectures (1926), where the two sides of his dialectical strategy--the objectification of emotion and the transmutation of thought into feeling--coalesce into a single comprehensive vision. Guided by the doctrine of the Incarnation and by the example of Dante, he asserts that poetry "elevates sense for a moment to regions ordinarily attainable only by abstract thought or on the other hand clothes the abstract, for a moment, with all the painful delight of the flesh." In Dante and his contemporaries, for whom "there is a system of thought to which is exactly equivalent a system of feeling," human emotions find their realization and arrangement in a systematic view of the universe, and each detail of the system has its precise equivalent in sensation and feeling. The poets of the Renaissance, by contrast, display the confusion that ensued from the dissolution of the Trecento synthesis, and this confusion is evident in their poetic style: "the acceptance of one orderly system of thought and feeling results, in Dante and his friends, in a simple, direct and even austere manner of speech, while the maintenance in suspension of a number of philosophies, attitudes and partial theories which are enjoyed rather than believed, results, in Donne and in some of our contemporaries, in an affected, tortuous, and often overelaborate and

ingenious manner of speech." Like Descartes, who claimed that
"what we know is not the world of objects, but our own ideas of
these objects," the Metaphysical poets also exhibit a dissociation
between subjective and objective realms that turns the objectification of emotion into a mere extension of individual personality. And by the nineteenth century this dissociation between
feeling and thought had become so extreme that a poet like
Laforgue found himself engaged in "a continuous war between
the feelings implied by his ideas, and the ideas implied by his
feelings":

> He had an innate craving for order: that is, that every feeling
> should have its intellectual equivalent, its philosophical justifica-
> tion, and that every idea should have its emotional equivalent, its
> sentimental justification. The only world in which he could have
> satisfied himself, therefore, was a world such as Dante's. . . . What
> he wants, you see, is either a *Vita Nuova* to justify, dignify and
> integrate his sentiments toward the jeune fille in a system of the
> universe, or else some system of thought which shall keep a place
> for or even enhance these feelings and at the same time enable
> him to *feel* as intensely the abstract world.

Whatever light this statement may shed on Laforgue, it is difficult to avoid reading it into Eliot's own previous works, for
behind this remark about his early mentor lies a long series of
poems marked by despair in the face of a world bereft of divine
sanction.

It is a long way from the language of Eliot's doctoral
dissertation to that of the Clark Lectures, but allowing for certain modifications, these two documents reveal a remarkable
consistency in outlook. Taken together, they display the complex
but systematic pattern of thought that informs Eliot's many
occasional essays both before and after his conversion. This pattern of thought was developed under the tutelage of Bradley and
other turn-of-the-century philosophers, but in a larger sense it
was a means of objectifying the emotional conflicts already evident in the early poems, which repeatedly express the agonizing
struggle between internal feelings and external behavior. Eliot
himself would later say "that in one's prose reflexions one may
be legitimately occupied with ideals, whereas in the writing of
verse one can only deal with actuality" (ASG 30). If we take him
at his word, we may regard the dialectical structure of his philosophical and literary prose as a conceptual articulation, or ide-
alization, of the personal emotions expressed in the poetry, and
recognize at the same time that the poetry exposes the emo-

tional core that is objectified, and to a certain degree sanctioned, by a coherent system of ideas.

WORKS CITED

Bush, Ronald. *T. S. Eliot: A Study in Character and Style*. New York: Oxford UP, 1984.

Costello, Harry T. *Josiah Royce's Seminar, 1913-1914: As Recorded in the Notebooks of Harry T. Costello*. Ed. Grover Smith. New Brunswick: Rutgers UP, 1963.

Eliot, T. S. "The Author of 'The Burning Babe'." *Times Literary Supplement* 1278 (29 July 1926): 508.

_____. *Knowledge and Experience in the Philosophy of F. H. Bradley*. Diss. London: Faber and Faber; New York: Farrar, Straus, 1964.

_____. "London Letter." *Dial* 71 (Aug. 1921): 213-17.

_____. "Note sur Mallarmé et Poe." *La Nouvelle Revue Française* XIV.158 (Nov. 1, 1926): 524-26.

_____. "Observations." *Egoist* 5 (May 1918) 69-70.

_____. "Poetry and Propaganda." *Bookman* LXX.6 (Feb. 1930): 595-602.

_____. "Reflections on Contemporary Poetry . . . I." *Egoist* 4 (Sept. 1917): 118-19.

_____. "Shakespeare as Poet and Dramatist." Unpublished Edinburgh University Lectures, 1937.

_____. "The Social Function of Poetry." *Adelphi* XXI.4 (July/Sept. 1945): 152-61.

_____. Unpublished notebooks. Berg Collection, New York Public Library.

_____. "Whether Rostand Had Something About Him." *Athenaeum* 4656 (25 July 1919): 665.

Schuchard, Ronald. "T. S. Eliot as an Extension Lecturer, 1916-1919." *Review of English Studies* ns 25 (May 1974).

Schwartz, Sanford. *The Matrix of Modernism: Pound, Eliot, and Early Twentieth-Century Thought*. Princeton: Princeton UP, 1985.

JEFFREY M. PERL

A POST-WAR CONSENSUS

All literature after 1945 is, in a sense, "holocaust literature," and *postmodern* is almost a synonym for *post-war*. The distinction between Evelyn Waugh after and Evelyn Waugh before V. E. Day may be as profound as the distinction between Elie Wiesel and Waugh or Paul Celan and T. S. Eliot. Until recently there has been little recognition that pre-war artists had post-war existence. Modernist survivors disliked their relegation, as Igor Stravinsky put it, "to an annex of the nineteenth century," and they did not, on the whole, admire what Stravinsky called "post-contemporary" art (Interview, Stravinsky and Craft 78). Yet beginning in the fifties Stravinsky adopted, in works like *Agon* and (most consistently) *Threni*, the serial method of composition that was crucial to post-war composers and that he had bad-mouthed ("a dead end") since its inception by Arnold Schoenberg ("Spring Fever," Stravinsky and Craft 30). Even Robert Craft, who encouraged this development, has wondered at its "real significance."[1] The phenomenon has an exact parallel in the career of Pablo Picasso. Until 1984, when the Guggenheim Museum mounted its exhibit, "Picasso: The Last Years," his late work was ignored or worse, and Picasso was bitter in the post-war decades because younger artists had chosen to desert him and the modernist mainstream for the alternative tradition of Marcel Duchamp.[2] His attitude is indistinguishable from that of Stravinsky, who felt that postmodern composers had abandoned

---

1. Robert Craft, jacket notes, *Threni*. Music by Igor Stravinsky, Columbia Records, MS 6065 (57-58). For Craft's influence on Stravinsky's adoption or adaptation of the twelve-tone serial method: Craft, *Present Perspectives: Critical Writings*.
2. Negative feeling about late Picasso was shared by the younger painters (a notable exception was David Hockney) with major critics like Clement Greenberg. The Guggenheim Museum/Gray Art Gallery show was preceded (in 1981) by an exhibition in Basel, "Picasso: The Late Work, 1964-1972," but it did not result in widespread revaluation. For Picasso's bitterness, see Richardson 21: Picasso "was bitter that his former constituency had forsaken him, especially now that he had made a major breakthrough and was doing what he felt was work of great innovative power. He was bitter, too, that young artists had gone after new gods, false gods--Marcel Duchamp in particular. Picasso had never taken Duchamp seriously, his camp followers less so. 'They've looted Duchamp's store,' he said of the Neo-Dadaists, 'but all they've done is change the wrapping paper.' " Picasso compared his own plight with that of Rembrandt's old age: 24.

him for Schoenberg or Anton von Webern, and Picasso too appropriated the language of the enemy. Several critics have noted allusions in his late works to Rembrandt and the old masters, but it is clear that Picasso was at least equally concerned with the young (see Cohen 30-40, and Schiff 59-61). His assertion that technique matters only "on condition that one has so much ... that it completely ceases to exist" was reminiscent of Jackson Pollock, and Picasso's last canvases have some of the vulgarity, harshness of color, and purposeful awkwardness of Abstract Expressionist painting (Richardson 27).[3] The cartoonish quality of Picasso's "musketeer" graphics and paintings may be ascribed in part to the influence of Pop Art. And the sudden appearance of musketeers in 1966--a staple of Dutch bourgeois painting in the work of a modernist whose taste ran to minotaurs--signaled Picasso's intent, like the intent of Pop Artists, to reconcile the savage *avant-garde* to the temperate values of the middle class (see Richardson 22).

The metamorphosis was not easy. Picasso had been a connoisseur of ritual violence and hieratic severity. Friends say his motivation for change was a fear of World War; and the catalyst, a long evening, at the time of the Cuban missile crisis (Daix 385) spent with slides of war paintings (Parmelin 73-76).[4] What followed was a series of drawings and paintings entitled, *Rape of the Sabines*, and Gert Schiff, who helped arrange the Guggenheim exhibit, sees in these a progression from cruelty to identification with the victims (14-15). John Richardson, describing how the artist weaned himself of the *corrida*, writes that Picasso substituted television wrestling for bullfighting and, in his paintings, musketeers for toreadors: "There is violence but it is more farcical than solemn; there are fetishistic costumes but they are more comic-strip than hieratic; and there are sexual overtones, but they are more honky-tonk than darkly sacrificial" (22). The *corrida* features of modernism, virtuosity and libido, were retired after the war. The transitional work for Stravinsky may have been his *Symphony in Three Movements*, composed between the siege of Stalingrad and the fall of Berlin. "Each episode in the Symphony," Stravinsky wrote,

> is linked in my imagination with a specific cinematographic impression of the war.... The square march beat, the brass-band instrumentation, the grotesque *crescendo* in the tuba, these are all related to those abhorrent pictures. (Columbia, MS 6331)

---

3. Cf. with Picasso's statement, Jackson Pollock: " ... it doesn't make much difference how the paint is put on as long as something has been said. Technique is just a means of arriving at a statement."
4. The evening was in Oct. 1962, and the paintings discussed were Poussin's *Massacre of the Innocents* and David's *Rape of the Sabines*.

But the *Symphony* does not sound a condemnation of war any more than *Le Sacre du Printemps* sounds a critique of human sacrifice. There are disquieting echoes of the *Sacre* in the *Symphony*: they manifest a prophecy vindicated, almost a sensibility fulfilled. Perhaps Stravinsky, like Picasso, turned from an idiom when he found it compromised. This is a pattern characteristic of post-war modernists. The last *Cantos* of Ezra Pound are shy and slim, and the great volume concludes, "To be men not destroyers" (Pound, *The Cantos* 802; see Perl 260-79).

Pound composed his finest poems in a U. S. prison camp. W. B. Yeats died some months before the war and Gertrude Stein some months after it. Virginia Woolf and James Joyce died in 1941, Paul Valéry in 1945. Literary history, at the end of the war, was a virtual clean slate, free of modernists, except that Eliot was alive and active, a modernist spy in the postmodernist world. He was dealt with accordingly:

> [H]e was extremely nervous about the treatment he was then receiving in America over the award of the Bollingen Prize to Ezra Pound. . . . [Eliot] was singled out for abuse: in fact, he seemed to receive more than Pound himself. . . . The *Saturday Review* was particularly hostile. . . . It suggested that 'this rootless expatriate' be at once dropped from the jury of the Library of Congress. The charge of antisemitism, and implied neo-fascism, was particularly serious just four years after the war. . . . At first he thought of resigning from the jury but then decided not to do so. . . . three months before the opening of *The Cocktail Party* in New York, he asked [his producer] to try to ensure that there would be no attempt to obstruct the production. (Ackroyd 297)

The conditions of Eliot's life after 1939, and his post-war development, resemble those of Stravinsky and Picasso, but his response to the war is better documented than theirs. A few months before the Nazi invasion of Poland, Eliot wrote that "The present state of public affairs . . . has induced in myself a depression of spirits so different from any other experience of fifty years as to be a new emotion" ("Last Words" 274). He termed the last three quartets "war poems" (they were published in 1940, 1941, 1942), and his lectures and essays of the period may be reckoned as war prose.[5]

The theme of Eliot's wartime writing, even of pieces with titles like "Johnson as Critic and Poet" or "What Is a Classic?", was that "germanism of the sensibility" ("Classic," OPP 69) is a vice and that a "general *autarky* in culture simply will not

---

5. "All the last three Quartets are in a sense war poems--increasingly. 'East Coker' belongs to the period of what we called 'the phony war' ": "T. S. Eliot talks about his poetry" 14.

work" ("Social Function of Poetry," OPP 13). He was appalled
by the destruction of Europe, the "mutilation and disfigure-
ment," but that is the nature of all wars and he was more
alarmed by the special, racist features of this one ("Classic,"
OPP 72). In a sequence of war lectures, delivered to Norwegians
(1943), Parisians (1945), and finally Germans (1946), Eliot
examined "the Germany of Hitler" and its racial and eugenic
doctrines ("Unity of European Culture," CC 196).[6] That he did
so in the context of explaining the social function of poetry and
the unity of European culture (these are the titles of the lectures) would have fooled none of his auditors:

> A superior language can seldom be exterminated except by exter-
> minating the people who speak it. ("Social Function," OPP 8)

This sentence is taken from Eliot's remarks on the value of
learning foreign languages, but it was published in a journal
whose other articles concerned the Gestapo, the "German mentality," and the Nazis' "treacherous attack" on Norway. *Extermi-
nation* was not a metaphor in 1943. Later, while the Nuremberg
Trials were in progress, Eliot lectured a German audience about
the "error" of assuming "that every other culture than that of
Germany was either decadent or barbaric" ("Unity of European
Culture," CC 196). "Let us," he said, "have an end of such
assumptions," and he underscored as his main point that no
national culture of Europe could survive without cultivating "the
sources which we share in common: that is, the literature of
Rome, of Greece and of Israel" (CC 190). Eliot did not, as on
other occasions, refer to the Bible or to the literature of Christianity, but rather, in a post-war address on German radio, to
the literature of Israel. He did this again, some years after, on a
visit to Germany--"It is because of our common background, in
the literatures of Greece, Rome and Israel, that we can speak of
'European literature' at all" ("Goethe as the Sage," OPP 245)[7]--
and on more than one occasion, during and after the war, he
made reference to "the common heritage of Jews and Christians" ("Letter to the Editor" 9). A decade of persecution and
genocide separated the delivery of these war lectures from the
publication of *After Strange Gods.* An insistent topic of Eliot's

6. The other lecture is "The Social Function of Poetry," OPP 3-16 (delivered in Paris, 1945; delivered
in less developed form to the British-Norwegian Institute, 1943, and excerpted in *Norseman* 6 [1943]:
449-571).
7. Eliot delivered this lecture at Hamburg University, May 1955. It was subsequently published as
"Goethe as the Sage," in *On Poetry and Poets.* He had already tried out the reference to Israel in an
article published during the war: "The Responsibility of the Man of Letters in the Cultural Restoration
of Europe," *Norseman* 248. Also in 1962 Eliot added the footnote on the Jews' European diaspora in
Notes towards the Definition of Culture, CC 144. For Eliot on the Jewish contribution to Western
civilization, see also "The Man of Letters" 341.

work, during the forties and fifties, was the "hatred of foreign-
ers" ("Responsibility of Letters" 337) and, in *Notes towards the
Definition of Culture*, the impetus of his new interest became
clear: "the deliberate destruction of another culture as a whole
is an irreparable wrong," Eliot wrote shortly after the war,
"almost as evil as to treat human beings like animals" (CC 140).

    The war altered Eliot's politics and his poetics more
fundamentally than his conversion had affected them. Catholicism, classicism, and royalism emerged from an intellectual process that began at Harvard and a psychological process that
began in childhood,

> But the torment of others remains in experience
> Unqualified, unworn by subsequent attrition. (CPP 133)

Eliot's acquiescence in democracy ("We all agree on the affirmation that a democracy is the best possible aim for society")
was announced on a lecture tour of America in 1950 and was a
more momentous development than is generally supposed (TCC
70).[8] An implication of his Ph.D. dissertation had been that--
since reality is conventional, and truth determined by conventions of language--it was necessary to maintain a rigorous and
exclusive vocabulary in order to have truth or reality at all. From
this perspective, pluralist democracy threatens the continuity
and even the existence of reality because it encourages the
claims of rival vocabularies and establishes the expectation of
their alternating dominion. But democracy, Eliot came to
believe after the war, was "not merely a form of government, but
a common ethos, a common way of responding emotionally,
even common standards of conduct in private life" ("Education," TCC 71). Democracy no longer seemed to Eliot a mechanism for the avoidance of commitment, of the selection of discourse, but as an instrument of its expression. Part of the reason
for his change of mind may be that democracy itself had
changed: in 1933 democratic elections brought Hitler to power,
and in Europe, during the years between the wars, a vote for a
political party could signify the voter's choice of an ethics, a
metaphysics, and a system of government. Eliot had held that
electoral politics conduced only to unbridgeable disagreement,

---

8. "The Aims of Education" (1950) 70. The change, at least, of tone is remarkable; contrast the sentence quoted with this passage from Eliot's "Commentary," *Criterion* 7 (1924): 235: "This aversion for
the work of art, this preference for the derivative, the marginal, is an aspect of the modern democracy
of culture. We say democracy advisedly: that meanness of spirit, that egotism of motive, that incapacity
for surrender or allegiance to something outside of oneself, which is a frequent symptom of the soul of
man under democracy." One scholar who has recognized the change in Eliot's position is Roger
Kojecky 205: "This is a different Eliot who can speak so cheerfully of liberal democracy."

indeed incommensurability, or else to frivolous dispute.[9] Following the war, democracy, at least in English-speaking countries, produced what Eliot called "significant disagreement": enough agreement about terms and values to make debate possible, sufficient divergence of method and purpose to make debate more than a sport (qtd. in Kojecky 180).[10]

Eliot adjusted to the logic of the situation. Democracy had the advantage of existence, and his endorsement disposed of the apparent contradiction between his distaste for theoretical worlds, as a philosopher, and his advocacy of them, as a social critic. Eliot determined, the war having proved major upheavals undesirable, that there were developments in modern life "which we must accept," but he discovered as well that democratic values fit closely with his philosophical position ("Education," TCC 96). More closely, it appears, than had his interim values: Eliot's post-war essays read more like the papers of his Harvard years than anything written between them, and they contain innumerable apologies for the tone and content of prior work.[11] In "The Aims of Education," the lecture series in which he explored the virtues of democracy, the controlling argument was that " ' education' is likely to mean, in practice, a compromise between what different people mean by it" (TCC

---

9. For the politics of normal and abnormal discourse, see Eliot, "Commentary," *Criterion* 39 (1931): 308; ASG 13.
10. Eliot, response of Jan. 1941, at a Moot group meeting, to a presentation by Karl Mannheim.
11. The late essays rewrite the early ones in somewhat the same way that, as Hugh Kenner has shown, Eliot's post-conversion poems revise pre-conversion works. See especially Eliot, "Last Words," *Criterion* 71 (1939): 272, regarding the obscurity and confusion of his political essays; "The Classics and the Man of Letters" (1942) 148, and "Milton II" (1947) SE 165 ff., for apologies to Milton (but see also "To Criticize the Critic," TCC 23-24, for Eliot's disclaimer of retraction); "Poetry and Drama" (1951), OPP, for apologies to Shaw (76, 87), Shakespeare (78), Yeats (82-83), and for criticism of *The Family Reunion* (90); "To Criticize the Critic" (1961), TCC 23, for an additional apology to Shakespeare and for second thoughts about Byron and Tennyson; "Goethe as the Sage" (1955), OPP, for apologies to Goethe (244, 256), Wordsworth and the Romantics (254); "What Dante Means to Me" (1950), TCC 130-32, for a quasi-apology to Shelley; the preface to *A Choice of Kipling's Verse* for his apology to Kipling; "The Unity of European Culture" (1946), CC 195-96, for the "failure" of the *Criterion*; "Education," TCC 62, 67, for criticism of *Notes towards the Definition of Culture*; "The Three Voices of Poetry" (1953), OPP 98-99, for criticism of *The Rock*; "The Frontiers of Criticism" (1956), OPP 111, for criticism of his 1923 essay, "The Function of Criticism," and 117 for the "truly embarrassing success" of his critical terminology; "A Note on *Monstre Gai*" 526, for the "*Times-Literary-Supplement*-leading-article manner" of his critical essays; "Preface to the Edition of 1964," UPUC 9-10, for criticism of his 1919 essay, "Tradition and the Individual Talent." And in "What Dante Means to Me," TCC 127, Eliot at long last included Homer, despite objections of temperament, in his list of the greatest poets. About these apologies and self-criticisms, Eliot made a number of general remarks: "The Music of Poetry" (1942), OPP 17: "I can never re-read my own prose writings without acute embarrassment"; prefatory note to *Selected Essays*, July 1950 ("I find myself at times inclined to quarrel with my own opinions, and more often to criticize the way in which they were expressed. . . . As one grows older one may become less dogmatic"); "Goethe as the Sage," OPP 256: "I have always found the re-reading of my own prose writings too painful a task," but cf. "Poetry and Drama" 75, where he says he has been "Reviewing my critical output for the last thirty-odd years." The most comprehensive explanation and apology are offered in "To Criticize the Critic," TCC 11-26. A breathtaking self-parody appears in "The Influence of Landscape upon the Poet," *Daedalus*, spring 1960: 420-21: "I managed to take up a good deal of time, I remember, by expatiating on the subject of my own ignorance in general, with particular reference to my ignorance of English Letter Writers. Whether the address was a success or not I do not know. You may suspect from this anecdote that what I am saying now is merely an elaborate way of saying that I have nothing to say. Not so."

104), and that "'equality of opportunity' . . . means different things to different people, and different things to the same people at different moments, often without our knowing it" (TCC 101). To judge by style or by slant, the date of these comments might be 1915 and, as contributions to public debate, they show how Eliot had by 1950 found the latitude at which perspectivism and pluralism meet. The perspectivist and the pluralist, having a special awareness of dissension, may be specially devoted, as a practical consequence, to the achievement of consensus. Eliot's metaphors for consensus had been absolutistic--a consensus achieved, for the skeptic, is a truth--and these uncongenial metaphors served to alienate a plurality from the consensus he described. His post-war metaphors were benign, even democratic. *The Oxford English Dictionary* became Eliot's favored illustration of consensus: the *O.E.D.* comprehends all mutations of definition, past and present, on the assumption that every usage, however eccentric or archaic, is valid and that, despite wide variation, "there is an implicit unity between all the meanings of a word" ("Education," TCC 67).[12]

This had been precisely Eliot's characterization of orthodoxy--the implicit consensus of diverse perspectives--but orthodoxy, whatever Eliot's intention, did not connote a human consensus. Eliot had depicted tradition (his secular synonym for orthodoxy) as "an ideal order" of "monuments,"

> which is modified by the introduction of the new (the really new) work of art among them. The existing order is complete before the new work arrives; for order to persist after the supervention of novelty, the *whole* existing order must be, if ever so slightly, altered; and so the relations, proportions, values of each work of art toward the whole are readjusted . . . . ("Tradition and the Individual Talent," SE 5)

Nowhere in this famous trope is there indication of how, or by what agency, such relations and values are adjusted--the key verbs are in the passive voice--but Eliot's dissertation, completed three years before *The Sacred Wood*, supplies the missing *whom*:

> An account of reality, or of any field of it, which has the appearance of going to the point of substituting a new type of objects for the old will be a true theory and not merely a new world, if it is capable of making an actual practical difference in our attitude

---

12. Cf. Eliot, "Johnson as Critic and Poet" (1944), OPP 218: "It is prudent, not simply to choose the set of definitions which we find most congenial, or to assume that that one is most exact which is most recent; but to collate all those of respectable authority of different ages. We find that these have a great deal in common."

> toward the old, or toward some already accepted object, so that
> there may be an identity uniting differences of quality. (KE 161)

"Tradition and the Individual Talent" applies this principle to
literature, with the crucial phrase, "our attitude," excised: literary tradition and religious orthodoxy do not modify themselves.
Eliot portrayed tradition as objective and anonymous, but that
was a tactic. It kept his motives obscure and permitted him, as
he later confessed, to adjust Georgian attitudes to modernist
needs.[13] His critical essays, often timed to precede new artistic
departures, prepared readers raised on Wordsworth and Rupert
Brooke for *Ulysses* and *The Waste Land*.[14]

But by the forties, that battle was won--"Prufrock"
was an anthology piece--and with Europe in ruins, Eliot
rethought both the nature of tradition and the achievements of
modernism. The revaluation was pervaded by a sense of moral
failure, and Eliot called the process a "moral necessity"
("Goethe," OPP 241); he had committed, in the campaign for
modernism, many "literary injustices" (OPP 244). In 1939, Eliot
had spoken of "an enormous catastrophe which includes a war"
and, after 1945, literary tradition remained a field on which the
war for Europe would be waged (qtd. in Kojecky 172).[15] Eliot
gave his last years to laying groundwork for a truce. He was conspicuously unsuccessful: his early criticism had been taken as a
battle plan, and his lieutenants were confused by the marshal's
white flag.[16] The reaction of William Wimsatt was typical:

> Let us pay the old possum, the aged eagle, the self-depreciatory
> and recantatory elder statesman, the tribute in 1966 of asserting
> that he himself has not had the right or the power to subvert his
> own image. We have taken his own radical, constructive, and accu-
> rate ... ideas of 1919, 1927, 1930, or 1935, far too seriously and
> with far too much advantage to the sanity of our own thinking
> about literature, to submit to any of his now pleasantly weary ges-
> tures of dismissal. (589)

The most important task of reconstruction, and the
most difficult to urge on disciples of his early prose, was to
revise the historical theory known as the "dissociation of sensi-

---

13. See "To Criticize the Critic," TCC 16: "I was in reaction, not only against Georgian poetry, but
against Georgian criticism; I was writing in a context which the reader of today has either forgotten, or
has never experienced."
14. For Eliot's critical maneuvers, see Perl 68-89. For the relation of "Tradition and the Individual
Talent" to *Ulysses*: 174-76. Cf. Eliot, "To Criticize the Critic," TCC 16: "in my earlier criticism, both in
my general affirmations about poetry and in writing about authors who had influenced me, I was
implicitly defending the sort of poetry that I and my friends wrote." The clearest instance of Eliot
essays that announce Eliot poems are "Dante" (1929) and the preface to *Anabasis* (1930), which prepare the reader for the departure of *Ash-Wednesday* (1930).
15. At the first meeting of the Moot group in 1939 after Britain's declaration of war on Germany.
16. For the degree to which this view of Eliot's criticism was inaccurate, see Perl 68-89.

bility" ("Metaphysical Poets" SE 247). Eliot had proposed that the English Civil War and, by implication, all the fratricidal wars of Europe after the Reformation, had disastrously split a unified cultural mind into opponent fragments: Catholic and Puritan, Tory and Whig, classicist and romantic. It was not that this thesis had been discredited by World War--the first war, in fact, may well have occasioned it--but that our civilization was past the stage where analysis of the problem could help to solve it. An idea has only so much reality, Eliot's dissertation argued, as it commands belief in its real existence: the "dissociation of sensibility" would not be resolved as a problem until it had been superseded as a concept. Eliot's first step, taken during the war, was to disclaim interest in cultural unity:

> A completely unified national culture, such as has been the ambition of German ideologues for the last hundred years and more, to bring about in Germany, tends to become ... a menace to its neighbors. What is not so immediately obvious is, that from a cultural point of view, a nation so completely unified is a menace to itself. ("Responsibility of Letters" 245)[17]

This reasoning made necessary the revision of prior critical judgments. In essays of the early twenties--"William Blake" (SE 275-80), "Andrew Marvell" (SE 251-63), "The Function of Criticism" (SE 12-22)--Eliot had written that, while the English language did not conduce to classic unity, the question is, "*not* what comes natural or what comes *easy* to us, but what is right?" ("Function of Criticism," SE 17). During the forties and after, Eliot praised English specifically for its diversity, taking variety to be a sign of life and classic unity its termination:

> We need not consider it as a defect of any literature, if no one author, or one period, is completely classical; or if, as is true of English literature, the period which most nearly fills the classical definition is not the greatest. I think that those literatures, of which English is one of the most eminent, in which the classical qualities are scattered between various authors and several periods, may well be the richer. ("What Is a Classic?" OPP 53; see also 55-56, 67-68. Cf. "Unity of European Culture," CC 187-89)

"Romanticism versus classicism" had been buried as an issue, but Eliot exhumed it briefly to apologize to injured parties (Shakespeare, Milton, Goethe, Wordsworth, Kipling, Yeats) and to argue, at some length, that no clear distinctions could be

---

17. Eliot developed this argument further in the "Unity and Diversity" chapters of *Notes towards the Definition of Culture*. He did not, however, concede at any point that the effects of the Civil War had terminated ("I question whether any serious civil war ever does end"): "Milton II," OPP 168.

drawn among the tendencies and schools of European letters. These were simply variations upon a theme:

> If we identify 'edification' with the propagation of the moral ideas of Johnson's time . . . we fail to see that it is merely our notions of edification that have changed. When Matthew Arnold said that poetry was a criticism of life, he was maintaining the standard of edification. Even the doctrine of 'art for art's sake' is only a variation under the guise of a protest; and in our time . . . the attempt . . . to express or impose a social philosophy in verse, indicate[s] that it is only the content of 'edification' that changes.
>
> If, therefore, we allow to 'edification' all the elasticity of which the term is capable, it seems to come to no more than the assertion that poetry should have some serious value for the reader: a proposition which will not be denied and which is therefore hardly worth affirming. ("Johnson as Critic and Poet," OPP 211)

Such agreement as exists will go unexpressed, yet diversity is expressive of unity. The cultivation of either "may lead to tyranny" (CC 123). This was a decidedly post-war conundrum, and its solution lay for Eliot in the province of ethics. During the war, Eliot brought his contextualist argument to bear upon human relations and began to picture literature as a human, rather than an impersonal, enterprise. The role of the poet or critic or reader is not to judge the products of human ingenuity, but to appreciate and learn from them. Unappealing artifacts and repellent claims are not errors, Eliot said, or will not seem so, "once we succeed in apprehending the point of view" ("Johnson," OPP 195). In concluding his "quarrel with Goethe" and the romantics, Eliot replaced the politics of tradition with an ethics of reading ("Goethe," OPP 243):

> we begin to enquire into the reasons for our failure to enjoy what has been found delightful by men, perhaps many generations of men, as well qualified or better qualified for appreciation than ourselves. . . . Differences which are unexamined never emerge from the obscurity of prejudice: the better we understand our failure to appreciate an author, the nearer we come to appreciation-- since understanding and sympathy are closely related. . . . And antipathy overcome . . . is an important liberation from a limitation of one's own mind. . . . I find that there may be a few authors whom I have never really known, in the sense of intimacy and ease, with whom I must settle my account before I die. ("Goethe," OPP 242-44)

It is no trick to learn what one already knows, nor to admire what one likes, and it is immoral to annihilate or banish phenomena that do not indulge the self. This ethics, scarcely original but in 1944 needing reiteration, Eliot extended and deepened under wartime pressure. "One needs the enemy," he said, and meant the verb literally: we cannot get along without that which we hate (CC 133).[18] It is not simply that a culture lives off internal friction, though Eliot made this claim as well, but that a human being in the process of maturing rejects in himself essential qualities that are recoverable only by engaging them in others. To meet one's castlings is uncommon in personal life--Eliot's last two plays are about this rare occurrence--but the opportunity is available elsewhere:

> In the perfection of any style it can be observed, as in the maturing of an individual, that some potentialities have been brought to fruition only by the surrender of others. . . . A literature is different from a human life, in that it can return upon its own past, and develop some capacity which has been abandoned. ("Johnson," OPP 191)

A national literature, Eliot held, was the "ordered though unconscious progress of a language to realize its own potentialities within its own limitations" ("What is a Classic?" OPP 58). An individual possessed for him a similar entelechy, and in one tender, awkward moment, Eliot exemplified in himself the identity of the two: "it came to me that 'Nature' to Wordsworth and to Goethe meant much the same thing, that it meant something which they had experienced--and which *I* had not experienced ("Goethe," OPP 254).

The need to share in the experience of others was a late product of Eliot's skepticism, of the position that "all possibilities should be explored" because there are, in the absolute sense, no realities ("From Poe to Valéry" [1948], TCC 42). He asked, for example, that moderns not discount a medieval interpretation of Virgil merely because it was incorrect. Its incorrectness was beside the point: that many sensitive, intelligent persons had believed it ("Virgil and the Christian World," OPP 136-38). This argument was an extension of democratic postulates to history. No citizen of the culture, alive or dead, should be disenfranchised, neither by majority will, nor by "proof" that his views are "wrong"--the assumption being that all perspectives are in some way valid and all in some way indispensable. Of contemporary distaste for Samuel Johnson, Eliot wrote that

---

18. Cf. "Cultural Diversity and European Unity," *Review-45*, summer 1945: 67: "If we had met only people who were wholly congenial, if we had come in contact only with ideas which we could accept, how much we should have missed!" Cf. also "Gordon Craig's Socratic Dialogues," *Drama*, spring 1955: 21: "I hope there will always be iconoclasts and malcontents and stirrers-up of strife. . . ."

> If we censure an eighteenth-century critic for not having a mod-
> ern, historical and comprehensive appreciation, we must ourselves
> adopt towards him, the attitude the lack of which we reprehend;
> we must not be narrow in accusing him of narrowness, or preju-
> diced in accusing him of prejudice. . . . The sensibility of any
> period in the past is always likely to appear to be more limited
> than our own; for we are naturally much more aware of our ances-
> tors' lack of awareness to those things of which we are aware, than
> we are of any lack in ourselves, of awareness to what they per-
> ceived and we do not. ("Johnson," OPP 187, 189. Cf. "Milton II"
> 167)

Eliot had been approaching this conclusion for years. He had
criticized friends, during the thirties, for narrowness of taste, but
now he felt himself a victim of prejudice as he himself faded into
history:[19] "Last season's fruit is eaten / And the fullfed beast
shall kick the empty pail. / For last year's words belong to last
year's language / And next year's words await another voice"
(CPP 141).

* * *

Eliot was conscious of living on into a postmodernist world, and
about this fate he had mixed feelings:

> As the taste for my own poetry spread, so did the taste for the
> poets to whom I owed the greatest debt and about whom I had
> written. Their poetry, and mine, were congenial to that age. I
> sometimes wonder if that age is not coming to an end. . . . And
> indeed it is to other poets than these that I am likely to turn
> now. . . . ("To Criticize," TCC 22)

He no longer turned, for instance, to Joyce, whose "monstrous
masterpiece," *Finnegans Wake* ("Frontiers" [1956], OPP 120),
confirmed Eliot's belief that modernism had gone too far
("From Poe to Valéry," TCC 41-42).[20] "One book like this," he
wrote, "is enough," and complained of its vastness, allusiveness,
and obscurity (OPP 119).[21] His mind, however, was not altogether on Joyce:

> I must admit that I am . . . not guiltless. . . . The notes to *The
> Waste Land*! . . . the remarkable exposition of bogus scholarship
> that is still on view to-day. . . . They have had almost greater pop-

---

19. Friends in the thirties (Ezra Pound and Herbert Read): UPUC 74-77. Eliot wrote of these lectures
in 1963: "I found to my surprise that I was still prepared to accept them as a statement of my critical
position."
20. Note, however, that Eliot had written three years earlier that "one *Inferno*, even by Dante, is
enough" and hence that the remark may not constitute an insult: "The Three Voices of Poetry," OPP
97.
21. Cf. Eliot's letter to Jack Dalton, *James Joyce Quarterly*, Fall 1968: 79-81. Joyce had his own doubts
about Eliot: see Nathan Halper, "Joyce and Eliot," *A Wake Newslitter*. 3-10; Aug. 17-21; Dec. 22-26.

> ularity than the poem itself.... I regret having sent so many
> enquirers off on a wild goose chase after Tarot cards and the Holy
> Grail. (OPP 121-22)

At the same time, Eliot's ardor for Henry James "somewhat flagged," and in his own verse, that of *Four Quartets* and the last plays, there is evidence of retirement from syntactic complexity and obscurity of reference (TCC 17). Eliot envisaged, and to some extent approved, a retreat from modernist sophistication. After *Finnegans Wake*, "a new simplicity, even a relative crudity, may be the only alternative" ("Classic?" OPP 60).[22] "I do not believe," he said of modernism, "that this aesthetic can be of any help to later poets," and in revising his early views of unsympathetic predecessors, he commended a new, or rather an old, set of qualities to his successors ("From Poe to Valéry," TCC 41). In Yeats' plays Eliot admired the increasing simplicity ("Yeats," OPP 305), and his chief criteria for excellence after the war--qualities he found in Johnson and in Kipling--were straightforwardness, clarity, and eloquence of communication ("Johnson," OPP 216-217; "Kipling" 294). In contemplating Milton, he advised future poets to develop "new and more elaborate patterns," though he still insisted on "a definite meaning expressed in the properest words" ("Milton II," OPP 183).

"Definite meaning" comes as something of a shock, particularly when in preference to "overtones, associations, and indefinite suggestiveness" ("Johnson," OPP 217). The common feature of Eliot's recommendations was that each expressed discontent with the poetics he had helped to construct. He was in this respect an active participant in the formation of postmodern aesthetics, although one of his motivations--dread "of being the *last* poet"--could give postmodernists no satisfaction ("Classic?" OPP 67). Eliot was diffident, in private as in public, about evaluating younger writers, but his opinion does not seem to have been positive; not even the jacket notes he wrote for Faber poets evince enthusiasm.[23] He wrote in 1947 of "the likelihood

---

22. Cf. "From Poe to Valéry," TCC 42. For a different view of the significance of the shift in Eliot's aesthetics, see Bush 191 ff.

23. Diffident: Valerie Eliot, letter to me, 10 Nov. 1983. (Cf. Ackroyd, 330-31.) In nominating "books of the year," during the fifties for *The Sunday Times*, Eliot recommended no books of poetry and reported that "I never read contemporary fiction" (24 Dec. 1950: 3; cf. 26 Dec. 1954: 6). His essay, "The Publishing of Poetry," *The Bookseller* 2450, is a model of condescension to the "young poet"; he writes, for instance, of making "tactful suggestions of detail" (1570). Allen Tate confirmed that "What he thought of 'us'--by us, I mean his old but slightly younger literary friends--we never quite knew because he never quite said" ("Postscript by the Guest Editor" to the Eliot memorial issue of *Sewanee Review* I [1966]: 383). Jacket notes: King's College Library, Cambridge, maintains a collection of Faber "blurbs," with markings by John Hayward that indicate the ones Eliot wrote. He appears to have saved his enthusiasm for contemporaries like Marianne Moore; of the younger poets, he seems to have been most impressed by Robert Lowell, but even for Lowell his praise was a bit pale ("a new idiom that echoed no other voice": *Faber and Faber List for Spring/Summer 1950*: 96). His opinion of contemporary criticism was no higher: "The Classics and the Man of Letters," TCC 151: "In the past twenty

that the development of poetry in the next fifty years will take quite different directions from those which to me seem desirable to explore" ("Milton II," OPP 167), and he replied, in 1953, to a question about post-war literary talent with the phrase, "I must confess . . . I don't see much" (Lehman 5). His concern was not exclusively for literature: he could conceive "a decline which would mean that people everywhere would cease to be able to express, and consequently be able to feel, the emotions of civilized beings" ("Social Function" OPP 15; Cf. CC 31, 91). "This of course," he said during the war, "might happen," and to ensure that it did not, Eliot imagined for his successors a culture after modernism, after the movement that had fancied itself the apotheosis and therefore the end of culture. Change, even change hostile to himself or to modernism, was not Eliot's fear: "this is a condition of human life," he wrote, "and what I am apprehensive of is death" (OPP 16).

A second motivation for poetic reform was moral. Eliot felt that his historical judgments and his judgments of other writers could themselves be judged by moral criteria; he was no less attentive to the ethics implicit in his verse. *After Strange Gods* is notorious for its condemnation of the immoral beliefs of other modernists, but after the war Eliot's moral concern was as much with form as with content and was directed less at others than at himself. His new canons of simplicity, directness, and "definite meaning" appear meant to quash Mallarmé's injunction to veil a poem and amaze the mob.[24] Symbolist snobbery was inconsistent with the lessons of a war that led Eliot to vote Labour (see Tate, "The New Criticism" 87). The *Quartets* play the old mode of poetry off the new--a highfalutin lyric about apocalypse and hollyhocks is followed in *East Coker* by measured words of disapproval:[25]

> That was a way of putting it--not very satisfactory:
> A periphrastic study in a worn-out poetical fashion,
> Leaving one still with the intolerable wrestle
> With words and meanings. . . . (CPP 125)

Eliot published his last significant poem in 1942, nearly a quarter-century before his death. He was unable to write poetry in the new mode, and brought cheerless tidings, after completing

years I have observed what seems to me a deterioration in the middle literary stratum, and notably in the standards and the scholarship which are wanted for literary criticism."
24. Stéphane Mallarmé, "Le Livre, Instrument Spirituel" (1895), *Igitur, Divagations, Un Coup de dés* 272. For a very different view of Mallarmé's aesthetics and of Eliot's relation to it, see Bush, *Modernism Reconsidered* 201 ff.
25. Note that the lyric of *East Coker*, part 2, may be to some extent a parody of the lyric of *Burnt Norton*, part 2, which was written before the war (1935).

the fourth quartet, about the possibilities for reconciling egalitarian morals with the axiology of high culture:

> If the reader says: "the state of affairs which I wish to bring about
> is *right* (or is *just*, or is *inevitable*); and if this must lead to a further
> deterioration of culture, we must accept that deterioration"--then
> I can have no quarrel with him. I might even, in some circum-
> stances, feel obliged to support him. (CC 89; Cf. "Classics and
> Letters" TCC 153).

Eliot did not dissent from the view that the war exposed a deep vein of immorality in the culture. Reforms made out of moral necessity would be, by definition, necessary--but that would not mean that the standard of culture thereby produced would not represent, in the context, a decline.

One solution might be to alter the context, such that moral art would be taken to be great art. (The aesthetics of socialist realism was a seeming case in point.) Eliot reasoned that this solution was impossible and its proposition hazardous. The alteration implied a new culture entirely and, new cultures taking centuries to grow, Europeans would in the meantime slip into the barbarism of which they had proved themselves capable. "No one society," Eliot thought, "and no one age of it realizes all the values of civilization. Not all of these values may be compatible with each other" (CC 91). For our society, the improvement of ethics might require the decay of aesthetics. All we could do, in that situation, would be "to improve such civilization as we have, for we can imagine no other" (CC 90). During the years he was making this argument, Eliot left poetry for drama. His post-war plays comprised a moral rather than an aesthetic undertaking: Eliot's term for this type of writing was "*applied* poetry" (Lehmann 5). These plays were intended, as a basis of counter-modernist reform, to reach a large audience in a popular genre. After decades of symbolism, modernism, and *épater les bourgeois*, he was determined "to improve such civilization as we have." The irony was that after the war the civilization was not quite what it had been, nor was the middle class, and that *En Attendant Godot*, not *The Confidential Clerk*, was the talk of 1953. The irony, on the other hand, is less impressive than the simple fact, which the mind can barely register, that Eliot's comedies and Beckett's were contemporaneous events. The aesthetic shortfall of Eliot's plays, and the knowledge that they were Eliot's--the work, that is, of a residual modernist-- have prevented our seeing them as documents of the origin and early development of postmodernism.

Eliot was a reader of "modern French plays," though evidently it was Sartre, not Beckett, who mattered to him: a predictable circumstance, determined by affinity ("Poetry and Drama" [1951], OPP 84-85). Eliot and Sartre were philosophers, students of Husserl and idealism, but in search of alternatives, and both were dramatists *à thèse* (Sartre, *Diaries* 183, 82 ff.). Each rejected belief in inherent meaning--each held that men make their own--and the two concerned themselves, on account of the war, with the ethics of that position. But the Existentialists, Eliot feared, had drawn the wrong conclusion; or, at least, *The Cocktail Party* was meant to refute *Huis Clos*:[26]

> What? Only two of you? I thought there were more; many more. [*Laughs.*] So this is hell. I'd never have believed it. . . . Hell is--other people! (*Huis Clos* [1945])

> What is hell? Hell is oneself,
> Hell is alone, the other figures in it
> Merely projections. (*The Cocktail Party* [1949], CPP 342)

In the Existentialist rhetoric of *les autres*, there was sufficient to alarm Eliot, who drew from the war lessons about interdependence and mutual respect. Sartre, beginning in his war diary, characterized human relationships in imperialist (his metaphor) and intrusive terms (*Diaries* 256). "He sees me, he speaks to me, at once he cuts into my very existence and I thrust myself like a knife into his"--this was Sartre's portrayal in 1939 of an ordinary conversation between himself and an army comrade (205). Freedom was the watchword of Existentialist ethics, but it was difficult to specify, in a world of victors and vanquished, in what freedom might consist. "Nothing," Sartre wrote during the war,

> is dearer to me than the freedom of those I love . . . but the fact is, this freedom is dear to me provided I don't respect it at all. It's a question not of suppressing it, but of actually violating it . . . there's no shadow of a doubt that that's what the desire to be loved means: to hit at the Other in the Other's absolute freedom. Such is the root of sadism, for example. . . . The broken victim who yields, the battered Jew who cries out 'Down with the Jews!', is still making a real choice. . . . That kind of freedom is subjugated *by itself*; it turns upon itself . . . to will its captivity. (256-57)

Human relations as a battle of wills--a not unfamiliar hypothesis. "I recognize," Sartre recorded in his diary, ". . . that

---

26. Eliot said that the line, "Hell is oneself," was meant to be "Contre Sartre": E. Martin Browne, *The Making of T. S. Eliot's Plays* 233. For a detailed comparison of Eliot's play with Sartre's, see note 30 and corresponding text. Cf. also the plays' concluding statements: "Well, well, let's get on with it"; "Oh, I'm glad. It's begun." Bernard F. Dick suggests that Eliot's play echoes *La Nausée*: "Sartre and *The Cocktail Party*," *Yeats-Eliot Review* 1978: 25-26.

there's a hint of fascism in my current thought" (146), and his observation that "in war, there are no innocent victims" (128) carried over into a more general belief that, given human free-dom, *"one never has any excuse"* (113). Sartre's heroic notion would appear to be the opposite of Jeffrey Masson's view, also formed with reference to Jewish suffering, that the world is rife with victims.[27] These opinions share, however, a presumption that hell is other people, and the fact that Sartre and Masson, despite wide differences, concur in it should enrich our sense of the term "resistance." *The Intellectual Resistance in Europe*, James Wilkinson's book, demonstrates in detail that the ideol-ogy of the Underground--its "mere inversion" of the Nazis' "Manichaean universe"--entered into and transformed the mainstream of modern ethics (264. Cf. Butler 7). Resistance intellectuals feared that the Liberation would mark, in Sartre's phrase, a mere dispersal, but their efforts to realize their agenda only perpetuated the self-contradictory stance into which the Nazis had forced them.[28] The Resistance was a moral elite of militant free-thinkers. Relativism entails a social context in which the madmen are genial: "That is not what I meant at all"--the beloved's reply to Prufrock--would not do as a response to Hitler. When Inez in *Huis Clos* refuses, out of enmity, to credit the story Garcin tells of himself, he is thrown back upon a choice which for the relativist is hell. He can insist that he is telling the Truth; he can try to conquer the adversary; he can accept the enemy's viewpoint. Incapable of selection, he settles into para-noia and what looks, in the age of Super Powers, to be a very cold war.

    The Cocktail Party plays out alternatives that Sartre did not entertain. Sainthood is one, defined as "despair": a dis-illusion so complete that the self loses need of a viewpoint (CPP 364). Celia Coplestone is the ultimate skeptic ("the dreamer is no more real than his dreams"), and her skepticism resolves a crisis that appears Existential (CPP 362): [29]

> And then I found we were only strangers
> And that there had been neither giving nor taking
> But that we had merely made use of each other
> Each for his purpose. (CPP 362)

---

27. *Diaries* 113: "Nothing is ever too much" for the free man.
28. All peaces to date have been mere dispersals": *Diaries* 163. Cf 197:"it's much easier to live decently and authentically in wartime than in peacetime." See also Wilkinson, 51 ff., for similar remarks of Beauvoir, Camus, and others.
29. Julia introduces the theme of Celia's skepticism: "My darling Celia, / You needn't be so sceptical" (CPP 299).

"That's horrible," she concludes, and asks, "Can we only love /
Something created by our own imagination?" The rivalry of
imaginations is what puts an end to Celia--Kinkanjans eat the
Christians who have eaten sacred monkeys--and, desirable or
not, transcendence is made conceivable. Neither victim nor victimizer, the disillusioned one transcends their game by living out
her empathy with both. But the Bodhisattva is, to say the least, a
rarity, and Eliot's real critique of Sartre is lodged in the parable
of Edward and Lavinia. The Chamberlaynes are borrowed characters: each enters the play in the throes of *Angst*; each views
the other as the Other.[30] Edward complains of his wife's

> oppression, the unreality
> Of the role she had always imposed upon me
> . . . she has made me incapable
> Of having any existence of my own. . . .
> She has made the world a place I cannot live in
> Except on her terms. (CPP 349)

Edward may have been modeled on Garcin, Sartre's cowardly
lion--the metaphorical doorway in Edward's "hell" speech is a
telltale steal from *Huis Clos*, and his image of Lavinia resembles
closely Garcin's of Inez.[31] These men regard themselves as
objects; their female counterparts as subjects, whose purpose is
subjection. The categories of Continental philosophy are projected onto the relationship of persons.

  Sir Henry Harcourt-Reilly, the "Unidentified
Guest," comes from another play entirely--Eliot's--and from a
different philosophical tradition. In his advice to Edward Chamberlayne, Reilly quotes F. H. Bradley: "my patients / Are only
pieces of a total situation / Which I have to explore. The single
patient / Who is ill by himself, is rather the exception" (CPP
350). Eliot had written of Bradley's "total situation" in an essay
of 1913, and Reilly applies his contextualist holism to the ethical
questions of marriage and divorce.[32] The Chamberlaynes, he
tells them, have together concocted their problem. There is neither victimizer nor victim, neither subject nor object, but simply
a marriage, a "total situation," in relation to which divorce
would be the origination of a dualism. Reilly has no patience for
theoretical distinctions. Lavinia is "exceptionally unlovable" and

30. For "the Other," see, e.g. Sartre, *Diaries* 137-38.
31. Doorway: CPP 342; cf. Garcin in Sartre, *No Exit*, CPP 42-43. Edward on Lavinia: CPP 343; cf. *No Exit*, CPP 43-47. See also note 26, and corresponding text. Cf. Edward's view of Lavinia and Garcin's of Inez with Michael's view of Lord Claverton, his father, in *The Elder Statesman*.
32. Eliot, "Degrees of reality," unpublished MS., 1913. John Hayward Bequest, King's College Library, Cambridge. Mrs. Valerie Eliot holds the copyright to this material and it cannot be consulted or reproduced without her permission.

Edward is "incapable of loving"; given the fact of their union, there is no problem to resolve:

> You could accuse each other of your own faults,
> And so avoid understanding each other.
> Now, you have only to reverse the propositions
> And put them together. (CPP 356)

"Understanding" means to place in context, to apprehend perspective ("Johnson," OPP 187-89, 201-02; 195), to overcome antipathy: such at least was Eliot's prescription for understanding "authors" ("Goethe," OPP 242-44). But this ethic places limits on one's freedom of belief and will; and it is on that ground that Edward shows resistance to it.[33] The response of Reilly--"you are not free, Mr. Chamberlayne"--is, or so it seems, the play's chill retort to Sartre (CPP 350).

Freedom is a post-war shibboleth, for obvious and compelling reasons. The word has political significance, more or less exact, but is extended with regularity and impertinence. Eliot's last plays dramatize the irrelevance of freedom, or free will, or free-thinking, to the conditions of our "relative world." Sir Claude Mulhammer, in *The Confidential Clerk*, repeats the Existential line--"If you haven't the strength to impose your own terms / Upon life, you must accept the terms it offers you"--and proceeds to show the stuff that Existentialists are made of (CP 234):

> I want a world where the form is the reality,
> Of which the substantial is only a shadow.
> . . . I loathed this occupation
> Until I began to feel my power in it.
> It begins as a kind of make-believe
> And the make-believing makes it real.
> . . . I believe you will go through the private door
> Into the real world, as I do, sometimes. (CP 236-37)

It is only other people who do not know what truth is. The Existentialist--magisterial free-thinker--is in effect a closet Platonist.[34] If everything is make-believe, nothing is gained by saying so. Only the disappointed true believer would harp on make-believe and playing roles; the make-believe might as well be called the Real, and one's role be termed one's Self. The argu-

---

33. Eliot's ethics of "understanding" extended to the process of his playwriting: see "The Three Voices of Poetry," OPP 103, and cf. Iris Murdoch, "The Sublime and the Beautiful Revisited" 257.

34. Free-thinker: even in the original sense--see Sir Claude on religion: CP 40. Note that Sartre admitted to a tendency toward philosophical absolutism, which he found it difficult to overcome: *Diaries* , 82-83.

ment that truth is fiction can be a tool of rhetoric for luring others from an established fiction to one's own.

But the truth returns to haunt Sir Claude and (in *The Elder Statesman*) Lord Claverton, who *in camera* have believed their fictions true, and each is horrified to find that reality is a function of consensus, a balancing of social roles, a synthesis of viewpoints reaching back in time and forward to the future. The resolution scene of *The Confidential Clerk* is virtually an election: the characters are canvassed to determine what they prefer reality should be. "I don't believe it," Sir Claude replies when his candidate is defeated: "I simply can't believe it. / Mrs. Guzzard, you are inventing this fiction / In response to what Colby said he wanted" (CP 286). Other people can be hell if what one wants is the freedom to impose one's will. Reality is not an imposition, nor--what amounts to the same thing--a discovery. Once consensus happens ("You have all had your wish / In one form or another," Mrs. Guzzard tells the company), the facts fall into line (CP 290). Facts are cheap, a set exists to support any interpretation, and the interpretation of the facts precedes them. Interpretation, furthermore, is a disingenuous wish. What remains, upon achievement of consensus, is for each participant to adjust: "We all of us have to adapt ourselves / To the wish that is granted," Mrs. Guzzard observes, and "That can be a painful process" (CP 284). Sir Claude rebels against the pains that most men take for granted. He does not want to acclimate to others' wishes, their neuroses, conflicting interests, self-destructive and unintelligent desires, historic arrangements, and unconscious agreements--the responsibilities and loss of freedom, in short, attendant upon the love of people. The same applies to Claverton, and Eliot sentences them both to the peace that "force of will" cannot obtain for independent and superior men (CP 266).

The domineering characters whom consensus overtakes are men of Eliot's own stature and generation (they are, precisely, elder statesmen), and these last plays are among his most autobiographical works. If the late plays comprise a response to Sartre, then Eliot's critique could only be that Sartre was too much like himself. The younger generation, in the plays, has no need for struggle with the old--Mrs. Guzzard neutralizes Sir Claude and Lord Claverton eliminates himself. Gone is the Oedipal ferocity of modernism: in *Purgatory*, the Yeats persona kills both his father and his son (see Perl 133-35, 280). Eliot's last plays, like Picasso's last paintings, efface their own self-portraits.[35] But this is at once a gesture of good will and of monition:

> I am not eager to rehearse
> My thought and theory which you have forgotten.
> These things have served their purpose: let them be.
> So with your own, and pray they be forgiven
> By others, as I pray you to forgive
> Both bad and good. (*Little Gidding*, CPP 141)

The consensus, among intellectuals in Europe, was that the defeat of Hitler would mean "a new order" (in Sartre's words [qtd. in Wilkinson 51]) or "a new civilization" (in Wiesel's [Wiesel 14]). Even Waugh was convinced there would be "something new" (though worse [*Letters* 214]). Eliot, who shared with the young the desire for atonement and reform, did not share this expectation (see, e.g., Eliot TCC 151 and Kojecky 198 ff). To sweep away and start again was a very old reflex: a tradition indeed, of which, Eliot held, the war was an expression (see note 15). The resistance to renewal, after the war, arose in quest of a new world order. Here is an irony that helps account for Europe's now frenetic, now languorous decline.

WORKS CITED

Ackroyd, Peter. *T. S. Eliot, A Life*. New York: Simon and Schuster, 1984.

Browne, E. Martin. *The Making of T. S. Eliot's Plays*. New York: Cambridge UP, 1969.

Bush, Ronald. "Modern/Postmodern: Eliot, Perse, Mallarmé, and the Future of the Barbarian." *Modernism Reconsidered*. Ed. Robert Kiely. Cambridge: Harvard UP, 1983. 191-214.

Butler, Christopher. *After the Wake: An Essay on the Contemporary Avant-Garde*. Oxford: Clarendon, 1980.

Cohen, Janie L. "Picasso's Exploration of Rembrandt's Art." *Arts Magazine* Oct. 1983: 119-126.

Craft, Robert. Jacket notes. *Threni*. Music by Igor Stravinsky. Columbia Records, MS 6065, n.d.

_____. *Present Perspectives: Critical Writings*. New York: Knopf, 1985.

Daix, Pierre. *La vie de peintre de Pablo Picasso*. Paris: Editions du Seuil, 1977.

Dalton, Jack. "A Letter from T. S. Eliot." *James Joyce Quarterly* Fall 1968: 79-81.

Dick, Bernard F. "Sartre and *The Cocktail Party*." *Yeats-Eliot Review* 1978: 25-26.

Eliot, T. S. "Books of the Year Chosen by Eminent Contemporaries." *Sunday Times* 24 Dec. 1950: 3.

---

35. Picasso: see e.g., "In the Studio" (painted 8 Nov. 1963), "The Artist at Work" (3 Feb. 1964), "The Sculptor" (26-27 Feb. 1965). On Eliot's self-effacement in the post-war years, cf. Wyndham Lewis in *Time*, 30 May 1949: 60: "When last I painted [Eliot] he still had--at least for me--a certain amount of uncouthness of the flesh about him, of the brazen and sardonic as well as the elegant ironic. This time I was painting a man who had passed through a white fire, who is specifically anointed."

_____. "Books of the Year Chosen by Eminent Contemporaries." *Times* 26 Dec. 1954: 6.

_____. "Commentary." *Criterion* Apr. 1924: 231-35.

_____. "Commentary." *Criterion* Jan. 1931: 307-314.

_____. "Cultural Diversity and European Unity." *Review-45* Summer 1945: 61-69.

_____. "Degrees of Reality." Unpublished ms., 1913. King's College Library, Cambridge.

_____. *Faber and Faber List for Spring/Summer 1950*. London: Faber and Faber, 1950.

_____. "Gordon Craig's Socratic Dialogues." *Drama* Spring 1955: 16-21.

_____. "The Influence of Landscape upon the Poet." *Daedalus, Journal of the American Academy of Arts and Sciences* Spring 1960: [420]-22.

_____. "Last Words." *Criterion* Jan. 1939: 269-275.

_____. Letter. *The Times* 24 March 1962: 9.

_____. "The Man of Letters and the Future of Europe." *Sewanee Review* 3 (1945): 341.

_____. "A Note on Monstre Gai." *Hudson Review* Winter 1954-55: [522]-526.

_____. Preface. *A Choice of Kipling's Verse*. By Rudyard Kipling. London: Faber, 1941. 5-36.

_____. "The Publishing of Poetry." *Bookseller* 2450 (1952): 1568-70.

_____. "The Responsibility of the Man of Letters in the Cultural Restoration of Europe." *Norseman* July-Aug. 1944: 243-48.

_____. "The Social Function of Poetry." OPP 3-16. Lecture. British-Norwegian Institute. 1943. Excerpted in *Norseman* 6 (1943): 449-571.

_____. "T. S. Eliot talks about his poetry." *Columbia University Forum* Fall 1958: 11-14.

_____. "The Unity of European Culture" ("*Die Einheit der Europaischen Kultur*"). Three broadcasts, delivered in German over German radio. Mar. 1946. Rpt. CC.

Eliot, Valerie. Letter to the author. 10 Nov. 1983.

Halper, Nathan. "Joyce and Eliot." *A Wake Newslitter* June 1965: 3-10; Aug.: 17-21; Dec.: 22-26.

Kojecky, Roger. *T. S. Eliot's Social Criticism*. New York: Farrar, Straus and Giroux, 1971.

Lehmann, John. "T. S. Eliot Talks About Himself and the Drive to Create." *New York Times Book Review* 29 Nov. 1953: 5, 44.

Lewis, Wyndham. "White Fire." *Time* 30 May 1949: 60.

Mallarmé, Stéphane. "Le Livre, Instrument Spirituel." (1895) *Igitur, Divagations, Un Coup de dés*. Paris: Gallimard, 1976. 266-72.

Murdoch, Iris. "The Sublime and the Beautiful Revisited." *Yale Review* Dec. 1959: 247-271.

Parmelin, Hélène. *Voyage en Picasso*. Paris: Editions Robert Laffont, 1980.

Perl, J. M. *The Tradition of Return: The Implicit History of Modern Literature*. Princeton: Princeton UP, 1984.

Pound, Ezra. "Notes for Canto CXVII et seq.," *The Cantos of Ezra Pound*. New York: New Directions, 1970.

Richardson, John. "The Catch in the Late Picasso." *New York Review of Books* 19 July 1984.

Sartre, Jean-Paul. *The War Diaries of Jean-Paul Sartre, March 1939-March 1940.* Trans. Quintin Hoare. New York: Pantheon, 1984.

Schiff, Gert. *Picasso: The Last Years, 1963-1973.* New York: George Braziller, 1983.

Stravinsky, Igor. Interview. *New York Review of Books* 1 Feb. 1968. Rpt. in *Retrospectives and Conclusions.* Igor Stravinsky and Robert Craft. New York: Knopf, 1969.

_____. Jacket notes. *Symphony in Three Movements.* Columbia Records, MS 6331, 1962.

_____. "Three Types of Spring Fever." HI-FI-Stereo Oct. 1964. Rpt. in Stravinsky and Craft.

Tate, Allen. "The New Criticism." Taped discussion. *The American Scholar Forum* Winter 1950-51: 86-104.

Waugh, Evelyn. *The Letters of Evelyn Waugh.* Ed. Mark Amory. New Haven and New York: Ticknor & Fields, 1980.

Wiesel, Elie. "Why I Write." *New York Times Book Review* 14 April 1985: 13-14.

Wilkinson, James D. *The Intellectual Resistance in Europe.* Cambridge: Harvard UP, 1981.

Wimsatt, William. "Eliot's Weary Gestures of Dismissal." Rev. of *To Criticize the Critic* by T. S. Eliot. *Massachusetts Review* Summer 1966: 584-91.

RICHARD SHUSTERMAN

REACTIONARY MEETS RADICAL CRITIQUE:
ELIOT AND CONTEMPORARY CULTURE CRITICISM

I

Though he is far better known and appreciated as a poet and critic of literature, T. S. Eliot devoted a great deal of thought and writing to social theory and cultural criticism. His active interest in this area links him to the tradition of Arnold, Ruskin, and Pater. But in reaction to what he sees as their humanistic religion of progressive culture and aesthetic fulfillment, Eliot presents a more conservative brand of cultural critique (see "Arnold and Pater," SE 382-93). His culture theory seems even more conservative than it actually is or need be, since it is highlighted by his explicit commitments to the conservative institutions of Anglicanism and royalty and to the Tory Party.

The result of this extremely conservative image is that Eliot's cultural criticism is taken seriously only by conservatives, most particularly conservative Christian thinkers. As for most of us secular progressives, we either try to ignore or factor out this aspect of Eliot the thinker, so that we may concentrate on his criticism, literary theory and philosophy without any threat of embarrassing encumbrance from conservative social theory and theology. Or instead we read all of Eliot in the light of his religious and political conservatism, usually with baneful consequences for our appreciation of his thought. Though the first option can be very fruitful--since most of Eliot's actual views and arguments in the philosophy of criticism do not in any way depend on his religious or political views and are often far from conservative--it is the latter path which is much more frequently pursued. One can clearly document how Eliot's outspoken conservatism in religion and politics is largely responsible for the relative unpopularity and disdainful dismissal of his literary theory and critical practice among today's secular literary theorists, most of whom see themselves as socially and politically progressive.[1]

If his political and religious conservatism presents such an obstacle to our contemporary appreciation of his literary criticism, it might seem an insurmountable check to the progressive appreciation and appropriation of his cultural criticism. Here there is just no way to bracket out political, social, and religious questions as marginal, for they are at the core of the theory and criticism of culture. Nor is there any way, even with the greatest possible ingenuity of reading against the text, to deny the conservative thrust of Eliot's views on culture. He clearly mourned the modern dissociation of sensibility and the disintegration of a unified European culture united under Christianity, and he sought to shore up and revitalize Western civilization through a return to a religion that was largely moribund for modern man. Moreover, he sharply and repeatedly rebuked the dominant contemporary liberal ideology of optimistic progress through the continued refinement of bourgeois institutions and ideals of individual fulfillment that were already and still are well in place. Is Eliot's cultural criticism then too conservative to be appreciated and appropriated by more progressive culture theory?

In this paper I wish to suggest it is not. Indeed, one could say paradoxically that precisely because Eliot is too conservative his views can support and converge with much of today's more progressive cultural criticism. For if we construe conservatism as the desire to conserve or preserve the status quo, then Eliot is not a conservative but a reactionary, who was as scornfully dissatisfied with the status quo as any radical revolutionary. But Eliot and today's radical cultural critics share more than a general disenchantment with society's status quo and ideology. They share a perception of its precise flaws and their causes, and, though to a much lesser extent, they even share some ideas as to how these flaws must be remedied. Eliot's arguments against the dominant bourgeois liberal ideology of his day, which remains the prevailing ideology of our own, can therefore be a resource and reinforcement to today's radical cultural critique. Indeed, if we take the root meaning of

---

1. I present some documentation of this in chapter one of my *T. S. Eliot and the Philosophy of Criticism*. My project in that book was to treat his views and arguments in literary theory in isolation from his religious and political beliefs, a reasonable and rewarding project since the former can be easily separated from the latter and formulated and defended independent from them. This of course is not a viable option with respect to the general theory of culture, especially since Eliot comes close to identifying culture with religion, when religion is widely conceived "as the *whole way of life* of a people, from birth to the grave" and culture is similarly holistically construed. Eliot does not quite identify the two but regards culture as the incarnation of a people's religion (CC 103-06).

"radical" seriously (i.e., its meaning as "root") then Eliot's reactionary rejection of the dominant bourgeois liberal ideology could be called a radical cultural critique of its own, one aimed at helping Western culture go better forward by going back to its healthier roots.

This way of approaching conservative thinking for progressive revolutionary thinking is suggested by one of our most important and radical contemporary critics of culture, T. W. Adorno. In a brief epigram from his *Minima Moralia*, this Frankfurt-School Marxist writes: "Not least among the tasks now confronting thought is that of placing all the reactionary arguments against Western culture in the service of progressive enlightenment" (192).

I propose in what follows to do this with Eliot; and by placing his cultural critique alongside Adorno's own views, I hope not only to show their remarkable convergence, and to promote progressive enlightenment, but to suggest how very relevant Eliot's thought remains, even when his operative recommendations often sound so impossibly repellent, hopeless, and outdated to our secular ears. My exposition of Eliot's critique of contemporary culture and its bourgeois liberal ideology will be developed through three interrelated areas of ascending specificity: fundamental philosophical presuppositions, the structure of society and the individual self, and finally the specific role of art in culture and in the critique of culture. I begin then with Eliot's critique of the philosophy behind bourgeois liberal culture.

II

1. One of the most general philosophical attitudes which Eliot sees and criticizes as fundamental to liberal ideology is its privileging of the individual subject. This bias toward the subject as the ultimate source and authority of truth can be traced back to the father of modern philosophy--Descartes. Eliot in his unpublished Clark Lectures was quick to identify and condemn him as originating "the disintegration of the intellect" of Western civilization by diverting "human inquiry from ontology to psychology."[2] Descartes' innovative notion was that what one really or most truly knows is not the objects of the world but one's ideas

---

2. Eliot's unpublished Clark Lectures were delivered at Trinity College, Cambridge, 1926 under the title *On the Metaphysical Poetry of the Seventeenth Century with special reference to Donne, Crashaw, and Cowley*. The typescript is in Kings College Library, Cambridge. In this paragraph I cite and paraphrase from the title page and pages 38-41, 44, 49, 51.

of those objects, and that therefore to study the world one must first and foremost study the contents and faculties of one's mind. Eliot lamented this move for having undermined the idea of a shared external world and the *"sensus communis"* of its dwellers which had previously helped unite Western civilization and make its art and language more powerful. With the loss of the shared objective world, "mankind suddenly retires into its several skulls"; the individual becomes the center of truth and reality, and thus ontology is superseded by what Eliot calls the "pseudo-science of epistemology" based on psychology. He regards this as a philosophical revolution more radical and momentous than Kant's later Copernican revolution, and one which "gave rise to the whole pseudo-science of epistemology which has haunted the . . . last three hundred years" of Western philosophy, including Kant. Eliot, moreover, notes that Locke (one of the fathers of liberalism) played a central role in continuing and reinforcing this subject-orientated epistemological bias with its representational theory of knowledge.

Eliot's critique of the Cartesian-inspired and liberal-supported interiorization of thought and subjectivization of authority was not confined to his Clark Lectures, but resounds throughout his critical corpus. Perhaps the most striking example is his sarcastic diatribe against Middleton Murry's faith in "the Inner Voice" of the individual as superior to the shared principles of tradition or to any "spiritual authority outside the individual" (SE 17-18). It is not surprising but most noteworthy that in denouncing the Inner Voice he concludes by giving it the name of "Whiggery" which is but a synonym for liberalism (SE 18). What also should be noted is Eliot's discomfort with the "inner/outer" dichotomy, a distinction basic to the Cartesian program of interiority, but one which Eliot regarded as philosophically invalid in any principled sense ("the distinction between inner and outer, which makes the epistemologist's capital, cannot stand . . ." [KE 138]). Indeed when he here employs it for the pragmatic purpose of polemics he construes in an almost transparently aporetic manner: "If you find that you have to imagine it as outside, then it is outside" (SE 15); a definition of outside that paradoxically relies on the inner voice of one's imagination.

The privileging of subject-based, psychologistic epistemology over ontology which Eliot so mourned has been severely challenged this century by thinkers like Heidegger and Gadamer who insist that our Being-in-the-world is always already presupposed in any thinking that we do, and by Wittgenstein who argues that to think any thoughts in any language pre-supposes for its very intelligibility our living in a social and prac-tical context, our inhabiting some form of life. Moreover, other (often Hegelianly inspired) contemporary philosophers have grown increasingly dissatisfied with the Cartesian view of the external world as mere lifeless and totally mechanical material extension. Such a view confines all spirituality to the psychology of the individual; spirituality becomes identified with personal subjectivity, and the sense of objective spirit and purpose in the world is lost. The further effect of this process of "the disen-chantment of the world" and the privatization of spirituality has been to make man feel increasingly alien in his natural and social world and thus ever more contemptuously manipulative and destructive of that world which is his only home (Adorno, *Dialectic of Enlightenment* 3). It has even made him feel alien in his own body and its feelings and senses which are identified with materiality.

     This brutal Cartesian division and impoverishing mentalization of man leads directly into the dissociation of sen-sibility that Eliot so sharply and repeatedly criticized. Further, the Cartesian privatization of spirituality and disenchantment of the world entails that the only conceivable meanings and values are those projected from the desires of individual psyches, a view which promotes a society torn by the war of subjective wills struggling to assert their private valuations rather than a com-munity united by a common ethos and shared set of values. We shall return at the end of this section to the dissociation of sen-sibility and dissociation of community, which Eliot (like Adorno) saw as deeply interconnected.

     What I want here to reiterate is that Eliot's condem-nation and challenge of Cartesian interiority--the privatization of thought and the subjectivization of knowledge and authority--is shared by the most powerful and progressive currents in con-temporary philosophy, currents as diverse as the Hegelian Marxism of Adorno, the pragmatist naturalism of Dewey, the ontological hermeneutics of Heidegger and Gadamer, and the historicist, culturally-sensitive linguistic philosophy of the later Wittgenstein. All these thinkers insist on the essential social and historical grounding of all human thought and experience. This theme, as I have lengthily argued in *T. S. Eliot and the Philoso-phy of Criticism*, is at the core of Eliot's thematization and mature theory of tradition--a notion whose very essence is socio-historicality.[3]

    Tradition for the mature Eliot is not the narrowly aesthetic and transcendent set of artistic monuments of "Tradition and the Individual Talent" which only the elite can attain through a "great labour" of "consciousness" (SE 4, 6). It is rather that full-bodied and immanent matrix in which we move and which we have grasped or imbibed largely unconsciously, but which prestructures our activity, experience and understanding of the world:

> What I mean by tradition involves all those habitual actions, habits and customs, from the most significant religious rite to our conventional way of greeting a stranger, which represent the blood kinship of "the same people living in the same place.". . . [A] *tradition* is rather a way of feeling and acting which characterises a group throughout generations; and . . . it must largely be, or . . . many of the elements in it must be, unconscious. (ASG 18, 31)

Eliot says essentially the same thing about culture (his later and perhaps less conservatively "loaded" term for tradition). It is not limited to high culture, which Eliot describes as simply more specialized and "more conscious culture" but includes the whole spectrum of the societal community's activities and thus can only be adequately defined or understood "in the pattern of the society as a whole" (CC 121, 95). He takes admirable care, as do contemporary sociologists of culture like Bordieu, to place the realm of individual high culture into the larger anthropological framework of a society's culture as a whole, insisting that we cannot understand the former without the latter.[4] Moreover, Eliot realizes that since culture forms the structural matrix of our experience or way of life, it is not something that can be wholly grasped and consciously controlled: "Culture can never be wholly conscious--there is always more to it than we are conscious of; and it cannot be planned because it is also the unconscious background of all our planning" including "the unconscious assumptions upon which we conduct the whole of our lives" (CC 170; TCC 76). Culture is a socially generated and historically structuring structure which inhabits and informs our most private thoughts and gives them a language without which they could not be articulated or thought. It therefore shows the folly of the isolated Cartesian *cogito*. Tradition or culture, then,

3. See chapter seven of that book, which is devoted to an analysis of the concept of tradition and where the philosophical views of Gadamer, Wittgenstein, and the pragmatists are related in detail to Eliot's theory of tradition.
4. See Pierre Bourdieu, *Distinction: A Social Critique of the Judgment of Taste*. Bourdieu's views are related to Eliot's theory of tradition and culture in *T. S. Eliot and the Philosophy of Criticism* 187.

is the Eliotic counterpart of a Heideggerian sense of Being-in-the-world or a Wittgensteinian inhabiting a form of life, though it is perhaps closest to the concept of tradition that Gadamer has recently made so influential in hermeneutics. In his attack on Cartesian epistemology and recognition of the necessary shared socio-historical context of thinking, Eliot joins ranks with some of the most progressive currents in contemporary philosophy.

2. Closely (though seemingly paradoxically) connected with the Cartesian project of knowing the world by examining individual consciousness and relying on the subject's reason and its capacity for clear and distinct ideas is the scientifico-philosophical ideal of knowledge of the world as it really is in itself independent from any particular human perspective or biased perception of it, the goal of attaining a perfect God's-eye view of the world free from human prejudice and distortion. The whole method and dynamic of Cartesian doubt and cognitive recovery is based on a clear separation between things as we see them (our ideas in our mind) and things as they really are (which our ideas can either accurately or inaccurately represent). For Descartes as for Galileo and most of modern science, the true world was not that grasped by the individual's senses but that which could be measured and explained by God's mathematical laws revealed by impersonal, universal reason. In short, we have here a picture of representational epistemology which has held us captive for centuries--a picture of human knowledge as a mirroring correspondence of reality where we aim to transcend all the socio-historical, personal, and even physiological contexts of our perception to see things with a perfectly pure mirroring gaze. What cannot detach itself from the personal context or be quantifiable or governed by mathematical law is relegated from the realm of knowledge and consigned to mere feeling or attitude. Fact is dirempted from value, and the latter is seen as essentially subjective, a matter of mere individual preference. This scientistic view of knowledge as mirroring correspondence, so basic to the philosophy of liberalism, was firmly rejected by Eliot, though for a brief and early period he toyed with such an ideal of pure knowledge as absolute impersonal correspondence to the real, advocating "a pure contemplation from which all the accidents of personal emotion are removed; thus we aim to see the object as it really is . . ." (SW 14-15).

Eliot, as I have elsewhere shown, quickly came to see the implausibility and gainlessness of the scientistic correspondence model of knowledge, and took a hermeneutical turn, insisting that our understanding must always be conditioned and limited by our concrete historical situation (see Shusterman 41-76, 107-33). We are all limited, by circumstances if not by capacity" (TCC 104). "[E]very effort to formulate the common element is limited by the limitations of particular men in particular places and at particular times" (UPUC 135). For this reason, he held that "pure literature is a chimera of sensation" (*Criterion* 3-4) and that pure artistic appreciation devoid of relationship to the socio-historical context and attitudes of the reader is an equally chimerical "abstraction" or "figment" (SE 231, UPUC 101). There is no perspectiveless knowledge, and to criticize at all "one must criticize from some point of view" (SE 96). And he later continued to maintain that "[we] have to see literature through our own temperament in order to see it at all, though our vision is always partial and our judgment is always prejudiced" ("Experiment in Criticism" 225).

Eliot, like Gadamer, does not mourn the fact that all our thinking is socio-historically conditioned and that it thus proceeds from basic cognitive prejudices. He instead recognizes how such prejudices provide the necessary directedness to the world and social context in which we must cope. The factoring out of the fruitful from the baneful prejudices is for Eliot (and Gadamer) the function of tradition and the tradition-informed but open-minded practical intelligence which must appropriate and interpret tradition in changing circumstances. Thus instead of the pure gaze and ideal of correspondence posited by the ideology of science, Eliot opted for a model of objectivity as consensus or shared belief which is implicit in his notion of tradition and his idea of the "common pursuit of true judgement." In his grasp of objectivity as constituted by solidarity and consensus, Eliot not only registers his debt to the community oriented pragmatism of Peirce and Royce but anticipates such contemporary approaches as Rorty's and Gadamer's.

Moreover, we must also note that his aim of consensus was later wisely tempered by an insistence on the tolerance of difference--that though we want some basic underlying unity we do not want an oppressive uniformity.[5] Here Eliot shows

---

5. Later, in *The Idea of a Christian Society*, Eliot continues to admit a secular alternative to Christianity as a possible source of cultural, societal regeneration from the negativity and fragmentation of liberalism: "My thesis has been, simply, that a liberalized or negative condition of society must either proceed into a gradual decline of which we can see no end, or (whether as a result of catastrophe or not) reform itself into a positive shape which is likely to be effectively secular. . . . But unless we are content with the prospect of one or the other of these issues, the only possibility left is that of a positive Christian society" (CC 20).

It is worth noting that Eliot later went so far as to recognize that class revolution might be necessary and justified for the regeneration of society, This could occur when "the ruling class" loses touch with the "essential interests" of society so that social "harmony" is "broken." "Or the social circum-

himself aware of another theme of contemporary cultural theory--the problem of respect for the Other and her discourse. In *Notes towards the Definition of Culture* Eliot expresses this most pointedly in his concern for and defense of weaker regional cultures and Third World cultures (both of which he terms "satellite" cultures) in the face of Western cultural imperialism (CC 127-29, 137-40). He was extremely worried, as was Adorno, of bureaucratic technocratic efforts towards the homogenization of culture advocated in the name of world unity, but more likely to result in an oppressive and lifeless uniformity. One such world-systematizing, totalizing ideology is that of science and technology.

3. In recognizing that there are no perspectiveless perspectives, that even science works within a socio-historical context and horizon of which it is often unaware, Eliot was bravely critical of science and its limitations at a time when it was still most unfashionable to be so. Before Hiroshima, before our growing sense of the social and ecological destruction caused by technological science, in an age where science was blindly worshiped by our liberal culture which regarded it as the unambiguous salvation of humankind and the sole key to all of its problems, Eliot spoke out against our unhealthy "exaggerated devotion to 'science' " ("Religion Without Humanism" 108).

The view that science stands pure, above and detached from the social conditions and human vicissitudes of inquiry, is given little credence by today's philosophers of science. But it was more or less unquestioned dogma when Eliot challenged it by asserting science's insufficiency and need to be guided by wisdom. Recognizing that science is not free from ideology and is itself an ideology which abstracts from the whole of the real, he warned that "practitioners of both political and economic science in their very effort to be scientific, to limit precisely, that is, the field of their activity, make assumptions which they are not only not entitled to make, but which they are not always conscious of making" (EAM 118). He moreover realized that none of us, not even the hard-nosed scientist, could "get on for one moment without believing *anything* except the 'hows' of science" ("Literature, Science, and Dogma" 242). Indeed, the very pursuit of science cannot exclusively rely on verified scientific knowledge and method. For any scientific theory or hypothesis needs to be interpreted into the real-world or laboratory

stances may alter, through economic or other developments, so that the centre of power shifts, or should shift, to another class. History has found various methods of dealing with a ruling class, when such a situation has arisen." These remarks are from a letter Eliot wrote in August 1943, which is reproduced in part in Roger Kojecky, *T. S. Eliot's Social Criticism* 191.

conditions for it to be tested and confirmed; and the determining of such conditions and assessment of confirmational testing require more than is given by the theory or by strict scientific method. Thus, philosophers of science like Putnam and Polanyi contend that even the exact science "typically depends on unformalized practical knowledge," on tacit socially acquired skills and sentiments, and that the scientist must *"rely on his human wisdom"* (Putnam 72-73).

4. Eliot, of course, was less concerned with science itself than with the society and liberal ideology which looked to it for all the answers. Here especially he felt that the liberal faith in science and in individual preferences was not enough. We cannot simply and uncritically accept the contingent, unexamined, and perhaps largely irrational hopes and wishes of all individuals as equally valid and then rely on science (political and technological) as a means to adjust them to a satisfactory optimum. For some of those unquestioned hopes are indeed a hopeless product of misinformation and manipulation. Social theory and reform must be critical and deal with values; it must face "the question: what is the good life?" and achieve some measure of ethical wisdom before it moves on to social engineering (EAM 119). "A really satisfactory working philosophy of social action, as distinct from devices for getting ourselves out of a hole at the moment, requires not merely science but wisdom"; and "wisdom, including political wisdom, can neither be abstracted to a science nor reduced to a dodge" (EAM 121).

What Eliot perhaps most greatly laments here is the sharp division of political and social theory from ethical thought and practice in our contemporary liberal culture, a division which is reinforced in our educational institutions where scientific "objective" facts are rigidly separated and isolated from human values and emotions which are considered to be utterly and irremediably subjective or private:

> The modern world separates the intellect and the emotions. What can be reduced to a science, in its narrow conception of 'science', . . . a limited and technical material, it respects; the rest may be a waste of uncontrolled behavior and immature emotion. (EAM 121)

Instead Eliot urges "that the classical conception of wisdom be restored," an idea of Aristotelian *phronesis* which is more than the cold, technical instrumental reason of "means" that Adorno so criticizes, but rather treats both means and ends, both action and feeling. It is a practical wisdom which involves more than theoretical truth and even more than action but also the development of character and the education and discipline of the emotions. For without such ethical development, "a moral conversion" involving "the discipline and training of emotion," the knowledge of social truths and mastery of techniques of social engineering cannot achieve true social regeneration. Eliot thought that such emotional discipline was so difficult for the modern mind as to be "only obtainable through dogmatic religion" ("Religion Without Humanism" 110). This, in key part, is Eliot's pragmatist justification for rejecting secular liberalism for a religious perspective which offers a definite, time-tested vision of the good life and a solid, reinforcing community and practice of its pursuit. The rejoinder of today's secular pragmatist is that dogmatic religion has been too dead to too many for too long to make it believable and in any way effective for ethical and social regeneration. We either need a more living and compelling myth or meta-narrative, or need to make do without any mythical support whatever in forging a better society and way of life.

Eliot, we should note, was well aware of these options. He felt that liberal individualism had so deeply fragmented our sense of community that we needed some communal myth to bind us together in a spirit of common social and individual regeneration. But he recognized that Marxism was very well-positioned and well-equipped to provide the needed binding narrative myth and utopian vision, which could appeal to both the intellectual and the common man. "The great merit of Communism is the same as one merit of the Catholic Church, that there is something in it which minds on every level can grasp. . . . Communism has what is now called a 'myth' " ("Commentary" [1933] 644). Had Eliot been a generation younger and still alive today, who knows if he would not have seen Marxism as a more promising and effective tool than Catholicism for a restitution of the deep sense of community and collective consciousness which both he and contemporary Marxists condemn liberalism for destroying?

What is clear is that he and Adorno think very little of the pseudo-individualism that bourgeois liberal ideology presents as perhaps its highest value and achievement. Adorno, like Eliot, condemns liberalism's view of intelligence as mere instrumental reason, advocating instead something like *phronesis*, an idea of a substantive reason (closer to *Vernunft* than to *Verstand*) that critically deals with values, ends, and feelings, and is morally informed and guided (see *Dialectic of Enlightenment* 3-42, 81-96). "Intelligence is a moral category. The separation of feeling and understanding . . . hypostasizes the dismemberment of man into functions. . . . It is rather for philosophy to seek, in the opposition of feeling and understanding, their--precisely moral-- unity" (*Minima Moralia* 197-98). We find in these remarks of Adorno an echo of Eliot's complaint against the modern separa- tion of intellect from emotions and values, which returns us to the theme of the dissociation of sensibility, a central theme shared by Eliot and Adorno and one that has clear social roots and implications.

5. When Eliot first launched this theme in "The Metaphysical Poets" (1921), he wrote: "In the seventeenth cen- tury a dissociation of sensibility set in, from which we have never recovered," a dissociation of thought from feeling (SE 247). While poets like Donne and Herbert could still "feel their thought as immediately as the odour of a rose" and express their feeling with lucid intellect, later poets could not fuse thought and feeling together: "they thought and felt by fits, unbalanced" (SE 247-48). Descartes, of course, was *the* philosopher of the seventeenth century, and, as we have already seen, in the Clark lectures of 1926 Eliot later blamed him specifically for originat- ing the split. Descartes not only insisted on the unreliability and fallaciousness of the senses, but he went further to equate human identity with thought. Through the *cogito* by which he proves his existence, he defines himself in "Meditation I" as essentially "a thinking thing"; and in "Meditation VI" he more explicitly argues for a complete dualism of mind and body, where human identity is identified with (since inconceivable without) mind, while the body is regarded as a contingent, often misleading, though closely connected appendage. The result of this bifurcation of the intellect from the bodily senses is that feelings and emotions, because of their association with the body, get relegated to inferior and irrational status; while ratio- nality becomes wholly disembodied and equated with only the abstractly logical and mathematical.

But Cartesian dualism is not the only source of mod- ern dissociation of sensibility. Eliot and Adorno both trace it to the Western individualism and functional division of labor. This too, as I earlier suggested, can to some extent be traced to Descartes--his privileging the individual subject over society and its cultural tradition as the axiomatic starting point of all inquiry and the standard of authority; and his division of the human individual into a bodily machine and a rationally thinking mind. The result of four centuries of increasingly individualist liberal ideology is that we have lost our sense of communal wholeness, our "natural collective consciousness" and "unconscious values" (CC 12, 14). Our society has become deeply and complexly fragmented into very poorly integrated functions and groups. The Cartesian division of thinking mind and bodily machine has been reified into a society of privileged managerial thinkers for whom the idea of manual labor is an insult and a contrasted mass of laborers who are treated as the unthinking machines which dictate their lives and to which they are compelled to assimilate their rhythms and psychic energies.

Even on the individual level, the complex functional division of modern life makes it difficult to maintain a satisfyingly integrated sense of self as one tries to adjust the rhythms and demands of being an impersonally efficient check-out cashier at the A&P, a patiently caring lover and mother, and a Ph.D. student of literature struggling to find a route to material security free from alienated labor. Eliot recognizes the intimate link between the dissociation of individual sensibility and that of our world, the fragmentation of self and society:

> I believe that at the present time the problem of the unification of the world and the problem of the unification of the individual, are in the end one and the same problem; and that the solution of one is the solution of the other. Analytical psychology . . . can do little except produce monsters; for it is attempting to produce unified individuals in a world without unity; the social, political, and economic sciences can do little, for they are attempting to produce the great society with an aggregration of human beings who are not units but merely bundles of incoherent impulses and beliefs. ("Religion Without Humanism" 112)

Adorno repeatedly makes the same connection between personal and social fragmentation, and, like Eliot, sees this dissociation of sensibility, issuing in lifeless thought and cloying, unintelligent artistic sentimentality:

> The assumption that thought profits from the decay of the emotions, or even that it remains unaffected, is itself an expression of the process of stupefaction. The social division of labor recoils on man. . . . The faculties, having developed through interaction, atrophy once they are severed from each other. . . .The socialization of mind keeps mind boxed in . . . as long as society is itself imprisoned. (*Minima Moralia* 122) One of the trivial triumphs of philistinism derives from the futile exercise of sorting out feeling and knowing. . . . This perspective is a distorted reflex of . . . the division of labor, a trend which has left its imprint even in subjectivity. . . . Modes of response which we subsume under the concept of feeling turn into enclaves of futile sentimentality as soon as they lose their relation to thinking. . . . The deadly dichotomization of

emotion and thought is a historical result that can be undone.
(*Aesthetic Theory* 454-55)

To speak, as Eliot and Adorno do, of the fragmenta-
tion of the self and its divided sensibility as "a historical result"
is to recognize the self as as social product, now the bitter, withered fruit of liberal individualism. Let us now turn more specifically to Eliot's critique of this phenomenon.

III

Bourgeois liberal individualism represents and congratulates
itself as a victory of emancipation toward the full autonomy of
individual human agents and an incipient promise of their happiness through the guarantee of their freedom to pursue it in
whatever form they see fit. Even critics of liberalism must admit
that this is far from a total misrepresentation. True emancipatory progress has been made by the bourgeois liberal revolution
in freeing individuals from the yoke of feudalism and oppressive
ecclesiastical institutions. But what critics like Adorno and Eliot
argue is that such gains of individual freedom have been largely
offset by serious losses of which liberal apologists are blithely
unaware but which exact from us members of liberal society a
painful price.
        It is worth noting and commending that Eliot does
not essentially base his critique of liberal ideology on the
assumption of the infallible truth of Christian dogma. His argument is not, as it were, that such happiness as secular liberalism
promises is paltry compared to the bliss of the hereafter and
constitutes both a threat to achieving that bliss and a departure
from allegiance to Church values presumed to have transcendental privilege. Instead Eliot provides a powerful imminent or
deconstructive critique by showing how liberalism is riven by
contradiction, does not really provide what it pretends to, and
thus fails by its own standards.
        1. The first point of critique is that liberal individu-
alism's promise of happiness has proven illusory. The dissolving
of societal bonds and overriding values to promote the private
pursuit of individual happiness has issued in a world of haplessly
lonely and unrewarded pleasure-seekers. The painful isolation
and fragmentation of modern individualist society is expressed
perhaps most powerfully in Eliot's verse, which so often portrays
a lonely, alienated individual desperately unhappy and desperately seeking to make real human contact, achieve real commu-

nity in a social world which neither provides it nor seems to allow it. We typically find either figures of isolation or arbitrary, lumpen aggregrates--not true, integrated groups: We encounter a lone whore in a lunar nightscape ("Rhapsody on a Windy Night"), a lonely aging socialite starving for friendship ("Portrait of a Lady"), an exotic collection of rootless cosmopolitans inhabiting the same house ("Gerontion"), a bunch of old hags "[g]athering fuel in vacant lots" ("Preludes" [CPP 13]), "a crowd" flowing over London Bridge (*The Waste Land*). Even the apparent social groups and connections are portrayed as artificial and elusive or illusory--like the mechanically peripatetic women talking of Michelangelo in "Prufrock" or the tawdry and meaningless coupling of the lonely typist and "the young man carbuncular" in *The Waste Land*.

Similarly in his prose, Eliot mourns the loss of community and solidarity induced by liberal individualism's "destroying traditional social habits of the people, by dissolving their natural collective consciousness into individual constituents" (CC 12). This loss of collective habits of feeling, action, and thinking is expressed not only in the unhappy, lonely alienation of the individual and in the social and political fragmentation and confusion he must deal with. It further issues in a loss of common meanings which renders language too hollow and vague for good prose or great poetry which, to achieve classic status, requires both "a common style" of language and "a community of taste" (OPP 57).

Eliot, moreover, provides an explanation of why liberalism's promise of happiness has failed: the majority of individuals are neither intelligent enough nor sufficiently self-reflective and self-critical to know what is good for them, to distinguish between what they want or think they want and what will really make them happy. Liberalism's doctrine that every individual can and should determine his own values and goals too often amounts to "licensing the opinion of the most foolish" (CC 12), with dire results for those foolish individuals and for society at large. Eliot explicitly addresses the "liberal-minded" faith "that if everybody says what he likes and does what he likes, things will somehow, by some automatic compensation and adjustment, come right in the end. " 'Let everything be tried', they say, 'and if it is a mistake, then we shall learn by experience' " (EAM 107). The problem which Eliot perceptively sees in this argument is that we are finite; our time for experiment is limited; our memory of past experience is fallible and fading; and our willingness "to learn ... from the experience of ...

elders" and past generations is increasingly diminishing (EAM 107-08). Life is not a controlled laboratory, and a bad experiment can be irremediably fatal.

2. If liberalism errs "in assuming that a majority of natural and unregenerate men is likely to want the right things" (EAM 141), Eliot also thinks it gravely errs in assuming that modern individuals are really as individual and autonomous as they like to think they are and that truth will emerge from an evolutionary struggle of truly independent thinking. "These liberals are convinced that only by what is called unrestrained individualism, will truth ever emerge. Ideas, views of life, they think, issue distinct from the independent heads, and in consequence of their knocking violently against each other, the fittest survive, and truth rises triumphant" (EAM 108).

The problem here is not so much "that the world of separate individuals is undesirable; it is simply that this world does not exist" (EAM 108-09). Modern life, as Adorno similarly insists, has become so pervasively programmed and administered by technocratic bureaucracy, the publishing and entertainment industry, and advertising that the individual is relentlessly exposed and assimilated into "a mass movement."[6] The public is "so helplessly exposed to the influences of its own time ... [that] it is more difficult to-day to be an individual than it ever was before" (EAM 109). The ideology of liberal individualism masks the conformist mob mentality of modern society, a mask which Eliot mordantly penetrates in his critique of liberalism's privileged "inner voice" of individuality: "The possessors of the inner voice ride ten in a compartment to a football match at Swansea, listening to the inner voice, which breathes the eternal message of vanity, fear, and lust" (SE 16). Adorno supplies the same savage attack on the pretensions of modern individualism, but even more pithily: "In many people it is already an impertinence to say 'I' " (*Minima Moralia* 50).

Both Eliot and Adorno see free-market capitalism, industrialization, and the related cult of "materialistic efficiency" and "mass suggestion" through advertising as largely responsible for undermining real individuality and independent thought. For Eliot "the tendency of unlimited industrialism is to create bodies of men and women--of all classes--detached from tradition, alienated from religion, and susceptible to mass sug-

---

6. Adorno's most concentrated critical analysis of the culture industry of entertainment and advertising is in the chapter with that title in *Dialectic of Enlightenment*. Eliot notes that through the secular totalizing bureaucracy of *étatisme* and the similarly regimenting and totalizing effects of industrialization, the treasured liberal "domain of 'private life' becomes smaller and smaller, and may eventually disappear altogether" (CC 14-15).

gestion: in other words, a mob. And a mob will be no less a mob if it is well fed, well clothed, well housed, and well disciplined" (CC 17). Already in his 1939 warnings of liberal society's smoothly seductive "regimentation and conformity, . . . puritanism of a hygienic morality in the interest of efficiency; uniformity of opinion through propaganda" which includes advertising and the art which "flatters the official doctrines of the time" (CC 18), Eliot was anticipating the consumer conformism of the fifties and our present yuppie age.[7] He sensed, well before Adorno, that today's individual owes his identity "to the forms of political economy, particularly to those of the urban market. . . . The individual mirrors in his individuation the preordained social laws of exploitation, however mediated" (*Minima Moralia* 148).

Though Adorno is ready to admit "reactionary criticism's . . . insight into the decay of individuality and the crisis of society," he attacks it for seeing these evils as the responsibility and failure of "the individual"; for thinking the problem is simply that today's individuals suffer from "neurotic weakness" and "mechanical emptiness" while those of past ages had greater strength and substance. In short, Adorno chides reactionary critique for not recognizing that it is not the individual but the ideological idolatry of individualism and the socially fragmenting manner of individuation which are primarily to blame. But Eliot can in no way be accused of this failure "to criticize the social *principium individuationis*" (*Minima Moralia* 149). He recognizes as much as Adorno that the individual self is not a foundational given but a social construct, "the result of the social division of the social process" (*Minima Moralia* 153). As early as his doctoral thesis Eliot asserted that the self and its most private thoughts could only be defined, identified, and articulated in terms of a common social world constituting a "community of meaning" that is "ultimately practical" in purpose (KE 161). "I only know myself in contrast to a world" and other selves or "finites centres" who collaborate to construct it (KE 152, 146).

Moreover, no less than Marxist thinkers, Eliot recognized that as the self was molded by society, "society [itself] is very deeply affected morally and spiritually by material conditions, even by a machinery which it has constructed" (EAM 140); and that, in Adorno's words, the liberal man's pursuit of

---

7. Eliot's critique of liberalism throughout the thirties (and later) must not be read as an endorsement of any sort of Fascism, which he most strongly deplored for its very similar "totalitarian worldliness." Indeed, Eliot remarks that he was stimulated to write *The Idea of a Christian Society* in 1938 out of his opposition to Hitler and his perception of England's moral weakness in the 1938 appeasement, a weakness he thought symptomatic of great social and cultural decay. See CC 16, 50-51.

freedom through the denial of all traditional social bonds and community roots, "only robs him of the strength for freedom" (*Minima Moralia* 149, 153-54).[8] For those traditional links of family, region, community, and culture are what serve to give an individual a meaningful differentiating substance so that he is not simply reduced to an integer of mass marketing and political regimentation. Someone deprived of those enduring social modes of self-definition is someone whose only values are those that today's admen proclaim are the real ones; someone who having lost his roots fears losing his very self and social status if he does not conform and keep up to date with the fashions and life-styles of late-capitalist consumerism. In a fairly obvious sense, such a someone is a nobody. It was this fear of the dehumanizing homogenization and totalization of society into an unstructured, ungrounded mass market and mass politic, one that could be too easily and violently manipulated, which made Eliot think that a traditional class society might be better than the continuing disintegration of liberal individualist society into an unsocial mass of non-individuals.

IV

In his critique of bourgeois liberalism's complacent pseudo-individualism and its smug conviction of perpetual improvement and progress, which blinds and deprives it of the sources and resources of older but still fruitful traditions, Eliot aims at regenerating a greater sense of community not only in the present but with our past. Art can provide an invaluable weapon for such a cultural critique. It serves to criticize present assumptions and social relations, partly by portraying past alternatives. Moreover, as the great communicator affording shared imaginative experience, art helps connect us to each other and to our past. I shall conclude this paper on Eliot's cultural criticism by briefly considering his views on the cultural functions and dangers of art which connect him once again with the Marxian cultural criticism of Adorno.

      1. Since Eliot is too often falsely maligned for being narrowly formalist and aestheticist about literature, it is impor-

---

8. "Not only is the self entwined in society; it owes society its existence in the most literal sense. All its content comes from society, or at any rate from its relation to the object. It grows richer the more freely it develops and reflects this relation, while it is limited, impoverished, and reduced by the separation and hardening that it lays claim to as an origin. Attempts like Kierkegaard's, in which the individual seeks abundance by retreat within himself, did not by accident end up in the sacrifice of the individual" (*Minima Moralia* 154).

tant to stress at the outset that he was very much alive to what Adorno similarly recognized as "the social essence of art" (*Aesthetic Theory* 20, 320). In insisting that major developments in art and criticism are largely "due to elements which enter from the outside," most especially "social changes" (UPUC 119, 11), Eliot recognizes with Adorno that social influences and contents are sedimented in and can be read from the very form of art.[9] Moreover, both recognize that the process of expression and sedimentation of social forces and content in the forms of art is not an instantaneous or fully willed and conscious one; and perhaps cannot be such if the expression is to be deep, genuine, original, and of enduring aesthetic value. For society itself, even in frenzied modern times, does not change in such an immediate and conscious way.

2. This introduces another common theme of Eliot and Adorno: the ardent and scathing critique of modern culture's worship of the superficially new. The theme in Eliot is most familiar from his advocacy of a deep common tradition over attention-seeking individual innovation in "Tradition and the Individual Talent"; but it runs throughout his work. Moreover, it is crucial to insist that Eliot was not against change, novelty, and artistic revolution *per se*, just against their willed and artificial manufacture for their own sake, and the tendency of their worship to issue in shallow imposters. Though he condemned the modern cult of artistic individuality (most viciously in *After Strange Gods*) and rejected mere surface "novelty as a sufficient criterion of excellence" (TCC 152), Eliot welcomed "the new (the really new) work of art," recognizing that if "it would not be new, . . .[it] would not therefore be a work of art" (SE 5). He similarly saw the need for "revolutionary theories" to supply "the violent stimulus of novelty" when a tradition became crustily complacent, since he realized that we must not "associate tradition with the unmovable"; for the word itself implies movement. Tradition cannot mean standing still (ASG 19, 25).

Eliot links the modern idolatry of artistic individuality and novelty to the decay of self and society which we have earlier traced. The same loss of our social sense of self through a liberal ideology that glorified our individuality has put us ago-

---

9. Eliot writes, for example: "Such changes as that from the epic poem composed to be recited to the epic poem composed to be read, or that which put an end to the popular ballad are inseparable from social changes on a vast scale, such changes as have always taken place and always will" (UPUC 11). And later, more globally: "Any radical change in poetic form is likely to be the symptom of some very much deeper change in the society and in the individual" (UPUC 66-67). It is worth noting that Eliot cites with approbation Trotsky's views on the deep dependence of art on social forces (UPUC 128). Cf. Adorno's *Aesthetic Theory* 298.

nizingly on the spot and at a loss to define that individuality which was once very substantively defined and integrated through meaningful social relations. Having lost a sense of themselves and the communal audience they once served, artists are driven to fashion and assert some "particularist" individuality to call attention to their work.[10] Similarly, with the loss of traditional social community, which involves community with the past, the artist is forced to seek only novelty which tends to condemn his search to "the ephemeral." For "the novelty of anything that is merely new produces only momentary shock: the same work will not produce the same shock twice, but must be followed by something newer" (TCC 152).

Adorno's savage condemnation of our worship of the superficially new is likewise connected with the liberal dissolution of communal society that ultimately results in the disintegration of the self. But he highlights more than Eliot the industrial and economic machinery driving the frenzied rhythms of the modern quest for novelty which only issues in the disguised and unsatisfying repetition of the old:

> The cult of the new ... is a rebellion against the fact that there is no longer anything new. The never changing quality of machine-produced goods ... converts everything encountered into what always was, a fortuitous specimen of a species, the *doppel-ganger* of a model. ... The new, sought for its own sake, a kind of laboratory product, petrified into a conceptual scheme, becomes in its sudden apparition a compulsive return of the old, not unlike that in traumatic neuroses. ... The decomposition of the subject is consummated in his self-abandonment to an ever-changing sameness." (*Minima Moralia* 235-38)

Even the quest for novelty (and individuality) in art is explained neither by the creative essence of art or even by the romantic myth of creative genius but instead by the cold and relentless logic of consumer capitalism:

> The phenomenon of novelty is a historical product. In its original economic setting, novelty is that characteristic of consumer goods through which they are supposed to set themselves off from the self-same aggregate supply, stimulating consumer decisions subject to the needs of capital. As soon as ... capital stops offering something new, it is going to lose ground in the competitive struggle. Art has appropriated this economic strategy. (*Aesthetic Theory* 31)

---

10. Eliot writes that a "tradition, simply by its influence upon the environment in which the poet develops, will tend to restrict eccentricity to manageable limits: but it is not even by the lack of this restraining influence that the absence of tradition is most deplorable. What is disastrous is that the writer should deliberately give rein to his 'individuality' that he should cultivate his differences from others; and that his readers should cherish the author ... because of them" (ASG 35; see also 68).

What, for Adorno, has more fully appropriated this strategy and has thereby thrived to hypertrophic dimensions is the so-called "culture industry" of low brow art and popular entertainment, whose commercialism and enormous influence have worked to undermine art's character while overwhelming its appeal and posture of relative autonomy.

But for all their recognition that art was corruptible and was indeed being corrupted by the corruptions of our socio-economic world, Eliot and Adorno still thought that art--in the form of high art rather than the culture industry's commercial entertainment--remains the greatest source of wisdom, an invaluable tool of critique, and one of our best hopes for spiri-tual growth and regeneration.[11] For high art resists more than anything else the pervasive logic of profit and materialistic effi-ciency. It is not aimed at the "box-office," at maximizing sales and profits, nor is it conceived and structured along guidelines determined by marketing research. The high artist of mod-ernism (a movement to which both Adorno and Eliot were dis-tinctly committed) will not lower his artistic standards just to cater or pander to the taste of the masses, even if he deeply hopes, as did Eliot, that such an audience might find satisfaction in his art.[12] For pandering to common taste and expectations is to give up art's crucial critical and emancipatory role which involves challenging our taste and presumptions, and instead to accept condescendingly that the general populace is simply and irremediably unfit for anything better or more difficult: that they deserve no better than what they have been socially constrained to expect or desire.

Eliot like Adorno reluctantly recognized the value of a cultural and artistic elite and "their labour in developing human sensibility, their labour in developing new forms of expression and new critical views of life and society" though he mourned that they were increasingly cut off from the general public, and thus that "commercial literature will continue to flourish and to pander, more and more severed from real litera-ture" ("Commentary" [1932] 678). But he would defend high art with Adorno's rejoinder: "The elitist segregation of the avant-

---

11. This point is argued in considerable detail in chapter six of *T. S. Eliot and the Philosophy of Criti-cism*, and in "Aesthetics, Ideology, and the Defense of Art," in B. Dziemidok and W. Truitt (eds.), *Art as a Social Phenomenon*, forthcoming from Haven.

12. Eliot felt that any poet would like to reach "as large and miscellaneous an audience as possible," though he should not achieve this by pandering compromise of his art. Indeed he asserts: "I myself should like an audience which could neither read nor write" (UPUC 146). Moreover, it is worth noting that both he and Adorno distinguish between genuine traditional popular art that is a deep expression of and response to the life of the people and the more modern and manipulatively commercial art of the culture industry. Both of them express an approbation of "music-hall" art (UPUC 148; *Aesthetic Theory* 156)

garde is not art's fault but society's. The unconscious aesthetic standards of the masses are precisely those society needs in order to perpetuate itself and its hold on the masses" (*Aesthetic Theory* 360).

Its strength to refuse and disappoint, even to shock the unconscious assumptions and expectations of its audience so as to stir them out of their complacency that everything is smoothly functioning, that it's business as usual, is one of the great values of high art. In its very distinction from reality, art represents a protest against and an alternative to a reality that we are programmed to feel is inevitable. And, for Eliot, much of the special value of past works of art is in showing us that other worlds with other values and assumptions are not only possible to conceive but were to a certain extent actually conceived and indeed in place. In this way art provides a route to self-knowledge, self-enlargement, and critical consciousness of our world. He therefore insists that "we also make the effort to enter those worlds of poetry in which we are alien" so that we can achieve a better and critical understanding of our own" ("Poetry and Propaganda" 602).

3. There are two more points where Eliot and Adorno see art as pointing a way to redemption by defying the unquestioned and virtually unconscious presumptions of our social ideology. First, in a world so totally committed to the idea of streamlined work and production, and to the means-end rationality and materialistic efficiency through which it is pursued, art with its essence of play and non-instrumental purposiveness represents a striking and challenging alternative. Both Eliot and Adorno emphasize art's character of play and its relative freedom from functioning for specific extrinsic ends. Eliot's remarks that "poetry is not a career, but a mug's game," "a superior amusement" (UPUC 147-48, SW viii), make this clear, as does his view that the poet should not pursue his work under the illusion that he is or must be performing the function of world-educator, world-legislator, or prophet.[13] And Adorno is even more explicit: play "is a necessary ingredient of art . . . [through which] art is able to atone for its illusory character" (*Aesthetic Theory* 57). "What lifts art above the context of immediate economic praxis and purposive behavior is the moment of play" (437).

---

13. Eliot criticizes the theories of Shelley, Arnold, and Richards with respect to their advocacy of such a grandiosely lofty function for literature in *The Use of Poetry and the Use of Criticism.* For a detailed account of Eliot's view of literature as a game, see my "T. S. Eliot on Reading: Pleasure, Games, and Wisdom," and chapter six of *T. S. Eliot and the Philosophy of Criticism.*

But again, this is not to say that art's eschewal of specific social aims to concentrate on its own play means that art fails to have and serve important functions. Indeed one such valuable social function is to be an implicit critique of society's relentless functionalism. As Adorno (who like Eliot deplores programmatically political art as propaganda) writes: "What is social about art is not its political stance, but its immanent dynamic in opposition to society. . . . If any social function can be ascribed to art at all, it is the function to have no function. By being different from the ungodly reality" of universal instrumentalism and profit-seeking, art negatively suggests the possibility of a more positive alternative (322). "To instrumentalize art [by giving it a specific function] is to undercut the opposition art mounts against instrumentalism" (*Aesthetic Theory* 442).[14]

4. In its integrated noncoercive form and its unity in variety, art represents yet another valuable contrast to the grim, fragmented, and brutally regimented social reality of our world. The polyphonic unity and harmony of a poem or musical work, where the individual words and notes seem freely to bond themselves together in the whole without thereby losing their specific value and identity is an implicit condemnation of the failure of our social union and a model of what ideal society could be. For Eliot, "it is a function of all art to give us some perception of an order in life, by imposing an order upon it" (OPP 86). And he repeatedly employs art's classic definition of formal beauty-- "variety in unity," "the ideal pattern of unity and diversity" (CC 198, 156)--to convey his sense of what the ideal society or culture would be.

Though Adorno agrees that the fictional order of art is much more harmonious, tolerant, and integrated than the deeply divisive classes and compartments and the savagely imposed conformist uniformities that modern society imposes, he is aware that art's form and order, however close to the ideal of nonrepressive union, cannot be wholly unrepressive. For as a product of social life, it inevitably bears to some extent the traces of repression and regimentation of such life:

> Form is the non-repressive synthesis of diffuse particulars; it preserves them in their diffuse, divergent, and contradictory condition. . . . This goes to show that form is the anti-barbaric dimension of art. Form ensures that art both shares in the process of civilization and criticizes it by its sheer existence. [Yet in imposing form on the flow of life and on natural materials, we can see] how repression is carried from reality into art works. . . ; it makes inci-

14. Hence for Adorno, "art's role in a totally functional world is precisely its afunctionality" (*Aesthetic*

sions in the living in order to endow it with language, but disfig-
ures it in the process. The myth of Procrustes tells a chapter of the
primal history of art. (*Aesthetic Theory* 207-08)[15]

5. To sum up, despite its essential social nature and
the repressive taint and limitation this entails, art remains--
through its fictional, playful, and formal aspects--a factor of
resistance and defiance to the totalizing pressures of the grim
and fragmented yet homogenized workaday world. It therefore
represents for both Eliot and Adorno the most promising source
of wisdom and truth. But neither of these canny thinkers is naive
enough to believe that such wisdom is purely, directly, and
unproblematically encapsulated in works of art and can be simply read off from them. For again, since art is an historical
(hence ideological) product, it must contain and purvey as much
blindness and falsehood, as truth. Its implicit refusal of the real
world so as to immerse itself and its audience in a fictional one
can as much encourage impotent escape and fantasy as promote
real critical enlightenment. Moreover, all too often, especially in
the low-brow art of the culture industry, the fictional world that
art offers is but a shallow, complicitous copy of the unreal "real"
world of the mass media, where even if the names and plots are
changed, the false assumptions and values are simply repeated
and confirmed if not exaggerated for the thrill of sensationalism
and the power of indoctrination. How then is art's claim to truth
and wisdom to be redeemed?

Eliot and Adorno again converge in the view that
art's truth content is helplessly mute on its own and is moreover
vulnerable to dangerous distortion. Art needs conscious ideological criticism for its truth to emerge, yet that criticism must
first be based on a full experience of the work's imaginative
world and the alternative assumptions and world-view it purveys.
Eliot and Adorno thus advocate a remarkably similar two-stage
theory of reading. In the first stage, we project ourselves into the
work and surrender ourselves to the author's vision, "when we
try to understand the rules of his own game, adopt his own point
of view" (OPP 164). For unless we at least provisionally accept
and surrender ourselves to the work's world and point of view,
we will be unable to get deeply involved in the work and thus, be
unable to understand it fully enough to appreciate the power of

---

Theory 442).
15. Adorno notes that with some of the powerful forms of classic works of art "their perfection monu-
mentalizes force and violence'" (*Aesthetic Theory* 229). But art remains superior to the social world in
that its repression is metaphorical and results in true integration and beauty. "Works of art cannot
help continuing the work of repressive reason, for they contain that moment of synthesis which helps
organize a totality. While disavowing real repression, art heeds the principle of repression in a
metaphorical, we might also say truncated and shallow-like, manner" (423-24).

its alternative vision. This primary process of imaginative self-surrender and self-projection into the work is similarly advocated by Adorno as the stage of imminent interpretive experience--"Verstehen" (*Aesthetic Theory* 177, 477). But, secondly, proper understanding of art requires that we go on to "another stage of self-consciousness" and critical reflection where we detach ourselves from the work we have entered and accepted in order to examine it "by outside standards" involving the wider contexts of the literary tradition and the extra-literary world (EAM 104, OPP 145; see Adorno's *Aesthetic Theory* 177-79, 346-47, 375-76, 387, 477-79; see also Shusterman, *Philosophy*, chapt. 6, and "Games and Wisdom").

Through this two-stage theory of reading, Eliot provides an admirably clear and sensible answer to the troubling old question (debated since Plato) of whether literature purveys valuable truth or misleading illusion. The cognitive value of a literary work depends not only on itself but also very much on how well its reader performs both stages of the reading process.

> It is simply not true that works of fiction, prose or verse, ... *directly* extend our knowledge of life.... Knowledge of life obtained through fiction is only possible by another stage of self-consciousness.... So far as we are taken up with the happenings in any novel in the same way in which we are taken up with what happens under our eyes, we are acquiring at least as much falsehood as truth. But when we are developed enough to say: 'This is the view of life of a person who was a good observer within his limits ... ; so what I am looking at is the world as seen by a particular mind'--then we are in a position to gain something from reading fiction ... ; but these authors are only really helping us when we can see, and allow for, their differences from ourselves. (EAM 104-05)

Adorno offers the very same two-stage, two-standpoint theory of aesthetic understanding though which we can extract the invaluable and not always intentional truth content of art. On the one hand, to understand a work of art one "must enter into the work," "give himself over to the work" (*Aesthetic Theory* 387, 346). But, Adorno no less that Eliot insists on the necessity of the second stage:

> A wholly immanent understanding of works of art is a false and deficient mode of understanding because it is under art's spell. ... This demand [for understanding] can be fulfilled only by a twofold approach: specific [immanent] experience joined to ... [critical] theory. ... The states of affairs discovered by immanent analysis have to be transcended in the direction of second reflection and emphatic criticism, which try to get at the truth content of the

work. . . . Those who have only an inside view of art, do not understand it, whereas those who see art only from the outside tend to
falsify it for lack of affinity with it. (*Aesthetic Theory* 177, 179, 477,
479)

Eliot wields this two-stage theory of reading as a
weapon of cultural criticism to account for and warn us of the
extraordinarily powerful and dangerous effect of trivial literature or commercialized art consumed for mere pleasure. Our
light "pleasure reading" has such a powerful effect on our beliefs
and attitudes because with such reading we typically do not
trouble ourselves with the second, critical stage; for we know we
are reading only for pleasure not for cognitive or ethical
enrichment. However, since any enjoyment or understanding of
art requires a first stage of imaginatively accepting and assimilating the work's world and outlook, omission of subsequent
critical reflection on these features will leave the attitudes or
beliefs expressed in the work dangerously active, unconsciously
and uncritically, in the mind of the reader. Hence it is "the literature that we read for 'amusement,' or 'purely for pleasure' that
may have the greatest and least suspected influence upon
us. . . [since it is] read in this attitude of 'purely for pleasure,' of
pure passivity" (EAM 106). And since popular contemporary literature, or more generally the popular art of the culture-indus-
try, is what we most often and easily consume in that passive
unreflective attitude, it "can have the easiest and most insidious
influence upon us" and thus "requires to be scrutinized most
closely."

Eliot here provides the literary critic with a crucial
role of cultural critique, exposing and critically examining the
ideologies which inform contemporary popular literature and
culture. If Eliot's own patently Christian execution of this task
seems to us awkwardly heavy-handed or superannuated, if not
sometimes painfully bigoted, this does nothing to invalidate his
general theoretical doctrine that art needs ideological critique
and that adequate, substantive literary criticism cannot ultimately afford to ignore it. Marxists and deconstructionists who
condemn Eliot's critical theory as insularly aestheticist, technical, and blind to the importance of the critique of ideas and ideologies in the criticism of literature are thus wildly off target.
Their difference with Eliot is not on the philosophical issue of
the relevance of ideology but rather on the particular ideology to
be used as a critical touchstone and pursued as a cultural end.
Indeed, as this paper has labored to show in connection with
Adorno, Eliot's cultural critique of bourgeois liberalism--its ide-

ology of individualism, scientistic instrumental reason, and pro-grammed production and consumption of the superficially new--is very much in tune with one of the most influential lines of contemporary Marxist cultural critique.

Thus, for us secular readers of Eliot who fancy our-selves socially progressive if not radical, Eliot's theory and criti-cism of culture need not be swept embarrassingly under the car-pet. It can rather be read with appreciation of its great merits and temporally very understandable limitations. In his dissatis-faction with the social and personal malaise of our modern world, Eliot still speaks to us as a contemporary. In his pene-trating imputation of so much of its unhappiness and evils to the ideology of bourgeois liberalism, he even speaks to us as an acute diagnostician and welcome ally. If his remedy of a return to a Christian society seems so implausible and unsavoury com-pared to our hopes of a more emancipated and secular socialist regeneration of society and culture, Eliot's own exemplary pose of quizzical, self-critical reflection should give us pause. We must continuously question how plausible and concretely desir-able are our often nebulous aims of radical social and cultural reform, no matter how firmly and doggedly we continue to desire and fight for them.

WORKS CITED

Adorno, Theodor. *Aesthetic Theory*. London: Routledge & Kegan Paul, 1984.

_____. *Minima Moralia*. London: Verso, 1978.

_____ and Max Horkheimer. *Dialectic of Enlightenment*. New York: Continuum, 1986.

Eliot, T. S. "A Commentary." *Criterion* July 1933: 644.

_____. "Experiment in Criticism." *Bookman* 70 (1929): 225.

_____. "Literature, Science, and Dogma." *Dial* 82 (1927): 242.

_____. "Religion Without Humanism." *Humanism and America*. Ed. N. Foerster. New York: Farrar and Rhinehard, 1930. 108.

Kojecky, Roger. *T. S. Eliot's Social Criticism*. London: Faber, 1971.

Polanyi, M. *Personal Knowledge*. London: Routledge & Kegan Paul, 1958.

Putnam, H. *Meaning and the Moral Sciences*. London: Routledge & Kegan Paul, 1979.

Shusterman, Richard. "Aesthetics, Ideology, and the Defense of Art." *Art as a Social Phenomenon*. Ed. B. Dziemidok and W. Truitt. New York: Haven, 1990.

_____. *T. S. Eliot and the Philosophy of Criticism*. New York: Columbia UP, 1988.

_____. "T. S. Eliot on Reading: Pleasure, Games, and Wisdom." *Philosophy and Literature* 11 (1987): 1-20.

NOTES ON CONTRIBUTORS

RICHARD BADENHAUSEN received his Ph.D. in English from the University of Michigan in 1989. He is currently Assistant Professor of English at Marshall University in Huntington, West Virginia.

SHYAMAL BAGCHEE teaches at the University of Alberta, Canada. Editor of the *T. S. Eliot Annual* (Macmillan Press, London), he has also edited *A Voice Descanting: Centenary Essays on Eliot and O'Neill in Perspective*. In 1988 the University of Arkansas awarded him an Eliot Centennial Citation and he will deliver the 1990 Eliot Memorial Lecture of the T. S. Eliot Society of America, St. Louis, Missouri.

JOSEPH BENTLEY died September 28, 1988. He was Professor of English at the University of Southern Florida (Tampa) at the time of his death. He published numerous books and articles on modern literature including *Reading* The Waste Land: *Modernism and the Limits of Interpretation*, which he co-authored with Jewel Spears Brooker.

JEWEL SPEARS BROOKER, Professor of English at Eckerd College, St. Petersburg, Florida, is past President of the T. S. Eliot Society. She edited *Approaches to Teaching T. S. Eliot's Poetry and Plays* and the forthcoming *The Placing of T. S. Eliot*. She couauthored *Reading* The Waste Land: *Modernism and the Limits of Interpretation* with Joseph Bentley. She is currently working on a book on mythical method in Yeats, Joyce, Eliot, and Pound.

RONALD BUSH is Professor of Literature at California Institute of Technology. His works include *The Genesis of Ezra Pound's* Cantos, *T. S. Eliot: A Study of Character and Style*, and *T. S. Eliot: The Modernist in History*. He is currently writing *Ezra Pound and the Ideologies of Modernism: Essays on the Major Poetry* and *The Composition of* The Pisan Cantos.

BARBARA EVERETT is Senior Research Fellow at Somerville College, Oxford University. Her works include *Poets in Their Time: Essays on English Poetry from Donne to Larkin* and *Young Hamlet: Essays on Shakespeare's Tragedies*.

HARVEY GROSS is Professor Emeritus of Comparative Literature at the State University of New York in Stony Brook. He is author of many works including *The Contrived Corridor: History and Fatality in Modern Literature, Sound and Form in Modern Poetry, A Study of Prosody from Thomas Hardy to Robert Lowell* and *Plans for an Orderly Apocalypse*. His extensive writings on music and culture include essays on both Wagner and Mahler.

JOAN FILLMORE HOOKER is an Adjunct Associate Professor of Humanities at New York University where she received the Siegel Award (1982) for distinguished undergraduate teaching in the humanities. She is author of T. S. Eliot's *Poems in French Translation: Pierre Leyris and Others* and is working on articles about the translations of "Journey of the Magi" and "A Song for Simeon."

CLEO McNELLY KEARNS is a Visiting Lecturer at Princeton Theological Seminary. She has written *T. S. Eliot and Indic Traditions: A Study in Poetry and Belief* and is working on *Kristevan Wisdom: Language, Art, and Religion*.

HUGH KENNER is Professor of English at Johns Hopkins University. He is the author of two landmark studies on Pound, *The Poetry of Ezra Pound* and *The Pound Era*. He has also written *Wyndham Lewis, Dublin's Joyce, Joyce's Voices, Ulysses*, as well as numerous other books and articles on modern poetry, including his recent study *Sinking Island* (1988). He has been a senior editor of *Paideuma* since its inception in 1972. His most recent work includes two books on Desmond Egan: *Desmond Egan: The Poet and His Work* and *The Selected Poetry of Desmond Egan*.

EDWARD LOBB is Associate Professor of English at Queen's University at Kingston, Kingston, Ontario. His works include *T. S. Eliot and the Romantic Critical Tradition* and a forthcoming collection of essays on Eliot's *Four Quartets*.

JAMES LONGENBACH is Associate Professor of English at the University of Rochester. He is the author of *Modernist Poet-*

ics *of History*, *Stone Cottage: Pound, Yeats, and Modernism*, and *Wallace Stevens: The Plain Sense of Things* (forthcoming).

LOUIS L. MARTZ has been teaching at Georgetown and Emory since retiring from Yale University, where he taught for forty years. His major books *include The Poetry of Meditation*, *Milton: Poet of Exile* and *The Poem of the Mind*, the last of which contains essays on Stevens, Eliot, Williams, and Roethke. He is editor of *H.D.: Collected Poems, 1912-1944* and *H.D.: Selected Poems*.

JAMES E. MILLER, JR. is Helen A. Regenstein Professor of English at the University of Chicago. He has written *T. S. Eliot's Personal Waste Land: Exorcism of the Demons*, *The American Quest for a Supreme Fiction: Whitman's Legacy in the Personal Epic*, and *Heritage of American Literature* (2 volumes) (forthcoming in 1991).

A. D. MOODY is Professor of English and American Literature at the University of York, England. He is the author of a wide range of works including *Virginia Woolf* and *Thomas Stearns Eliot: Poet*. In addition to being a keynote speaker at The National Poetry Foundation's T. S. Eliot Centennial Celebration, he was the Eliot Memorial Lecturer at the Centenary Celebration of the T. S. Eliot Society in St. Louis, September 24, 1988. He is currently working on *How to Read Ezra Pound*.

RUSSELL ELLIOTT MURPHY, Associate Professor of English at the University of Arkansas at Little Rock, is editor of the *Yeats Eliot Review*. He is author of both fiction and scholarly works which include the novel *Spent* and *Structure and Meaning: An Introduction to Literature*. He is currently working on a novel entitled *That Spring in Daytona Beach* and a study of Yeats' use of Byzantium in his poetry and prose.

JEFFREY M. PERL is Professor of the Humanities at the University of Texas (Dallas) and founding editor of *The Postwar Review*. His works include *The Tradition of Return* and *Skepticism and Modern Enmity: Before and After Eliot*. He is in the process of writing *The Other Tradition: Antagonism and Ambivalence in Modern Literary Culture* and *Two Windows on St.-Denis*.

J. P. RIQUELME is Duwain E. Hughes, Jr. Distinguished Professor of English and Chair of the Department of English at Southern Methodist University, Dallas, Texas. Among his many works are *Teller and Tale in Joyce's Fiction: Oscillating Perspectives* and *Harmony of Dissonances: T. S. Eliot, Romanticism, and Imagination*. He is working on books about Oscar Wilde, Samuel Beckett, and W. B. Yeats. He also plans to write commentaries on Wolfgang Iser and on the Konstanz School of literary theory.

SANFORD SCHWARTZ is Associate Professor of English at Pennsylvania State University in University Park, Pennsylvania. He is author of *The Matrix of Modernism: Pound, Eliot, and Early Twentieth-Century Thought*. His works in progress include a book entitled *Between Philosophy and Literature*.

MOHAMMAD SHAHEEN is Professor of English Studies at the University of Jordan in Amman. He is an Associate for *Paideuma* which has published a number of his studies over the years. His works include *The Modern Arabic Short Story*. He is currently writing a book on Pound and Medieval Thought and translating both Pound and Eliot into Arabic.

RICHARD SHUSTERMAN is Associate Professor of Philosophy at Temple University. He is author of *The Object of Literary Criticism*, *T. S. Eliot and the Philosophy of Cubism* and editor of *Analytic Aesthetics*.

W. B. WORTHEN is Associate Professor of English at the University of Texas at Austin. His works include *The Idea of the Actor: Drama and the Ethics of Performance*. He is currently completing *Modern Drama and the Rhetoric of Theater*.

INDEX

Entries in the index consist mainly of proper names, book titles, musical compositions, concepts, places, and selected historical events. Eliot's works are arranged alphabetically in the body of the index and are not indexed under his name. Authors and works which appear in Works Cited are not included in the index.

p. 45 Duality
p. 73, 75 (old or new)

p. 109 syntax, prosody,
patterns of imagery

p. 116 Tiresias, the whithered
conscience of a ruined culture

p. 119 an act of evocation

p. 121